MW00738059

CHATHAM, N. J. THE VALLEY OF THE PASSAIC

View from the Tower of Jacob Vanderpoel's Residence, 1873.

From Hoyt's Pen and Pencil Pictures on the D. L. & W. Railroad.

HISTORY

OF

CHATHAM, NEW JERSEY

BY

AMBROSE E VANDERPOEL
MEMBER OF THE NEW JERSEY HISTORICAL SOCIETY

PRINTED BY
CHARLES FRANCIS PRESS
NEW YORK

CONTENTS

Contents

CHAPTER I

THE Borough of Chatham is situated in Morris County,
on the west side of the Passaic River, and is traversed
by the main road leading from Elizabeth to Morristown
The Passaic at Chatham is the boundary between Morris
County on the west, and the counties of Essex and Union
on the east, the two latter being separated by the highway
Shortly after the opening of the 19th century, a section of
the road in the older part of the village was acquired by
the Morris Turnpike Company, and became a turnpike
It is now officially called Main Street within the borough
limits, but on the east side of the river the name Morris
Turnpike is still retained, although the company whose title
is thus perpetuated has ceased to exist, and while such
designation therefore is no longer accurate, we will often
find it convenient to refer to the street as the turnpike in the
following pages

Prior to the coming of the white men, the aborigines
had made a permanent trail, called the Minisink Path,
across the State of New Jersey, from the Delaware River to
the ocean, which was regularly traveled by the Minisink
Indians on an annual excursion to the seashore, as well as
by local tribes on shorter journeys or war expeditions   The
path crossed the Passaic at Chatham by means of a natural

ford about four rods below the Main Street bridge [1] The ford was called by the white men the Minisink Crossing; and the name seems to have been applied also to the neigh-boring settlement which in the aftertime became the village of Chatham The first settlers were attracted by the water-power afforded by the Passaic for the operation of saw- and grist-mills, and the selection of this particular place as a village site was doubtless due to the existence of the Indian trail, which was the only avenue in this part of the Province whereby the primeval forest could be readily penetrated, and was naturally followed by the pioneers when they en-tered this region

In early writings reference is occasionally found to "the country of the Minisinks." The territory of this tribe lay beyond the Kittatinny Mountains, on either side of the Delaware River, extending from the Water Gap to the Lackawaxen These Indians journeyed to the ocean every summer for the combined purposes of fishing, clam drying, salt water bathing, and the gathering of shells for the manu-facture of wampum The clams were dried upon pieces of bark, and carried away [2] The Minisink Path leading to the sea commenced at Minisink Island in the Delaware, ran through Culver's Gap and past Culver's Pond to the Musconetcong River near Lake Hopatcong, and thence, by way of the Succasunna Plains, Dover, Morris Plains, Mon-roe and Madison, to Chatham. Crossing the Passaic at the latter place, it followed the approximate line of the Morris Turnpike through the gap of Hobart Hill, and curved toward the south just before reaching the Rahway River in Springfield It then maintained a southerly direction to the Raritan River, which it crossed at a point about three miles above Perth Amboy, and, skirting the shore of Raritan

[1] Essex County Road Book, A B 34
[2] Ellis's Monmouth County, 9

FORD OF THE PASSAIC

Bay, it led to Middletown and thence to the Highlands of Navesink [1]

The Minisink Path, as its name implies, was more than a scarcely perceptible trail, which could be discerned and followed only by the practised eye of the Indian, if we may judge by the manner in which it is referred to in early records, and delineated upon ancient maps, it was a well-beaten track, which, in all probability, was worn below the level of the adjacent soil by the tread of tribal generations It was so well known and so clearly defined that it at once became a recognized landmark when the country was explored, and was soon converted into a road by the settlers in various localities along its length—at first as a mere bridle-path for travelers on horseback, and later as a widened and improved thoroughfare for the passage of vehicles It is represented in Chatham by Main Street and King's Road, and in Madison by King's Road and Park Avenue,- although the modern highway is very much straighter than the aboriginal path, which, like all Indian trails, pursued a devious course in order to avoid natural obstacles, and to reach the most advantageous places for fording the streams

The first settlement in the locality where Chatham now lies sprang up in close proximity to the Passaic, and gradually spread along the road in each direction from the stream

---

[1] Morristown Year Book, 1911, 99, Whitehead's East Jersey under the Proprietors, 28, and map at p 118; Whitehead's Perth Amboy, 268 One of the affidavits to the Elizabethtown Bill in Chancery was made by Jeremiah Osborn of Morristown, at that time (1741) 86 years of age, who stated, among other things, that the Minisink Path "went near as the road now goes," east of the Passaic at Chatham He had reference to the road which antidated the Morris Turnpike, the general course of which was the same as that of the turnpike, though it was not so straight

[2] In Madison the path ran close by a celebrated spring which flows from the hillside near the northeast corner of Park and Ridgedale Avenues It is said that the first settlers suspended a bottle from a neighboring bush or tree to be used in drinking from the spring, and from this circumstance the name of Bottle Hill, as Madison was formerly called, originated Traditions vary, however, respecting the origin of the name

The early village was thus divided by the river into two sections, which were probably about equal in population and extent, and were often distinguished, during and after the Revolution, as "Chatham, Morris County," and

Ancient Signet Ring

"Chatham, Essex County." Gordon's New Jersey Gazetteer, published in 1834, and Barber & Howe's Historical Collections of New Jersey, dated ten years later, state that the Passaic River flows *through* the village; and the former work, in its description of Springfield Township in Essex County, mentions "part of Chatham" as one of the villages of that township. But at a later period the increase of population, and the consequent growth of towns and villages, caused their boundaries to be more sharply drawn; and as a result, the corporate limits of Chatham are now confined to the west, or Morris County, side of the Passaic, while the adjacent territory on the opposite side forms part of other municipalities.

In the year 1664, the Dutch colonies in America, known as the New Netherlands, passed from the possession of Holland to that of England, and were granted by King Charles II. to his brother, the Duke of York, in whose honor the name of New York was adopted. During the same year the Duke conveyed to Lord John Berkeley and Sir George Carteret that part of his holdings in the New World which lay west of the Hudson River between Delaware Bay and "the northermost branch of the said Bay or River of Delaware, which is 41° 40′ of latitude"; Berkeley and Carteret thus becoming the original proprietors of the province thereafter known as Nova Cæsarea or New Jersey. This territory was subsequently divided into two provinces, called East Jersey and West Jersey, which, by transfers from the original grantees, came into the possession of a large number of proprietors; East Jersey being governed by a board of twenty-four, having its seat of government at Perth Amboy while the affairs of West Jersey were administered at Burlington by a much greater number The line of partition between the provinces soon became a subject of dispute and it was altered more than once in an attempt to effect a division which would be acceptable to both proprietaries As a result of these changes, the site of Chatham, which, owing to its geographical position, was properly a part of East Jersey was included at one time in the western colony

The two provinces were created in 1676 by agreement between Carteret and the West Jersey proprietors the latter having acquired the interest of Berkeley On July 1 of that year a deed of partition was executed in London, known in history as the Quintipartite Deed from a descriptive word used in the document itself in reference to the five contracting parties which provided, in effect that New Jersey should be separated into two equal portions—the eastern half being the share of Carteret—and that the dividing line between them should start from the point on the Delaware River which the grant of the Duke of York had named in latitude 41° 40′ North, and should run straight to the most southerly point on the east side of Little Egg Harbor It was soon found, however, to be extremely difficult if not impossible, to make a fair and equal division when the country was an unexplored wilderness, about which reliable information could not be obtained, and owing to the want of accurate surveys, a question arose as to the proper location of the partition line The following excerpt from a letter addressed to the East Jersey proprietors in England, at a later date, illustrates the difficulties which the situation presented

And thirdly some other precise bounds needs be appointed for the north end of the two provinces, than what the deed of Partition mentions for as to it bound viz 41 deg. & 40′ our Surveyor tells us it is not to be found on any branch of delaware river as the deed mentions, for no branch is in yt latitude in the true and proper Sense of a branch, wch is a stream coming out of the river yt makes a true branch but no such can be found in yt latitude, or near to it, only the Surveyours found some brooks running into the river but where they Joined to the river was farre from ye latitude And Indeed it is very disputable & unclear what is delaware river itselfe above the falles for two great streams meet farre beyond the falles northerly, and which of these is delaware river, cannot be easily determined, but rather seemeth Impossible for the name delaware was only given to it as it extended from the falles to the sea fourthly seeing the deed of Partition is grounded on a false mapp, and a wrong account of the country, as to its Survey, and delaware river itselfe was supposed to have a branch in that latitude, and yet hath none, we Judge yt any Judge will Say, the deed of Partition must be wholly laid aside and a new line of devision ordered to be run if yt already run in great part, doe not stand, and if a new line must be run, we are ready to think yt by equal devision the new line shall be more favourable to east Jersey than this already agreed & run in part but nothing can be certainly affirmed till west Jersey be surveyed as well as east Jersey [1]

Several ineffectual attempts were made by the two proprietaries to agree upon the points between which the partition line should run, and at length the question was submitted to arbitrators, who decided that the boundary "shall runn from ye north side of ye mouth or Inlett of ye beach of little Egg Harbor on a streight lyne to Delaware river north north west and fifty minutes more westerly according to naturall position & not according to ye magnet whose variation is nine degrees westward"[2] This course however, inclined much too far toward the west, and gave East Jersey more than an equal moiety In 1687, George Keith, surveyor-general of East Jersey, undertook to run the line, commencing at Little Egg Harbor and surveying northward to a point on the south branch of the Raritan River near the present village of Three Bridges Had the course

[1] New Jersey Archives, Ser 1, II, 21 Original in Library of the New Jersey Historical Society
[2] New Jersey Archives, Ser 1, I, 524

been continued to the Delaware, the eastern division would have contained nearly 27,000 acres more than an equal half of the Province, and the injustice of such a partition became so apparent that the West Jersey proprietors would not allow him to proceed Keith's line is perpetuated by the present boundary between the counties of Monmouth and Ocean on the east, and Burlington on the west, and his survey may be traced upon a modern map of New Jersey by continuing this line southward to Little Egg Harbor, and northward to the Raritan in Hunterdon County

With the view of making a more just and equal division, another agreement was entered into in London on September 5, 1688, between Dr Daniel Coxe, governor of West Jersey, and Robert Barclay, governor of East Jersey, in behalf of their respective boards of proprietors This agreement affirmed the Keith line as far as the same had been surveyed, and provided that the boundary, when continued from the point on the Raritan where Keith stopped, instead of running straight to the Delaware, should pursue a devious course, in such manner as to increase the area of West Jersey The line, it was declared, should be drawn from the northern extremity of Keith's survey, by way of the north branch of the Raritan River, to the head waters of the Passaic, thence down the latter stream to its junction with the Pequannock, thence up this river to the 41st degree of north latitude, and thence along that parallel to the Hudson [1] Prior to the adoption of this partition, the present county of Morris, or at any rate a large part of it, was regarded by the East Jersey proprietors as included in their possessions but by the selection of the Passaic River as a section of the boundary, Morris County as a whole was ceded to the western province

This division was duly accepted and for many years the West Jersey authorities exercised control and jurisdiction over the region where Chatham now lies, yet the agreement

[1] Smith s New Jersey, 197

was not entirely satisfactory, and the boundary long continued in dispute   The East Jersey proprietors, claiming
under the grant of the Duke of York to latitude 41° 40'
North on the Delaware River, maintained that to be the
"north partition point", and in 1719 an act of the Assembly
was passed providing that the boundary should be a straight
line drawn from that point to Little Egg Harbor   The line
was not actually run until the autumn of 1743, when John
Lawrence surveyed it from the harbor to a point on the
Delaware a little north of latitude 41° 12'   This partition
has always been recognized by East Jersey, although it gave
the western province a territorial advantage   Lawrence's
line bisected Budd's Lake in the westerly part of Morris
County, and consequently the east part of the county, including the site of Chatham, which had been ceded to West
Jersey by the Coxe-Barclay agreement of 1688, was once
more embraced in the eastern division

The proprietors of East Jersey acquired their interest
in the Province as a real estate speculation which promised
handsome returns   The transfer from Carteret's representatives involved but little expenditure; immense quantities
of land could be bought from the Indians in exchange for
merchandise of trifling cost, and the land, when surveyed in
parcels of a size convenient for development and cultivation,
could be conveyed to settlers at prices which would yield
large profits   Needless to say, the proprietors strongly opposed all attempts on the part of individuals to usurp their
prerogatives by purchasing land directly from the natives,
as many of the pioneers were disposed to do

The history of Chatham may be said to commence in
1651, when a large tract of land in this vicinity was bought
from the Indians   In the latter part of that year Cornelis
Van Werckhoven, a *schepen* (magistrate) of Utrecht in
Holland, obtained from the Amsterdam Chamber leave to
establish two colonies or manors in the New Netherlands,

and to carry out his plan he employed Augustine Heerman, a prominent resident of New Amsterdam, to make four purchases of Indian lands, two being in New Jersey and two on Long Island   The first tract lay in eastern New Jersey, fronting on Staten Island Sound, and was encompassed by the Raritan River, a creek called Pechciesse, and a straight line drawn from the source of one to the source of the other In after years the question was raised whether the name Pechciesse had been applied to the Passaic River as was commonly supposed, or to the Rahway River, which was thought by some to correspond more accurately with the description in the deed   If the latter stream was meant, the conveyance included the region where Chatham is situated, but if the tract was bounded by the Passaic, the site of Chatham lay immediately outside of its confines No attempt to colonize this district was made during the Dutch occupancy of the New Netherlands, for the Amsterdam Chamber, upon learning of Heerman's purchases, considered it inadvisable to allow so much land to become the property of a single individual, and accordingly permitted Van Werckhoven to retain only one of his tracts, compelling him to relinquish the others   He chose one of the plots on Long Island, and the title to the other three reverted to the aborigines [1]

In the autumn of 1664, shortly after the Dutch possessions in America had passed into the hands of the English, a tract of land which apparently included the site of Chatham was again sold by the Indians   In this transaction, which is known in history as the Elizabethtown Purchase, the territory was acquired by a party of English colonists from Long Island, who had formed an association for the purpose of establishing a settlement in the fertile and inviting region beyond the Hudson   They founded the city of

[1] Hatfield's Elizabeth, 20, 21, O Callaghan's New Netherlands, 187; Letter No 2, appended to Answer to Elizabethtown Bill in Chancery

Elizabeth, N J, and were called the Elizabethtown Associates   Their purchase included approximately 500,000 acres, extending from the mouth of the Raritan to the mouth of the Passaic—about seventeen miles—and running westward into the interior double that distance, being in part the same property which the Indians had sold to Heerman thirteen years before   It embraced, on paper, the whole of the present county of Union, and parts of Essex, Middlesex, Somerset, Hunterdon and Morris   The conveyance was sanctioned by the local authorities, Governor Richard Nicolls of New York (whose jurisdiction included New Jersey), issuing a patent or grant to the associates officially confirming their title [1]

This transaction was antedated by the sale of the entire Province of New Jersey by the Duke of York to Berkeley and Carteret (intelligence of which had not yet reached America), and, therefore, from the standpoint of the home government, was illegal and void   At first the proprietors did not question the validity of the Indian deed and the Nicolls grant, but it was not long before the inevitable controversy arose between them and the Elizabethown associates respecting the title to the soil—a quarrel which continued with ever-increasing bitterness for a full century, and was finally set at rest only by the War of Independence   Both parties lost little time in selling lots suitable for plantations, causing disputes between the settlers, some of whom had purchased their land from the proprietors, while others had bought the same plots from the associates

Although the Indian deed and the Nicolls grant were so drawn as apparently to convey a tract extending westward about thirty-four miles from tidewater (i e , double the distance from the mouth of the Raritan to the mouth of the Passaic), the assertion was afterwards made by the savages that the western limit of the purchase was the

----

[1] Hatfield's Elizabeth, 29, 36

COLONIAL MANSION ON THE EAST RIVER, NEW YORK

Minisink Path, just west of the Rahway River in the present township of Springfield—only seven or eight miles from the original settlement of Elizabethtown. The general course of the path in that locality was approximately north and south; and the Indians insisted that the land lying beyond the trail had not been conveyed to the associates; the truth of this statement being admitted by many of the whites.

As the town of Elizabeth increased in size, the associates caused the land lying toward the west to be surveyed in small lots, which were divided among their number and sold by them to settlers; these surveys extending in the course of time to the Rahway River. Although this district was clearly included in the Eliza-bethtown Purchase (being east of the Minisink Path) it had been occupied to some extent,

Colonial Weather-Cock

prior to these surveys, by planters holding grants or leases from the proprietors, who naturally resisted the attempts of the associates to dispossess them; the disputes being aggravated by costly and protracted litigation.

The opening up and settlement of the country lying beyond the Minisink Path, and extending to the Passaic opposite the site of Chatham, occasioned further disputes of similar nature; these difficulties arising during the administration of Gawen Lawrie, who was appointed deputy governor of East Jersey in 1683. Upon his arrival from England, Lawrie established his residence in Elizabeth; and

during his term of office he adopted a policy of conciliation
in all his dealings with the associates, making no effort to
contest the validity of their title   On the contrary, he
requested some of their leaders to point out the town limits
to him, saying that he wished to buy of the aborigines, in
behalf of the proprietors, some land lying west of the Elizabethtown Purchase   The associates were unable to comply
immediately with his request, since their western bounds had
never been definitely fixed, and they assembled the Indian
sachems to guide a party of the townspeople into the wilderness for the purpose of indicating and marking the limits of
the town

The party consisted of Richard Clarke, Jr , Captain
John Baker, Jonas Wood, Stephen Osborn, Joseph Meeker
and Joseph Wilson, together with two boys, Richard Baker
and John Cromwell, who went to see the woods, and the
Indians were led by Wewanapo, a cousin of one of the saga-
mores who had signed the Indian deed Setting out on July
16, 1684, they went "to a Plain back of Piscataway, to a
marked tree with some stones about it and a stake by the
tree," and thence "forward towards the Green River, near
where it comes out of the mountain, and lodged by the river-
side that night, and the next day they made a circle or compass along the foot of the mountain, by the directions of
the Indian, till they came to the Minisink Path, and then
came down to Elizabethtown " Scarcely had this territory
been explored when a controversy arose concerning it   The
associates maintained that, according to an admission of
Wewanapo, this compass included only a part of their holdings, and that the town lands in point of fact were much
more extensive, while, on the other hand, the proprietors
alleged that Captain Baker and his companions had bribed
the savages to designate a large area lying entirely beyond
the limits of the town, to have then and there bought this
additional land of the red men, and to have afterwards represented it to Lawrie as part of the Elizabethtown Purchase

There is reason to believe that this contention was well founded, because Baker was convicted of having violated the provisions of a recent law which prohibited individuals from buying Indian lands, and because the tract which Lawrie subsequently purchased of the savages appears to have been in part the same as that located by the exploring party.[1]

The tract which Lawrie bought for the proprietors extended from the Rahway River in what is now Springfield Township to the Passaic River opposite the site of Chatham The line of the Minisink Path from Springfield to Chatham, corresponding roughly with that of the Morris Turnpike, formed his northern boundary The northwest corner of the tract was indicated by a marked walnut tree standing near the path, on the east side of the Passaic, below the present Main Street bridge, and another corner or angle was fixed by a marked birch tree near a watercourse then called Wahackick Creek, in New Providence[2] This land was included—nominally at least—in the Elizabethtown Purchase of 1664 (although the associates had not caused it to be surveyed and settled), but Lawrie was assured by the Indians and by some of the whites that such was not the case It reached from Chatham to Bound Brook, and parts of it were soon occupied by settlers who claimed under proprietary right.[3]

The territorial extent of the township of Elizabeth was not legally determined until 1693, when its limits were fixed by legislative enactment. In October of that year an act of the Assembly was passed providing that

[1] Hatfield's Elizabeth, 228, 229, Elizabethtown Bill in Chancery, 54, Tanner's New Jersey, 76

[2] Elizabethtown Bill in Chancery, 56, 114

[3] Joseph Harrison, in an affidavit appended to the Elizabethtown Bill in Chancery, stated that about 40 years before (that is, about the year 1700), Theophilus Pierson, when negotiating with the Indians for the purchase of a tract lying west of Newark, was told by them that they had sold the land south of the Minisink Path and between the rivers (which he understood to be the Passaic and Rahway Rivers), to Governor Lawrie, for one Mrs Haige, a Scotch woman

The Township of Elizabeth-Town, shall include all the Land from the mouth of Raway River West to Woodbridge-Stake, and from thence Westerly along the Line of the County to the Partition Line of the Province, and from the mouth of the said Raway River, up the Sound to the mouth of the Bound-Creek, and from thence to the Bound-Hill, from thence North-west to the Partition Line of the Province [1]

As this statute was subsequent to the Coxe-Barclay agreement, which declared the Passaic to be in part the partition line of the Province, the river now formed the west boundary of Elizabeth township This boundary was again officially defined in 1739, when Elizabeth was incorporated as a free borough by a charter granted by King George II, declaring the western limit of the municipality to be the Passaic River from the mouth of Dead River to the Minisink Crossing [2] Thus the early settlement on the east side of the Passaic, which, during the Revolution and for many years afterwards, was considered part of Chatham, lay at the time of which we write within the corporate limits of Elizabeth

In the autumn of 1736 the associates continued their surveys from the Rahway River to the Passaic They did not extend their operations down the latter stream quite as far as the Minisink Crossing, but adopted as their northern boundary a line drawn to the Passaic at Chatham in the vicinity of the Watchung Avenue bridge, and their survey covered the greater part of the valley above that point It included much of the land which Lawrie had bought of the Indians, which was already occupied in part by settlers holding proprietary grants, and the action of the associates in selling the lots into which their survey was divided provoked fresh quarrels and renewed litigation, the hostility between the two factions resulting in serious riots in the village of Turkey, as New Providence was then called

---

[1] Hatfield's Elizabeth, 240
[2] *Ibid*, 320

For many years the courts were occupied with suits
and counter suits between rival claimants to the soil   While
similar causes of action arose and were brought to trial in
other parts of the Province, the strife seems to have been
most vexatious in Essex County, particularly in regard to
the Elizabethtown lands

At length a suit was commenced by the East Jersey
proprietors against some of the people of Elizabeth which
was designed to finally determine their long-continued controversy   In this proceeding they filed the famous Elizabethtown Bill in Chancery—a document prepared in the
most thorough and painstaking manner, which, in setting
forth the grounds and particulars of their demand, recited
in detail the history of Elizabeth, enumerated all noteworthy
events which had any bearing upon the subject of land titles,
reviewed the pretensions of the associates and those claiming under them, and mentioned the numerous suits which
had been previously brought to try the question of owner-
ship   Some conception of the enormous labor involved in
its preparation may be gained from the fact that three years
were devoted to the work, and that in manuscript form it
covered 1500 pages   The bill was filed in 1745, and was
printed during the two years next ensuing   In printed form
it is a folio of 124 pages with double columns, having an
appendix of 40 pages, together with explanatory maps

The formal denial of its allegations was set out in the
"joint and several answer" of 449 freeholders and inhabitants of Elizabethtown named in alphabetical order, which
was filed in 1751, and printed the next year in form similar
to that of the bill itself, though containing only 48 pages.
This document also reviewed the history of the town, so that
the bill and answer constitute one of our chief sources of
information respecting the colonial history of northern New
Jersey, although their allegations, being naturally biased,
must be accepted with due caution

The proprietors chose an opportune time for the prose-

cution of this suit   The provincial government was then
administered by Lewis Morris, who had presumed (without due authority, it was said) to establish a court of
chancery, and to exercise the prerogatives of chancellor
He was himself the holder of land by proprietary right,
and, under the circumstances, it seemed almost certain that
his decision would be in their favor   Morris died, however,
in 1746, and the reins of government passed into the hands
of Jonathan Belcher, who, as a resident of Elizabeth, was
thought to be in sympathy with the associates   Probably
for this reason the case was not brought to trial before
him   While the suit was still pending, the attention of the
litigants was distracted by the outbreak of the French and
Indian War, and soon afterwards came the popular excite
ment and indignation caused by the passage of the Stamp
Act, and augmented by subsequent oppressive legislation, followed by the War of Independence   During these troublous
times the people had no desire for litigation   All proceedings in the suit were suspended, and after the close of
the Revolution they were not renewed, for under the new
conditions incident to a republican form of government, a
judicial decision respecting colonial land titles would have
possessed but little value [1]

The lands lying on the east side of the Passaic at Chatham in the neighborhood of Main Street bridge are believed to have been first occupied by settlers holding proprietary grants based upon the Lawrie purchase of 1684
The earliest survey to an individual in this locality, as appears from the East Jersey records, was to Dr John Johnson, by virtue of a warrant of the proprietors, dated June
6, 1701, and recorded in Liber O of East Jersey Surveys,
page 209   The deed reads in part as follows

The Proprietors of ye province of East New Jersey To all persons to whom these presents shall come send Greeting   Know yee

[1] Hatfield's Elizabeth, 369-372

MAP OF THE JOHNSTON TRACT

Showing Chatham Bridge in the Southwest Corner.
From Original in Possession of the Dickinson Family.

Legend: May 3d, 1749. Surveyed for Andrew Johnston Esqr the above tract at Passaik
river in the County of Essex . . . . bearers were James Mitchel & . . . . . er Raymond

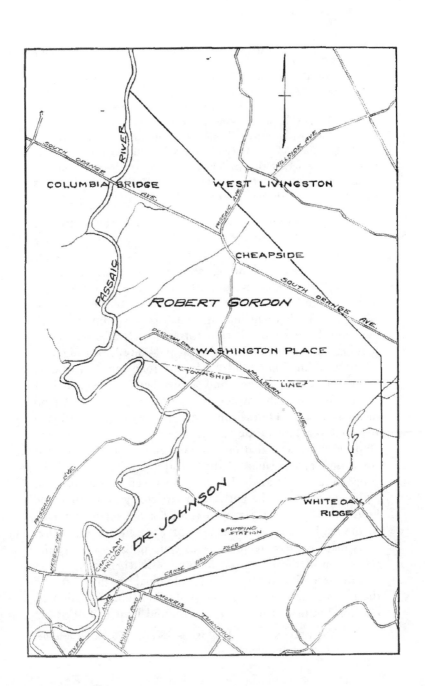

that wee ye sd prop Have Granted Released & Confirmed and by
these presents Do grant Release & Comfirme Unto John Johnston of
ye County of Monmouth Esqr In right of headland All that tract
of land Scituate Lying & being in ye County of Essex Beginning
upon passaick River fifteen chaines above where ye Minisinks road
to Elizabeth Town Crosseth ye sd river & from thence running North
fifty six degrees Easterly one hundred thirtie six chaines & an half
from thence running north fifty two degrees westerly to sd passaick
river & thence up ye river to where it beganne [1]

Dr Johnson's boundary line, as thus defined,
started at the Passaic approximately fourteen chains above
Main Street bridge, and, crossing the turnpike at or near the
mouth of the River Road, it ran to a point in the neighborhood of White Oak Ridge, whence it turned toward the
northwest and continued straight to a point on the river not
far from the dividing line between the townships of Millburn and Livingston It thus formed a triangle, having its
base on the Passaic and its apex near White Oak Ridge

Dr John Johnson (Johnston or Johnstone), a leading
citizen of Perth Amboy and a member of the board of
proprietors, was the owner of several large tracts of land
in East Jersey He died in 1732, and his eldest son dying
the same year, his property was inherited by his second son,
Andrew, who was also one of the proprietors, and served
for a time as chairman of the board Andrew caused the
property above described to be resurveyed and mapped in
1749, possibly for the purpose of correcting an error made
by the surveyor in 1701, who recorded the superficial area
of the land as 410 acres instead of 558, the correct figure
This map, or a contemporaneous copy of it, is now in the
possession of the Dickinson family of Chatham

The second transfer to an individual in this part of
the Passaic valley was a grant "unto Sir Robert Gordon of
Gordonston in ye Kingdome of Scotland Esqr in full of his

[1] Liber G of East Jersey Deeds, p 361, in office of the Secretary of State
Whitehead's Perth Amboy, 68, 72

first division of Land in ye sd province," of a tract surrounding the Johnson property. Its description reads "All that tract of Land Scituate Lying & being upon ye South side of passaick river Contaning after allowance for barrans &c fifteen hundred acres Beginning at ye upper Corner of John Johnston's land above where ye path from Elizabethtown to Minisinks Crosseth ye sd river from thence runing north seaventy Eight deg. Easterly one hundred Sixty Seaven Chaines from thence north one hundred chaines thence north fourty four deg westerly to ye sd passaick River from thence up allong ye river & sd John Johnston's land to where it begann "[1] This boundary commenced at Dr Johnson's upper corner, embraced the village of White Oak Ridge, and thence ran northwardly and northwestwardly, between Cheapside and West Livingston, to a point on the river about half a mile below South Orange Avenue. Although the description is not wholly free from ambiguity, it was doubtless the intention of the proprietors to exclude the Johnson tract, and to sell only a strip of land surrounding it, for the previous transfer was legal, and they could have conveyed to Gordon a valid title only to the property lying outside of Johnson's boundaries.

The Gordon family eventually sold the property to one Rockhead, who conveyed it in small plots to the pioneers. The early surveys show that the plantations bought by the first settlers in the neighborhood of the turnpike from the crown of Hobart Hill to the Passaic were bounded by the Gordon line and not by that of Johnson.

Neither Johnson nor Gordon, as far as we know, lived in this vicinity. Their purchases seem to have been a mere speculation. The first settler on the east side of the river at this point is believed to have been Samuel Carter, whom

[1] Book C of Patents, p 241, in office of the Secretary of State. The survey is recorded in Liber O of Last Jersey Surveys, p 213, following that of Dr Johnson

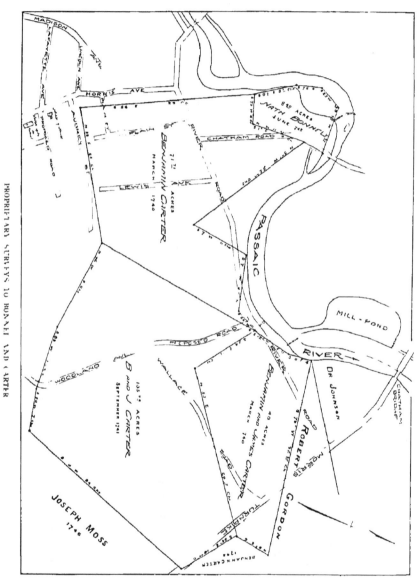

PROPRIETARY SURVEYS TO BONNEL AND CARTER

Drawn Over a Modern Map of the City

we find living on what is now the Vanderpoel homestead farm as early as 1726, when the primitive road which succeeded the Minisink Path was officially surveyed as a public highway [1] When and under what circumstances Carter acquired his property the records do not show It lay within the Johnson tract, his house standing between the road now represented by the turnpike and Johnson's southern boundary; but no record of a survey or conveyance of his plantation has been found.

In 1740, 1741 and 1742 several neighboring plots were conveyed by the proprietors, in some cases to Benjamin Carter alone, and in others to James and Benjamin Carter as joint purchasers The Carter family thus acquired large tracts on the east side of the Passaic opposite Chatham Their holdings lay immediately south of Gordon's line, extending from the river about 40 chains eastward, diagonally crossing the line of the turnpike, and running into the present golf links of the Canoe Brook Country Club Their lands also extended up the river, so that, with the exception of eight and a half acres fronting upon the stream near the present Summit Avenue bridge, they owned practically the entire valley in what is now the city of Summit from the vicinity of Morris Avenue to the Morris Turnpike The tract of eight and a half acres which they did not own was conveyed by the proprietors on June 30, 1748, to Nathaniel Bonnel, a millwright of Elizabeth [2] It is now the property of the Commonwealth Electric Company, and is occupied in part by a power station

[1] Essex County Road Book, A B 34
[2] East Jersey Surveys, S 2, 279

CHAPTER II

First Settlements in Morris County—Purchases of Indian Lands by
the Pioneers—Purchases by the West Jersey Proprietors—
Allotment of the Land—Proprietary Surveys in Chatham—
John Budd an extensive Landowner—Settlement of Chatham—
Counties and Townships instituted—Chatham formerly known
by various Names—Its present Name adopted

ALTHOUGH the Indian deed and the Nicolls patent
were so drawn as to include in the Elizabethtown purchase a large part of what is now Morris County, the
associates do not appear to have ever laid claim to the lands
lying beyond the Passaic River at the Minisink Crossing
That locality was occupied under proprietary grants   It was
during the period when the Passaic formed in part the
dividing line between East and West Jersey that the colonists established the settlement from which the Borough
of Chatham has developed

Much uncertainty exists concerning the date when the
first settlers entered the territory now called Morris County
According to Barber & Howe's Historical Collections of
New Jersey, a party of pioneers from Elizabeth, Newark,
East Hampton, L I, and New England, accompanied by
a few Englishmen, established themselves upon or near the
Whippany River as early as 1685, having been attracted
by the inviting appearance of the country and the fertility
of the soil, but especially by the rich deposits of iron ore
in the Morris County hills   They and their descendants
are said to have built so many forges in various places for
the manufacture of iron, that the locality was known as
"the Old Forges" for many years   Dr Samuel L Tuttle,
in his History of the Madison Presbyterian Church, locates

one of these early forges on or near the site of the grist mill at Chatham bridge

But the assertion that the white men secured a footing in this region at so early a period is not corroborated by other historians   Rev Jacob Green, in a historical sketch of the Presbyterian church of Hanover, written in 1767, and compiled largely from the parish records, gives the date of the first settlement in the county as 1710   Dr Joseph F Tuttle, a former pastor of the Presbyterian church at Rockaway, who made an exhaustive study of the subject, discovered that the earliest record date is that of a conveyance of land "near a place called Whippenung," in May, 1715, although he found traces of a settlement by five or six families in Pequannock Township, in the same county, as early as 1700 [1]

The West Jersey proprietors, like those of the eastern division, strongly opposed individual purchases of land from the Indians, and at an early date caused laws to be passed restraining such conveyances   These laws were re-enacted after the surrender of the proprietary government to Queen Anne, and although occasional attempts were made to evade them, their existence rendered it impossible for the settlers to acquire a title which would be officially recognized until the proprietors had bought the land from the savages, and had surveyed it into small parcels to be placed upon the market   An Indian deed to an individual possessed no legal validity unless previously authorized or subsequently confirmed by the authorities

There is reason to believe that in a few instances where land in this region was bought by the pioneers from the natives the site of Chatham was included in the transaction, but it is impossible to locate with certainty the property conveyed, for the descriptions in the Indian deeds were in-

[1] Sherman's Historic Morristown, 5, N J Historical Society Proceedings, Ser 2, II, 52

variably drawn in a most vague and careless manner. The
points of the compass were not definitely stated, the various
monuments referred to were in most cases merely posts,
marked trees, or heaps of stones, and when streams or hills
were mentioned they were often called by Indian words
bearing no resemblance to their present names. It is doubtful if greater accuracy was possible, owing to the lack of
exploration, or if it was considered necessary when the
country was so sparsely settled.

The most noted of these illegal conveyances was the
New Britain purchase, the deed of which is preserved in the
library of the New Jersey Historical Society. By this instrument which is dated August 13, 1708, a tract of land
about 18 miles square, called by the Indians *McKseta
Cohunge*, and by the whites New Britain was conveyed by
one Tapkaow and fifteen other savages to Peter Fauconnier
May Bickley, Ebenezer Wilson and Lancaster Symmes, all
of the city of New York, and Nathaniel Bonnel of Elizabethtown—a party of speculators who bought in anticipation of
large gains to be realized from the sale of farm sites to the
settlers. The boundary line of the property ran from a
point near Lake Hopatcong southwestwardly about 19 miles
to Peapack, thence due east 17 miles, thence due north 18
miles through the Great Swamp, the Passaick and Wey-
penunk Rivers, and along the east side of the latter stream,
and thence due west about 14 miles to the point of beginning.
It may be noted, as an evident inaccuracy of this description
that a course of 17 miles due east from Peapack would have
continued the purchase across the Passaic River into Elizabeth Township, though there is no reason to believe that
such was the design of the contracting parties. It is much
more probable that the tract was intended to adjoin, without
overlapping, the territory of Elizabeth. There can be little
doubt that the site of Chatham was included in this conveyance. Fauconnier and his companions sold plots upon

the tract to some half-dozen settlers, who, owing to the
illegality of the original purchase had considerable difficulty
in securing from the proprietors a subsequent confirmation
of their titles, but none of these plantations was located in
the immediate vicinity of Chatham

From an examination of the West Jersey records we
learn that during the opening years of the 18th century steps
were taken by the proprietary body to purchase and develop
Indian lands in the northern part of the Province. Aroused
by the knowledge that several planters who claimed under
deeds of the aborigines were settling in West Jersey the
proprietors decided in the spring of 1709 to secure as much
land as the natives could be induced to sell, and large purchases were accordingly made in 1712 and 1713, the savages
conveying practically all the territory they had not already
sold in the present counties of Morris, Sussex and Warren.
The speculation seems to have been very profitable, in view
of the fact that the proprietors estimated the cost of the
purchases at about six shillings per 100 acres and fixed the
price at which similar quantities of land should be sold to
the settlers at £35 [1]

During the years 1714 and 1715 the property thus
acquired was surveyed and divided into lots or tracts in order
that it might be justly and equally apportioned among the
members of the West Jersey proprietary who had joined in
its purchase. The minutes of the board indicate that the
allotment of the land was thus provided for

Sep 11th 1714. A full Council being met this day in order
to consider further of the method to be taken for dividing the last
purchase from the Indians in the most equal and impartial manner
It is agreed that the Division shall be in the following manner

That the whole quantity subscribed for or to be subscribed and
paid for before the time hereinafter appointed for drawing Lots shall
be divided into   Lots of 1250 Acres each

[1] West Jersey Proprietary Minutes, III 43, 46

That the Lots shall be numbered 1, 2, 3, &c until the full quantity subscribed for shall be made up

That such Props as have less than 1250 Acres or thereabouts can join their rights with others to make up the quantity not exceeding 100 Acres more or less

That the several Purchasers who have paid or who shall pay towards said purchase shall faithfully and impartially draw their Lots without any preference and according to the order or succession of their numbers which they draw shall have warrants granted them and may proceed in the same order to have their lands surveyed in such places as they choose

That none shall be allowed to take up above 10 Acres of Meadow or rich low land in each 100 Acres which they survey and not less than the quantity contained in their Lot shall be laid out in one Tract

That those who dislike their Lots when drawn may reject them and may take up Rights in any other part of W Division or in said Purchase after all those that approve of their Lots and proceed to survey are surveyed

That the said Lots shall be drawn at Burlington the 28th inst and that "The Council" meet on the 27th [1]

The land now included in the corporate limits of the Borough of Chatham lay in three tracts, the drawing of which by certain of the proprietors marked the first conveyance to individuals of land on the west side of the Passaic at and near the Minisink Crossing of which a definite and reliable record remains The first tract, which is designated in the proprietary surveys as Lot No 36, and which fell to the share of John Budd, embraced the northern part of Chatham, the second being a portion of Lot No 44, surveyed to Abraham Chapman, included the Stanley section of the borough, and the third, which lay between them, and was conveyed to John Hayward, contained the site of the early settlement The northeast corner of Chapman's lot, where it joined that of Hayward, touched the river at a point in

[1] West Jersey Proprietary Minutes, III, 68

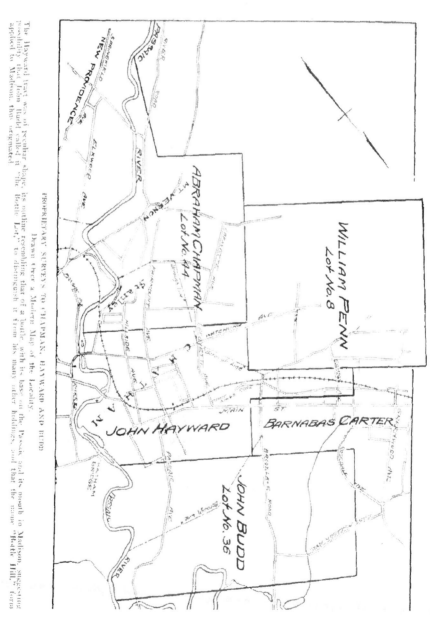

PROPRIETARY SURVEYS TO CHAPMAN, HAYWARD AND BUDD
Drawn over a Modern Map of the Locality.

The Hayward tract was of peculiar shape, its outline resembling that of a boot with its heel on the Passaic and its mouth in Madison, suggesting, possibly, that from Budd called it "the Boot Lot," to distinguish it from his many other holdings, and that the name "Budd Hills" was applied to Madison, that originated.

the Stanley millpond a short distance above the Watchung Avenue bridge, and the boundaries of the three tracts have been worked out by reference to that point

Lot No 36 was surveyed to John Budd on May 13, 1715 It consisted of 1250 acres (less 87 which had been previously seated by Samuel Carter), having a frontage of over a mile on the river, and extending northwestwardly as far as East Madison, and while its boundaries cannot be located with absolute precision, owing to the propensity of the early surveyors to select as their monuments nothing more permanent than trees and posts, we know that it included the territory now called lower Chatham and adjacent parts of the Borough of Florham Park [1]

Abraham Chapman's land, a portion of Lot No 44, which lay much farther up the river, was surveyed to him on August 23 of the same year Its area was given as 833 acres, though in point of fact it was much larger Its boundary line began on the Passaic above the Watchung Avenue bridge, and ran northwestwardly, a little north of Willow Street, to a white oak corner tree standing about as far from the river as Division Avenue, although the corner was some distance south of the southern extremity of that highway Here the tract adjoined Lot No 8, described as lying at the head of the Great Swamp, which had been previously surveyed to William Penn Turning at right angles, the line then ran 114 chains toward the southwest, along Penn's property, to a corner post whence it returned by two courses to a point on the river perhaps half a mile above the New Providence bridge [2] Chapman sold this property to William Oldden (Oulden) of Piscataway [3]

The third lot—that of John Hayward—is the tract in which our interest centres, for it embraced the heart of

[1] West Jersey Surveys, B, 37
[2] Ibid, A 183
[3] New Jersey Archives, Ser 1, XXIII 345

the early village   This land apparently was not included in
the original surveys, but was a remnant left between the
tracts adjoining   Concerning it the following entry occurs
in the council minutes of the West Jersey board of proprietors under date of August 22, 1715

John Budd & Richard Bull request in behalf of Capt Johnson
——Lucars ———Young & ———Crane that they may have
the liberty to purchase and lay a Right on 1250 Acres of land by
the Minisink Path between Govr Penn's Lot at the 'Head of the
Great Swamp" and John Budd's Lot in one piece or else to take
such smaller pieces of vacant lands between surveys already made
to make up the same quantity provided they transfer and deliver up
& release the Deed of Indian Purchase of the Lands of Whippany
commonly called "Cail's Purchase ' Ordered that lands be appro-
priated to them when Rights appear to be made them and they release &c as above said [1]

In compliance with this order it is believed, 1600 acres
or thereabouts were surveyed to John Hayward on May
22, 1716   The conveyance included three plots, of which
the first is the object of our inquiry   It consisted nominally
of 870 acres and bordered upon the Passaic between the
tracts of Chapman and Budd, having a river frontage of
more than a mile, and extending northwestward into the
present Borough of Madison   Its northern boundary
touched the Passaic near the mouth of the mill-race below
Main Street bridge   It was bisected by the Minisink Path,
now represented by Main Street and King's Road '
In the course of the allotment of lands among the West
Jersey proprietors and by subsequent purchases, John Budd
a merchant of Philadelphia, who at the time was one of the
most wealthy and influential members of the board became
the individual owner of several tracts in various localities,

[1] West Jersey Proprietary Minutes, III, 141
[2] West Jersey Surveys, B, 49

aggregating fully 15,000 acres most of which lay in what is now Morris County. For some reason, now unknown, he did not always take in his own name the land allotted to him; we find in the records occasional mention of lots surveyed to other persons "in right of John Budd." This procedure was adopted in the case of Hayward's property at Chatham, which seems to have belonged to Mr. Budd though surveyed to another. John Hayward was one of the early settlers, a carpenter by trade, who lived in Newark at the time of this purchase, but became a resident of Whippany as early as 1717.[1] The records do not show that he ever lived upon or sold the tract where Chatham now lies, and as Mr. Budd seems to have regarded the land as his own and to have disposed of it to the settlers at his pleasure, the inference is that Mr. Hayward appeared in the transaction merely as his representative.

A large collection of business papers of John Budd relating to his real estate was formerly possessed by one of his descendants, Frank M. Budd, of Chatham, but was unfortunately destroyed in the burning of the latter's residence in 1884. The collection included an immense number of memoranda, letters, accounts, land warrants, surveys, maps, deeds, powers of attorney, cancelled mortgages, assignments, leases, etc., dealing with lands in many parts of West Jersey and Pennsylvania, chiefly in the neighborhood of Whippany, and contained much valuable data respecting the settlement of Chatham. Among others were two undated maps, thought to have been drawn in June, 1748, which together covered the Hayward tract, giving the names of the settlers and the location of their plantations. Neither these maps nor any of the other papers indicated the date when the Hayward property was divided and sold, but there is reason to believe that the earliest sales were not made prior to 1720 or 1725.

[1] Budd Papers, Package 21, Nos. 12, 13.

We have seen that the conveyance of Lot No 36 to
John Budd in 1715 excepted a plantation of 87 acres previously seated by Samuel Carter, who thus appears to have
been the first settler on the west side of the Passaic where
Chatham now lies   No record has been found showing the
location of his farm, but as he was one of the first purchasers of land in the Hayward tract, where his holdings lay
on the north side of Main Street and King's Road,[1] extending from Passaic Avenue to Black Brook (now called Day's
Brook), it is reasonable to suppose that the plantation which
he had previously seated in Lot No 36 adjoined this
property on the north

Mention should also be made of John Day, the pioneer
who gave his name to the settlement   John and Daniel Day,
former residents of Long Island,[2] were the first to locate
near the river in the Hayward tract   The time of their purchase is not known, but as a reference to Daniel was found
in the Budd papers under date of 1728, it is assumed that
that year, or the year preceding, marked their arrival in this
region   From one of the maps above referred to, and from
some of the other papers of John Budd, it was ascertained
that John Day owned a farm of approximately 100 acres
lying on both sides of Main Street, having a frontage
on the river of some 3,000 feet, which ran down the
stream from a point a short distance below the upper
dam of the Chatham grist mill, and extending toward
the west to a small brook which crosses Main Street near
the corner of Minton Avenue. His residence stood on the
south side of the former street a few rods west of the

---

[1] Main Street and King's Road are mentioned together in this connection because the colonial highway is represented by the former from the
river to the corner of Washington Avenue, and by the latter from the corner
of Lafayette Avenue to Madison Between Washington and Lafayette
Avenues its line has been obliterated The section of Main Street west of
Washington Avenue was not opened until a much later date

[2] Lewis Publishing Company's Morris County, I, 282

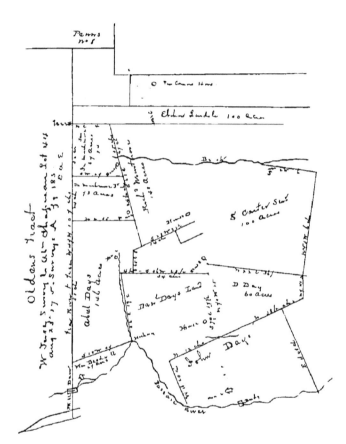

MAP OF CHATHAM, EASTERN SECTION
From the Budd Papers

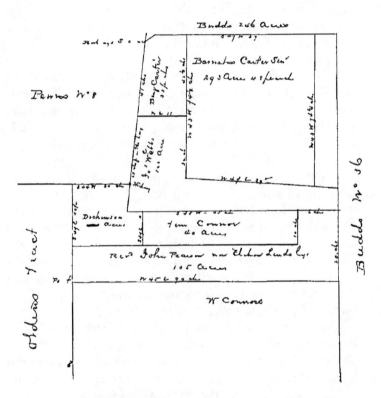

MAP OF CHATHAM, WESTERN SECTION
From the Budd Papers

river Adjoining this farm on the south and west was the plantation of Daniel Day, about 150 acres in extent, which was divided by Main Street into two unequal portions South of the road it stretched up the river from John Day's upper corner to the approximate line of Raymond Street, with its western boundary near Fuller Avenue On the north side of Main Street it extended from John Day's line as far west as Passaic Avenue, where it adjoined the Carter property mentioned above, and although the course of the latter street does not correspond exactly with Daniel Day's boundary, there is little doubt that it was originally a lane separating these ancient farms The holdings of both John and Daniel Day were not confined on the north by the side line of the Hayward tract, but extended irregularly a few rods into Lot No 36

The road now known as Main Street was laid out soon after the founding of the settlement, the bridge being constructed on John Day's property about four rods above the Minisink Crossing The name of John Day's Bridge was given to this structure, and later to the settlement itself The bridge was probably so called because of the proximity of Mr Day's residence, although the name may indicate that it was built by him to facilitate the transportation of his farm- and garden-produce to Elizabeth and Newark

The first mill in this locality was built by William Broadwell, who, on May 31, 1737, bought of John Budd a plot of 27 acres in the southeast corner of the Hayward tract, extending along the river from the Stanley millpond to the point where the stream approaches the railroad The map found among the Budd papers, which was thought to have been drawn in 1748, showed that the mill had been erected prior to that time, the dam being on or near the boundary between the tracts of Hayward and Chapman, in which vicinity a dam has been maintained until modern times

Regarding the sales to the early settlers of plantations in Lot No 36, definite information is not obtainable   From the Budd papers it appeared that on December 11, 1730, Samuel Lum, a weaver of Elizabeth, purchased of John Budd for £95 a parcel of land known as Stephen's Neck (a name applied to the east end of Lot No 36), extending from the river to Black Brook   It was described in the deed as "bounded Southward and Westward by land said Budd sold to John Day, Danl Day and Samuel Carter, and Eastward by Passayck River, and westward by Black Brook, exclusive of said Brook, and Meadow sold John and Danl Day & Joseph Jump, and Saml Carter as per their Deeds "[1]   The holdings of John and Daniel Day and Samuel Carter which adjoined this property on the south were the plantations they had bought in the Hayward tract, and the deed to Mr Lum indicates that the Days and Joseph Jump had bought lots lying west of Black Brook in Lot No 36 [2] The location of these farms, however, cannot be ascertained

[1] Package 20 The deed was witnessed before Joseph Bonnell, judge of the Essex County Court of Common Pleas, June 19, 1737

[2] Joseph Jump at one time owned a plot of 50 acres on the south side of Main Street between Fairmount and Lafayette Avenues Following is a memorandum of his deed found among the Budd papers

Package 19, No 2, May 10, 1728   John Budd of Hannover for £25 Deeds Jos Jump, late of New England, now of Hannover, 50 Acres opposite Saml Carter & 8 Acres on Passaick River in the Neck, being same as was surveyed for John & Jos Carter, with 2 Acres which was surveyed for Danl Day

The lot on Main Street was acquired by John Carter, who disposed of it as follows

Package 17, No 16   Sept 17, 1729 John Carter of Hannover Deeds Nathl Cogswell of said Town, Blacksmith, for £30, 55 Acres in Hannover, 50 Acres lying on S side of King's Highway to E Town Beginning at Post by a small Run 4 Pearches up the Run from Saml Carter's lands, thence by S side Highway, S 41° E, 28 Pearches, thence S 68° E, 100 Pearches by said Road, thence S 22° W 60 Pearches, thence N 68° W, 80 Pearches, thence S 22° W, 20 Pearches, thence N 68° W, to aforesaid Run of Water & down same to beginning Also 5 Acres on N side said Road   Witnessed by Ephm Sayre

Package 17, No 17   1732 Cogswell Deeds Peter Vantilburg 30 Acres on S side & 5 on N side of above land

Package 20, No 15 1735 Vantilburg Deeds to Benj Parkhurst the said 35 Acres

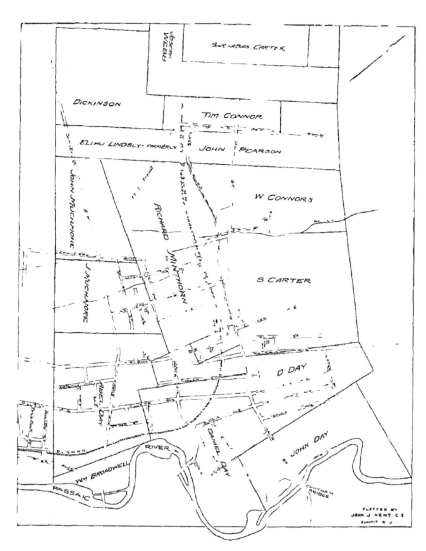

JOHN BUDD'S MAP OF EARLY PLANTATIONS
Drawn Over a Modern Map of Chatham

Three years later Samuel Lum bought the Carter property in the Hayward tract—a farm of 100 acres—which as already stated, butted on the north side of Main Street and King's Road from Passaic Avenue to Black Brook. Mr Carter had previously sold this property to Joseph Lyon of Newark, who, on February 19, 1733, conveyed it to Mr Lum for £52. This deed was also found among the Budd papers [1]. As a result of these purchases, Samuel Lum's holdings extended from the Passaic in lower Chatham and Florham Park to Main Street

The present homestead farm of the Budd family on Passaic Avenue is located in Lot No 36—presumably in the section known in colonial days as Stephen's Neck—and

Package 17, No 18 1736 Parkhurst Deeds the same to John Budd

The following survey, while not connected with the history of Chatham, is of sufficient interest to warrant its insertion here, as it is believed to have been the first survey to an actual settler in this part of Morris County It was made by Joseph Harriman, surveyor, of Elizabethtown, but not signed by him, and not recorded among the West Jersey surveys It was declared irregular, and the land was resurveyed under West Jersey rights Budd Papers, Package 21 No 7 At Whipeny Laid out for John Cramer Beginning it a White Oak stake in a large meadow, thence S 9° W, 116 chains, thence S 86 W, 71 chains, then N 13 E 149 chains, thence S 66 E, 61½ chains to the place it first began April ye 14th day 1710

Memorandum   800 Acres surveyed to J Cramer
    78 was due him
    ———
    722
    33 retd to S Potter Jany 14, 1717 18
    ———
    689
    150 P Keighley
    ———
    539
    40 to Potter
    ———
    499 To Ford & Hayward

[1] Memorandum of Samuel Lum's second deed found among the Budd papers

Package 20 Feby 19th 1733 Joseph Lyon of Newark to Samuel Lum of Elizabethtown for £52 Tract of land in Hanover on North side of Highway leading from Passaick River to ye Plantation of Barnabas Carter Begin at the second brook which crosses said Highway from said River thence on said Highway S, 40 E 7 chains, thence on same S 68 E, 23 chains thence N 23 E, 36½ chains, thence N 53 W, 26 chains, thence S 22 W, 16 chains to said Brook, thence on Brook to beginning 100 Acres formed part of the plantation sold by John Budd to Samuel Lum Dr John C Budd, a grandson of the proprietor, came into possession of the property by his marriage to Miss Mary Lum, and the presence of Samuel Lum's deeds among the Budd papers is explained by this marriage

During the closing years of the 17th century, when the partition line of the provinces followed the Passaic River for part of its distance, and the site of Chatham was consequently in the western colony, the division of West Jersey into counties and townships was commenced The earliest counties were Gloucester in the south, formed in 1677, and Burlington in the north, dating from 1694 The limits of the latter as originally laid out being quite indefinite, an attempt to legally determine them was made in 1710, and although the language of the statute was not wholly free from uncertainty, its intention was that Burlington County should completely cover the northern half of the Province

In 1713-14, upon petition of the settlers inhabiting the northern parts of West Jersey, who objected to traveling so far to attend sessions of the county court, a large section of Burlington was set off and erected into a separate county called Hunterdon, which was bounded on the south by Assunpink Creek (a tributary of the Delaware at Trenton), and embraced the entire territory of the Province to the northward The gradual increase of population led to further recognition of the needs and convenience of the inhabitants by the erection of Morris County, which was carved out of Hunterdon in 1738-9 The new bailiwick contained not only its present area, but also that of the more recent counties of Sussex and Warren It was named in honor of Governor Lewis Morris, during whose administration it was formed

One of the first townships created in the upper portion of West Jersey was called Whippenong It lay to the northward and eastward, including the region where Chatham is situated, and is said to have been laid out about 1700 Its name was changed to Hanover probably about 1721 References to Hanover Township occur as early as 1722 in Volume II of the Hunterdon County court minutes, but the first volume, which doubtless recorded the formation of the township and its subsequent change of name, is missing, and a diligent search in 1879 failed to bring it to light

The Morris County Court of General Sessions convened at Morristown, for the first time it is believed, on March 25, 1740, and proceeded as its initial step to divide the county into three townships to be known as Pequonnock, Hanover and Morris By this action the former township of Hanover was greatly reduced in size Pequonnock lay in the extreme north and east, between the Pequonnock and ˙Rockaway Rivers, and the other two embraced the remainder of the county, being separated by the road which ran through the centre of Chatham The dividing line was thus laid out

And that a Certain road from the Bridge by John Days up to the Place where the Same road passes between Benjamin and Abraham Persons and thence up the Same road to the Corner of Samuel Fords fence, thence Leaving Samuel Ford to the right hand thence running up to the road that leads from the Old Iron Works toward Succasunning Crossing Whippenung Bridge and from thence to Succasunning, & from thence to the great Pond on the head of Musconecong, do part the Township of Hanover from the Township of Morris, which part of the County of Morris Lying as afd to the Southward and Westward of Said Roads, lines & places is Ordered by the Court to be and remain a Township, District or Precinct, & to be Called & Distinguished by the name of Morris Town [1]

The fact that the village of Chatham on the west side of the Passaic was divided between the townships of Hanover and Morris, accounts for its representation by the

[1] Morris County Oyer and Terminer Minutes, I 1

committee of observation of each of these districts during
the early days of the Revolution

With the increase in population incident to the opening
up of a new country, the settlement afterwards known as
Chatham continued steadily to grow, and as we approach
the Revolutionary period we find it a flourishing village,
having its nucleus at the bridge, extending perhaps three-
quarters of a mile in each direction along the highroad, with
scattered dwellings up and down the river, and containing
stores, taverns, grist-, saw- and fulling-mills, blacksmiths'
shops and other local industries The settlement, however,
lacked a definite and distinctive name It was originally
known both as John Day's Bridge, and as the Minisink
Crossing, although the latter appellation probably referred
to the ford of the Passaic more particularly than to the
village itself, but during the late colonial period these names
appear to have fallen into disuse, the settlement being somewhat vaguely denominated "On Passaic River" An early
mention of the hamlet thus designated is found in the diary
of Captain John Montresor, who noted therein the expenses
of a journey from Philadelphia to New York at the time of
the erection of the fort on Mud Island in the Delaware
River, probably in the latter part of April, 1771 He wrote:

Expenses for Self, Servant & horses on ye road Ferriages—
from Phila to New York for one chais and horse for self and 1
Horse for Servant.

Neshaming	. .	One Shilling, one penny Pennsylva
Trent Town	. .	3 do one do do
Brunswick		1 do Eleven do
P'Suck		24 coppers
Hackinsack	.	2 Shilling & 8 coppers
Powles-hook		6 do & 1 copper
Boats Crew white oak Barge		1 guinea
do of one of the Island		1 do

Expenses from Phila to Boston and return—Twice [1]

[1] New York Historical Society Collections, XLV, 416

The stopping-place which he calls "P'Saick" was doubtless the settlement which in time became the village of
Chatham. The present city of Passaic was then Acquackanonck.

In the *New York Gazette* of July 26, 1773, Stephen
Ball advertised for sale his residence &c. at Passaic River,
on the main road from Morris Town to Elizabeth Town;
the property being 12 miles from Elizabeth Town, 13 from
Newark, a gun shot from a saw
mill, grist mill, and market, and
within one and three quarter
miles of South Hanover Meeting,
by which he meant what is now
known as the Madison Presbyterian church. He added that as
he intended to move to the Mis-
sissippi in the early fall, he would
sell very cheap.

Colonial Tankard

When communication with
the cities became more frequent,
the term "On Passaic River" was
found to be too indefinite; and the settlers decided that their
town had attained a size and importance which entitled it to
a more distinctive name. Accordingly, on the 19th of November, 1773, at a meeting held for the purpose, they agreed
to call it CHATHAM, in honor of Sir William Pitt, Earl of
Chatham, who had won the gratitude and esteem of the
colonists by his parliamentary activities in their behalf when
their rights and interests were menaced by the oppressive
policy of the government. Public notice of this important
step was given by advertisement inserted in the *New York
Gazette* of December 6, 13 and 20, 1773, which read as
follows:

TO THE PUBLIC.

Whereas the inhabitants of a certain village, situate at Passaik-

River, on the main road that leads from Elizabeth-Town to Morris-
Town, found themselves under a considerable disadvantage from the
place's not having a particular name, as the river runs through the
country 40 or 50 miles, and letters directed to persons at Passaik
River only, would be sometimes carried above and sometimes below
them; upon which the principal freeholders and inhabitants assembled
together on Friday, the 19th. inst, and unanimously agreed to
call it Chatham; and all persons that should hereafter direct letters,
or anything else to any person living at or near the above place, are
desired to direct at Chatham, on Passaik River.[1]

[1] This advertisement also appeared in *The New York Journal or General
Advertiser* of November 23, 1773.

CHAPTER III

Commencement of the Revolution—Committees of Safety—Repression of Toryism—The Liberty Pole—Military Organizations—Chatham a Militia Station—The Bridge Carefully Guarded

BUT little can now be learned of the part taken by the citizens of Chatham in the series of events which led to the severance of allegiance to the British crown, but we know that, as an initial step, they joined the people of the neighboring villages in the formation of committees of observation, and committees of correspondence. These committees were organized by the people, without official authorization, in the counties and townships of the Province, and were composed of the most influential men in each community. They were originally designed simply to voice public opinion, and to this end they passed resolutions, in the early days of their existence, consisting of protests against the oppressive acts of the government, accompanied by declarations of loyalty to the king, but in some instances (as in the case of the Committee of Morris County) they were vested by the people with legislative powers, subject to the control of the Provincial Congress, and after independence was declared they became the recognized head of the local government. Captain Stephen Day, of Chatham, was a member of the Committee of Hanover Township, representing that part of the village which lay west of the river and north of Main Street.[1]

When war with the mother country was found to be

---

[1] Lee's New Jersey as Colony and State, II, 47, Minutes of the New Jersey Provincial Congress and Council of Safety, II, 52, Sherman's Historic Morristown, 161

inevitable, the people of Chatham embraced the cause of
liberty with fervor and enthusiasm There were doubtless a
few persons in the community who remained loyal to the
crown, but their number seems to have been insignificant,
and, in fact, it is highly probable that those who were not in
sympathy with the popular excitement soon found it prudent
to make no mention of their views, for at an early period of
the Revolution laws were enacted for the restraint of disaffected persons, the severity of which legislation increased
as time went on, until at length toryism was punished by
banishment from the State and forfeiture of lands and
goods After the close of the war the newspapers of New
Jersey published an occasional advertisement announcing the
sale of the property of some turbulent royalist, who, owing
to his disloyal utterances, or his activities in the interests of
the British, had been adjudged an enemy of his country,
whose lands were declared forfeited to the State One of
these advertisements, published November 15, 1786, in the
New Jersey Journal of Elizabeth, is quoted in illustration

CONFISCATED ESTATES in the County of Essex, to be
sold at public vendue

    *   *   *   *   *   *   *   *   *   *   *

Also all the property of William Wright, of, in and to a certain piece of land within the bounds of Elizabeth Town, at a place
called Chatham, which land was formerly sold by Matthias Winans
to William Wright by a deed bearing date the 20th day of October,
1776, and now forfeited to the state by William Wright

SAMUEL HAYES,
Agent for Essex County [1]

[1] In the *New York Gazette and Weekly Mercury* of September 28 1776,
Ezekeal Ball of Newark Farms (now Hilton) offers a reward of $2 for
the return of a heifer and calf strayed from the pasture of Matthias Wynants
of Chatham, the reward to be paid by himself or by Mr Wynants or by
Dr Ball at Chatham This pasture was doubtless part of the farm referred to in the text William Wright had tried to dispose of his property
during the Revolution, but apparently without success In the *New Jersey
Gazette* of August 5, 1778, he advertises for sale a plantation of 81 acres
at Chatham, Essex County, there being 50 acres of English meadow, 8 acres
of plow land, and the rest wood land

Dr James Thatcher, in his Military Journal, describes in the following words the treatment meted out to those who refused to support the cause of the colonies at that time of intense feeling and excitement His statement has reference to an entirely different part of the country, but the conditions which existed in this vicinity were precisely similar

The man who does not acquiesce in the theme of liberty is marked by the vigilant eye of suspicion, or stigmatized as an enemy to his country Liberty poles are erected in almost every town and village, and when a disaffected tory renders himself odious by any active conduct, with a view of counteracting the public measures he is seized by a company of armed men, and conducted to the liberty pole, under which he is compelled to sign a recantation, and give bonds for his future good conduct In some instances, of particular stubbornness and obstinacy individuals have been imprisoned, or their names have been published in the newspapers as enemies to their country It has indeed unfortunately happened, that a few individuals, in consequence of their own indiscretion, have been the subjects of a more rigorous procedure Having fallen into the hands of those whose zeal has transported them beyond the bounds of moderation, they have received from the rabble a coat of tar and feathers, and in this predicament have been exposed to the scoffs and ridicule of the populace Such examples have the effect of striking terror into the hearts of all the disaffected, and of restraining the whole party from acting against the general sense of the people

A prominent tory of Morris County whose name has come down to us was Thomas Eckley, an English gentleman who had purchased the homestead farm of Peter Smith on the road from Hanover to Florham Park Mr Eckley was one of the leading citizens of Hanover in colonial days, and had served the community as a lay judge of the county courts [1] He is described as 'a man of considerable property and not a little hauteur" [2] and he was

[1] Munsell's Morris County (1882), 75
[2] Jones s Ashbel Green, 33

most strongly and bitterly opposed to the rupture with the
mother country   So freely and aggressively did he express
his opinions that his neighbors became greatly incensed, and
they discussed the advisability of taking drastic action
against him   A rumor of the threatened movement having
reached Elizabeth, Elias Boudinot of that place, a member
of the Essex County Committee of Correspondence, hastily
dispatched a letter to the corresponding committee of Morris County, protesting against such step   A draft of this
letter has been found among Boudinot's papers, and is given
below   It bears no signature, but is known to be in his handwriting

Gentl
     We have been much surprised, by an information just received
from a Mr Morrell of Chatham given to his Brother of this Town,
that there is a determination of a considerable number of your
County, to raise a Liberty Pole at Chatham to morrow and from
thence they are to proceed to Mr Thomas Eckley, where it is supposed they intend to offer Violence to his Person on account of some
imprudent Expressions said to be inimical to the Liberties of this
Country, and that this determination is in Consequence of an Example said to be set by our own People here, with regard to Dr
Chandler
     Deeply impressed therefore with a sense of the unhappy Conse
quences that must necessarily attend a Proceeding of this kind with
regard to our Comon Cause, we are at the Trouble and Expense
of an Express to you on this occasion, beseeching you immediately to
exert yourselves to prevent a Measure that if adopted by the friends
of Liberty will be such a Stain to our Characters as Men & Christians, that it may in the End deter every good Man from joining
with us   It is our honor that while we are engaged in so glorious
a Struggle for what is more dear to us than Life, that even our very
Enemies in the midst of us enjoy that Peace & Liberty which we so
ardently wish for ourselves
     As to the Precedent alledged to be drawn from our Example
respecting Dr Chandler, nothing can be more untrue   The fact

stands thus a Number of Men from a small distance from the Town having been under Arms all day towards Evening some of them became rather intoxicated with Liquor and being urged by a Person who was incapable of the exercise of his reason, (and we are afraid in order to answer some private design) marched away suddenly to Dr Chandler's House, without the least suspicion of the Committee as to their design They were immediately followed by the Committee who arrived time enough to send them back before they entered the Doctor's Yard, by which means all violence was prevented And we are unanimous in discountenancing every Act of Violence to the Person or Property of any man whatever as a Measure eventually necessary to our union & Success and directly contrary to your & our resolutions and as there is no opposition to our publick Measures either with you or us we cannot think that Liberty Pole Meetings can be necessary or any way serve the comon cause and if the People will undertake & carry on every or any publick Measure without the advice of the Committee chosen by themselves it will be impossible to perfect any Plan for the general good

These are our Sentiments wrote in a great hurry, which we communicate to you as Brethren, from the earnest desire we have to preserve a similarity of Sentiment and Practice among all the friends of Liberty in this Colony
Sunday Evening Aprile 30 1775
To Committee of Morris County

The outcome of this occurrence is thus described by Dr Ashbel Green, a son of Rev Jacob Green, the Revolutionary pastor of Hanover church

Before long, this Englishman became so publickly audacious, that some young and ardent whigs, in a neighbouring town, were reported to have declared that they would tar and feather him This report came to his ears on a Saturday evening, and it frightened him half out of his life He came to my father on the following Sabbath morning, in the greatest trepidation imaginable He acknowledged that he had done wrong in speaking against the American cause, said he was sorry for his imprudence and violence, and was willing to promise, most explicitly and solemnly, that if he might be forgiven,

and be permitted to live in peace and safety, he would be silent on
the American controversy in future, and would, in all respects, de-
port himself inoffensively   Such was the substance of his communication, for I pretend not to give his words   He entreated my father
to write down this humiliating statement and read it publicly from
the pulpit that morning, and he promised to attend, and stand up
in the face of the congregation, and own the whole as his own
voluntary act and deed   My father, I believe, had not heard a word
about the tarring and feathering of his alarmed visitant, till he
heard it from himself, and was rather disposed to dissuade him from
a public confession, although he had witnessed his imprudence, and
did not know but he might be in danger of what he so greatly feared
As the tory insisted upon making a public confession and retraction,
my father told him to write it   This he was not well able to do,
and urged my father to write it for him, which was accordingly
done, in strict conformity with his dictation   Agreeably to his
promise, he appeared in the church, and rose up in his pew before
the congregation, when my father began to read his paper, and at
the close of the reading, he assented distinctly to its contents, as containing his voluntary confession and promise   I was present, and
saw and heard what I now write   But the matter did not end here
The alarmed and anxious tory took the paper which my father had
read, and hurried to the town from which the threatening had come,
that he might have done there, in the afternoon service, what had
already been done in the morning, in the place of his residence   But
the minister of the town assured him that what he had heard had
been greatly magnified, and that nothing had taken place in that
town to render necessary any such public transaction as he had
solicited, and he refused to read the paper   Whether what was done
in my father's church really saved him from tar and feathers, or
whether his own fears had precipitated him into an unnecessary act,
I know not   But I know that he lived many years on his farm in
my father's neighbourhood, without any disturbance, and died there a
considerable time after the close of our revolutionary war.
And I know, that although my father played him no trick in the
matter of his public confession, yet when he found he was in no

danger, he seemed to suspect it, and treated my father with greater distance after, than before that occurrence.[1]

The above incident is mentioned by Rev. Dr. Joseph F. Tuttle, who adds that the proposed act of violence emanated from some "hot bloods" of Morristown, and that the clergyman who was requested by Eckley to read the confession in the afternoon service was Rev. Timothy Johnes of that place,[2] but Dr. Tuttle gives no authority for this statement, and in the light of Mr. Boudinot's letter, indicating that the threatenings proceeded from Chatham, it seems more likely that the application was made to Rev. Azariah Horton, pastor of the Presbyterian church of Madison. There being no church edifice in Chatham at that time, this village was included in the Madison parish.

Whether the liberty-pole referred to by Mr. Boudinot was raised at that time or at a later date, is a question which unfortunately cannot be answered. We know that there was such a pole in Chatham during the Revolution, for it is mentioned more than once in a local newspaper of the period, the *New Jersey Journal,* but the time of its erection and removal cannot be ascertained. We are able to fix its location, however, with some degree of accuracy. In the *Journal* of April 13, 1779, the executors of Mrs. Eunice Horton advertised the sale of part of her effects "opposite the Liberty-Pole." From Dr. Samuel L. Tuttle's History of the Madison Presbyterian Church it appears that Mrs. Horton lived and died on the property adjoining on the east the former Presbyterian parsonage in Chatham, and from other sources we learn that the former parsonage is now the residence of Frederick S. Tallmadge of East Main Street. As the articles advertised for sale consisted of personal effects and household goods, there is scarcely room for doubt that the vendue

[1] Jones's Ashbel Green, 34-36
[2] Annals of Morris County, 45, Harper's Magazine, XVIII, 292

was held in Mrs Horton's house, in front of which, as is
inferred from the advertisement, the liberty-pole stood   It
may have been raised in the road, but if placed upon private
property, its site is the land now owned by Clark C Cyphers,
on the north side of Main Street about twenty-five rods west
of the river

The Revolutionary citizens of Chatham did not confine
their activities in the cause of freedom to the raising of a
liberty-pole and the disciplining of tories they proved their
patriotism in a more conclusive and practical way by enlist-
ing, and rendering valiant service in the army, some of them
joining the Continental troops, and many others enrolling
themselves in the militia   These were the two chief branches
into which the military of New Jersey was divided in Revolutionary days. the Continental troops corresponding to the
regular army of modern times, and the militia being a force
designed more especially for home defense, whose members,
as originally planned, were to confine their operations to
their own State, although circumstances occasionally arose
which necessitated their presence beyond its borders   Besides
these there were bodies called the State troops, and the
minute men, but both of the latter organizations were composed of soldiers drawn from the militia

The Continental troops originated in October, 1775,
when Congress recommended the Province of New Jersey
to recruit men "at the expense of the Continent" for the
national army, the call being for two battalions of eight companies each, a company to consist of 68 privates   One
battalion was raised in each of the two divisions of the
Province, and they were therefore distinguished as the First,
or Eastern, and the Second, or Western, their respective
colonels being Lord Stirling and William Maxwell   During
the following June a third battalion was organized, having
eight companies of 78 privates each, and commanded by
Colonel Elias Dayton   The first and second battalions were

discharged in the autumn of 1776, and the third in the following spring

The troops raised in response to this call of Congress constituted what was officially termed the "first establishment," the contingent of this State being designated as the First, Second and Third Battalions, First Establishment, New Jersey Continental Line

The second establishment was formed in the autumn of 1776, the Continental Congress calling for 88 battalions to be raised in the several States, of which New Jersey's quota was 4   Their commanders were commissioned by Congress, and those of the New Jersey battalions were Colonels Silas Newcomb, Israel Shreve, Elias Dayton and Ephraim Martin   These four battalions constituted what is known in history as the Jersey Brigade   William Maxwell, who had been promoted to the rank of brigadier-general, commanded the brigade until July, 1780, when he resigned, and Colonel Dayton succeeded him

About the time that men were recruiting under the second call of Congress, Colonel Oliver Spencer, of the New Jersey militia, raised a battalion of approximately 150 troops for the Continental service   As the second establishment consisted of four battalions, Spencer's is sometimes referred to as the Fifth

The third and last establishment of the New Jersey Continental line was organized in the spring of 1779, and consisted of three regiments commanded respectively by Colonels Matthias Ogden, Israel Shreve and Elias Dayton Many recruits for these regiments were obtained from the militia, and among those taken from the Eastern Battalion of Morris County we find the names of some residents of Chatham, namely   Gilbert Bonnel, Eb McDonald and James Richardson of Captain Carter's company, and Philip Lunney and Wright Reading of Captain Ward's company

The militia antedated the Continental army   Bodies

of citizen-soldiery existed in the Province during the late colonial period, but upon the outbreak of the Revolution this arm of service was greatly enlarged, and put upon a much more effective basis, recruits being eagerly sought for, and new companies and regiments raised   In June, 1775, the Provincial Congress enacted that, "for the purpose of defending American freedom," one or more companies of militia, each consisting of 80 men from 16 to 50 years of age, should be raised in every township or corporation, allotting a certain number of regiments or battalions to each county   Essex County was to furnish two regiments, with the privilege of forming them into four battalions, and Morris County one regiment or two battalions   Two battalions were accordingly organized in Morris County, distinguished as the "Eastern" and "Western," in the first of which several Chatham men were enrolled

Each soldier was required to provide himself with a musket or fire-lock and bayonet, a sword or tomahawk, a steel ramrod, worm, priming-wire and brush, a cartouche-box to contain 23 rounds of cartridges, 12 flints and a knapsack, and to keep in his house one pound of powder and three pounds of bullets   Any man who was eligible for militia duty and who refused to bear arms was required to pay to the township committee four shillings Proclamation money per month, as an equivalent for personal service

At first the citizens were merely "requested" to join the militia; but as time went on the laws became more and more stringent, until practically every eligible man was compelled to render military service   Although the militia was a local organization, properly within the exclusive control of the State legislature, yet we find the Continental Congress occasionally passing a law for its regulation   For example, the penalties imposed for the failure of militiamen to attend musters and reviews were fixed by the federal authorities, and consisted of fines varying in amount according to the rank of the offender In 1780 fines were imposed upon nearly all the able-bodied men of Pequannock Township, Morris County, about 300 in number, for neglecting to turn out at the time of the battle of Springfield These delinquents were chiefly of Dutch descent, and seem to have taken but little interest in the struggle for freedom [1]

The men enrolled in the militia were not required to render constant service, but were called at certain times for short periods or tours of military duty, the object of this arrangement being to interfere as little as possible with their usual occupations In 1776 they were divided into two classes, each of which served one month and was then relieved by the other During a great part of the war the militia served on this basis of monthly classes

In the summer of 1776 the peril of New York caused the Continental Congress to call upon the States for 13,800 militia Of this number, New Jersey furnished 3,300 They were divided into 5 battalions of 8 companies each, with 78 privates in a company, and their term of service was limited to December 1st of the same year The Essex County troops formed a battalion of 3 companies, and one of the other battalions consisted of 4 companies of Morris County and 4 of Sussex

In 1778 the militia of the State was reorganized and formed into 2 brigades, the troops of Bergen, Essex, Middlesex, Morris, Somerset and Sussex forming one, and those of the other counties the other In 1781 the number of brigades was increased to three, called the Upper, Middle and Lower Brigades, the first including the troops of Morris and Essex Counties

Independent companies of artillery and troops of horse were raised from time to time in various parts of the State, either by direction of the governor or by special laws

The minute men were so called because required to

[1] Rivington's *Royal Gazette* No 397, July 19, 1780

serve at a minute's notice whenever and wherever they might
be needed   They were organized in response to a call of the
Continental Congress, nearly 4,000 being drawn from the
New Jersey militia and formed into 62 minute companies,
of which the counties of Morris and Essex each furnished
six   These men were given precedence over the common
militia, and their term of service was limited to four months
They were to hold themselves in readiness for instant service, and, in case of alarm, to rendezvous at the homes of
their captains

Owing to the danger to which the State was exposed when
both New York and Philadelphia were in the hands of the
British, and to the fact that the system of monthly service
required of the militia interfered with the cultivation of the
farms, it was found necessary from time to time to embody,
for limited periods, a certain number of troops for special
service   These organizations were designated the State
troops, although also known as New Jersey Levies and Five
Months Levies, and were composed entirely of volunteers
from the militia   They were chiefly employed in the portions of the State which were particularly exposed to the
enemy, although they were prepared to extend their service
to the adjoining States if occasion required

In the summer of 1776 Congress decided to reinforce
the army in the field with a new species of troops of an inter-
mediate grade, who, it was believed, would be more permanent than the militia, and more easily recruited than the
Continentals   This organization was called the Flying
Camp   It was a sort of outpost, having its headquarters at
Perth Amboy, N J, and was designed, as its name
implied, to be suddenly moved to any place where reinforcements were needed   For this service 10,000 men were
called from the States of Pennsylvania, Delaware and Maryland, and 2,000 were detached from the New Jersey militia
The Jerseymen comprised 30 companies of 64 privates each,

Morris County furnishing two companies and Essex three [1]

Few of the patriots of 1775 were more actively interested in recruiting and organizing the militia of northern
New Jersey than was Lord Stirling of Basking Ridge
Owing to his energy and assiduity in this direction, as well
as to the experience he had gained in the French and Indian
War, he was chosen colonel of the First Somerset County
battalion, which he had been instrumental in raising, and it is
said that he supplied arms at his own expense to such of the
men as could not otherwise obtain them [2] In March, 1776,
he was commissioned brigadier-general, and placed in command of the first two Continental regiments raised in this
State, but his interest in the militia was not abated by his
transfer to the more important branch of the service
Among the papers of General Washington now preserved in
the Library of Congress there is a paper entitled "Alarm
Posts and Plans of Rendezvous of the Militia at New
Jersey," which is thought to have been sent him by Lord
Stirling, as a copy of it is found in a collection of Stirling's
letters in the library of the New York Historical Society
The original is indorsed with the date May, 1780 It reads
as follows

COUNTIES & COLONELS

MIDDLESEX—North of Raratan

Colonel Webster	To assemble at the Short Hills and Quib-
	ble Town To have some small Parties
	of the most trusty men to watch the mo-
(1)	tions of the Enemy and to give him fre-

---

[1] Speaking of the Flying Camp, Henry Belcher, an English writer, says
'The Flying Camp is a pet phrase of Congress It was an imaginary force
evoked out of the riff-raff of the militia of the Middle States with a view
of forming the *franc-tireur* class of combatant, every man of which should,
according to military custom, have been shot on capture But the Flying
Camp, about which so many directions are given in the Journal of Congress,
appears to have been a *chose gatée* "—*The First American Civil War,*
II, 179

[2] Griswold's Washington and the Generals of the Revolution, I, 171

quent information which he is to communicate to the Commander in Chief as soon
as possible

(2)   If he finds the Enemy advancing into the
Country to endeavor to keep on one or
both their Flanks and as near their Front
as possible, and to keep up a constant fire
with small Parties in different places

(3)   If they keep towards the Mountains and
seem to intend to penetrate them He is to
possess himself of the gap they move towards and give them all the annoyance
and obstruction in his Power

MIDDLESEX—South of Raratan

Colonels Wilson   To assemble at Brunswick and South
and Scudder   Bridge And further to act according to
(1) (2)   Circumstances most effectually to distress
and annoy the Enemy

ESSEX—Southern Part and Middle Part

Colonel Jaques   To assemble at Connecticut Farms, Wt
Field, Springfield and Mountain Meeting
House   (1) (2) (3)

Colonel Cortland—   To assemble Part in the Hills in the Rear
Northern Part   of Newark, and Part at the Heights near
Docti Roaches above Aquackanonck
(1) (2) (3)

SOMERSET—North of Raratan

To assemble Part at Capt Tingleys near
Quibble Town gap, and Part at Turkey
Meeting House to have a particular attention to all the gaps and Passes of the Mountains between Quibble Town and Turkey
(1) (2) (3)

SOMERSET—South of Easton

> To assemble at the landing Bridge and Part at Bound Brook
>
> (1) (2)

Colo Vandyke

> It He finds the Enemy are pushing towards the Mountains He is to move his Regiment within the Mountains, and to act in connection with Colonel Frelingheisen in opposing them

BERGEN COUNTY

Colo Dye

> To assemble on the Heights near Hackensack new Bridge Early to send out one Party to the little Ferry and another towards Closter to prevent the Enemy turning his right or left
>
> (1) (?) (3)

MORRIS COUNTY

Colo Seeley

> The lower Part to assemble as soon as possible at Chatham and Bottle Hill
>
> (1) (2) (3)

The Upper Part
Colo Monson   (4)

> To assemble as soon as possible at their usual Places of Meeting, and to march by Companies by the shortest Roads to Morris Town and there take further orders

SUSSEX

Colo Seward &
Colo Webster
at Phillipsburg

> To assemble at their usual Places of Meeting by Companies and to march by the shortest Roads to Morris Town and there take further orders

HUNTERDON COUNTY

Colo Beaver

> To assemble at German Town and to march by Veal Town to Morris Town

| Colonel Taylor & Lt Col Chamberlin | To assemble at Reading Town Meeting House and to march by Pluckimin Toumin's Tavern and Baskingridge Meeting House to Morris Town |

HUNTERDON COUNTY

| Colonel Phillips | To assemble at Hopewell and to march by Somerset Court House and Bound Brook to Morris Town |

BURLINGTON COUNTY

| Colo Wm Shrive Colo Thos Reonalds | To assemble at Princeton and to march by Somerset Court House and Bound Brook to Morris Town |

| Colo Holmes | To assemble at South Amboy and along the shore towards Middletown |

| Colo Hendrickson Colo Saml Toumin | To assemble at Middletown Tinton Falls, Shrewsbury and Deal To watch the Motions of the Enemy, and in Case of their Landing to give them all the annoyance in their Power [1] |

We learn from local tradition and from references to the village in Revolutionary correspondence, military orders, soldiers' diaries, and news-items contained in public prints, that Chatham was the scene of much activity during the war, and was regarded as a place of considerable importance from a military standpoint It was known as a "common station of the militia guard,"—other similar posts being Newark, Elizabethtown, Springfield, Lyons Farms, Woodbridge and Rahway—and there is no doubt that soldiers were stationed here during the greater part of the Revolutionary period In view of the stringency of the laws governing military service, we may be reasonably sure that every able-bodied man of Chatham fought for his country at

[1] Washington Papers in the Library of Congress, B XI pt 2, 369
[2] Condit Genealogical Notes

some time during the war, but details are not obtainable, because the existing muster-rolls are very incomplete

An interesting source of information relating to the Morris County militia is a manuscript volume called the "Condit Genealogical Notes" in the library of the New Jersey Historical Society. It is a memorandum-book written by Dr Lewis Condit of Morristown, containing abstracts of affidavits made by Revolutionary soldiers when applying for pensions, many years after the close of the war (1833 to 1840), when the veterans were advanced in life, and needed financial assistance. The notes or abstracts from the original affidavits were apparently preserved by Dr Condit because of their data concerning the old families of Morris County, and they possess interest from a genealogical, as well as a historical, standpoint

The veterans in their affidavits describe their services in a very general way, for so many years had elapsed since the occurrences referred to that most of the details had been forgotten. They make frequent mention of Chatham as a place where the militiamen were enrolled, stationed, or discharged, but these references are very meager and fragmentary. Among those who performed one or more tours of duty at Chatham were Captains Artmas Day, Josiah Hall, Timothy Tuttle and Jonas Ward, Lieutenant Phineas Farrand, Ensign Abram Harrison — O'Hara, a subaltern of cavalry, and privates John Ball, James Doty, Joseph Kitchell, Luke Miller, Amos Potter Samuel Shipman, Benjamin Thompson and Robert Young. James Doty, Luke Miller, Samuel Shipman and Benjamin Thompson enlisted at Chatham, and Luke Miller received his discharge here [1]

The affidavit which is most complete as to details in Dr Condit's book is that of Daniel Skellinger of Chatham. He was born March 12, 1757, at Canterbury, Connecticut,

---

[1] Nathaniel Sayre was another militiaman who performed a month's tour of duty at Chatham, Springfield, etc, in the autumn of 1776 —*Banta's Sayre Genealogy*, 207

fourteen or fifteen miles from Norwich, and lived there until two years of age, when his parents removed to Bridgehampton, Long Island He came to Chatham in the spring of 1776, and during the ensuing summer joined Captain N B Luce's company of Colonel Martin's regiment as a volunteer. He fought in the battle of Long Island during his first tour, marching through Morristown, Newark and Powles Hook to New York and thence to Long Island, staying in New York one night He arrived on the island a week before the battle, in which his company and regiment participated, and left the island the night before Washington withdrew He had served six weeks when discharged

His second tour was in September, when he was stationed at Elizabethtown for guard duty under Captain Nathaniel Horton, Colonel Drake and General Heard He also served one month in November, doing guard duty at Elizabethtown under Captain Horton. He was at Elizabethtown when Washington retreated through New Jersey, but did not follow him he was discharged and went home

In the spring of 1777, probably in March, the weather being cold and windy, he served a month under Captain Torry and General Winds at Van W [illegible] In time of planting corn (May) he was out one month, going to Elizabethtown and then to Newark for guard duty In time of cutting grass (the latter part of June) he was called for guard duty under Captain Horton, Colonel Drake and General Winds In August and September he served a month at Elizabethtown under Captain Horton and Colonel Drake, and in November a month under Captain Horton at Elizabethtown doing guard duty

He was out one month in March and April, 1778, performing guard duty at Elizabethtown under Colonel Drake In May and June he served a month under Captain Horton and General Winds Started for Mon[mou]th battle, but as a result of information received on the road, General

Winds returned to Elizabethtown, where Skellinger stayed out the month. His station was a little west of the town. In August he served a month at Elizabethtown under Horton, Drake and Winds, and in November marched to Elizabethtown, Newark and Acquackanonck under Horton, when Jerry Bell was accidentally shot and killed.

In the spring of 1779 he performed a tour under Captain Horton at Elizabethtown, doing guard duty. In June or July he served a month under Captain Torry, marching against the Indians who had burnt the Minisink settlement on the Delaware. General Winds commanded. They marched by way of Dingman's Ferry, but found that the Indians had retired.

In the spring of 1780 he served a tour at Elizabethtown under Captain Horton. In June he fought at Connecticut Farms when the place was burnt and Mrs. Caldwell shot, and also served at Springfield after that village was destroyed. His company had been lying at Elizabethtown. He served at least two tours at Elizabethtown in the summer and fall after Springfield was burnt.

He is corroborated by the testimony of Elisha Skellinger. They were both in the battle of Long Island, in Captain Luce's company of Colonel Martin's regiment. Elisha continued with the army under Washington through the summer at Fort Washington, White Plains and (after crossing the Hudson) beyond New Brunswick. He was discharged near New Brunswick, and returned home. He remembered seeing Daniel in the battle of Springfield, and knew of his going to Minisink.

The selection of Chatham as a station or rendezvous of the militia was largely due to the fact that the Passaic bridge on the main road was considered by the authorities to be a point of vital importance which must be carefully guarded. There was a similar structure at Turkey, now New Providence, and another at Hanover, but Chatham bridge, being

on the direct road from Morristown to Elizabeth, and
thence by water to New York, seems to have been considered the principal entrance to Morris County, and for
this reason, particularly exposed to an advance of the
British, who were believed to be constantly awaiting a favorable opportunity to invade this part of the State, for the
purpose of destroying the stores and powder-mill at Morristown It is evident from the records now available that
the greatest care was taken in guarding Chatham bridge
Whenever an advance of the enemy was apprehended, a
formidable body of troops was stationed here, though their
number was reduced when hostilities in this region temporarily ceased.

The necessity of placing a guard at this point was
perceived soon after the commencement of the war by
Colonel Benoni Hathaway of Morristown, and a militia
company under Captain Timothy Tuttle of Whippany was
one of the first detachments stationed here for the purpose
Dr Samuel L Tuttle, in his historical writings, mentions an
incident occurring at Chatham bridge which caused much
excitement at the time It was the shooting of Breese Williams, who attempted to force his way over the bridge in
defiance of the sentries, two brothers named John and Jacob
Garrigus Williams, who was intoxicated, insulted and
abused the sentinels upon their refusal to allow him to pass,
and at length he seized the musket of one of the guards and
tried to wrest it from his hands, when the other soldier,
fearing that he would succeed in his purpose, shot him in the
groin and inflicted a fatal wound [1]

The circumstances of this tragic episode are described
somewhat differently by J Percy Crayon in his Rockaway
Records of Morris County Families That author states
that the Garrigus family was of French Huguenot descent,

[1] Historical Magazine, Ser 2, IX, 331, Affidavit of Robert Young in
Condit Genealogical Notes

living in Philadelphia during the colonial period, that Jacob Garrigus, the first of the name in Morris County, settled near Rockaway upon what was afterwards known as the Peck farm, on the road to Littleton, and that he and his sons, David, Jacob, Jr., John and Isaac, were soldiers in the Revolution, serving in the companies of Captain Robert Gaston and Captain Josiah Hall

It is related [continues Mr. Crayon] that when David was doing duty as guard one Foster Williams, son of Samuel, of Shongum had laid a wager with some of the Company, that he could take David's musket away from him while he was on his post. He came up and demanded his musket, but David well knowing the penalty resisted, when Williams undertook to deprive him of his musket by force, and was shot, so that he died a few hours after for his rash wager

The death of Williams produced a deep impression upon the soldiers then stationed in the neighborhood, and it is mentioned in several of the affidavits contained in Dr. Condit's book

The assertion has been made by historians of recognized authority that one of the sentries posted at Chatham bridge was Ashbel Green, the fifteen-year-old son of Rev. Jacob Green, pastor of the Hanover Presbyterian church, and that he arrested a stranger who attempted to cross the river without giving the countersign, but the writer of these pages is of the opinion that this is an error, and that the above incident in the life of Dr. Green occurred upon the bridge at Hanover in the neighborhood of his home

The supposition that Green was stationed at Chatham is based solely upon a statement contained in his autobiography. Describing his early home at Hanover, he writes

You know that the place of my birth and boyhood was in East New Jersey, within a mile of the line which divides the counties of

Essex and Morris, my paternal residence was in the latter of these counties. This location placed our family, at a certain period, in very hazardous circumstances, for on the retreat of General Washington, and the pursuit of the British army, from the Hudson river to the Delaware, we were within twelve miles of the enemy's line of march

After alluding to a rumor that a party of British light horse was about to raid the village of Hanover for the purpose of seizing some of the leading patriots, of whom his father, owing to his prominence in the American cause, was certain to be one, and describing the flight of his parents, who remained in hiding until the report was proven to be groundless, Dr. Green continues

It was at this eventful period, that the whole militia of the upper part of New Jersey were called into active service, and left their houses and families, with no other protectors than boys, and old men no longer capable of public military duty   The tories, too, who had remained, and had kept silence through fear, now made a merit of their known opinions and feelings, and sought to recommend themselves to the British, by giving them every information which was calculated to aid their cause and injure ours   To prevent this, as far as possible, the old men and boys of our neighbourhood kept guard, at a bridge over the Passaic river, which was the usual passing place from the county of Morris to that of Essex, where the British troops were in force   At the station where this guard was kept, I stood sentinel, in my fifteenth year, in as cold a December night as our climate almost ever knows   I arrested one man, who was going to the bridge   He was very loth to be stopped, but as he had not the countersign, I presented my bayonet, which my previous training had taught me to do *secundum artem,* and he yielded at once, and I conducted him to the officer of the guard   Whether he was going to the British or not, I am not sure, although the circumstances were suspicious [1]

The author conceives that Dr. Green's words "our

[1] Jones's Ashbel Green, 56, 58

neighborhood," as well as his context, indicate that the bridge he referred to was the structure at Hanover, and not the one at Chatham The latter was considered of sufficient importance to be guarded by regularly enlisted soldiers, and if the absence of troops at any time had necessitated the employment of boys and aged men as sentries, it seems much more likely that the boys of Chatham would have been chosen rather than that Green would have been sent for Moreover, had the doctor, at so tender an age, been sent a distance of five miles from home to perform military service at night in a strange village, the incident would have made so deep an impression upon his mind that he would have been almost certain to mention it The only reference to Chatham in his autobiography is contained in his recollection of the battle of Springfield, at which time he was eighteen years of age, and regularly enrolled in the militia He writes "June 23d, 1780 Alarm—marched to Chatham, from thence to the left of Springfield."[1] As he thus records the mere fact of passing through Chatham, it seems hardly possible that he could have been regularly employed in guarding the bridge at this place without making more particular allusion to the circumstance

Owing to the vigilance of the sentries at Chatham bridge, to the presence of troops in the village, and to the enemy's hesitancy to enter the defiles of the Short Hills between Springfield and Chatham, where they might be easily led into ambush, the British never succeeded in penetrating Morris County, although an advance upon Morristown was repeatedly attempted, and was constantly feared by the patriots Dr Joseph F Tuttle is the authority for the statement that shortly after the battle of Springfield, in June, 1780, a British detachment was sent to Chatham for the purpose of exchanging prisoners The troops stationed in the village at the time were commanded by General Wil-

[1] Jones's Ashbel Green, 119

liam Winds, of Rockaway, to whom the British officer
jocularly remarked that he purposed to dine with him the
next day in Morristown—a taunt which drew from the
sturdy patriot the retort that if the Englishman dined in
Morristown next day, he would sup in h—l next night.[1]

[1] Annals of Morris County; Revolutionary Forefathers of Morris
County; Washington in Morris County.

CHAPTER IV

JOHN BUDD AND HIS DESCENDANTS

MENTION has been made in a previous chapter of John Budd, a wealthy merchant of Philadelphia, and a member of the West Jersey board of proprietors, who at one time owned the entire district embraced in the older part of the Borough of Chatham, and was probably the most extensive landowner in the present county of Morris He was a son of Thomas Budd of Burlington and Philadelphia, and traced his descent from John Budd, Earl of Berkshire, whose eldest son fell in the battle of Barnet

THOMAS BUDD, the founder of the family in America, was the son of a clergyman of the same name, rector of Martosh parish in Somersetshire, and afterwards a minister among the Quakers The son emigrated to America in 1668, and settled in Burlington, N J, whither he was followed a few years later by three of his brothers He was a successful merchant, residing in Burlington until 1690, and thereafter in Philadelphia, where he died in 1697 From an early date his name is closely associated with the history of West Jersey He was a leading member of the council of proprietors, having acquired a propriety in 1676, and when the first form of government was established in the colony he was instrumental in framing a code of laws He married Susannah ————, and had four children John, Thomas, Mary and Rose [1]

[1] Tanner's New Jersey, 15, Smith's New Jersey, 134, New Jersey Archives, Ser 1, XXIII, 70, Lee's Genealogical History of N J, 434, 944

JOHN BUDD, eldest child of Thomas Budd, became a
resident of what is now Morris County, N. J., about the year
1721, establishing his home in Hanover Township approximately two miles from Morristown His wealth, business
interests, and connection with the proprietary body gave him
a prominence in the community which was soon recognized
by his selection for public office, and in 1728 we find him
serving as a justice of the peace of Hanover Township and
a judge of the Hunterdon County courts When Morris
County was set off from Hunterdon he was appointed one
of its judges, and held his seat on the bench until the
September term, 1747 Upon his removal from Philadelphia he renounced the religion of the Friends, and
united with the Presbyterian church at Hanover, which he
represented in the Synod of Philadelphia in 1722, 1723,
1724, 1728, 1729 and 1730 [1]

His residence in Hanover Township stood on the rising
ground not far from the northeast corner formed by the
intersection of the road from Morristown to South Orange
(the old Columbia turnpike), and the road now called Park
Avenue, leading from Madison to Monroe He died about
1754, and was buried in a family cemetery on his farm.
When the road to South Orange was converted into a
turnpike its line was straightened where it crossed the Budd
property, leaving a narrow gore of land between the new
highway and the former road This gore, which lay south
of the turnpike and east of Park Avenue, contained the place
of Judge Budd's interment, but no trace of his grave can
now be seen

John Budd married, 1st, Rebecca, daughter of John
Smith of Bristol, R. I.; 2d, Sarah Cosens [3] The latter survived him, and married, as her second husband, John Scott,

---

[1] Wickes s History of Medicine 173
[2] Budd Papers, Package 13 No 43
[3] New Jersey Archives, Ser 1, XXX, 73

who had been Judge Budd's business manager The judge had children

1 JOHN, a physician of Salem, N J, who went to Charleston, S C, shortly before the Revolution, and served during that war as a captain in the Fourth South Carolina Artillery

2 THOMAS, a physician of Hanover, and a surgeon in the navy, who perished in the blowing up of the *Randolph* in an action with a British frigate

3 WILLIAM, who went to England

4 BERN (Bernard or Barnabas), a physician of Morris County

5 SUSANNAH, married —— Stewart, whose children founded the town of Stewartsville N J

6 CATHERINE, married David Gould of Morris County, and removed to Charleston, S C.[1]

DR BERN BUDD was born in 1738, and died in 1777 He studied under Dr Chiven of Hibernia, near Rockaway, N J,[2] and became a physician and surgeon of exceptional skill He lived near his father's residence, about two miles from Morristown in the vicinity of Monroe, having received a portion of the homestead farm as his inheritance [3] His recognized ability and engaging personality won for him a large and lucrative practice which extended throughout the southeastern section of Morris County, including the village of Chatham, and so highly was he esteemed, that a serious difficulty with the government, in which he became involved during the late colonial period, caused no diminution of his practice His name appears first among the fourteen founders of the New Jersey Medical Society in 1766 He

[1] New Jersey Archives, Ser 1, XX, 208, Ibid, XXII, 58, Ibid, XXIV, 354, Ibid, XXV, 435, Wickes s History of Medicine, 171, 178, Heitman s Historical Register, 130, Lee's Genealogical History of N J, 1311 Budd Papers, Package 21, No 18

[2] Wickes's History of Medicine, 173 Tuttle's Revolutionary Fragments, No 5

[3] Budd Papers, Package 16

participated in the Revolutionary struggle, entering the service of his country on September 12, 1777, as a surgeon of Winds' brigade of Morris County militia   He died of putrid fever on the 14th of the following December, and was buried in the family cemetery on his father's farm, but his grave was not marked with a monument, and its location has been lost [1]

Dr Budd married Phebe Wheeler of Morris County, and had children 1, John C , 2, David; 3, William, 4, Sarah, 5, Mary - John and David entered the medical profession, the former practising in Morris County, and the latter in Brooklyn, N Y

DR JOHN C BUDD, born in Morristown, May 26, 1762, died in Orange, January 12, 1845, was the first member of his family to reside in the neighborhood of Chatham   By his marriage with Mary, daughter of Moses Lum, he came into possession of the property now known as the Budd homestead farm, which lies just beyond the borough limits on Passaic Avenue, and is part of a large tract which was sold by his grandfather, Judge Budd, to Samuel Lum, one of the first settlers [3]

[1] Biographical Encyclopaedia of New Jersey, 388 , Stryker's Officers and Men of New Jersey in the Revolution, 376 , Morristown Bill of Mortality

[2] Wickes's History of Medicine, 173 , Budd Papers, Package 21, No 18

[3] Passaic Avenue, it is believed, was originally a private lane leading from the farm to the village   It was known for many years as Budd Lane —so called in honor of the Budd family in general, and of Dr John C Budd in particular—and its change of appellation is much to be regretted The original names of ancient roads often possess a historic significance and value which should not be lightly disregarded or lost through meaningless changes   In this instance no valid reason is assigned, or can be imagined, for the adoption of the name "Passaic Avenue" In its present application it is not especially appropriate, nor is it in anywise distinctive of this municipality, since it is a street name which Chatham shares with many other towns in the valley of the Passaic   But the name of Budd as applied to this highway speaks to us of a titled family of England, a pioneer family of America, whose members from the earliest times have been makers of New Jersey history, who were numbered among the founders of Morris County, and who have been identified to a marked degree with the origin and growth of Chatham

Dr Budd served in the militia during the Revolutionary War He was a student of Dr John Condit of Orange, and became one of the most celebrated practitioners of medicine and surgery in northern New Jersey Many young doctors studied the rudiments of their profession under his tuleage He is described as of medium height, and stout, with a large head inclined to baldness, and a cheerful, kindly face He was perfectly erect, even at the advanced age of 82 His manner was somewhat brusque and stern, belying a sympathetic and benevolent disposition He possessed a keen sense of humor, and generally preferred fun to professional toil, but he nevertheless devoted himself conscientiously to his practice, which was very widely extended He had two famous prescriptions one he called his Tincture Botanæ, and the other his Diabolical Pill "The first," he said, "I give when I don't know what else to do, for it emmenagogue, sedative, cathartic, tonic and expectorant, and cannot fail to hit somewhere"[1]

"Old Dr Budd," as he was invariably called during the later years of his life, was reputed, in those days of ignorance and superstition, to have control over the powers of darkness, and to be able to summon at will supernatural visitants from the infernal regions—a reputation doubtless gained through his love of practical jokes Dr J Henry Clark describes in the following anecdote how Dr Budd was once frightened by an apparition of his own contriving He was returning home one Saturday night from a professional call at the Short Hills, and when passing Day's tavern near Chatham bridge he was surprised, in view of the lateness of the hour, to see a light in the window Stopping to investigate, he learned that several guests of the hotel persisted in playing cards in the parlor, despite the protests of Mrs Day, who wished to close the house for the night At

[1] Stryker's Officers and Men of New Jersey in the Revolution, 524, Clark's Medical Men of New Jersey, 24, Munsell's Morris County, 198 Biographical Encyclopaedia of New Jersey, 388

her request Dr Budd remonstrated with the gamblers, pointing out that, as it was after midnight, they were desecrating
the Sabbath, and intimating that the devil might appear if
they did not desist, but they responded only with gibes and
jests, observing that he afforded an example of "Satan re-
proving sin," and the doctor determined to produce an
artificial demon to frighten them from the premises

Asleep on the floor of the bar-room were some boys
employed as chimney-sweeps, who were returning from New
York to spend the Sabbath   Dr Budd awakened one of the
smallest, who readily agreed, for a gratuity, to represent the
devil coming down the chimney, providing himself for this
purpose with a pair of trace-chains, and a fresh cowhide
having the horns and hoofs attached, which he found in the
barn   The huge, old-fashioned chimney, before which the
card party was seated, communicated also with the room adjoining Sending Mrs Day's son to extinguish the fire in the
parlor, and to tell the card players that if they would not
cease their sport, they should at least have no fire, the doctor
conducted the chimney-sweep to the adjoining room, directing him to ascend the flue of the chimney to its junction with
the flue from the parlor, and to descend through the latter,
rattling his chains the while, until he was sufficiently low to
display the cowhide in the fireplace

Dr Budd then returned to the unwelcome guests to
observe the result of his stratagem, and he soon became so
deeply interested in watching their game that he forgot to a
great extent the intended movements of his accomplice   The
latter found the chimney so hot that he was unable to maintain his position and to play his role as agreed, and he suddenly tumbled down into the fireplace   So hideous was his
appearance in the dim candle-light, covered with the hide,
blackened with soot, and enveloped in a great cloud of dust,
that for a moment the doctor himself was considerably
startled   The gamesters were extremely terrified, and left

the house with the utmost precipitation, while Dr Budd, recovering from his own fright, hastened to bar the door against them

Throughout the village the appearance of the devil to the Sabbath-breakers was believed to have been a veritable visitation of Satan It caused much excitement, and awakened renewed interest in religion, resulting in several conversions It was chosen by the pastor of a local church as the subject of a sermon, which, however, he was dissuaded from preaching by Dr Budd [1]

Dr John C Budd married (1) Mary Lum, (2) Betsey Cohert, a widow of New York His children (last two by second marriage) were.

1 BERN W, a physician of New York, m Catherine dau of David Reynolds of Madison
2 JOHN S, m Charlotte dau of Aaron M Ward
3 MARY C, m John Meeker
4 JOANNA VASHTI, m (1) Parrot Reynolds, (2) Noble Barry
5 JANE CAROLINE, m Israel Dickinson
6 VINCENT B m (1) Nancy, dau of John Ward, (2) Jane, dau of Rev John Hancock
7 PHEBI, m (1) Edwin Tryon of Connecticut, (2)——— —Lounsbury of Michigan
8 SUSAN A, m Ambrose Bruen of Madison
9 ELIZA, m Stewart Marsh a physician of Rahway, N J
10 SARAH, m George Severn of Elizabeth, N J
Frank M Budd, the present owner of the homestead, is a son of John S, and a grandson of Dr John C -

THE HORTON FAMILY

On the southerly side of East Main Street, near the site of John J Muchmore's present home, stood the Horton residence in Revolutionary days [1] The head of the Horton family in this region was Rev Azariah Horton,

[1] Clark's Medical Men of New Jersey, 26

[2] Littell's Passaic Valley Genealogies, 121, Lee's Genealogical History of N J, 1311

[3] Tuttle's Madison Presbyterian Church, 116

who enjoyed the distinction of being the first American missionary, and was for many years the pastor of the Presbyterian church of Madison, N J   He was born in the ancient
town of Southold, Long Island, March 20, 1715, the son
of Jonathan and Mary Tuthill Horton, was educated at
Yale College, graduating in 1735, and was ordained by the
Presbytery of New York in 1740   He declined a desirable
charge on Long Island to take up the work of a missionary
among the Indians of that region, particularly those of the
Shinnecock tribe [1]

In those days there was in Edinburgh, Scotland, an
organization known as the Society for Propagating Christian
Knowledge, which, together with other activities of similar
character, maintained missionaries among the North American Indians   A committee of this society, consisting of
several eminent clergymen of New York and vicinity,
recommended Rev Azariah Horton and Rev David
Brainard for this service, and the former was the first missionary appointed   His charge extended along the southern
shore of Long Island from Rockaway to Montauk Point—
a distance of over 100 miles—and he traversed the entire
district four or five times a year, living with the Indians, in-
structing them in the art of reading, and preaching to them
almost every day [2]

Mr Horton commenced this work in 1741, and continued it for nine years, with the exception of 1742, when
he journeyed to the "forks of the Delaware" (the junction
of the Delaware and Lehigh rivers at Easton), to prepare
the savages for the ministry of Mr Brainard

His work among the Long Island Indians was abandoned in 1750, their number having been greatly reduced by
death or removal to other parts of the country, while those
who remained seemed but little moved by his exhortations

[1] Prime's Long Island, 104, Whitaker's Southold, 263, 266
[2] Wm P Tuttle in The Madison Fagle, June 10, 1898, Gillies' Historical
Collections, II, 408, 409

For a short time he supplied a church connected with the Presbytery of Suffolk, and in 1751 or 1752 accepted a call to the Presbyterian church of Bottle Hill, now Madison, N J, of which society he was the first regularly installed pastor This pulpit he filled until November, 1776, when he resigned his charge, and took up his residence in the home of his son Foster in the village of Chatham, which at that time was included in the Madison parish [1]

During the following winter, when Washington's army was encamped in Morris County, an epidemic of smallpox broke out, making fearful ravages, not only among the troops, but also among the civilians, in whose houses many of the soldiers were quartered As the Madison pulpit was still vacant, Mr Horton faithfully resumed his pastoral duties, and labored heroically among the victims of the dread scourge, until he himself contracted the disease, and died in Chatham on March 27, 1777, at the age of sixty-two His grave in the Madison cemetery is marked by a handsome monument, the gift of an unknown gentleman who came to that village about 1855 or 1860, and obtained permission to erect this memorial above Mr Horton's final resting place [2]

Mrs Horton was a Miss Eunice Foster of Shinnecock, near Southampton, Long Island She is described as a very energetic and well educated woman, who, during her husband's ministry in Madison, took a deep and active interest in the work of his church The pastor's salary was small, and to partially relieve him from the expense of maintaining the family and educating the children, his wife opened a general store in Madison This enterprise proved successful, and she realized enough from the profits of the

[1] Tuttle's Madison Presbyterian Church, 22
[2] Tuttle's Bottle Hill and Madison, 52, 53, Horton's Horton Genealogy, 184

business to purchase a valuable property in Chatham.[1] After the removal of the family to the latter place, she again engaged in trade, at this time in partnership with her son Foster; dealing in drygoods, staple groceries, and numerous articles of household use; the store being (probably) located in an extension or wing of her residence.

Eunice and Foster Horton were frequent advertisers in the *New Jersey Gazette* of Trenton, and also in the local newspaper, the *New Jersey Journal*. Mrs. Horton died August 14, 1778, in the fifty-seventh year of her age.

Some uncertainty exists concerning the children of Reverend Azariah Horton. In his will he mentions four sons: Jonathan, Azariah, James and Foster; and three daughters: Eunice, Mary and Hannah. It is claimed, however, that there were other children. Caleb Horton, an ensign and

OLD-TIME CANDLESTICK

later a captain in the western battalion of Morris County militia, is said to have been a son of the clergyman;[2] while in the Horton Genealogy by George F. Horton, mention is made of a son Charles, a surgeon in the Revolutionary army who died in service, and of a daughter Charlotte who married —— Chrystie. According to the late William P. Tuttle, of Madison, who devoted many years to the most painstaking historical research, Mr. Horton's daughter Charlotte died unmarried, and his daughter Eunice married —— Tuttle, of Hanover Neck or Whippany, N. J.[3]

[1] Tuttle's Bottle Hill and Madison, 51.
[2] Sherman's Historic Morristown, 363.
[3] *The Madison Eagle*, June 10, 1898.

The assertion has been made that Dr Jonathan Horton, an army surgeon in the Revolutionary War, was Pastor Horton's eldest son, but this is an error Mrs Horton, who died in 1778, referred in her will to her deceased son Jonathan, while the surgeon of the same name was assigned to the general hospital of the Northern Department in 1779, and died in 1780 [1] It is probable that the doctor, as regards his military services, has been confused with the Charles Horton mentioned in the Horton Genealogy The writer of these pages finds no record of a surgeon named Charles Horton in the army of the Revolution

Azariah Horton, the clergyman's second son, is said by Mr Tuttle to have kept a store in Madison at one time He occupied a position of trust and confidence in the Continental army, holding the rank of lieutenant-colonel attached to the commissary department, and was doubtless a prominent and influential citizen, yet it is impossible to learn very much about him In the list of Pastor Horton's children contained in the Horton Genealogy, Azariah, Jr , is not even mentioned, nor does his name appear in Stryker's Officers and Men of New Jersey in the Revolution He graduated from Princeton College, of which his father was one of the founders, in 1770, and received the degree of A M in 1773 [2] During the Revolution he entered the army, and acted as deputy commissary general of musters from June 9, 1777, to January 12, 1780, when the department in which he served was discontinued [3] The *New Jersey Journal* of Chatham published on May 11, 1779, this item

CHATHAM, May 11 The Honorable Congress have appointed Col Azariah Horton D Commissary general of Musters, and the

---

[1] Heitman's Register of Continental Officers, 301, Stryker's Officers and Men of New Jersey in the Revolution, 73

[2] Alexander's Princeton College in the Eighteenth Century

[3] Statement contained in his memorial to Congress —*Papers of the Continental Congress, No 41, II , 293*

Commander in Chief has ordered accordingly that he be obeyed and respected as such

Colonel Horton made his home in Philadelphia after the close of the war, and presumably died in that city

Foster Horton was a merchant of Chatham   He was a leader in his father's parish, and a respected citizen   After his mother's death he continued the business which she had established in Chatham, trading alone until June, 1791, when he formed a partnership with Samuel Sheppard, who was also a merchant of this village, under the firm name of Horton & Sheppard [1]

Mary Horton, born 1752, died February 16, 1783, married Jacob Morrell who lived next door to her father in Chatham, and Hannah Horton, born 1757, died July 24, 1844, married, 1st, —— Phinney, and 2nd, Captain Lewis Woodruff, of Elizabeth, N. J

JACOB MORRELL

Jacob Morrell, mentioned above as having married a daughter of Reverend Azariah Horton, was a son of Thomas and Judith Morrell, who were numbered among the early residents of Long Island, and whose family consisted of five sons Jonathan, born 1726, Jacob, born 1728, Samuel, born 1733, Robert, born 1737, and Thomas, born 1739 [2]

Jacob, the second son, was a resident of Chatham in Revolutionary days, being the owner of the property adjoining the Horton home on the west   His house is still standing, and is now occupied by Frederick S Tallmadge   When and under what circumstances Mr Morrell settled in Chatham, is not known   We find him living in New Jersey as early as 1773, when he advertised a reward

[1] *New Jersey Journal*, No 402, June 29, 1791
[2] Morrell's Ancestry of Daniel Morrell, 45

of $10 for a runaway slave named Hagar, who was under a warrant for theft Mr Morrell described himself in the advertisement simply as a resident of Morris County, for the village of Chatham had not yet received its present name [1] He was enrolled among the freeholders entitled to vote for representatives in the Provincial Congress at an election held in Morristown May 27, 1776 [2] but the fact that he was thus listed does not necessarily indicate that he was then a resident of Morristown for in the early days only one polling place was provided in each county, and the electors of the entire district were obliged to go to the county seat to cast their votes

The Morrell mansion in Chatham was originally larger than at present, and was an uncommonly fine dwelling for the period of its erection It was occupied for a time by General Washington, who, in all probability, chose it as his headquarters because it was then the most commodious private residence in the village It is alleged that the frame of this house dates from 1740 [3] Although the building has been somewhat altered, its general outline and appearance remain unchanged A covered porch with seats on either side has been replaced by a modern piazza, the parlor windows have been enlarged and extended down to the floor, and a bay window has been added at the east end of the house At the opposite end there was formerly a large and roomy extension, which was doubtless a store in Revolutionary days, and was used for that purpose by Mason Ferris during the middle of the last century but the extension was purchased many years ago by Charles Farmer, who cut it away from the main building and removed it to a lot on the west side of Passaic Avenue south of Centre Street, where it still remains, converted into a residence It has been altered for the accommodation of two families, but originally contained only a single apartment

[1] *New York Gazette,* May 24, 1773
[2] Sherman's Historic Morristown, 194
[3] Hampton's Historical Discourse 7

Mr Morrell did not take a leading part in the military activities of his day, and, aside from the fact that he was once the host of the illustrious Washington, he was an inconspicuous figure in civil life   We learn from his frequent advertisements in the *New Jersey Journal* that he was a merchant of Chatham, dealing principally in groceries, dry-goods, hardware, seeds and plants   In 1781 the cards of Samuel Alling first appear in the newspaper, announcing that he is keeping the store formerly occupied by Jacob Morrell, but as the latter's advertisements continue, it is clear that he had not at that time retired from trade   He probably remained in business until 1790, when he advertised the sale of his house, with a large nail shop, and four acres of land

Mr Morrell died at his home in Chatham, February 23, 1814, at the age of eighty-six   In his will he named five children   Calvin, Charlotte, Jane, Charles and Polly, his sons-in-law, Henry King[1] and Aaron Brookfield, being appointed executors   His son, Charles, a resident of Morristown, had a daughter, Louisa Frances, who married Benjamin L Cuyler, and was the mother of Rev Theodore L Cuyler, D D , an eminent clergyman of Brooklyn, N Y [2]

GENERAL ELIAS DAYTON

The name of Colonel (afterwards General) Elias Dayton, one of the most celebrated officers of the Revolution whom New Jersey produced, is closely connected with Chatham during the later years of the struggle for liberty He was a native and prominent citizen of Elizabeth, but toward the close of the Revolution he established a temporary home near Chatham, this step being taken partly because of the insecurity of his native city, which was particularly exposed to the incursions of the British, and partly

[1] Husband of Charlotte.
[2] Nicholl's The Earliest Cuylers in Holland and America, 47, Cuyler's Recollections of a Long Life, inscription on Jacob Morrell's tombstone.

because his military duties required his continual presence in this vicinity

Colonel Dayton (to give him the title by which he was known while a resident of Chatham, for he did not become a general until about the end of the war) was born May 1, 1737, the son of Jonathan Dayton, one of the pioneer settlers of Elizabeth On March 19, 1759, he entered the military service of the Province as a lieutenant, and a year later was promoted to a captaincy in the Jersey Blue regiment, attached to the regular British troops in the French and Indian War He fought under General Wolfe on the Plains of Abraham, and in 1764 was placed in command of an expedition against the northern Indians near Detroit, for which service he received official commendation

In December, 1774, he was chosen a member of the Committee of Correspondence, upon which committee his father, then over 74 years of age, also served Early in 1775 he became the colonel of a regiment of militia which numbered among its members several who had fought with him against the Indians In the following autumn he was appointed muster-master, and assisted in recruiting the first two regiments of Continental troops raised in New Jersey He was commissioned colonel of the Third Continental regiment in February, 1776, and a little later was given the command of the operations against the tories and Indians in the Mohawk valley During this campaign he built Fort Schuyler, on the site of Fort Stanwix at Rome, and Fort Dayton at Herkimer

Colonel Dayton succeeded General Maxwell in command of the Jersey Brigade on June 20, 1780 He participated in every battle of the Revolution in which the New Jersey line was engaged, notably Ticonderoga, Brandywine, Germantown, Monmouth (where his command was the first to attack the enemy), and Yorktown In 1783 he was one of two brigadier-generals appointed for New Jersey

to the Continental army, and ten years later was commissioned major-general of the Second Division of the New
Jersey militia, holding this office until his death

Colonel Dayton is described as courteous, ingenuous,
unassuming and scrupulously upright   In person and bearing he closely resembled General Washington, the likeness
between the two officers being so strong that when their
backs were turned it was difficult to distinguish them   The
enemy was thought to have been deceived at times by this
resemblance, and to have made Colonel Dayton the special
object of their marksmanship, mistaking him for the
commander-in-chief; for his horse was shot beneath
him in the battles of Brandywine, Germantown and Springfield, while his coat was riddled with bullets

Before and after the Revolution, Colonel Dayton was
engaged in business as a merchant of Elizabeth, at first
alone, and afterwards as a member of the firm of Elias
Dayton & Son   He was elected to Congress in 1779, but
declined the honor, though he was a delegate in 1787   He
served for many years in the State Legislature, and was
mentioned for the United States Constitutional Convention
in 1787, but declined in favor of his son Jonathan   He also
held office in his native city, being mayor of Elizabeth from
1796 to 1805, with the exception of one year   He was a
staunch member of the Presbyterian church, and was long
the president of its board of trustees   Upon the formation
of the New Jersey Society of the Cincinnati, he was chosen
its first president, and held this office until his death, which
occurred October 22, 1807

Colonel Dayton married a Mrs Rolfe   His children
were 1, Jonathan, 2, Hannah, who married Colonel Matthias Ogden, 3, Elias Bailey, 4, Sally, who married Isaac G
Ogden of New York, 5, William, 6, Horace, 7, Aaron, and
8, John [1]

---

[1] Clayton's Union County, 96, 240, Appleton's Cyc of American Biography, Hatfield s Elizabeth, 651-2, Drake's Sketches of the Revolution, 93, 95

GENERAL ELIAS DAYTON.
From Clayton's History of Union County.

Colonel Dayton's home near Chatham was located on the south side of the turnpike about half a mile east of the river   The property is now included in the corporate limits of Summit   It was known for many years as the Muchmore farm, and is now owned by John R Todd   An occasional reference to Dayton's residence at Chatham may be found in a manuscript volume, now in the New York Public Library, which originally belonged to Sir Henry Clinton, and contained the reports of his spies   Under date of April 4, 1781, is this statement

Col Dayton is ill at Chatham   He has but one company of light Infantry with him

And in the following June we find the following entry·

Col Dayton lives at Chatham with his family and pays occasional visits to Camp   Col Dehart commands in his absence

Part of Colonel Dayton's correspondence of the Revolutionary period is quoted below   While the contents of the letters are of little historic value, the fact that they were written at, or addressed to, Chatham during the War of Independence gives them a certain local interest   The first two are found among the Washington papers in the Library of Congress, the others are in the possession of the author

TO GENERAL WASHINGTON

Chatham May 4th   1780

Sir

By intelligence received this morning it appears that the enemy have a number of boats in readiness to move from N York this evening probably with about 1500 men, their object supposed to be our provision at Brunswick, as Capt Ross who commands the armed sloop in the Kils mentioned to a person I sent over on Monday last he then expected our stores in Brunswick were in their hands

In consequence of the intelligence I have sent an express to the commanding officer at the post and waggons are now going by order of Mr Caldwell sufficient I hope to load up all the provision this night I should have gone immediately to my Regiment had I not the promise of hearing from the other side by sun rising tomorrow morning

I have the honor to be Your Excellencys most Humble servant

ELIAS DAYTON

[Addressed]

His Excellency General Washington

TO GENERAL WASHINGTON

Chatham June 4th 1780

Sir

Since writeing yesterday I have received the enclosed letter and paper from New York forwarded by a person I believe to be a real friend The person who handed me the enclosed informs me that a party from Staten Island were in Elizabeth Town last night and carried of a number of horses to the Island

I have the honor to be your Excellency's Most obedt Humble servant

ELIAS DAYTON

[Addressed]

His Excellency General Washington

FROM CAPTAIN WILLIAM SHUTE

[Addressed]

Colonel Elias Dayton,
Chatham

[By] Col Shreeve

Jersey Camp Jany 8th, 1781

Dr Colo —

Yours of the 31st Ultimo came to hand this evening by Major Hollinshead

My not acknowledging the receipt of the Continental Mue before this, must be imputed to forgetfullness she has arriv'd and I flatter myself will answer every present purpose

Am very sorry the Beef answer'd not your expectation, if it had, it would not of answer d mine, but I assure you, it was the best in my possession

From the Fifty head since receiv'd, I little expect one (only) may be taken that will answer your purpose, he must be slaughter'd tomorrow as I have nothing for him to subsist on, two Quarters of which shall be laid aside for your use

Should be happy in complying with your requisition with respect to Candles but I have not one on hand, neither have I recen'd any since arriving in Jersey last, the first I procure shall be at your service   On receipt of this if no opportunity should offer to forward the flour to Elizth please to take the weight, and make use of it

I am Sir with respect, your hbe Servt

WILLIAM SHUTE

FROM COLONEL SYLVANUS SEELY

[Addressed]
    Colo Dayton,
       Chatham
Dear Colo

I have Just time to inform you that we have received information that 60 Sail of Transports under convoy of the Rainbow and Confederacy Sail'd yesterday for London having on board the fleet allmost all the Navell Prisoners Officers and all

Gell Arnold has arrived from Virginia with twenty five Sail of Transports with his Litehorse on board —for the Purpose of Recruting them —this may be relyed on

All the Troops on Staten Island have Certainly remained down to the flage Staff

I have the Honour To be with the Highest Esteem Your Most Obedent H St

                S SFIY

Colo Dayton
    Jan th 11th 1781

All the British are absolutely on board and goeing on board S Arbethnot is comsairy of for the French fleet that Expected

[Indorsed on outside] Wm Jones Jno Coningham Wm
Jibbs & Saml Gray, Cosat A sergeant who is a british dester [de-
serter] six weeks or 2 months since attempted to go to the enemy by
way of Amboy.

FROM CAPTAIN NATHANIEL LEONARD

[Addressed]
    Colo Dayton
        Chatham

                          Jersey Hutts 21st March '81
Sir,
    Tomorrow morning I expect to set out for the purpose of re-
cruting, Brunswick landing Bound brook & from thence to Germantown, I mean to make my rout, my party is Compleat except a fifer
which I yet want, and as there is but one to the Regt at present, it
cannot Suploy me, unless the Colo will see propper to let David
Rogers of Mr Shute's Comd return to Camp with the bearer, the
Regt can then spare me Cremer, a fifer who is well aquainted in the
Nabour hood ware I am going and may be of singelar service to the
party money I have not as yet but expect it on my arrival at one
of the above mentioned places
    I am Sir your Very He servant

                                   N LEONARD
Colo Dayton.
[Indorsed] From Capt Leonard, March 81, Recruiting

FROM CAPTAIN WILLIAM SHUTE

[Addressed]
    Colonel Elias Dayton
        Chatham

                          Jersey Camp 11th June 1781
Sir,
    Agreable to your directions I waited on Doct Little who col-
lected Six horsemen whom together with himself accompanied me
the rout directed by you Benjamin Sweeny was not at home, &
from the best accounts I cannot suppose he had been in that Quarter
since Saturday morn   at Sharps I call'd next, who lives this side of

Wisers Mills, he was not at home tho expected every minute, I proceeded to the Tavern near one Mile further at which place we tarried to refresh, and employ'd a person of that neighborhood to watch his return home, but to none effect from this Tavern I proceeded with two horsemen on Schuyle's Mountain for the High Dutcher by name Philip Terrabarrier found the description of his situation very accurate, tho he possitively denies the charge on my [paper torn] to the valley Doct Little had heard nothing of Sharp, as it was evident he was in the neighborhood I did not like to return without him, and as Doct Little was acquainted with the family, I begg'd of him alone to wait on Mrs Sharp & prevail on her to inform him where her husband was, which he did, and by issuing her he wanted Sharp for an evidence, & by depositing his arms in her desk, she consented to shew him the way to her husband through a thick wood and over a Mountain—before examing Sharp I found he had been with the Horse Thieves at one Bartum Beams on fox hill, altho I had not his name on the list I thought proper to take him with the others on our return to black River about 2 o Clock this morning I surrounded old McSweeny s house in hopes of finding Benj at home, but was disappointed, I gave the old gentle man to understand that his son Caleb was the person I wanted

Col D'Hart knows nothing of the Prisoners nor of the Person to support the charges, & expects you will order them, as you think necessary Sharp I have put in Irons,—the other two appear to be inoffensive creatures, and considerably aged this is all the paper I can procure

I am Sir with respect your very hbl Sert

WILLIAM SHUTE

FROM LIEUTENANT SAMUEL SEELY

[Addressed]
    Colo Dayton
        Comdt 2 B G

                                        Hackinsack

Dear Colo
    As I thought it very necessary that you should have the earlyest information—

I took the liberty to inform you and I believe from good Authority, that a fleet anchored Day before Yesterday at the Hook and is
Generally supposed to be Lord Cornwallis's From Virginia   there is
four thousand Troops on board, it is reported more, but I believe
from what I can gather, there is no more than the above mentioned
Number   Some say from the west Indies this you can put your
own construction on

  this day I saw william day, who will see you tomorrow three
Oclock in the afternoon

  I am with Capt Outwatter and shall remain with him untill
the Colo shall come down, or send

Your H St

SAML SEELY

Hackinsack,

July the 27th 1781

[Indorsed] Permit the bearer to pass to camp and pass the Guards
at any time of night

SAML SEELY Lieut

1st Jersey Regt

FROM ELISHA BOUDINOT

[Addressed]
  Col Elias Dayton
  Chatham

Hanover 22d Decr 1781

Dear Sir

  The Bearer Mr H B desires me to write you on a particular
Subject relative to him   He has been my Neighbour for some time
he is a Man of considerable Property, and far above the stile of the
generalty of those employed in that Way, and which made me sur-
prized at his making any offers of that kind   I have always found
him a kind and an obliding Neighbour   His Character in a political
Way has not escaped the Tongue of Slander, but supposing him
even to have *traded* which is the most that has been said yet his
property is a sufficient Tie of his Attachment, and his Connections
are such (from his Information) that I should think every good use
might be made of him, and he is capable of Observation & distinguish-
ing Circumstances, which you cannot often meet with

Mrs. Boudinot desires her best Compliments to Mrs Dayton, and if good Sleighing, We should be happy to see you next Week and in that Case shall expect it, and if you come in the Morning, it will render it less fatiguing to Mrs. Dayton

I am sir with Esteem

Yours most Obt Servt

ELISHA BOUDINOT

Col Dayton

FROM CAPTAIN ROBERT NICHOLS

[Addressed]

Coll Dayton
Chatham

Dr Coll,

Sir

You will pleas to Recolect that after My Return from Philadelphia on the Unhappy Affair of Caleb Bruen that I Acquainted you that the Grand Dificulty With the Marques Mr Peter's Presedent of the Bord of War Govenor Reed & Genl Potter Vice President of the Council War by What Means We should get the Enemy To make the first offer of Exchange As they did not hold Bruen as a prisoner of War, but all as one gave their word in Case such purposel Could be obtained from the Other Side, if theay ware not Directly Repugnant To All Rules of War they would Do all in their power To Efect an Exchange, Now Sir you know Best Whether you Can help him or not I am sencable of your feelings for Poor Bruen & Need not Say any thing To Excite you thereunto, but with Respect Remain your Huml Servt

ROBT NICHOLS

Newark 30th Decr 1781
Coll Dayton
Chatham

P S

Enclosed I send the Certificate I Obtained from the Marques Chuse Rather you should keep it than myself if you Please

DRAFT OF A LETTER FROM

COLONEL DAYTON TO GENERAL WASHINGTON

[This draft is not signed   It formerly belonged to Rev Dr Sprague
of Albany, N Y, an early collector of autograph letters, by whom it is
indorsed "The within is the writing of Genl Elias Dayton "]

Chatham Feby 8th 1782

Sir

    I have received the letter which contained your Excellency's
orders for the releif of the garrison at Wyoming   I expected the
N york line would have been ordered to releive them but as your
Excellency is pleased to order it otherways I would ask permission
to releive the officers only as the men at that place are fit for garrison
duty and no other   I have therefore delayed the marching of the
men until further orders   I have reason to beleive the men at
Wyoming will be contented to remain with a new set of officers   I
have at this time about one hundred men at Eliz Town and Newark
which number I thought necessary (during the severe frost) to prevent the robers from the other side plundering & abusing the friends
to the states, they have had a very good effect, we have made prisoners one Doctor two Negroes & four privates, & killed one   I have
had one rase after a party of them on the salt Marsh for two miles I
got one black & 1 white prisoners & took from them eight sleds loaded
with hay   The matter with respect to flags I expect will be settled
at least so far as respects Mr Skineis negotiations, but Skinner has
been absent at Goshen this week or more   enclosed is the particular
cantoonments of the troops in N Y & vicinity, handed me by a good
man

    I have also an accurate map of the fortifications at Brooklyn
given me by the same person but will take a safer opportunity of
conveyance   We have had from three to six deserters from the
enemy every day since the river has been froze

[Indorsed] Copy sent Gl Washington Feby 8. 1782

FROM COLONEL ISRAEL SHREVE

[Addressed]

Colonel Elias Dayton
Commandin the Jersey line
at Chatham

Burlington County 24th Feby 1782

Sir

The bearer George McDonald Quarter Master Serjant to your Regiment claims his Discharge for the following reasons — in the year 1776 he Served in the 4th Virginia Regt as a Serjant, in January following he came to me (his time being out) and desired me to recommend him for an Ensigncy in my Regt the Regt being full of Officers that failed I Advised him to Inlist untill a Vacancy should happen, which for some time he declined saying he could git a Commission in the Pennsylvania line, which I believed to be true as that Line was not near full, but as he had lived with me from nine years of age untill he was 22, he chose to be with me, upon my promiseing him a Commission the first Vacancy, If agreeable to the Officers of the Corps he agreed to Inlist upon the following Conditions, to be Quarter Master Serjant untill promoted, But If that should fail to Serve three years (unless I should sooner Leave the Service) and If I continued he to have his Discharge any time after three years Service when he should Claim it I then filled up a printed Enlistment for the war haveing no other by me he hesitated to Sign it untill I asured him it would make no Difference, and made not the least Doubt but he would be Commissioned the first Vacancy, and If that Should fail it would always be in my power to Discharge him — his being promoted has failed he Claimed his Discharge at Pompton huts a Little before the Revolt, I put him off untill I Left the Service, not Chuseing to do any thing that Should incur Censure, (notwithstanding all Some unprincipled officers Was pleased to falsly Asseit) in June last McDonold petitioned the assembly on the Occasion (as he was Circumstanced Somewhat Different from others) I was Called upon for Information which I give as near as may be to what I have here wrote the Members of the Assembly was unanimously of Opinion that he Ought to be Discharged, but was at a Loss to fall upon any mode for that purpose, without Involving in much Difficulty it was thought best to Inform the commanding Officer of the

Regiment, as it Seemed to Lay with him   the Campaighn Just then, beginning to be Active It was not Done   the above are facts which I am ready to testify to If Required

I am Sir with Respect your Most Obdt Servt

ISRAEL SHRLVL

Colonel Dayton

COLONEL DAYTON TO GENERAL WASHINGTON

[In handwriting of Captain Jonathan Dayton]

Chatham May 14th 1782

Sir,

I have received your Excellency's letter of the 7th with the proceedings of a court martial enclosed, which proceedings the court were of opinion from the nature of the oath they had taken, they could not communicate to any person until the Commander in chief's pleasure should be known   they therefore dispatched them to Head Quarters without my knowledge   When your Excellency returned them to me the first time I pointed out to the President the improprieties in them and desired him to assemble the court, to reconsider and revise them   they did so and sent them oft a second time without my knowledge for the same reason as before   Under these circumstances therefore I conceive that I cannot be censured for the misconduct and inattention of the court in a matter which could not have come within my notice

Your Excellency's apprehensions that the Jersey line have been so much neglected as to be unprepared for the field gave me no small degree of pain   I am however very happy that an official report of their appearance and situation is before this made by Colonel Stewart which I flatter myself will quiet your Excellency's apprehensions, to which I am compelled to observe, illnatured reports and misinformations must have given rise   The report of this gentleman will, I hope create in your Excellency a more favorable opinion of the zeal of the officers of the Jersey line, who are, I am confident exceedingly sollicitous to demean themselves in such a manner as may in every instance meet the approbation of their commander

I have just received the orders for preventing all communication with the enemy by flags, which your Excellency may be assured shall be most strictly obeyed. The following was extracted from a London paper of the 2nd of April and forwarded to me thro' a private channel, I thought it very proper that I should transmit it to your Excellency that you might place such reliance upon it as your Excellency should think just   "In last Thursday's Council the first of the new administration, the expediency of the immediate removal of the chief part of the British army from the Continent of North America was the only matter of importance debated, when the Cabinet came to an unanimous resolve of ordering the Garrisons of New York & Charlestown to be evacuated & the troops to be embarked for St Lucia & Barbadoes under the convoy of the whole British fleet which will be ordered to sail from the West Indies for their protection previous to the setting in of the Hurricane season, towards the middle of summer   The necessary transports are now providing for the above service   The Garrisons of Halifax & Quebec are still to be held & strongly reinforced "

The last letters I forwarded from Sir Henry Clinton to your Excellency had been five days in my possession, & could not have been sent on sooner unless a man had been hired for that particular purpose

[Indorsed] Copy sent Gl Washington May 14th 82

CAPTAIN JONATHAN DAYTON

Jonathan Dayton, the general's eldest son, was also a soldier of the Revolution   He was born in Elizabeth, October 16, 1760, graduated from Princeton College in 1776, and during the same year was commissioned ensign in his father's regiment, the Third New Jersey A few months later he became regimental paymaster, was promoted to the rank of lieutenant in 1777, and to that of captain-lieutenant in 1779   During the latter year he was appointed aide-de-camp to General Sullivan with the rank of major, on the expedition against the western Indians   He was commis

sioned captain in the Third New Jersey, of which his father
was still the colonel, in March, 1780, was taken prisoner at
Elizabeth in the following October, but was exchanged soon
afterwards, and served in the army until the end of the war

At frequent times during the Revolution, notably while
the Dayton family resided in the neighborhood of Chatham,
the captain was accustomed to act as his father's secretary,
and military letters are still extant which were signed by
Colonel Dayton, though written by the hand of Jonathan

After the war Captain Dayton took a prominent part
in the affairs of the State and nation He was elected to the
Assembly, and was speaker of that body in 1790 He
represented New Jersey in the convention of 1787 for the
formation of a Federal constitution He was elected to
Congress in 1791, and served four terms in the House of
Representatives, being speaker from 1795 to 1799, and
from 1799 until 1815 was a member of the United States
Senate

He was interested with John Cleve Symmes and others
in the purchase and development of military lands in the
Middle West, and the city of Dayton, Ohio, was named in
his honor While in the Senate he formed an intimate
friendship with Aaron Burr, and became involved in the
latter's scheme of empire without realizing its pernicious
nature He loaned Burr money to forward the project, and
was thus compromised with him in the charge of treason
Dayton's indictment was never tried, but his political career
was blighted by this scandal

His death occurred on October 9, 1824. He is described as a man of impressive appearance and manners—
a gentleman of the old school, who retained in his household, dress and deportment the formality of Washington
and Franklin He was familiarly nicknamed "the last of the
cocked hats "[1]

[1] Nelson's Biographical Encyclopædia of New Jersey 82 Hatfield's
Elizabeth, 662

COLONEL SYLVANUS SEELY

The most distinguished officer, and the one holding the highest rank in the Revolutionary army, who was a permanent resident of Chatham, was Colonel Sylvanus Seely, a veteran of the French and Indian War. He was out-ranked, it is true, by Colonel Dayton, who, toward the close of the Revolution, was promoted brigadier, but for Dayton, Chatham was merely a temporary place of residence, while Seely made the village his permanent home.

During the Revolution Colonel Seely lived on the south-west corner of the highways now known as Main Street and Fairmount Avenue[1] That he was a tavern keeper by occupation is affirmed by a well-established tradition, supported by advertisements of West Indian rum and French brandy which he occasionally inserted in the *New Jersey Journal*[2] In 1785 he bought at sheriff's sale a plot of twenty acres owned by Matthias Woodruff, extending from East Main Street to the Passaic, between the home of Foster Horton and the mill property, and tradition states that he kept a tavern upon this lot, standing on the south side of the road about 500 feet west of the river[3]

Colonel Seely seems to have commenced his career in the Revolution as a captain of militia. His name first

[1] Erskine's Army Maps, No 75-A, in library of the New York Historical Society

[2] The following advertisement indicates that he resided in Chatham as early as 1774

Notice is hereby given to the creditors of William Jinings, late of Morris-Town, that they are desired to bring in their accounts at the house of Sylvanus Sealy tavern-keeper, at Chatham, in Morris-County, on the 30th day of this instant, where due attendance will be given, at 10 o'clock in the morning, by us

JONATHAN STILES,
PHILIP V CORTLAND,
ABRAHAM CANFIELD,
Auditors

Morris-County, August 6th, 1774
—Dunlap's Pennsylvania Packet August 15, 1774

[3] Morris County Record of Deeds, A 155, Gardner's Historical Dis-course, 7

appears in the muster rolls as a captain in the battalion
known as "Heard's brigade," receiving his commission on
June 14. 1776 [1] though he held the rank for several months
prior to that date   He was ambitious to command a company of Continental troops, and to this end he presented
the following recommendation to the New Jersey Provincial
Congress, which was read before that august body on
February 7. 1776   As the village of Chatham lay on both
sides of the dividing line between the townships of Morris
and Hanover (in the former of which he resided) he caused
the petition to be signed by the authorities of both municipalities, thinking by that means to make it doubly
efficacious, but his hope was not realized, so far as the public
records show

Gentlemen
    The Bearer Hereof Capt Seely an Inhabitant of this Town-
ship & a Capt of Militia under the provincial Congress being a
Stranger to your Board & desirous of raising a Company to serve
in the continental Service has requested of this Committee a Recommendation   In consequence of which we beg Leave to recommend
him to you, & to say in his Favour that he is an Honest Man firmly
attached to the Liberties of his Country, & a Man who from his
former Services for two years in the last War has approved himself
a Man of Courage & Resolution & therefore we deem him fit &
worthy of Holding a Capt's Commission in the above Service & to
assure you that we doubt not but he would raise a Company in a
Short Time
        Signed by Order of the Committee of the Township of Morris
                            JABEZ CAMPFIELD *Clark*

Morris Town Feby 5 1776
To the President & Members of
the provincial Congress of the
Province of New Jersey
    We the committee of the Township of hanover haveing perused

[1] Stryker's Officers and Men of New Jersey in the Revolution, 355

the above Recommendation and Do approve of the same and Recommend him accordingly

Signed by Order

MATTHEW BURNET *Chairman* [1]

Colonel Seely afterwards served as captain in the Eastern Battalion of Morris County militia He was commissioned first major of this organization on May 23, 1777, and became its colonel on the 13th of the following November [2] He is referred to in Symmes biographical sketch of Colonel Oliver Spencer as having assisted the latter in the capture of nearly 100 mounted Waldeckers in a skirmish near Springfield [3]—doubtless the encounter which was reported in the *Pennsylvania Evening Post* of January 23, 1777, as occurring on the 5th of that month, and resulting in the death of 8 or 10 Waldeckers and the capture of the remaining 39 or 40, with two officers, by a force not superior in number, without sustaining the least damage

But Seely is chiefly remembered as the colonel of a battalion of State troops, for it was in this capacity that his most active and important services were rendered This position he held from 1779 [4] until (probably) the close of the Revolution Much of his correspondence with the civil and military authorities is still extant, and indicates that he was engaged for a considerable time during the later years of the war in endeavoring to prevent intercourse between the tories of New Jersey and the British in New York and on Staten Island Besides carrying information to the enemy, the loyalists were extensively engaged in "London trading" as it was called, which consisted of buying from the English certain articles which had been declared contraband, and

---

[1] Papers of the Provincial Congress, No 96, in library of the New Jersey Historical Society

[2] Stryker's Officers and Men of New Jersey in the Revolution, 355

[3] New Jersey Historical Society Proceedings, Ser 2, 253 (1886)

[4] New Jersey Archives, Ser 2, IV, 6

smuggling the goods within the American lines, where they could be sold at a handsome profit This nefarious business was strictly forbidden under severe penalties A letter written by Governor Livingston to General Heath, dated September 15, 1781, thus alludes to Seely's activities in checking this traffic

By the last returns I had of what we call our three months men, I doubt not the five hundred are by this time complete They are under the command of Collo Sylvanus Seely whose head quarters are at Connecticut Firms, about four miles from Elizabeth Town, and about seven from Staten Island From these he keeps constant outposts and pickets along the line, to prevent the incursions of the enemy, and to suppress the illicit infernal trade that is carried on with them He cannot, I think, be more advantageously posted in any part of this State for either of these purposes, and we should be very unhappy to think that he should be ordered out of it, not only because the men are expressly raised upon General Washington's requisition, grounded upon his professed design to attack New York, but also because not being able to complete our quota from the militia, I ordered several companies of our State regiment there on those lines, and raised for the very purpose of defending our frontiers, to join him, and which accordingly now make a considerable part of his corps While they remain on their present station, they will, I hope, prove sufficient to repel any excursions made by the enemy's partizan parties, and that you will in case of greater force endeavor on reasonable notice to succour and support the militia according to your kind promise, for which I acknowledge myself under the greatest obligations to you [1]

During the winter of 1779-80 charges of dereliction were preferred against Colonel Seely, upon which he was tried by court-martial, but the accusations were not sustained The records do not tell us where the inquiry took place, beyond the bare statement that the proceedings were held at Chatham, but there is little doubt that the court sat

[1] Massachusetts Historical Society Collections, Ser 7, V, 255

in one of the taverns of the village   Following are resolutions of the Legislative Council (corresponding to the
present State Senate) of February 25, 1780

A message was received from the House of Assembly by Mr
Sharp and Mr Foster in Words following
Whereas His Excellency the Governor has laid before the Legis-
lature sundry Charges exhibited against Sylvanus Seeley, Colonel of
the First Regiment of Militia in the County of Morris and re-
quested their Determination is to the Mode of Trial, whether by
Impeachment or by a Court Martial
  Resolved, That His Excellency the Governor be requested to
call a Court Martial as soon as possible for the Trial of Colonel
Sylvanus Seeley
  Resolved, That the Legislature will make Provision for the
Payment of all reasonable and necessary Expenses of the Members,
Witnesses and others necessary attending at such Court, and that
His Excellency be requested to lay an Account of the same before the
Legislature for that Purpose, as soon as possible after they are in-
curred
  Ordered, That Mr. Sharp and Mr Foster do carry the above
Resolution to the Council, and request their concurrence therein

  March 3, 1780
  The Council having taken into Consideration the Message of
the House of Assembly of the 25th of last month, relative to re-
questing the Governor to call a Court Martial for the Trial of
Colonel Seeley,
  Resolved, That the House concur in the Resolution therein
contained.
  Ordered That Mr Ogden do wait on the House of Assembly
and acquaint them therewith
  Mr Ogden reported that he had obeyed the Order of the
House.

  In compliance with the resolutions of the Council,
Governor Livingston issued a proclamation in these terms

A General court-martial of the State, of which Col Neilson is appointed President, is ordered to sit at Chatham, on the 27th instant   Colonels Frelinghuysen and Van Dyck, Lieut Colonels Jacob Crane and Benoni Hathaway   Majors William Davison and Joseph Lindley, and Captains Peter Latham, Daniel Cook, Garven M'Koy, Stephen Monson, Joseph Beech and James Kean, are appointed members   Mr Wilcocks is appointed to act as Judge Advocate of this court

By order of his Excellency Governor Livingston, April 10 1780 [1]

The judgment of the court was thus confirmed by a subsequent proclamation of Governor Livingston

By His Excellency the Governor

A General Court-Martial of the state, whereof Col John Neilson was appointed President, having been ordered by the Governor for the trial of Col Sylvanus Seely, on the 27th day of April last, on the following charges against him while commanding the State Regiment in Elizabeth-Town, in the latter end of the year 1779, viz

1 That he suffered goods and merchandise to be landed from the enemy's flag-boat within our lines thereby permitting an illicit trade to be carried on between the inhabitants of this state and the enemy

2 That he suffered those who came with a flag, some of whom were fugitives from this state, frequently to tarry all night on shore without any necessity, giving them an opportunity to hold conferences with the disaffected inhabitants, to gain intelligence, transact commercial affairs, and promote desertions from our troops

3 That he partook of this illicit trade himself, having goods taken out of the flag-boat and carried to his quarters

4 That of his own authority he gave permission to persons to go to the enemy, either to stay with them or return, and also gave permits to persons of suspected characters to pass his guards, who carried provisions to the enemy

5 That he authorized privates in the regiment to exercise com-

[1] New Jersey Archives, Ser 2, IV, 297

mand, and to rank and draw pay as officers, contrary to the constitution of the state, the law for raising the said regiment to the damage and expense of the state

And the said Court having met and proceeded to the trial of the said Col Seeley, upon the several charges aforesaid, pronounced their sentence or judgment, by which they unanimously declare, "that the said Col Sylvanus Seely is not guilty of any one or more of the said charges but on the contrary that during his command at Elizabeth-Town, he is entitled to the character of a good soldier, a vigilant officer, and faithful citizen and as such deserves the gratitude of his country', which sentence or judgment I do approve of

Trenton, 27th May, 1780 [1]   WM LIVINGSTON

In the Proceedings of the Legislative Council and of the General Assembly mention is made of certain expenses incurred in this matter, which were ordered paid by the State treasurer

4th To William Wilcocks, Esquire, for Expences and Fees as Judge Advocate, at the Trial of Colonel Sylvanus Seeley, by a Court-Martial held by Order of the Legislature in May last £546 13

5th To William Campfield for Expences for himself and Horse, going Express to notify Witnesses to attend the Trial of Colonel Seeley, in May last, £37 10

6th To Colonel John Neilson for the Use of himself and the Members of the Court-Martial appointed for the Trial of Colonel Sylvanus Seeley, in May last, £1875

During the following year Colonel Seely presided at a court-martial in Chatham for the trial of Lieutenant-Colonel Jacob Crane Captain Isaac Gillam and Lieutenant John Burnet, all of whom were officers of the Essex County militia, though Crane and Gillam also served for a time with the State troops The finding of the court is thus set forth in a proclamation of Governor Livingston, published in the New Jersey Journal on December 26, 1781

[1] New Jersey Archives, Ser 2, IV, 402

By His Excellency the Governor

Head Quarters, Trenton, December 14, 1781

At a General Court Martial, whereof Colonel Silvanus Seely was President, held at Chatham, the twenty-third day of October last by order of his Excellency the Governor, and continued by several adjournments, Lieutenant Colonel Jacob Crane was tried upon the following charges

1st That he traded with the enemy when commanding officer at Elizabeth Town in the year 1780

2d That he allowed others to trade with the enemy while commanding officer at the same place, in the year aforesaid

3d That he was so disguised with liquor when on Staten Island, under the command of General Dickenson, as to be wholly unfit for duty, and also at other times, when commanding officer at Elizabethtown in 1780

4th For unofficerlike behavior in an attack of a party of Refugees in Elizabeth Town, with a superior force under his command

The court having maturely deliberated upon the evidences, are of opinion, and do accordingly find, that Lieutenant Colonel Crane is guilty of the first and second charges, and that the said Colonel Crane is not guilty of the first part of the third charge nor of the fourth charge

And the said Court do sentence the said Lieutenant Colonel Crane to be publickly reprimanded by his Excellency the Governor

By the same Court Martial was tried Captain Isaac Gillam, upon the following charges

1st For a neglect of duty in a variety of instances

> 1 In staying a great part of his time since his late appointment in the twelve months' service of the state, at home
>
> 2 In going home and continuing there several days and nights when he knew that a number of vessels were coming up Newark bay, towards Newark and had got to the mouth of the river
>
> 3 In drawing provisions for himself and men without having the proper necessary returns, or knowing how many men he had on duty, or in town

4 In not calling the muster-roll, or knowing who appeared on the parade and did duty

5 In not sending out patrols, or placing centries, and not visiting them when placed

2d For giving unnecessary and unreasonable furloughs to his men

3d For not supporting authority and discipline in his company

4th For ungentlemanly and unofficerlike behavior to Lieutenant Burnet

5th For giving permission to a number of persons to go into and return from the enemy's lines.

6th For encouraging, protecting and supporting the illicit trade and intercourse with the enemy, and for the sake of a bribe, releasing and discharging a quantity of goods seized by some of his men, on the way from the enemy's lines, by which means the state is deprived of a considerable sum of money, and the punishment of offenders evaded

The following two charges were made by the court

7th For leaving his company when on it's march to Dobb's Ferry in the month of August last, without permission

8th That before and on the march of the said company to Dobb's Ferry, the said Captain Gillam did begin and excite a mutiny, and that at the same time and place he did join in a mutiny, and that also knowing of an intended mutiny, he did not, without delay, give information thereof to any superior or commanding officer, nor endeavor to suppress the same

The court having maturely considered the evidence offered on the several charges against Captain Isaac Gillam do find him of the first charge guilty in the fourth instance

In the first   instance not guilty.
       second   ditto   not guilty.
       third   ditto   not guilty
       fifth   ditto   not guilty
Of the second charge   not guilty
       third   ditto   guilty
       fourth   ditto   guilty
       fifth   ditto   guilty
       sixth   ditto   guilty.

seventh ditto   not guilty
eighth ditto   guilty

And it is adjudged by the same court that the said Captain Isaac Gillam be deprived of all and every military commission which he holds in the service of this State

And by the same Court Martial was tried Lieutenant John Burnet, upon the following charges

1st   For disobeying the orders of Captain Isaac Gillam, his superior officer

2d   For giving the soldiers of the said Captain's company strong liquor, to induce them to sign a paper which tended to encourage a mutiny

3d   For ordering said soldiers to mutiny

4th   For neglect of duty in suppressing the illicit trade with the enemy.

5th   For refusing to deliver up the muster roll to Captain Gillam

6th   For abusing the character of the said Captain Gillam

The court having considered the evidence, do find Lieutenant Burnet of the

First   charge   guilty
Second   ditto   guilty
Third   ditto   not guilty
Fourth   ditto   not guilty.
Fifth   ditto   guilty
Sixth   ditto   not guilty

And the said Court do sentence the said Lieutenant John Burnet to be cashiered

The Governor having duly considered the evidence produced to the said Court Martial, and the several sentences and acquittals of the same, approves of and confirms the sentence and adjudication of the said Court against Captain Isaac Gillam (whose several offenses do not admit of the least palliation, and which he could not have imagined that any officer of the militia of this state would have stained his character or disgraced his country) and orders the same to take place accordingly

Relative to the sentence passed by the said Court on Lieutenant-Colonel Jacob Crane, he thinks it more favorable than an officer

of his rank had reason to expect for so atrocious a crime as that of
trading with the enemy, and allowing others to trade with them (an
offense not only extremely injurious to his country, which had reposed
so great confidence in him, but which it was an essential part of his
duty and a grand object of the post he occupied to suppress) and for
which, as well as for the other offense proved against him, he is hereby
publicly reprimanded

With respect to the sentence passed by the said Court on Lieutenant John Burnet, it is with great regret that the Governor
finds that an officer who has distinguished himself for his zeal and
activity in the service of his country, should so far forget the absolute
necessity of maintaining subordination and discipline as to disobey
the orders of his superior officer, and whatever allowance may be
made for the precipitation of youth, or personal provocations offered,
the public interest indispensably requires so pernicious an example
to be uniformly discountenanced, and he therefore approves of and
confirms the sentence passed by the said Court Martial on the said
Lieutenant John Burnet, and orders the same to take place accordingly

WIL LIVINGSTON

The Gillam court-martial is mentioned in the Condit
Genealogical Notes described in a preceding chapter It is
briefly referred to by Joseph Lyon, from whose pension
affidavit Dr Condit copied the following statement

Enlisted for a year under Capt Neale who resigned before the
Co was filled up & Gillam was elected Capt in his stead & Lyon
served the whole year under him Gillam never headed his Co at
all, was accused of being coward by Lieut Burnet & Shea Burnet
took command Gillam was tried by C Mart at Chatham & broke

Colonel Seely married Jane ———— He had three
sons and four daughters, namely JOHN WILLIAMSON,
THOMAS JONES, who married Hannah ————, GEORGE F,
SUSANNA, married Solomon Moore; SOPHIA, married
James, son of Captain Enos Ward of Chatham, ELINOR,
married ———— Howell, and ELIZABETH, married Eliph-

alet, son of Ephraim Miller of Smalley's Bridge, Somerset
County, N J

After his marriage Mr Miller resided in Chatham, on the
south side of East Main Street, west of the home of Jacob Morrell
On May 27, 1811, he married Mary daughter of Isaac Beach of
Troy, N J By his first wife he had children CHRISTOPHER
SEELY, BENJAMIN FRANKLIN, CORNELIA ELIZA

Colonel Seely lived in Chatham for many years after
the close of the Revolutionary War, eventually removing
to Pennsylvania   John Littell, in his Genealogies of the
First Settlers of Passaic Valley, states that he "went to the
Beech Woods" with David Oakley In 1810 he was living
in Bethany, Pa , where he owned a grist- and saw-mill, and
he died there on March 28, 1821[1]

[1] Will of Sylvanus Seely, probated in Wayne County, Pa , Littell's
Passaic Valley Genealogies, 293, 305, 462, *Palladium of Liberty,* June 11,
1811, August 12, 1815, Morris County Record of Deeds, S 453
   The following advertisement appeared in the *New Jersey Journal* of
January 3, 1804 To be sold on reasonable terms or exchanged for property
in Essex or Morris County, A part or whole of 5000 acres of valuable land
situated in the waters of Lackawanna Creek which is navigable for rafting
timber to Philadelphia For information apply to Mrs Seely at Chatham,
N J , or to Capt John Howell, or to the subscriber on the premises in Wayne
Co , Pa
                                        SYLVANUS SEELY

CHAPTER V

DR PETER SMITH

DR PETER SMITH, an eminent physician of Chatham, and a surgeon in the Revolutionary army, was a son of Peter Smith, Jr, one of the early residents of Hempstead, L I[1] According to one biographer of the family, his mother was Rebecca Vanderpool of Albany, N Y,[2] but by the weight of authority she was Rebecca Nichols, eldest child of Isaac Nichols, 3d, of Milford, Connecticut[3]

The marriage of Peter Smith, Jr, and Rebecca Nichols was performed at Hempstead in 1732 At a later date they made their home in Hanover, N J Their children, whose names often occur in the Revolutionary history of eastern New Jersey, were probably born at Hempstead They were:

1 JACAMIAH, married Phebe—— He kept a tavern at Connecticut Farms in colonial and early Revolutionary days, but in 1781 was located in Elizabeth, where his hotel was the starting point of the Philadelphia stages He took an active interest in public affairs, and was at one time colonel of the Elizabethtown troops

2 URIAH, married Abigail Allen of Hanover He was a farmer of Northfield, N J

3 HEZEKIAH, of whom more hereafter

4 OBADIAH, married —— He was a farmer of Canoe Brook, now Livingston, N J

[1] Torrey's Ancestors and Descendants of Humphrey Nichols, 11
[2] Guild's Chaplain Smith and the Baptists, 21
[3] Torrey's Ancestors and Descendants of Humphrey Nichols, supra

5 SARAH, married Epaphras Cook, a farmer living between Livingston and Hanover. He subsequently moved with his family to New York, residing in Wooster Street

6 MARY, married Samuel Ellison, a farmer who lived near Chatham His farm lay on the Morris Turnpike in Millburn Township, and now forms part of the property of the Canoe Brook Country Club His residence stood near the main entrance of the club, about half a mile east of Chatham bridge

7 PETER, the subject of this sketch

8 CATHERINE [1]

The farm which Mr Smith purchased upon his removal to New Jersey lies on the road leading from Hanover to Florham Park It is known as the Meeker farm, having been owned for many years by the late Carnot and William Meeker It is now the property of Carnot M Ward The Smith residence is said to have stood near the site of the Meeker barn [2] Mr Smith offered the property for sale, by advertisement inserted in the *New York Journal or General Advertiser* of April 20, 1769, describing it as a tract of 360 acres on Passaic River, with a dwelling house almost new, situated on an eminence commanding a pleasant prospect, a large barn, two young orchards, 100 acres of wheat land and 50 acres suitable for hemp, the property lying 13 miles from Newark, 18 from Elizabethtown, and within half a mile of Mr Green's meeting house, having reference to the Hanover Presbyterian church, of which Rev Jacob Green was then the pastor [3]

Mr Smith died January 16, 1771, and was buried in the village cemetery at Hanover After his death his wife resided with her children who had married and settled in the vicinity She died at the home of her son Peter in

---

[1] Torrey's Ancestors and Descendants of Humphrey Nichols, 17-19, New Jersey Archives, Ser 2, V 188

[2] Torrey's Ancestors and Descendants of Humphrey Nichols, 12

[3] New Jersey Archives, Ser 1, XXVI, 416 He had previously advertised the property in *The New York Gazette and Weekly Mercury* of March 7, 1768 —*Ibid*, 68

Chatham, November 4, 1788, and was interred beside her husband in the Hanover cemetery [1]

Dr Peter Smith, the youngest son of Peter Smith, Jr , was born February 18, 1748, and died April 16, 1818   He married on August 12, 1771, Susannah, daughter of Rev Aaron Richards, who served for many years as pastor of the Presbyterian church of Rahway, and supplied the pulpit of the Madison church during the Revolution   She was born in 1756, and died October 20, 1785   His second wife, Phebe Potter, was a resident of Madison, and when the Potter farm was divided upon her father's death, Dr Smith received a portion of the property   The farm consisted of several hundred acres, fronting upon the Convent Road (now Park Avenue), near the property of the late Edward V Thebaud   Dr. Smith lived for a time in Madison, or Bottle Hill as it was then called, but a great part of his married life was spent in Chatham.[2]   At an early period of the Revolution he offered his services to his country in the following terms

To The Honourable Provincial Congress for New Jersey
Gentlemen

I Should be fond of Engageing in the Continental Service for the Defence of American Liberty as a Surgeon

I am Gentlemen your Most Obedient Humble Servent

Morris County   PETER SMITH
Jany 30, 1776

Recommended by the Following Gentlemen

Jacob Moriell	Nathl Bonnel
Amos Potter	Benjamin Bonnel
David V. D Pool	Stephen Day
Thomas Darling	Matt Wynans
Jonen Stiles	Silvanus Seely
Wm Darling	David Bruen
John Roberts	Jacamiah Smith

Nath C Martin [3]

[1] Torrey's Ancestors and Descendants of Humphrey Nichols, 12
[2] Ibid., 19
[3] Papers of the Provincial Congress No 90, in library of the N J Historical Society.

Dr Smith was a man of means and importance, and was considered one of the most skillful physicians in the State He was described by his grandchildren as a quiet, dignified and reserved individual, whom they regarded with great veneration He was one of three judges of the Court of Common Pleas which sat at Morristown twice a year, a fortnight at each term, and it is said that the doctor's opinion usually took precedence over that of his colleagues, for he was a fluent talker and could win anyone to his side with a few words

After the close of the Revolution, Dr Smith decided, for reasons which are not now known, to remove to Flanders, N J There he resided until his death, but his interment was made in the cemetery at Madison, where his wife was also buried From the advertisement which he inserted in the *New Jersey Journal* of Elizabeth, published March 14, 1792, when preparing to change his residence, we have the following description of his property

To be SOLD at PUBLIC VENDUE, *On Saturday the 17th day of March, at 3 o'clock in the afternoon*

The House and Lot of Land, whereon the subscriber lives, in Chatham, on the main road leading from Morris-Town to Elizabeth Town, containing about 3 acres of excellent land The house is very convenient, containing six rooms, two fire-places, a good cellar, and a good garden, a well of water that never fails, and on the premises is a good barn, and a shop, together with other buildings and a number of fruit trees ——It is an excellent stand for business, and would suit a silversmith, sadler, or shopjoiner as they are much wanted in the place The conditions made known on the day of sale, and the payments made easy to the purchaser, as the money is not wanted

Chatham, March 5, 1792　　　　　　　PETER SMITH

It appears, however, that Dr Smith did not leave Chatham until three or four years later

Children of Dr Peter Smith by his first marriage

1   CATHERINE, married Baldwin Wood of Spring Valley, N J

2   FANNY, unmarried, who lived at Chatham with Charlotte Smith, widow of her brother Frederick

3   ELIZABETH, b April 18, 1778, d July 25, 1849 While the family lived in Madison she was known as "the beauty of Bottle Hill" She married, April 9, 1796, Jacob, son of David Vanderpool of Chatham The marriage is said to have been hastened owing to her father's desire to remove to Flanders Her husband was born May 6, 1776, and died December 13, 1856 He was a shoemaker by trade After his marriage he built and occupied the house on East Main Street now owned by Mrs Louise G Collins, but soon afterwards removed with his family to New York, residing at 14 Catherine Street, where he opened a shoe store At a later date he became a dealer in coal, eventually selling out to Jeremiah Skidmore, whose business is still conducted under the firm name of Jeremiah Skidmore's Sons Mr Vanderpool was at one time an officer in the Custom House at New York

4   WILLIAM

5   FREDERICK C H, b April 24, 1781, d May 31, 1809 Married, April 28, 1805, Charlotte, daughter of Captain William and Nancy Day of Chatham. She was b October 25, 1785, d December 10, 1849

6   SUSANNAH RICHARDS, b April 21, 1781, d. January 10, 1854 Married, February 26, 1803, Foster, son of Captain William and Nancy Day of Chatham He was born in Chatham March 6, 1781, and died in Elizabeth June 26, 1845

Children by second marriage

7   POLLY, married Samuel Burroughs

8   REBECCA, married 1st, June 24, 1821, Anderson Lewis of Livingston, N J, 2d, ——— Van Sicklen [1]

Some of the descendants of Frederick and Susannah Smith, who married into the family of Captain William Day of Chatham, are described in the following interesting article published in a local newspaper

[1] Torrey's Ancestors and Descendants of Humphrey Nichols, 19, *New Jersey Eagle,* June 29, 1821

FIVE GENERATIONS OF A CHATHAM FAMILY.

A family of five living generations is exceedingly rare. There was once such a family in Chatham, containing an unbroken line from the great-great-grandmother down to the great-great-granddaughter. They are shown in the accompanying picture, which is reproduced from a copy of a daguerreotype. The original picture was taken many years ago, and four or five of the persons are dead. The surviving one is Mrs. Sarah Purdy. She was the mother of the little girl in the picture. At the time it was taken her name was Mrs. Crane, for she has married since then.

It was in 1853 that the daguerreotype was taken, and the event was one of the greatest importance in the history of the family. Every member of it was born and died in Chatham. The family was generally known as the Days, for the three eldest members of it lived in the Day homestead. Mrs. Crane and her daughter lived in another house close by. Chatham in those times did not have many things to be proud of, but it did have the five living generations, and it honored them fully. It is said that the peaceful little community at the foot of Long Hill was even prouder of the five generations than it had been only a few years before of Captain Day,

Courtesy of the Newark *Sunday Call.*

THE FIVE GENERATIONS

a veteran of the Continental army, who had fought valiantly against Great Britain

Captain Day passed away in 1853, leaving a widow, Mrs Nancy Day, who was the great-great-grandmother of the five generations She was in that year 95 years old Her daughter was Mrs Sally Crane, aged 77 years The next youngest, or Mrs Day's granddaughter, was Mrs Nancy Gardiner She was 49 years old Then came Mrs Sarah Crane, who bore her grandmother's name, having married a second cousin Her age was 31 years The little girl in the picture was Joanna Crane, 8 years old

The Crystal Palace Exposition was held in New York in 1853 The managers of it heard of the five generations in Chatham and wanted to know if they would not allow a daguerreotype to be taken The matter was discussed and they all consented except Mrs Nancy Day, but after much persuasion Mrs Day finally consented The exposition people were notified, and two men were sent to Chatham to take the picture That day was long afterwards talked of by the five generations Such a hurry and bustle in the household had never been known Each of the ladies had on her best black silk and the little girl her smartest frock and such other adornments as befitted the occasion It was explained to the men with the camera that Mrs Sarah Crane's eldest daughter, Julia, aged 12, was away, on a visit, so Joanna took her place Great, indeed, was Julia's grief and vexation when she returned home a few days later and learned what she had missed

Mrs Day died three years afterwards, aged 98 years The little girl followed her a few months later The next to depart this world was Mrs. Sallie Crane, who lived to be 97 years old Then Mrs Gardiner aged 94 years, died in 1898 Mrs Sarah Crane, the survivor, was 80 years old last month, and she gives promise of living as long as any of those heretofore mentioned Her residence is the old Day homestead She enjoys the best of health, is spry and has all her mental faculties About a year ago she went to Kansas City on a visit, making the journey there and back unaccompanied The owner of the picture is J C Bower, of Newark [1]

[1] *The Chatham Press,* March 22, 1902, reprinted from the Newark *Sunday Call*

REVEREND HEZEKIAH SMITH, D. D

Rev Dr Hezekiah Smith, elder brother of Dr. Peter Smith, was a brigade chaplain in the Continental army, and one of the most eminent clergymen of the Baptist denomination in New England　He was born at Hempstead, L I , April 21, 1737　His family moved to New Jersey during his boyhood, and he was a familiar figure in Chatham in early days

At the age of nineteen Hezekiah was deeply stirred by the preaching of Rev John Gano, the first pastor of the Baptist church of Morristown, and he was led to unite with the church, being one of Mr Gano's first converts in this locality　He had a strong desire for a college education, to which his parents were opposed, but his father's consent was at length obtained, owing in part to the persuasion of Mr Gano, and he entered the sophomore class of Princeton in 1759, graduating three years later　He afterwards entered the ministry, and in 1765 became the pastor of a newly organized Baptist church at Haverhill, Mass , which he served until his death [1]

Dr Smith married, June 27, 1770, Hepzibah, daughter of Jonathan Kimball, Jr , of Haverill [2]

Like many other clergymen of his day, Dr Smith served as an army chaplain during the Revolutionary war Shortly after the outbreak of hostilities he was commissioned chaplain of a battalion commanded by Colonel John Nixon, in which organization there were many soldiers from Haverhill　He was afterwards assigned to the Fourth Continental Infantry and later to the Sixth Massachusetts; becoming brigade chaplain in 1778　He remained in the army until the fall of 1780, participating in a number of the principal battles fought in the northern States [3]

[1] Guild's Chaplain Smith and the Baptists, 21 , Sherman's Historic Morristown, 81
[2] Torrey's Ancestors and Descendants of Humphrey Nichols, 18.
[3] Heitman's Historical Register, 503

For many year Dr Smith kept a diary, which has been published in book form,[1] and contains many interesting references to his experiences during the Revolution He was a warm friend of Washington, and speaks in his journal of dining with him on more than one occasion, and when the general passed through Haverhill in 1789, he visited the former chaplain at his home From the diary we learn that Dr Smith was accustomed to travel about the country as an evangelist, before and after the war, and in the course of these journeyings he made frequent visits to his relatives and friends in "the Jerseys" The following record of his movements in this region is made up of entries appearing in various parts of the journal, the dates indicating that the incidents referred to occurred at widely varying periods of his life The months and years are here inserted for the guidance of the reader.

Thurs, 24 [February, 1764] Went to my father's in Morris County Mon, [March] 15· Preached at Jeremiah Sutton's at Long Hill from Isa 9 67 Thurs, [April] 5 Went to my father's, and Fri, 6 I preached in Mr Green's meeting house, from John 3.3 The congregation was much affected

Wed, 7 [November, 1764] Went to my father's—Thurs, 8 Visited Obadiah Smith, Happy Cook,[2] and Elizabeth Cook, and returned to my father's In the evening was visited by Happy Cook and his wife and Mr Parrot and his wife

Wed, [September 11, 1765] Went to my father's—Thurs, 12 Visited Obadiah Smith and Happy Cook and their families —Fri, 13 In the evening I preached at Happy Cook's from Col 3.4

Mon, 6 [October, 1766] I preached at my father's a sermon from Ps 23.1 After sermon, I baptised my mother in Passaic River In the evening, I preached at Happy Cook's from, "Let the inhabitants of the rock sing"

[1] Guild s Chaplain Smith and the Baptists
[2] Epaphras Cook, his brother-in-law

Dr Smith again visited New Jersey in the spring of 1776, at which time he mentions selling his negro slave "Cato," a boy about fourteen years of age, to his brother, Dr Peter Smith of Chatham, for $125   The entries in his journal are as follows

Wed , 29 [May] Went to my brother's, Dr Smith at Chatham, and preached that evening at his house from Eph 6 11 —Thurs , 30 Went to see my mother and brethren, and preached that evening at my brother Uriah Smith's, from I John 3 14 Fri , 31· Preached a sermon at Happy Cook's from Joshua 1 7 and that evening another sermon at Dr Smith's, from Joshua 1 7

Wed , 21 [August] Went to my mother's at Cheapside Wed , 4 [September] Went to Brother Ellison's   Lodged there two nights and visited my relations and preached Thursday evening

Mon , 9 Went to my mother's Tarried there till Wednesday, when I went to Mr Halsey's at Scotch Plains   Sat , 14 Went to my mother's at Cheapside —Sab , 15   Preached two sermons in Mr Green's meeting house, in Hanover —Mon , 16   Visiting my relations

Mon , 17 [April, 1779] Went to see my relations in the Jerseys, and that evening married Daniel Zeleff and Sarah Smith, both of Knewbrook [1]—Tues , 18   Preached a sermon at brother Obadiah's at Knewbrook, from Ex 15 2   After sermon went to see my mother —Wed , 19 —Sat , 22   Tarried at my brother Peter's with whom my mother now lives in Chatham —Sab 23   Preached two sermons in the Presbyterian meeting house at Bottle Hill from Isa 12 2 and Eccl 12 13, 14, and in the evening at Chatham at Dr Smith's, from Rev 15 3

Fri , 23 [September, 1785] To Happy Cook's at Knew Brook, to see my mother   Tues , 27   To brother Peter's at Chatham Preached from Hos 14 9   Fri , 30   Preached at Short Hill, from Luke 14 23   Mon , [October] 10   Preached

[1] Canoe Brook is a stream in Essex County which rises in Livingston Township and empties into the Passaic a short distance below Chatham In former times the name was also applied, in a general way, to the territory through which the stream flows, including the villages of White Oak Ridge, Northfield and Livingston, but as used by Dr Smith, the name seems to be confined to Livingston and the region lying between that place and Hanover

at Uriah Smith's from I John 5 3—Tues, 11 Preached
a sermon at Happy Cook's, from Job 14 14, and in the evening at
Obadiah Smith's, from Isa 61 10—Wed, 12 Preached at Mr
Dunham's, from Acts 16 31, 32, and in the evening at Happy Cook's
from 2 Cor 13 11

Thurs, 10 [September, 1789] Went to Kennewbrook to
Happy Cook's—Fri, 11 Went to my brother Peter Smith's, at Chat-
ham Preached an evening lecture, from Solomon's Song, 2 10, and
the next evening at Happy Cook's from the same text—Sab, 13
Preached at Kennewbrook, from Isa 28 16, Mark 16 16, and 1
Tim 1 15

Fri, 14 [September, 1792] Went to Kennewbrook, New
Jersey—Sat, 15. Preached at Uriah Smith's from Rev 3 19—
Sab, 16 Preached two sermons at Kennewbrook, from Matt 25 2
and John 5 29

Sat, 25 [September, 1802] Left New York and went to
Brother Ellison's at White Oak Ridge—Sab, 26 Preached three
sermons, two at Northfield meeting house, from Gen 45 26, and
one at Brother Cook's from Isa 40 1.—Mon, 27 Preached a sermon at Uriah Smith's, from Jer. 31 3—Tues, 28 Preached a sermon at Northfield meeting house, from Heb 13 20, 21—Wed, 29.
Preached a sermon at Brother Ellison's, from Isa 3 10, 11—
Thurs, 30, Preached a sermon at Chatham, from Heb 2.3

This tour in the autumn of 1802 seems to have been
Dr Smith's last visit to his relatives in New Jersey He
died at Haverhill on January 24, 1805

Andrew Sherburne, who served in the navy during the
Revolution, and in after life entered the ministry, speaks in
his autobiography of his meeting with Dr Smith He
writes

In the autumn of the year, [1787] Doctor Hezekiah Smith, of
Haverhill, passed through Cornish, [Maine] on his return home
from a journey to the north He was, doubtless, one of the most
accomplished and most pious ministers of the age He put up with
old Mr Joshua Chadbourn, who lived at that time in an ordinary

log cabin   They had had some acquaintance some years before, in Sanford, where there had been a reformation   Dr Smith was a fine-looking man, and genteel in his deportment   I was surprised to see how perfectly at home he seemed to be in the humble cottage, but I was astonished when I heard him preach   He came late on Saturday evening, preached three times on the Sabbath, and left us on Monday morning   His preaching caused my very soul to tremble   I have a perfect recollection of his text to this day [1]

Dr Smith's personal appearance was thus described by his friend Dr Baldwin, a member of the Baptist Society of Boston

In stature Dr Smith was considerably above the middling size, being about six feet in height, and well proportioned   His voice was strong and commanding, and his manner solemn and impressive   His countenance, though open and pleasant, was peculiarly solemn and majestic   In his deportment, he was mild, dignified, and grave, equally distant from priestly hauteur and superstitious reserve   He never thought religion incompatible with real politeness, hence the gentleman, the scholar, and the Christian were happily blended in his character

He was further described by Rev Dr Laban Clark of Middletown, Conn, as "a man of venerable appearance and stately form—robust, but not corpulent, his locks white as wool, his eyebrows retaining their natural dark hue, his face full and fair, bearing almost the flush of youth, and beaming with intelligence and good-will, and his manner grave and dignified, as well befitting the office of an ambassador of God "[2]

REVEREND JAMES CALDWELL

A famous character of Revolutionary history, who spent much time in Chatham during the War of Independ-

[1] Memoirs of Andrew Sherburne, 149
[2] Guild's Chaplain Smith and the Baptists, 376

ence, was the Reverend James Caldwell of Elizabeth, the Pastor of the First Presbyterian church of that city, who acted as chaplain of various military organizations raised in this part of the State, and also served in the commissary department and quartermaster's department of the army "The Fighting Chaplain," as he is known in history, was the son of John and Margaret (Phillips) Caldwell His ancestors were French Huguenots who, having been obliged to flee from France after the revocation of the Edict of Nantes, established a home in Scotland, and later, to escape the persecutions of Claverhouse, sought refuge in County Antrim, Ireland From thence John Caldwell emigrated to America in 1700, with his wife, several children and four unmarried sisters, and settled at Chestnut Level, Lancaster County, Pennsylvania, afterwards removing to what is now Charlotte County, Virginia, and making his home at a place known as "the Caldwell Settlement," on Cub Creek, a tributary of the Staunton River Here James was born in April, 1734, the youngest of a family of seven children

James was prepared for college by Rev John Todd, a protegé of Rev Samuel Davies At the age of fifteen he entered the College of New Jersey, then located at Newark, graduating in 1759, studied theology under President Davies, and was ordained by the Presbytery of New Brunswick in 1760 He was appointed to supply vacancies in the South, especially in the Carolinas, but in the autumn of 1761 he accepted a call to the Presbyterian church of Elizabeth, N. J, at an annual salary of £160, and was installed during the following spring [1]

In 1763 Mr. Caldwell was united in matrimony with Hannah, daughter of Judge John Ogden of Newark, and a younger sister of Jemima Ogden who married, as her

[1] Hatfield's Elizabeth, 513, 514, Wheeler's The Ogden Family in America, 96

second husband, Stephen Day, a leading citizen of Chatham.[1]

The Caldwell family and many other patriots of Elizabeth were obliged to leave their homes upon the advance of the British into New Jersey in November, 1776, and to seek safety among the hills bordering the Passaic River in a remote section of the old township of Elizabeth then called Turkey and now New Providence   The parson, however, carried on his pastoral duties in and near Elizabeth whenever a withdrawal of the enemy rendered his return to the city reasonably prudent

During 1778 and the first half of 1779 Mr Caldwell lived with his family at Springfield, and subsequently, for about a year, at Connecticut Farms, now Union, these places being as near to Elizabeth as he could safely approach   At the time of the battle of Connecticut Farms, June 7, 1780, Mrs Caldwell was murdered by a British soldier, and shortly after his bereavement the chaplain bought a house in New Providence and resided there until his death

Mr Caldwell commenced his military career in the winter or spring of 1776, when he accepted the position of chaplain of the Third battalion of New Jersey Continentals, of which organization most of the officers and many of the privates were numbered among his parishioners   The Jersey Brigade, to which this battalion was attached, marched to relieve the northern army then besieging Quebec, and the chaplain saw considerable service in the field during the summer, returning to Elizabeth in the early

---

[1] Judge Ogden is known in history as "John Ogden of Newark"   In the Essex County court minutes he is mentioned continuously as justice, judge, &c, from 1742 to 1776   In 1740 he joined with his uncle Josiah and his brother Uzal in the purchase of the Ringwood property and the organization of the Ringwood Mining Company, his interest in which he retained until 1765   He married Hannah, daughter of Jonathan Sayre   His sons were all patriots with the exception of Jonathan, who held the rank of surgeon general in the British army, and was later a judge in Newfoundland —*Wheeler's The Ogden Family in America, 65, Mrs Ellet's The Women of the Revolution, II, 107*

tall He was discharged with his battalion in November
of the same year, but, while the records are silent on the
point, there seems to be no doubt whatever that he continued
to act as an army chaplain, though perhaps unofficially, up
to the time of his death [1]

Mr Caldwell's military activities were not limited to
the duties of chaplain· he also served in various other
capacities In some of the battles of the Revolution, notably
at Connecticut Farms and Springfield, he participated in the
actual fighting We are all familiar with the anecdote of
the latter engagement related by Dr Nicholas Murray, and
repeated in every publication in which the chaplain's name
occurs, namely that when the troops exhausted their supply
of wadding, Mr Caldwell hastened to the Presbyterian
church of Springfield and returned to the firing line with his
arms filled with Isaac Watts' psalm-books which he dis-
tributed to the soldiers to be torn up and used as wadding,
shouting "Now put Watts into them, boys!"[2]

In the Journals of Congress under date of March 15,
1777, there is a record of the payment to him of $200 for
extraordinary services, and on May 27 of the same year
Congress ordered the sum of $4,873 54 to be paid him
"for the services of a company of light horse of Essex
County in the State of New Jersey, commanded by Capt
Jacob Wynans their horse hire and expenses " On September 17, 1778, Congress directed one million dollars to be
advanced to the quartermaster-general, and for the purpose of distributing this money, and settling and paying the
accounts of the department, deputy quartermasters were
appointed thoughout New Jersey and Pennsylvania, one of
whom was "Doctor James Caldwell at Elizabeth Town,"
whose district included the counties of Middlesex, Somerset,

[1] Hatfield s Elizabeth, 525, 527
[2] New Jersey Historical Society Proceedings Ser 1, III, 79
[3] Hatfield s Elizabeth, 526

Essex, Morris, Bergen, Hunterdon and Monmouth in the former State[1] He seems to have served in this capacity with the honorary rank of colonel, for in military correspondence he is addressed and referred to by this title He resigned from the quartermaster's department in the spring of 1779

Mr Caldwell was also prominent in civil life He was elected one of the trustees of Princeton College in 1769—just ten years after his graduation—and we find him serving as clerk of the board of trustees in 1776, 1778 and 1779[2] During the latter year he was chairman of the Essex County Committee of Correspondence About that time Congress resolved to borrow $20,000,000 to meet the expenses of the war, the raising of money by taxation alone having been found too slow to be practicable, and Governor Livingston of New Jersey thereupon appointed discreet and trustworthy persons in the several counties of the State to receive subscriptions to this loan and to transmit the same to the loan office, Mr Caldwell being his selection for Essex County[3]

The highest civil office held by Parson Caldwell was that of member of the Legislative Council, as the State Senate was then called In the autumn of 1780 he was elected to represent Essex County, and took his seat on October 26th This office he held until his death, appearing in the council chamber for the last time on October 5, 1781[5] While a member of the council he was one of the three commissioners appointed by that body for the purpose of liquidating and settling the deficiencies of the pay of the New Jersey troops—a task which, owing to the great depreciation of the Continental currency, and the mutinous temper

---

[1] New Jersey Archives, Ser 2, II, 452
[2] Hatheld's Elizabeth, 522, New Jersey Archives, Ser 2, I, 547, II, 151, III, 191
[3] New Jersey Archives, Ser 2, III, 501
[4] Ibid, 559, 595
[5] Hatfield's Elizabeth, 528, Proceedings of the Legislative Council

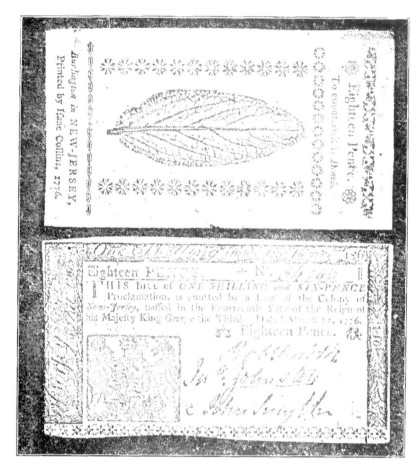

CONTINENTAL CURRENCY

of the soldiers, was one of great delicacy He served as clerk of the New York Presbytery in 1781 [1]

The character of Parson Caldwell combined in equal degree the qualities of clergyman and soldier, and he was most zealous and efficient in each capacity Ever ready to discharge the duties of a minister of the Gospel, and holding religious meetings whenever opportunity offered, in churches, in private dwellings or in the open air, he was also prepared to fulfil his military obligations at a moment's notice His services in the commissary department were of the greatest value The people held him in so much respect and esteem, and had such implicit confidence in his integrity, that his appeals for provisions for the army were always complied with, upon whatever guaranty he could give as to pay And when the passions of the soldiers were aroused to a state bordering upon mutiny, owing to the inability of Congress to pay them for their services, the chaplain was able, by his patriotic speeches, to calm their resentment and persuade them to remain loyal to the cause they served In fact he played so important a part in the struggle for liberty as to excite the especial animosity of the British, and it is said that with the single exception of Governor Livingston, for whose arrest or assassination the enemy offered a reward, there was no one in this region whom they were more anxious to capture than "the Rebel High Priest" So great was Caldwell's danger from this source that when preaching in Colonel Hatfield's storehouse in Elizabeth, after his church had been burned by the enemy in 1780 he deemed it necessary to place his pistols beside him on the pulpit, while sentries kept guard at the door [2]

Dr Samuel L Tuttle mentions an incident which illustrates the reverence and love with which the chaplain was generally regarded It was announced one day that he was

---

[1] *New Jersey Journal*, No 112, April 11, 1781

[2] New Jersey Historical Society Proceedings, Ser 1, III 77, Hatfield's Elizabeth, 527

to preach in the open fields not far from Chatham bridge
A multitude of people assembled from every quarter, and
while a man was erecting a temporary stage for the speaker,
an old soldier elbowed his way through the crowd, and upon
learning that a platform was being built for Mr Caldwell,
he exclaimed, "Let me have the honor of serving as his platform! Let him preach to-day standing upon my body!
Nothing is too good for Parson Caldwell!" with other expressions of similar character, showing his profound respect
for the warrior priest [1]

A Memoir of Rev James Caldwell, from the pen of
Dr Nicholas Murray, contains the following observations

So deep was the impression made by this man upon the minds
of the youth of his charge, that after a lapse of sixty years their
recollections of him are of the most vivid character   His dress, appearance, conversation, manner of preaching texts, are as fresh in
their minds as things of yesterday   And with a singular unanimity
they agree in the following description of him   He was of the middle
size, and strongly built   His countenance had a pensive, placid
cast, but when excited was exceedingly expressive of resolution and
energy   His voice was sweet and pleasant, but at the same time so
strong that he could make himself heard above the notes of the drum
and the fife   As a preacher he was uncommonly eloquent and pathetic, rarely preaching without weeping himself, and at times he
would melt his whole audience into tears   The venerable Dr Green,
now going on to his ninetieth year, says that the impressions made
by one sermon by Caldwell preached in Chatham in 1779 or 1780
have never been effaced from his mind

He was among the most active of men, and seemed never wearied by any amount of bodily or mental labor   Feelings of the most
glowing patriotism and of the most fervent piety possessed his bosom
at the same time, without the one interfering with the other   He was
one day preaching to the battalion—the next marching with them
to battle, and, if defeated, assisting to conduct their retreat—and
the next administering the consolations of the gospel to some dying

[1] Historical Magazine, Ser 2, IX, 333

parishioner His people were most ardently attached to him, and the army adored him   Let his name be held in perpetual remembrance [1]

Dr Murray relates an amusing anecdote of Parson Caldwell and one of his parishioners, Abraham Clark of Elizabeth, a signer of the Declaration of Independence, and for many years a member of Congress While serving in the commissary department the chaplain had an office and provision store at Chatham, over the door of which he displayed the sign "JAMES CALDWELL, D Q M G," having reference to his rank of deputy quartermaster-general Seeing Mr. Clark approaching the door one day, he went to meet him, and found him intently gazing at the sign "What are you looking at so earnestly?" asked Mr Caldwell "I am looking at those letters," responded his visitor, "and I am striving to comprehend what they mean" "Well, what do you think they mean?" asked the chaplain "I cannot conceive," was the reply, "unless they mean 'Devilish Queer Minister of the Gospel'" Parson Caldwell was much amused by this novel interpretation, and he joined with his friend in hearty laughter

Some of the circumstances of the case point to the possibility that Dr Murray is mistaken in placing the scene of this episode at Chatham, and suggest that the incident happened, not in this village, but in Springfield where Mr Caldwell then lived We know that the chaplain had an office in Springfield, for he mentions it in the advertisements relating to the business of the quartermaster's department which he inserted in the newspapers, and it seems unlikely that he maintained another office at the same time in the neighboring village of Chatham, unless required to do so by conditions which do not now appear In his advertisements he names a number of cities and villages where he purposes

[1] New Jersey Historical Society Proceedings, Ser 1 III 77 The township and city of Caldwell, in Essex County, received their name in memory of the Fighting Chaplain

to attend from time to time, "for the convenience of the inhabitants," in the discharge of his official duties, but in this
list of town-names no mention of Chatham is made   The
fact, too, that Mr Clark, as well as Mr Caldwell, resided
temporarily in Springfield when the activities of the enemy
compelled them to leave Elizabeth, adds weight to the supposition that the incident in question happened there
Nevertheless, Dr Murray's statement has never been questioned, but, on the contrary, it is corroborated by William
P Tuttle, author of Bottle Hill and Madison, who says that
the anecdote was related to his father by an eyewitness as
having taken place in Chatham

Allusion has been made to the murder of Mrs Caldwell
in the battle of Connecticut Farms   The family at that time
occupied the Presbyterian parsonage at the Farms, which
Mr Caldwell had rented during the preceding summer [1]
When the approach of the enemy was announced, the
chaplain placed his older children in a wagon in his possession as commissary, and sent them for safety to the home
of his friend, Deacon Ephraim Sayre of Bottle Hill [2] but the
two youngest remained with their mother   Mr Caldwell,
upon leaving his house to take part in the impending battle,
urged his wife to seek safety in flight, as their neighbors had
decided to do, but she preferred to remain, believing that, as
a non-combatant, she would be safe from bodily injury, and
hoping that her presence would be the means of protecting
the house from pillage

When the battle was about to commence, Mrs Caldwell
and her children, with their nurse, Catherine Benwood, and
a housemaid named Abigail Lenington retired to a bedroom
at the rear of the house, which being enclosed by stone walls
with only a single window, afforded protection against
random bullets   The party occupied this room when the

[1] Hatfield's Elizabeth, 491
[2] Mrs Ellet's The Women of the Revolution, II , 108, 111

enemy retreated through the village, the ladies sitting upon
the bed, and the nurse holding the youngest child in her
arms   The housemaid, upon looking out of the window,
suddenly exclaimed that a red-coat soldier had jumped over
the fence and was approaching the house with a gun   A
moment later he appeared at the window and taking deliberate aim at Mrs Caldwell who had risen to her feet, he
discharged two bullets, both of which entered her body   She
fell backward upon the bed and expired almost immediately
The house was then plundered and soon afterwards set on
fire   Mrs. Caldwell's body was removed, and lay for a time
in the road, but at length two civilians carried it into the
house of Captain Henry Wade on the opposite side of the
street, which was one of only two buildings in the village
which escaped the flames [1]

It was generally supposed that the murderer recognized
Mrs Caldwell, and shot her to gratify the hatred which the
enemy harbored toward her husband, but it is not certain
that he was actuated by such motive   The British claimed
that she had been killed by a random bullet fired from the
direction of the American lines, and in order to refute this
assertion, Mr Caldwell, a few weeks later, prepared and
published a detailed statement of the case, supported by the
affidavits of the two maids, proving that the homicide was
intentional   From this source many of the above facts are
taken

During the night after the battle, the chaplain lodged
in a house on the Short Hills, in a state of extreme anxiety
respecting the fate of his wife and children   He had retired
to rest when he overheard two soldiers in the adjoining room
discussing the rumored death of Mrs Caldwell   He immediately entered their room in great agitation, and im-
plored them to tell him all that they had heard   They en-

[1] *New Jersey Journal*, No 81, September 6, 1780, Barber's New Jersey
Historical Collections, 197

deavored to calm his fears, and persuaded him to return to
his bed, assuring him that the rumor was not substantiated,
and was probably untrue The next morning he procured a
flag, and hastened to Connecticut Farms He perceived from
a distance that the village had been laid in ashes, and was
not long in verifying the afflicting report of the preceding
night [1]

The recollection of Parson Caldwell's son Josiah regarding the tragedy and his movements at the time is thus
recorded in Mrs Ellet's valuable history, The Women of the
Revolution About sunrise on the fateful day, when it was
learned that the British were approaching, Josiah left his
father's house, and, joining the villagers who were driving
their cattle to safety, he accompanied them as far as Springfield There he saw his father with a 6-pound cannon which
had been formerly used as an alarm gun He then proceeded to the house of Deacon Sayre at Bottle Hill, and a
day or two later he and his sister Hannah set out on foot to
return home On their way they met their nurse Katy, with
the two youngest children, in a chair belonging to Mr Caldwell She informed them of their mother's death, and
urged them to return with her to Bottle Hill The little
girl yielded and was taken into the conveyance, but Josiah insisted upon continuing his journey Upon reaching the
Farms, he was conducted to the house to which his mother's
remains had been taken, and found his father, who had arrived a short time before, standing beside the bed upon
which her lifeless form reposed

Mrs Caldwell was survived by nine children ranging
in age from two to sixteen years, one son having died in
infancy We learn from Littell's Passaic Valley Genealogies,
page 153, that after her death the children were all taken to
the home of Stephen Day of Chatham, whose wife was a
sister of their mother The Day homestead stood upon the
property now owned by the Ogden Memorial Presbyterian

[1] Barber's New Jersey Historical Collections, 197

church, but nearer the road than the church edifice   How long the Caldwell children lived in Chatham at that time is not stated, but they probably remained here until their father bought a house and established a home at New Providence

On November 24, 1781, Mr Caldwell was shot and instantly killed at Elizabeth Town Point by an American soldier named James Morgan   It was commonly believed that the assassin had been bribed by the enemy to commit the crime, but no proof that such was the case could be obtained   His motive, in fact, has always remained a mystery, although part of the evidence adduced at his trial seemed to indicate that he shot the parson to gratify a private grudge, because Caldwell, as deputy quartermaster-general, had failed to tender him his pay with the regularity he desired   A report of the tragedy, which has been accepted as substantially accurate, is quoted from the *New Jersey Journal* of November 28th

It is with the utmost pain and distress that we inform our readers that the Reverend Mr Jas Caldwell of Elizabeth-Town was most inhumanly and barbarously murdered on Saturday last by a soldier belonging to the year's men at that place

This worthy gentleman being informed of the arrival of a young lady in a flag from New York, at the Point whose family had been peculiarly serviceable to our unhappy fellow-citizens, prisoners with the enemy proposed waiting on her and conducting her to the town, as a grateful acknowledgement of the services offered by her family as above mentioned   He accordingly went to the Point in a chair for that purpose and after the young lady had got in the chair, the sentinel observing a handkerchief tied up in a bundle in her hand, told Mr Caldwell he must seize it in the name of the state, on which Mr Caldwell jumping out of the chair, said if that was the case, he would return it to the commanding officer, who was there present, but as he stepped forward, another impertinently told him to stop, which he immediately did, but notwithstanding, the soldier, without farther provocation, raised his gun and shot him

dead on the spot The villain was immediately seized and secured
He made but a very indifferent excuse for his conduct, and still remains very sullen and obstinate After his being secured, it appeared
by several evidences that, though a soldier with us for near twelve
months past, he had been seen in New York within a fortnight past,
and, from several other circumstances, there seems just grounds of
suspicion that the wretch had been bribed to commit this abominable
deed

Morgan was confined for a time in Springfield, later in
Burlington, and finally in Westfield, where his trial was held
He expiated his crime on the gallows January 29, 1782,
upon a spot a little west of the town of Westfield, which was
long known as Morgan's Hill [1]

Mr Caldwell s body was removed to the house of Mrs
Experience Noel, widow of Garret Noel, on Jersey Street,
Elizabeth, where the funeral was held on November 27th,
the services being conducted by Rev Dr McWhorter of
Newark The administration of the chaplain's estate, and
the guardianship of his orphaned children were undertaken
by his warm friend Elias Boudinot As the estate proved
insufficient for the maintenance and education of the
children, a subscription for the purpose was taken up, among
those who contributed being General Washington, whose
donation amounted to twenty or twenty-five guineas [2]

The lives of the Caldwell children are briefly outlined
as follows

1 MARGARET PHILLIPS, her grandmother's namesake, born
January 23, 1764 died January 3, 1831 She was educated at Miss
Hedden's select school in Newark She married December 2, 1837,
Isaac Canfield, a farmer and storekeeper of Malapardis, N J, and
later a merchant of Morristown He had fought in the Revolution,
and served as major of the Morris Battalion from 1807 to 1812
He is said to have introduced the Virginia crabapple into Morris
County

[1] Hatfield s Elizabeth, 532 n Barber s N J Hist Collections, 169
[2] Hatfield's Elizabeth, 532, 534, Boudinot's Elias Boudinot, 207

2   JOHN DICKINSON, born January 29, 1765, died May 11, 1766

3   HANNAH, born September 20, 1767, died February 20, 1825   She married 1st (1790), James R Smith, 2d (1820), Dr John Richardson Bayard Rogers   Mr Smith was a merchant of New York, and one of the proprietors of the Tontine coffee house   He resided on Pearl Street, and later on Broadway   Dr Rogers was an eminent surgeon, a graduate of the University of Edinburgh, and a professor in Columbia Medical College   His father, Rev John Rogers, D D, pastor of the old Wall St church, was the founder of Presbyterianism in New York

4   JOHN EDWARDS, born February 2, 1769, died March 9, 1819 After his father's death he was placed under the care of Dr Mc-Whorter   The Marquis de Lafayette, out of regard for Parson Caldwell, obtained from Mr Boudinot permission to adopt the chaplain's eldest son   John accordingly accompanied the Marquis on his return to France in 1782, and became a member of his family   He returned to America in 1791, and made his home in Philadelphia, where Boudinot was then living   There he married, in 1801, Louise ———, who died within a year, leaving an infant daughter In June 1801, he was appointed consular agent of the United States for San Domingo, W I   His subsequent home was in New York He married, as his second wife, Hannah, the daughter of Rev Nathan Ker of Goshen, N Y, and widow of Theodorus Van Wyck He eventually renounced Catholicism, which he had embraced in France, and united with the Cedar Street Presbyterian church in New York, of which he soon became an elder   He was a distinguished philanthropist   He was one of the founders of the American Bible Society and until his death its general agent   He established *The Christian Herald,* and edited and published the first five volumes of that periodical

5   JAMES BAXTER, born January 8, 1771, died February 12, 1826, was a lawyer of Woodbury, N J, and for several years a judge of Gloucester County   His wife's name is not known

6   ESTHER FINLEY, born October 26, 1772, died in Lebanon, Ill, Sept, 1844   She married May 16, 1798, Dr Robert Finley of Basking Ridge, N J, afterwards president of the University of Georgia

7   JOSIAH FLYNT, born in Elizabeth, N J, August 23, 1774,

died in Washington, D C, November 15, 1859 After his parents'
death he was adopted by General Benjamin Lincoln, who placed him
in school at Hingham, Mass He was afterwards bound as apprentice to a hatter of Boston, from whom he ran away, and followed
the sea for many years He commanded his own ship during the
wars of Napoleon, and had many narrow escapes from capture by
both French and British frigates Upon retiring from a seafaring
life he resided in Washington, D C He married, November 27,
1815, Maria Helen Magruder of Alexandria, Va He held a clerk-
ship under the Federal government for thirty years, being connected
with the Post Office Department

8   ELIAS BOUDINOT, born April 3, 1776, died in Washington,
D C, May 31 1825 He was adopted by Mr Boudinot, whose
namesake he was He graduated from the College of New Jersey
in 1796, studied law with Mr Boudinot and inherited his fine law
library He married 1st, Elizabeth Boyd, 2nd, Ann Lingan
He was one of the founders, and also corresponding secretary, of
the American Colonization Society, and in acknowledgment of his
services in this capacity, a town in Liberia, Africa, was named in his
honor He served as clerk of the United States Supreme Court
from 1800 to 1827, and after the capitol had been burned by the
British in 1814, the court met for a time in his house, 204-206 New
Jersey Avenue

9   SARAH OGDEN born in Springfield, N J, June 12, 1778,
died August 25, 1826 She married, April 24 1800 Rev John S
Vredenburg of New Brunswick, N J, for many years pastor of
the Reformed Church of Somerville

Her seventh child Elizabeth married Rev John Edgar Freeman Mr and Mrs
Freeman went as missionaries to India and perished in the Sepoy Mutiny at Cawn
pore June 13 1857

10   MARIA, born in Connecticut Farms, September 29 1779,
died in New York City, April 5, 1852 After her father's death
she was adopted by Mrs Noel She married, October 22, 1804,
Robert S Robertson of the mercantile firm of Robertson & Kelso of
New York Mr Robertson failed in 1823, and thereafter secured
employment in the U S Custom House, which he retained for many
years [1]

[1] Hatfield's Elizabeth 534 & seq, Wheeler's The Ogden Family in
America, 161 & seq, Tuttle's Bottle Hill and Madison, 62, Barber's New
Jersey Historical Collections, 169, Banta's Sayre Family, 100

CHAPTER VI

The Signal Station on Hobart Hill—Location of the Alarm Post—
Description of the Beacon—Orders and Correspondence respect-
ing the Construction of Alarm Posts—The Alarm Guns "Old
Sow" and "Crown Prince"—Erection of a Monument

OUR Revolutionary forefathers did not rely solely upon
the troops at Chatham to prevent a British invasion
of this part of Morris County they perceived at an early
period in the war that some means should be provided for
quickly arousing the entire countryside, and assembling the
militia, whenever an advance of the enemy was attempted
A chain of alarm posts equipped with beacons was accordingly established upon the hilltops of northern New Jersey,
from one of which to another the tidings of the enemy's
movements could be readily signalled One of these stations
—the one from which an alarm was most frequently given
when this part of the State was threatened, and which, in
consequence, is most often mentioned in local histories—was
placed on the summit of a ridge known as Hobart Hill,
which is crossed by the Morris Turnpike leading from
Chatham to Springfield, about two miles southeast of
Chatham bridge This ridge forms a connecting link between the Short Hills of Essex County and an elevation in
Union County upon which the present city of Summit is
built Dr Hatfield calls it "Prospect Hill" in his History
of Elizabeth, and the name has been adopted by subsequent
writers, but during the War of Independence it was usually
included in the general name of the Short Hills, of which it
is, in fact, a part It was more particularly defined in military
correspondence as "the heights of Springfield," "the heights
above Springfield," "the Short Hills back of Springfield,"

and "the pass in the mountains", although the latter term
was generally confined to the notch or gap through which
the turnpike runs   The present name was bestowed in
honor of Rev Dr John H Hobart, bishop of the Protestant
Episcopal diocese of New York, who, after the close of the
Revolution, built a summer home upon the crest of the ridge
on the north side of the turnpike in the Brantwood district
of Short Hills, where the residence of C L Roche now
stands

Rev Dr Samuel L Tuttle gives a description of the
alarm post which is sufficiently interesting to be quoted at
length   He writes

While the Army was encamped here, a Company of armed sentinels was stationed on the crown of Short-hills, at a point about four
rods South of the main road, and nearly in front of the residence
of the late Bishop Hobart   This point commanded a view of the
entire country East of the mountain, including New York Bay,
Staten-island, Newark Bay, Newark, Elizabethtown, Springfield,
and, in fact, the entire seaboard in the vicinity of New York, so that
the slightest movement of the enemy, in all that wide region, could,
without difficulty be detected   It also commanded a view of the
entire region West of the mountain, to the crown of the hills which
lie back of Morristown, and extending to Basking-ridge, Pluckamin,
and the hills in the vicinity of Middle-brook on the South, and over
to Whippany, Montville, Pompton Ringwood, and, across the State-
line, among the mountains of Orange-county, New York on the
North

On that commanding elevation, which could, itself, be seen on
both sides of the Short-hills, over all this wide extent of territory, the
means were kept for alarming the inhabitants of the interior, in case
of any threatening movements of the enemy, in any direction   A
cannon—an eighteen-pounder called in those times "The Old Sow"
—fired every half-hour, answered this object during the day-time and
in very stormy and dark nights, while an immense fire, or beacon-
light, answered the end at all other times   A log-house or two, it
is believed, with fire-places and accommodations for sleeping, were

erected there for the use of the sentinels who, by relieving one another at different intervals, kept careful watch both by day and night
—their eyes continually sweeping over all the vast extent of country
that lay stretched out like a map before them

The beacon-light was constructed of dry rails, laid up in a
crib-fashion around a high pole This was filled with various com-
bustible materials, while a tar-barrel was placed upon the top of
the pole When the sentinels discovered any movement of the enemy,
of a threatening character either the alarm-gun was fired or this
mass of combustibles was set in a blaze, so that tidings were spread
almost instantaneously over the whole region

There are several persons still living in this place [1855] who
remember to have heard that dismal alarm-gun booming, and to
have seen those beacons sending out their baleful and terrific light,
from that high point of observation; and who remember also to have
seen the inhabitants, armed with their muskets making all possible
haste to Chatham-bridge and the Short-hills, the places of rendezvous
in such cases, to prevent the enemy from crossing over into this
valley Every ear was open at all hours of day and night, to catch
the first note of warning from that old field-piece, whose sound was
known by all, and there were but few moments during the watches
of the night in which there were not anxious eyes peering through
the darkness towards the East, to see whether or not that beacon-fire
was burning [1]

Rev Dr Joseph F Tuttle while a resident of Rockaway, N J, also collected much valuable data relating to
the Revolutionary history of Morris County, and although
his researches were chiefly confined to the western part of
the county, his writings contain in the following paragraph
a reference to the beacon on Hobart Hill

That there was a system of beacon-lights there can be no doubt,
although, unfortunately the most of those are dead who could give
us information about it, and there are no documents describing the
various points where these lights were kindled Of one, we have some
knowledge Seven miles North of Morristown, near the present

[1] Historical Magazine, Ser 2, IX, 325

Rail-road Depot at Denville, is a mountain which rises abruptly
to a considerable height, from which you can see the Short-hills On
this point there was a beacon-light, managed by Captain Josiah Hall,
whose descendants still reside in the vicinity A fire from this point
would be seen from the top of Green Pond mountain, several miles
farther North, and a fire on that mountain would probably reach
the portion of Sussex-county where the brave Colonel Seward,
grandfather of Senator Seward, resided Tradition says that such
was the case, and that, often, at night, the tongue of fire might be
seen leaping into the air on the Short-hills, soon to be followed by
brilliant lights on Fort-hill, on the Denville-mountain, the Green
Pond-mountain, and on the range of mountains on the Orange-county
line To many it has seemed inexplicable, and it was so to the enemy,
that they could not make a movement towards the hills of Morris,
without meeting the yeomen of Morris, armed and ready to repel
them I have conversed with several old men who have seen the
roads converging on Morristown and Chatham lined with men who
were hurrying off to the Short-hills to drive back the invaders The
alarm-gun and the beacon-light explain the mystery [1]

Dr Ashbel Green, in his autobiography, mentions the
signal station on Hobart Hill, but he is in error in stating
that its site afterwards became the country residence of
Bishop Hobart The bishop acquired the adjacent property,
but his residence stood upon the opposite side of the turnpike Dr Green writes

The alarm gun, an iron eighteen pounder, was placed on the
highest point of what are called the Short Hills in the neighbourhood of Springfield, N J Bishop Hobart, after the war, purchased
the site and made it his country residence A lofty pole was placed
by the side of the cannon, with a tar barrel on the top, which was
set on fire when the gun was discharged The report of the gun
and the flame of the tar barrel were heard and seen to a great distance in the surrounding country The militia companies had each
its place of rendezvous to which they hastened as soon as the alarm
was given The Short Hills were a kind of natural barrier for

[1] Historical Magazine, Ser 2, IX, 372

the camp and military stores at Morristown A hundred men might
have defended some of the passes over these hills against a thousand
A British detachment once reached Springfield and burnt it, but no
British corps ever ventured into the Sand Hills In a clear day,
with a good telescope, the city of New York may be seen from these
heights When encamped at Morristown, General Washington occasionally rode to these hills to make his observations. The first time
I ever saw him was on one of these occasions He was accompanied
by the Marquis de la Fayette as he was then called, and who looked
like a mere boy [1]

Local tradition is so clear and positive regarding
Washington's practice of riding from Morristown through
Madison and Chatham to the Short Hills for the purpose
of observation, that Dr Green's statement is hardly needed
in corroboration The fact is also mentioned by Dr Joseph
F Tuttle, who tells us that Mrs Washington sometimes
accompanied the general on these trips "It was no unusual
thing," he writes, "to see General Washington and his accomplished lady, mounted on bay horses, and accompanied
by their faithful mulatto 'Bill' and fifty or sixty mounted
guards, passing through the village with all eyes upon
them," and speaking of Mrs Washington, he says "She
was a graceful and bold rider, and when the weather became

[1] Jones's Ashbel Green, 96

[*] The commander-in-chief's guard was a famous organization As originally formed in 1776 it consisted of a major's command—180 men—carefully chosen from the regiments of the various States, the selection being
confined to native Americans who were handsomely and well made, young
and active, and measuring from five feet eight inches to five feet ten inches
in height In the spring of 1777 it was increased to 250 men, but reduced to
the original number a year later, and in 1783, the last year of service, further reduced to 64 noncommissioned officers and privates The first captain-
commandant, as the leader was called, was Caleb Gibbs of Rhode Island,
who was succeeded by William Colfax one of his lieutenants, at the close
of 1779 The command was made up of both infantry and cavalry, the
former guarding the headquarters, while the latter accompanied the general
on the march and when reconnoitering, being also employed as patrols,
videttes, and dispatch-bearers

The only resident of Chatham who was a member of this distinguished
corps was Private Benjamin Bonnel, but as he did not join it until the
spring of 1782, long after Washington had left this region, he was not
one of the 'fifty or sixty mounted guards" mentioned by Dr Tuttle, who

mild, sometimes accompanied her husband in his rides to the
Wicke Farm or the Short Hills, and until recently there
were those still living who remembered to have seen her
riding on horseback, and by the engaging courtesy with
which she bowed to the humblest soldier or other person she
chanced to meet, she won all hearts to herself "[1]

Dr Tuttle records the fact that on one occasion when
General Washington was visiting the Short Hills, he was
discovered in a retired place in the vicinity of the signal
station on his knees and in prayer, after which he arose, and
seating himself upon a neighboring rock, he sang Watt's
version of the 102d Psalm, common meter, 1st part   This

accompanied the general on his trips to the Short Hills   Bonnel's war
record is as follows

Enlisted for the war August 9, 1777, as private in the 3rd company, under Captain Conway, later Captain Mead, of the 1st New Jersey regiment,
Colonel Matthias Ogden, attached to General Maxwell's brigade   Deserted at Brandywine, Del, September 11, 1777, rejoined April 1, 1778
Fought in battle of Monmouth, June 28, 1778   Promoted corporal January
21, 1780   Fought at Connecticut Farms, June 7, 1780, and at Springfield,
June 23, 1780   Deserted December 13, 1780, rejoined in January, 1781, and
reduced to the ranks   Detached at Morristown February 26, 1781, to Captain Jonathan Forman's (the 1st) company of the 3rd battalion of Lieutenant-colonel Barber's 1st brigade in General Muhlenberg's 1st division of
light infantry, commanded by General Lafayette   Fought at Green Springs,
Va, July 6, 1781, and at Yorktown, October 19, 1781   Transferred at Newburgh, N Y, April 30, 1782, to the commander-in-chief's guard, under
Lieutenant-colonel William Colfax   Furloughed at Newburgh June 6, 1783,
until the ratification of treaty of peace   Discharged November 3, 1783
    —Lossing's Biography of Washington, II, 177 n , Godfrey's The Com-
    mander-in-Chief's Guard, Littell's Passaic Valley Genealogies, 46

His name appears in the following advertisements
    THREE HUNDRED DOLLARS REWARD   DESERTED from Capt
Mead's company the 12th instant, Benjamin Bonnel, John Burnett, and John
Yherts, belonging to the 1st Jersey regiment   Any person that will appre-
hend and secure the above deserters shall be entitled to the above reward
                                                    G MEAD, Capt
December 19, 1780
                    —The New Jersey Journal, No 97, December 27, 1780
    SUSSEX ss   WAS committed to the gaol of this county the 31st of
December last, the three following soldiers belonging to Captain Mead's
company, of the first Jersey regiment viz   Benjamin Bonnel, John Burnet
and John Yherts, who were lately advertised in the New-Jersey Journal as
deserters
Newtown, Jan 7 1781   JAMES MORROW, Gaoler
                    —The New Jersey Gazette, No 164, February 14, 1781
    [1] Historical Magazine, Ser 2, IX, 325, Harper's Magazine, XVIII, 301

anecdote was authenticated by a Mrs. Sayre, wife of
William, and mother of Calvin Sayre, all of Columbia (now
Florham Park), N J , who identified it with a place near
Springfield, and with the time of the last battle at that
village [1]

The site of the signal station is now occupied by the
residence of Henry B Twombly on Hobart Avenue, in the
city of Summit. The beacon stood about an eighth of a mile
south of the turnpike (upon a spot which is much higher than
the notch through which that highway runs), beside an
ancient lane or by-road, now represented by Hobart Avenue,
which formerly left the turnpike near C P Bassett's present
gateway, and led in a southerly direction along the ridge
The pole which supported the tar-barrel was placed just
inside the fence on the west side of the lane   In altering
this by-way into a city street, its line was moved toward the
east, consequently the site of the beacon is much farther
from the road at present than was formerly the case

It would be difficult to find in this entire region a place
which offered better facilities for watching the movements
of the enemy, and of alarming the inhabitants   The spot
was evidently selected with care   not only is it one of the
highest elevations along the ridge, where the light of the
beacon would be most conspicuous, but it is the point from
which the most extended view can be obtained   Farther
north the outlook toward Elizabeth and New York is obstructed by the hill at Millburn, while the choice of a more
southerly location would have caused the end of Long Hill
at Chatham to conceal the signal light from a large portion
of Morris County   In after years the prospect in each direction became considerably obscured by a dense growth of
timber, which still remains in part, but during the Revolution the hill probably was not so heavily wooded

According to local tradition, the signal station on

[1] Revolutionary Fragments of Morris County, No 13

Hobart Hill was established soon after the capture of New York by the British in the autumn of 1776   Colonel Drake, in his Sketches of the Revolution and Civil War, expresses the opinion that the alarm post was placed there by Colonel Jacob Ford, Jr , in the latter part of 1776, when he, with a brigade of militia, was stationed at Chatham, and that an alarm was first given by this means when a British force advanced to Springfield on December 17th of that year   But although it is probable that the station dated from that period, it would seem that the series of beacons of which the one on Hobart Hill formed part was not constructed until later

In the winter of 1778-9 much attention was given to the establishment of alarm posts and beacons upon the most conspicuous hills throughout this region, and an active correspondence on the subject was maintained between General Washington and his subordinates   Several letters were exchanged by the commmander-in-chief and Lord Stirling, for the latter was much interested in the plan, and some of the officers who were charged with the construction of the beacons were ordered to apply to him for particular directions, although in certain parts of the State the work was supervised by Stirling himself   The manual labor was performed by fatigue parties of approximately twenty-four men each, detached from the regiments which were encamped nearest to the points selected [1]

The method by which the beacons were constructed is set forth in a military order found among Lord Stirling's papers, and quoted as follows by Mr Lossing in his Pictorial Field Book of the Revolution. [2]

Among other orders issued by him at that time were several respecting beacons and alarm posts   From one of them, in possession of the son of Colonel Aaron Burr, I copied the annexed sketch,

[1] Washington Papers in Library of Congress, B, VIII, pt 1, 573.
[2] Vol II, 808.

made by the pen of Lord Stirling, together with the full order

"Each of the beacons are to be of the following dimensions at bottom, fourteen feet square, to rise in a pyramidal form to about eighteen or twenty feet high, and then to terminate about six feet square, with a stout sapling in the centre of about thirty feet high from the ground   In order to erect them, the officer who oversees the execution should proceed thus   he should order the following sized logs to be cut as near the place as possible   twenty logs of fourteen feet long and about one foot diameter, ten logs of about twelve feet long, ten logs of about ten feet long, ten logs of about nine feet long, ten logs of about eight feet long, twenty logs of about seven feet long, twenty logs of about six feet long   He should then sort his longest logs as to diameter, and place the four longest on the ground, parallel to each other, and about three feet apart from each other   He should then place the four next logs in size across these at right angles, and so proceed till all the logs of fourteen feet be placed   Then he is to go on in the same manner with logs of twelve feet long, and when they are all placed, with those of a lesser size, till the whole are placed, taking care, as he goes on, to fill the vacancies between the logs with old dry split wood or useless dry rails and brush, not too close, and leaving the fifth tier open for firing and air   In the beginning of his work, to place a good stout sapling in the centre, with part of its top left, about ten or twelve feet above the whole work   The figure of the beacon will appear thus.

The two upper rows of logs should be fastened in their places with good strong wooden plugs or trunnels "

These beacons [adds Mr Lossing] were erected upon hills from the Hudson Highlands through New Jersey by way of Morristown, Pluckemin, and Middlebrook, and upon the Neversink Hills at Sandy Hook They were to be used as signals denoting the approach of the enemy, for the assembling of the militia at certain points, and to direct the movements of certain Continental battalions

When alarm posts had been established in Somerset and Middlesex, General Washington decided that the system should be extended to some of the other counties He accordingly communicated to Governor Livingston a plan for the construction of a chain of beacons throughout the State, and on April 9th, 1779, the execution of the project was intrusted to General Philemon Dickinson,[1] who, during the preceding December, had been appointed chief signal officer of the Continental army for the Middle Department "The line of communication," says Mr Walton in his History of the United States Army and Navy, "extended from Newburgh-on-the-Hudson, through Orange and Rockland Counties, along the ridge of the Ramapo Mountains and by an indirect course to Princeton and Trenton This line was about a hundred and fifty miles long, and all communications between the Eastern, Middle and Southern Departments passed over it "

GENERAL HEARD TO COLONEL HOLMES

Monmouth County,
Rocky Hill 12th April, 1779

Sir,

I have this Day rec'd Orders from Maj General Dickinson to execute the within plan In consequence of which I desire that you

---

[1] Historical Magazine, Ser 2, IX, 371

On January 8, 1781, it was reported to the Legislative Council that there was due to John Webster, for erecting a beacon on the Short Hills, by order of Governor Livingston, the sum of 17 pounds, 17 shillings and 9 pence, and on October 6, of the same year, the sum of 8 pounds 16 shillings was reported due to Captain Joseph Horton, for himself and others employed in building a beacon in 1779

instantly on receipt of this letter the Beacons & give the Necessary Orders for the rendezvous of the Militia in case of alarm which are within your District agreeable to the inclossed directions You will emediately Order the Officers Commanding Companies to have their men's Arms put in the best of Order you must Keep an exact account of the expence attending the fixing of these Beacons which you will be pleased to transmit me regularly Drawn out and properly Certified if the Beacon should be Nearest to you I desire you will set fire to it or the officer nearest to it upon proper Occation

I am, Sir, Your most obt Servant,

Nathaniel Heard
Brigr Genl

N B

I am surprised that you have not sent me Returns of the state of your Regt I beg you will send me a Return of the state of the Regt imediately I desire you will send me word by Express as Soon as the Beacons are Erected

To Colo Holmes

Alarm Posts or places where the Militia New Jersey are to assemble on the first alarm which Will be given by fires on the Mountain at the places agreed on

[Here follow directions for each county]

Morris County

the Southern District to assemble at Turkey Meeting House and to proceed to the Gap on the Road to Springfield

The Middle District to assemble at Chatham to proceed toward Springfield

The Northern District to assemble near the mouth of Rockaway and to proceed over the Mountain towards Newark Mountain Meeting House

Essex

To settle their Alarm Posts with General Maxwell

*   *   *   (*   *

signals on which the Militia are to assemble—

No 1—A large fire on the Mountain in the Rear of Pluckemin

No 2—One do on the prominent part of the Mountain sted Gap

No 3—do on the most conspicuous part of the mountain Mordicais Gap (Alias Waynes Gap)

No 4—one do near Lincolns Gap

No 5—one do near Quibble Town Gap

No 6—one do on the Hill near the Road to Basking ridge about four Miles North of Colo Van Hornes, which is plainly seen at Morris Town & the Country on the side

No 7—One do on the Remarkable Tree on the Hill Toward Princetown

No 8—Another do on the Hill in front of Martin Tavern short Hills

these fires should be made of Logs intermixed with Brush square at Bottom about sixteen feet & to Diminish as they rise like a pyramid & should be 18 or 20 feet High

It is proposed that preparation should be made to make the like signals in the other following places in this state

No 9—at the point of the Mountain North of Springfield about a mile.

No 10—on the Top of the Hill about a Mile south East Catham Bridge

No 11—at Coopers Wind Mill on long Hill at Corns Ludlows [1]

No 12—at the point of Kenneys Hill at Morris Town

No 13—on the highest point of Pidgeons Hill about four miles North West of Morris Town

No 14—On the Highest part of Schylors Mountain North West of Pluckemin 12 Miles

No 15—On the Hill 10 Miles west of do.

No 16—on the Southernmost part of Cushahvick Hills

No 17—On the Hill N W of Fleming Towns

No 18—On the N W point of Sowerland Hill

No 19—On the most conspicuous place on the Height of Amwell looking southward

No 20—Near Prince Town looking southward

No 21—on Centre Hill in Monmouth

No 22—on Middleton Hill

No 23—on Mount Pleasant

---

[1] The Laws of 1780, Chapter LVII, provided for the payment to Colonel Sylvanus Seeley the sum of 56 pounds, 8 shillings and 9 pence, paid to John Roll for building a beacon on Long Hill, and for six cords of wood

These three last should be fired only when the Enemy invade Monmouth County south of Raritan or on the first appearance of any force of the enemy going up Amboy Bay [1]

Besides the company of sentinels who had charge of the alarm gun and beacon, small bodies of troops were occasionally stationed on Hobart Hill, which was an advantageous point for planning and executing sudden movements against the enemy. General Washington, in a letter to General Stephen of May 24, 1777, referring to the posting of Continental troops, says "Some men will be sent to possess the Pass of the Mountain, in some advantageous spot, between Springfield and Chatham" ,[2] and similar references are found in other military documents

LIEUTENANT-COLONEL ZEBULON BUTLER TO GENERAL WASHINGTON

Sir   Chatham May 29th 1777

Pursuant to orders received from your Excellency, by the hand of Major General Lincoln I have marched with the 3 detachments from Connecticut Regiments   Part of the Westmoreland Independent Companies have joined me as was ordered, & more will be this day

I am now encamped upon the Heights between Chatham & Springfield, Gen Stephens had left this place before my arrival & I am destitute of any orders,   My Quarter Master (by my discretion) waits on your Excellency for Orders, many of the Soldiers in the Independent Company's have received no Clothing since they entered the Service which was in Sept last many of their arms are defective & useless, they are also destitute of tents & every kind of Camp equipage, hope therefore your excellency will give special directions, how & in what manner they are to be supplied with those articles

I am with the greatest esteem your excellency's

ZEBN BUTLER [3]

[1] Stillwell's Historical & Genealogical Miscellany, III, 342
[2] Washington Papers in Library of Congress, B III, pt 1, 210
[3] Ibid , 16, 8

Colonel Butler probably remained until the 12th of June, when he was ordered by Washington to take post at Morristown, with his regiment and his two independent companies, to guard the stores at that place [1]

GENERAL WASHINGTON TO GENERAL ST CLAIR.

Headquarters, Middlebrook, 29th May, 1779

Sir.—

You will be pleased to march immediately with the division under your command, by way of Quibble Town and Scotch Plains, and take post on the heights between Springfield and Chatham, till further orders, or till some enterprise of the enemy shall make a sudden movement necessary.[2]

* * * * * * * * *

In a letter written by St Clair to Washington, dated Springfield, January 31, 1780, we find this paragraph

The Signals for calling out the Militia have been very much neglected, and are down in some Places and I cannot find who has Care of them   I have requested Mr Caldwell to have them reestablished and proper Persons appointed to give the Alarm in case of Necessity, but I am not certain but this may interfere with some Regulation of the State, which some time ago, put that Matter into the Care of the Militia Generals, and it has gone into the Hands of the subordinate officers in gradation untill it is nobody's Business[3]

FROM ONE OF ST CLAIR'S ORDERLY BOOKS

Division Orders, Springfield, February 16 [1780]

A corporal and six men to be sent to the Mountain to take charge of a piece of ordinance   He will call on Mr Caldwell at Springfield who will give him directions respecting the fixed signals to proclaim an alarm[4]

[1] Washington Papers in Library of Congress, B III, pt 2, 71
[2] Smith's The St Clair Papers, I, 471
[3] Washington Papers in Library of Congress, 35, 238
[4] Connecticut Men in the Revolution, 137

On March 11th Washington wrote to Baron de Kalb, who had then succeeded St Clair in command of the post at Springfield

There were certain Signals established for alarming the Militia in case of a serious movement, but I fear they have of late been neglected and have got out of repair Mr Caldwell can inform you better than any person where the Signals were placed and of the methods fixed upon for communicating the Alarm to the Country I must request you to apply to him for the necessary information upon the subject and to lose no time in having matters so arranged that we may upon the shortest notice call in the force of the Country You are not to depend upon the Militia for doing this, but send parties to repair any of the signals which may want it You will be pleased to communicate any intelligence which may reach you as speedily as possible Be pleased to inform me immediately of the situation in which you find the signals from Mr Caldwell's report [1]

Baron de Kalb replied

Mr Caldwell being at Philadelphia I conferred with Colo Jaques, of the Militia of Essex County on the Subject of the Signals established for alarming the Country I here inclose a copy of them in all the parts of this State I understand that those hereabout though neglected are not much impaired I will take care to see them repaired in Essex and Middlesex Counties, by the Persons appointed thereto

SIGNALS ON WHICH THE MILITIA ARE IMMEDIATELY TO ASSEMBLE

A Large fire on the mountain in the rear of Pluckimin

one on the mountain near Steals Gap

one on the mountain near Moidicas or Wayn Gap

one near Lincolns Gap

one near Quibble Town Gap

[1] Washington Papers in Library of Congress, B XI, pt 1, 441

one on the Hill the road to Baskinridge four miles north of Col
    Van Horns

one on the Hill towards princetown

one on the hill in front of martin's Tavern near short hill

    It is further proposed that preparations should be made to make
the like signals in the following places in this State—
    at the point of the mountain north of springfield one mile un-
der the care of Capt Gillam
    On the top of the Hill one mile south East of Chatham Bridge
under the care of Capt Horton
    at Coopers windmill on Long Hill
    at the point of Kennys Hill at morristown
    on pidgeon Hill four miles north west of morristown
    on Schuylers mountain N W of Pluckimen 12 miles
    on the Hill 10 miles West of Do
    on the South Point of Cushatunk Hill
    on the N W point of the Southern Hill
    on the high hill N W of flemingtown
    on the Hyhts of Amwell—looking southward
    near princeton looking Southward
    on Carter Hill in monmouth on middleton hill
    on mount Pleasant [1]

    A few days later (March 21st) Washington wrote to
De Kalb that the country people refuse to seek safety in
flight, in case of incursions, until the last moment, so that
it is necessary to keep a close watch upon the enemy, in
order to give the inhabitants timely warning, and although
Washington does not think that the British would attempt
anything while the commissioners appointed to negotiate an
exchange of prisoners are sitting at Amboy, still this is a
mere opinion, and De Kalb's vigilance must not be relaxed
"You will, no doubt, have the signals in the utmost state of
preparation," he continues, "and keep a small party stationed
with the alarm-guns below Chatham "[2]

[1] Washington Papers in Library of Congress, 36, 158
[2] Spark's Writings of Washington, VI, 489

The only officer having charge of the signal station on Hobart Hill whose name has come down to us is Captain Joseph Horton of Colonel Moses Jaques' regiment of Essex County militia   There is no evidence, however, that he had command of this post during the entire war

The beacon stood on property owned in Revolutionary days by Richard Swain, who is said to have served in the army with the rank of gun-master, and who, with one of his neighbors, John Pike, was detailed to take charge of the alarm gun   On February 25, 1779, upon the occasion of a British raid having for its object the surprise of Maxwell's brigade at Elizabeth and the capture of Governor Livingston, the signal gun was discharged, and an accident happened which resulted in Pike's death   It was his duty to swab the cannon, and in his haste and excitement he failed to do this thoroughly   While the gun was being reloaded, a premature discharge occurred, and Pike, who was standing directly in front of the muzzle, received mortal injuries, while Swain lost the thumb of his right hand [1]   The application of Pike's widow for a pension is taken from the records of the Essex County Court of Quarter Sessions   It is dated April 12, 1781

Jemima Pike Widow of John Pike late of the Township of Elizabeth Town, deceased having produced to this Court a Certificate from Benjamin Bonnel & James Campbell, Esq'rs two of the justices of the peace of the county of Essex, living in the township of Elizabeth Town, that the sd Jemima Pike was in their belief, the lawful Wife and now is the real Widow of the sd John Pike, & has her legal residence in the township of Elizabeth Town af'd   And the sd Jemima Pike having also produced a Certificate from Captain Joseph Horton of Col'n Moses Jaquis's Regiment of Essex County Militia, setting forth that the sd John Pike was a private

---

[1] *The Summit Herald*, October 17, 1896   According to a tradition of the Swain family, the cannon was placed on the western slope of the hill, toward Chatham, and not, as is generally supposed, beside the beacon on the summit

in his Company, and was stationed at the Short Hills in the sd County of Essex in the Winter of the year 1779, in order to attend the Beacon and Alarm Gun placed on the first mountain in the sd County, & to fire the same in case of Alarm or Invasion from the Enemy, & that on the twenty fifth day of February, in the Year of our Lord, one thousand seven hundred and seventy-nine, the Enemy having landed a party of men at Elizabeth Town, the sd Alarm Gun was ordered to be fired, in doing of which the sd John Pike was unfortunately wounded, & in three days afterwards died of the Wounds he then received and prayed a certificate for half pay, &c , Whereupon the Court considering the above Certificates, certify that the said Jemima Pike, is entitled to receive the half pay of a private to the artillery, from the sd twenty Eighth day of February atd agreeable to the statute of New Jersey in such Case lately made & provided

The certificate of the Essex County court was presented to the General Assembly on May 23, 1781, whereupon it was ordered that a warrant should issue in favor of said Jemima Pike for the sum of 25 shillings per month, being the amount of her late husband's half pay, she to draw the sum from the treasury monthly during her widowhood

The alarm gun at Hobart Hill, mentioned in the writings of Dr Ashbel Green, already quoted, was an iron eighteen-pounder popularly called "the Old Sow" This cannon, however, was not retained here during the entire period of the Revolution. Although definite information respecting it is lacking, we have reason to believe that it was brought to the signal station toward the close of 1777, and that it remained but little over two years The time of its arrival is inferred from the following reference contained in the minutes of the New Jersey Council of Safety,[1] under date of November 17th, 1777

His Excellency produced to the Board a letter from the Revd

[1] Vol III, 162

Mr Caldwell to Majr Genl Dickinson, dated the 22 October last, containing his report to Genl Dickinson who had been requested by the Board to inform them of the most proper place to fix beacons, and appoint alarm posts, by which it appears to the Board most expedient to remove the piece of Cannon now lying at Princeton, to the mountain that nearly divides the space between Elizabeth and Morristown, to be put under Guard of the Man who lives where the said Cannon is to be fixed and a few of his neighbors who ought to be exempted from Military Duty, That it would farther be proper to erect a *pile* on the Hill near where Mr McGee formerly lived, whence the Guard from the said Mountain may see the fire or smoke and by that means know that the Guns fired at Elizabeth Town, are intended for an alarm & upon that signal fire the Cannon on the Mountain The Council hereupon agreed That Mr Caldwell be desired to carry the above Plan into execution and to transmit to the Board an account of the expenses attending the same

The origin and meaning of the name "the Old Sow," which was applied to the alarm gun on Hobart Hill, has been the subject of much speculation and discussion, three theories being advanced to explain its significance A supposition which is quite generally entertained is that the patriots facetiously compared the sharp, whip-like cracks of the muskets to the squealing of little pigs, and the deep-throated roar of the signal gun to the grunting of the parent beast Another interpretation is given by Mrs J C Elmer of Springfield, in a communication published in the *Summit Herald* of October 31, 1896, namely that the cannon was so called because, not being mounted upon a carriage, its recoil when discharged caused it to root up the ground. This fact, she added, had been ascertained many years before by her husband, who had devoted much time to historical research A third, and perhaps the most reasonable, explanation is that suggested by Rev William Hoppaugh of Springfield, a former pastor of the Presbyterian church of that place, who points out that iron founders apply the name "sow" to the channel which leads

from the smelting-furnace to the pig-bed, and also to a piece
of metal cast in this channel, and he thinks that in the case
of the alarm gun, the name had reference to its mode of
manufacture, or to the variety of iron of which it was made

Considerable doubt exists concerning the subsequent
disposition of the "Old Sow " No trustworthy record has
been found, and traditions are so conflicting as to appear
unreliable A cannon was left at Hobart Hill when the war
was over, and lay upon the ground near the site of the
beacon for many years—the late Smith Taylor, who lived in
the neighborhood, used to say that he had often caught rab-
bits in its barrel, where they had sought shelter during a hunt
—yet this was not the "Old Sow," but a smaller cannon, a
six-pounder called the 'Crown Prince,' which was captured
from the British at Springfield in 1780 Tradition says that
the latter gun was used for a time at the signal station in
place of the "Old Sow"[1] (though failing to give the date of
the substitution or the reason for the change), and that the
original alarm piece was lost overboard from a sloop in
Newark Bay, before the cessation of hostilities, and never
recovered

Leaving the realm of tradition for the firmer ground
of written history, we learn that in the winter of 1780, when
Washington's army lay at Morristown, a carefully planned,
though unsuccessful, attempt was made to surprise the
British outposts on Staten Island The officer in command
of this expedition, which set out from Morristown on
January 14th, was Lord Stirling, who, on the eve of his departure, wrote to General Washington a letter containing
the following paragraph

There is at the short Hills, an Eighteen pounder which we intend to make use of. She probably is without ammunition Will
your Excellency have the goodness to order a supply as expeditiously

---

[1] As an illustration of the conflict of traditions, reference is made to
the assertion that the 'Crown Prince" was used as an alarm-piece, not at
the Short Hills, but upon Kimball Hill near Morristown

as possible? If there are no Eighteen pound shot, twelves will be better than none [1]

Although this letter furnishes the reason for a substitution of alarm guns on Hobart Hill, it throws no light upon the ultimate fate of the "Old Sow." Still, in the absence of definite information, we may readily assume that the cannon was taken by Lord Stirling on his expedition, and that his troops, when driven back from Staten Island, were obliged, in their hurried retreat, to leave the gun in the hands of the enemy. But as this movement took place in the middle of January, and the cannon called the "Crown Prince" was not captured from the British until the following June, there was an interval of five months during which the signal station must have been supplied with a third alarm piece, the identity of which cannot be ascertained.

Regarding the later history of the "Crown Prince" there is no such uncertainty. It remained near the site of the beacon until 1818, when General Benoni Hathaway of Morristown, who had won renown in the Revolution, presented it in charge to Lieutenant-Colonel William Brittin, then commanding the First or "Middle" regiment of Morris County militia. The latter removed the gun to his home in Madison, and placed it in his barn. Thereafter it was used for the firing of salutes in patriotic celebrations, being frequently borrowed for this purpose by the people of Chatham, New Providence, and other neighboring towns. At length it was taken to Morristown, where its booming announced the arrival of General Lafayette on his visit of 1825. It soon became the fashion to fire the cannon at political meetings, and it was frequently stolen and concealed by both Whigs and Democrats. At one time it was carried about a mile out of town, spiked, and buried in the ground for a year or more, either to prevent its use by the opposite political party, or to preclude its return to Madison, as the

[1] Washington Papers in Library of Congress, 35, 88

rivalry for its possession ran high between the two municipalities   Upon another occasion it was thrown into the
pond of the grist-mill on Speedwell Avenue for similar
reasons   About 1835 it was taken up to Fort Nonsense,
and a deliberate attempt was made to burst it, by
loading it with a double charge of powder, filling it with
stones and sods well rammed down, and then burying it
in the ground with the muzzle downwards   A slow match
was applied, and a tremendous explosion ensued, but it was
found that the gun had simply kicked itself out of the
ground, and was entirely uninjured

In 1871, when the monument was erected in the park
to the memory of the Morris County soldiers who fell
during the Civil War, the "Crown Prince" was mounted upon
a carriage made at the Speedwell iron works, and placed
in front of it   This position, however, was not considered
particularly appropriate, for the gun had no connection with
the War of the Rebellion, and on October 9 1890, it was
presented to the Washington Association of New Jersey by
William Jackson Brittin of Madison, a son of Colonel
Brittin, whose family still regarded it as their property,
when, with the consent of the town and county authorities,
and the approval of the local Post of the Grand Army of the
Republic, it was removed to the grounds of Washington's
Headquarters, where it may now be seen [1]

The pole supporting the tar-barrel remained for
several years after the close of the Revolutionary War
Upon its removal, the hole in which it had stood was filled
with stones, and continued to be plainly visible until 1896,
when the New Jersey Society of the Sons of the American
Revolution decided to mark the spot, and preserve its historic memories, by the erection of a monument   For this
purpose the society chose an unhewn boulder weighing about
three tons, which was presented by Hon   Nathaniel Niles

[1] *The Jerseyman,* October 10 and 17, 1890

THE "CROWN PRINCE"

of Madison, upon whose lands it was found, and it was
placed upon a foundation of solid masonry covering the site
of the beacon, with a handsome bronze tablet, bearing an
appropriate inscription, riveted upon its face.

1776
HERE IN THE TIME OF THE REVOLUTION
STOOD THE SIGNAL BEACON AND BY ITS
SIDE THE CANNON KNOWN AS
"THE OLD SOW"
WHICH IN TIME OF DANGER AND INVASION
SUMMONED THE PATRIOTIC
"MINUTE MEN"
OF THIS VICINITY TO THE DEFENSE OF THE
COUNTRY AND THE REPULSE OF THE INVADER

THIS MONUMENT IS ERECTED BY THE NEW JERSEY SOCIETY OF THE
SONS OF THE AMERICAN REVOLUTION AND DEDICATED TO
THE MEMORY OF THE PATRIOTS OF NEW JERSEY
1896

October 19, 1896, the anniversary of the surrender at
Yorktown, was the day set apart for the dedication of the
monument   The ceremonies began with the unveiling of a
shaft in the Revolutionary cemetery at Springfield, followed
by appropriate services in the Presbyterian church of that
village, and the members of the society, accompanied by
their guests, then proceeded to the summit of Hobart Hill
to dedicate the monument on the site of the signal station
The committee in charge consisted of A W Bray, William
M. Dean, John Farr, H P Toler, H J Barrell, William P
Tuttle and James C Holden   According to the statement
of contemporary newspapers, the spectators numbered one
thousand, which, allowing for the exaggeration common to
such reports, may be understood as meaning about two
hundred and fifty   Among those present were repre-

sentatives of many patriotic societies, including the Daughters of the American Revolution, the Society of Colonial Wars, the Order of Founders and Patriots of America, the Washington Association of New Jersey, and the New Jersey Historical Society   A speaker's stand had been erected near the monument, and the neighboring trees were tastefully draped with the national colors

The exercises were simple but impressive   The opening address was delivered by John Whitehead, the venerable president of the society, and he was followed by William P Tuttle, who, in a scholarly and carefully prepared speech, reviewed the circumstances under which the signal station was established, described the beacon and alarm gun, and related several interesting anecdotes connected with the Revolutionary history of the spot

At the time of the erection of the monument there were two persons still living who remembered having seen the tar-barrel surmounting the lofty pole, which remained long after the war   One was Mrs Experience Swain of Summit, then eighty-six years old (a daughter-in-law of Richard Swain, the Revolutionary gun-master), and the other was Mrs Nancy D Gardiner of Chatham, who was born in 1802 and had therefore attained the age of ninety-four The latter used to say that the tar-barrel, which overtopped the tallest trees upon the ridge, could be plainly seen from her window in Chatham, and that it was not removed until she was more than twenty years of age [1]

The land upon which the monument was placed belonged at the time to the late Dr William H Risk of Summit   Unfortunately the society did not purchase the property, but merely obtained the doctor's permission to put the boulder there, with his assurance that it would not be disturbed during his lifetime   At a later date, an effort was

[1] *The Summit Herald*, October 17, 1896, *The Madison Eagle*, November 20, 1896

THE OLD SOW MONUMENT

made by a Summit newspaper to interest the public in securing the title to the lot, either by some society or by the
municipality, so that the future of the monument might
be assured, but sufficient interest in the project could not be
aroused, and after the death of Dr Risk the land was sold
to Henry B Twombly, who removed the boulder, and built
a handsome residence upon the spot where the beacon stood
The bronze tablet mentioned above has been preserved, and
now adorns the wall enclosing Mr Twombly's door-yard

One of the cannons captured from the French in the siege of Louisburg was called the
Old Sow —*Harper s Magazine*, XXI ,96 The rarity of the name suggests that this
was the gun of the same appellation afterward used as an alarm piece on Hobart Hill
We may readily surmise that it was brought to New Jersey by some of the colonial
troops in the French and Indian War   A British cannon employed in the defense of
Quebec in the Revolution and afterward captured by the Americans is now preserved
at Elizabeth, N J, and the gun of Louisburg may have made a similar journey

CHAPTER VII

Operations in the Autumn of 1776—Gen Washington's Retreat to
the Delaware—Local Militia Assembled—Gen Lee takes Post
at Chatham—Brief Sketch of his Career—His Insubordination
—The British try to Reach Chatham—First Battle at Springfield—Arrival of Col Vose's Detachment from Ticonderoga—
Threatened Advance by the British upon Morristown—Gen
Maxwell takes Command of the Local Troops

THE village of Chatham first appears prominently in
Revolutionary history during the autumn of 1776
Although many of the patriots of this vicinity had enlisted
and rendered active service at an earlier date, and the
villagers had thus been brought in touch with the struggle
for liberty, the actual fighting up to this time had been more
or less remote, and they had had no reason to fear for their
personal safety. But following the operations in the neighborhood of New York during 1776, the scene of hostilities
was suddenly transferred to New Jersey, the American
army was driven back to the Delaware River, leaving this
portion of the State entirely exposed to the ravages of the
enemy, the first engagement at Springfield occurred in an
attempt on the part of the British to reach Chatham, and
the people of this village found the war brought almost to
their doors

This was perhaps the darkest period of the Revolution
The disastrous campaign on Long Island closed with the
abandonment of New York, and was shortly followed by
the defeat at White Plains, the loss of Fort Washington,
and the evacuation of Fort Lee. The patriots of New
Jersey were thoroughly disheartened, and regarded their
cause as practically lost, many who had previously been

loud in their protestations of loyalty to the colonies now seeking the protection of the British authorities, and renewing their allegiance to the crown Washington found his army decreasing almost daily, through desertions, and the withdrawal of troops whose term of enlistment had expired, and being unable to gather recruits to fill his depleted ranks, he was compelled, by a superior force to commence his memorable retreat from the Hudson to the Delaware, leaving the eastern part of New Jersey at the mercy of the enemy, who followed closely in his rear [1] For, although one detachment of Americans had remained at North Castle, a second at Fort Washington and a third at Peekskill, they were not sufficiently numerous to protect the inhabitants of this region

Perceiving that a British invasion of New Jersey was imminent, Washington had written from White Plains to Governor Livingston, as early as the 7th of November, urging the necessity of preparing the militia to take the place of the New Jersey troops whose term was about to expire, and of warning the inhabitants living near the water to hold themselves in readiness to remove their stock, grain and personal effects upon the earliest notice He pointed out the value of forage to the enemy, and advised that what could not be removed with convenience should be destroyed without the least hesitation [2]

Governor Livingston promptly issued instructions respecting the calling out of the militia to cover Washington's retreat, and to assist in attempting to check the advance of the British Matthias Williamson, at that time brigadier-general of the New Jersey militia, to whom the governor's instructions were addressed wrote as follows to Colonel

---

[1] In order to expedite this retreat, Washington divided his army into two columns, one of which passed through Springfield within five miles of Chatham.—*Mellick's The Story of an Old Farm, 320*

[2] Hatfield's Elizabeth, 446

Jacob Ford, Jr, of Morristown, under date of November 26th

Sir

By express just now received from his Excellency Governor Livingston, I am desired to call out all the militia of the State; therefore on receipt hereof, you are ordered to bring out all the militia in your County immediately, and to march them down to Elizabethtown and see that each man is furnished with a gun, and all his ammunition, accutrements, blanket, and four days' provision, and when they arrive to join their respective companies and regiments

I am, sir, your humble servant,

M Williamson

P S

Sir

You will please to send two men off to your County, express, with your orders to have these orders immediately put into execution Order the express to call on me, to take a letter to Sussex [1]

Williamson wrote to Washington from Morristown on December 8th that, pursuant to the governor's instructions, he had issued orders to the commanders of militia to draw out their battalions and join either Washington's army or his own troops as most contiguous   He added that very few of Essex and Bergen had responded, as many of the inhabitants of those counties, who had been thought staunch Whigs, had now forsaken the American cause, and that although Colonel Symmes of Sussex had joined, the number of his privates was inconsiderable, so that the force at Morristown consisted principally of a regiment of Morris County militia, numbering perhaps 800 officers and men, under Colonel Ford, to whose zeal and influence with the people the preparations for defence at that place were chiefly due   He continued

Colonel Ford has had the command since we arrived here   I

[1] American Archives, Ser 5, III, 1120

took so great a cold on the late march, which fell into my limbs, as
has in a great measure confined me to my room, and disabled me from
joining the brigade I rode out yesterday about four miles to Passaick,[1] our chief post, and taking fresh cold, am now entirely confined
to my room [2]

A brigade of militia was soon assembled, consisting of
the Morris County regiment under Colonel Ford, who was
the brigade commandant, a battalion from Sussex County
under Colonel John Cleve Symmes, and a battalion from
Essex County under Oliver Spencer, who had previously
served as major in the First Essex regiment, and was now
appointed to this brigade with the rank of lieutenant-colonel
The force numbered in all about 1,000 men, who, marching
from Morristown through Chatham, took post in the neighborhood of Springfield to watch the movements of the
enemy [3]

While these events were in progress, Chatham was
visited by General Charles Lee, who paused here for a few
days in the course of his march through northern New
Jersey to join the army of Washington

General Lee is a romantic, but by no means pleasing,
character of Revolutionary history   Though a resident of
Virginia at the time of which we write, he was in no way
related to the celebrated family of the same name in that
State   He is variously described by his many biographers
as an Englishman, an Irishman, and a Welshman, the weight
of authority giving Cheshire, England, as his birthplace, and
the year 1731 as the date of his nativity [4] He was an im-
perious, quarrelsome and vindictive man, tall, lank and
hollow-cheeked, with a discontented expression of counten-

[1] Chatham

[2] American Archives, Ser 5, III, 1120

[3] Hatfield's Elizabeth, 450, Gales's Spencer

[4] Jones's New York in the Revolution, II, 350, Paulding s Washington,
I, 262, Schroeder's Washington, II, 30, Doyle's Steuben, 105, Belcher's First
American Civil War, II, 192

ance, slovenly in dress, boorish in manner, and coarse, vulgar
and profane in speech   In temper he was sour and morose,
but, although he scarcely ever laughed, and seldom smiled,
he possessed a cynical wit, and delighted in making sarcastic
and insulting remarks in his harsh, rough voice   One of
his most marked characteristics was an extreme fondness for
dogs, and he was accompanied by three or four of these
animals upon all occasions [1]

But with all his faults, Lee was a brilliant, dashing
officer of unquestionable ability, being regarded by the
English and by many Americans as the most talented general
in the Continental army   A soldier from his youth, he had
fought in many countries and under several flags   He
obtained a commission in the British army, through family
influence, when only eleven years of age   At twenty-four he
commanded a grenadier company of the Forty-fourth regiment during the French and Indian War, at which time the
Mohawk Indians adopted him into their tribe, giving him the
very appropriate name of "Boiling Water"   As a colonel, he
fought under General Burgoyne in the war with Spain, dis-
tinguishing himself in the campaign in Portugal   For two
years he was attached to the staff of the King of Poland,
and in 1769 he was appointed a major-general of the Rus-
sian army, serving in the war with the Turks   He is afterwards heard of in Hungary, France and Switzerland, where
his irascible and pugnacious temperament involved him in
frequent quarrels, brawls and duels [2]

At an early period of his career Lee became interested
in English politics, taking a stand strongly opposed to the
party then in power   Through anger and disappointment
at failing to obtain promotion in the British army, he fiercely
attacked the ministry in the columns of the press, and for a

[1] Fiske's American Revolution, I, 152, Sear's Pictorial Revolution, 275,
Abbott's Washington, 299

[2] Mellick's The Story of an Old Farm, 337, Doyle's Steuben, 105,
Schroeder's Washington, II, 34

MAJOR-GENERAL CHARLES LEE

From a drawing by Barham Rushbrooke in Girdlestone's *Lee the Author of Junius*. Though designed as a caricature, it was declared by Lee's acquaintances to be "the only successful delineation either of his countenance or person"

time was suspected of being the author of the famous Junius letters which appeared in 1769 Coming to America shortly before the Revolution, he heartily espoused the cause of the patriots, not through sympathy with the principles involved, but rather for personal aggrandizement, and to gratify his animosity toward the home government He soon became an acknowledged leader of the colonists, who were impressed by his military record, awed by his braggadocio, and misled by his infinite self-confidence; and upon the outbreak of hostilities he was commissioned a major-general by the Continental Congress In marked contrast with the unselfish devotion of the patriots, whose labors and sacrifices in the cause of freedom were offered without thought of recompense, Lee's cupidity demanded a payment by Congress of $30,000 to compensate him for the forfeiture of his estate in England, which, as Trevelyan points out, was neither a rich nor an unencumbered possession, and for the surrender of the half pay which he drew as a retired British officer He aspired to the position of commander-in-chief, and was intensely chagrined at being outranked by General Washington and General Artemas Ward [1]

When the army crossed the Hudson after the defeat at White Plains, Lee's division remained on the east side of that river During the retreat to the Delaware, Washington considered his situation to be so critical that Lee's support was most urgently needed, and in the course of his march he wrote from Hackinsack, Newark, New Brunswick and Trenton, desiring that officer to follow and join him as quickly as possible Lee, however, was extremely tardy in obeying these orders His command on the Hudson was practically independent, and he had no wish to merge it in the forces of Washington, whom he regarded with envy and contempt He accordingly returned evasive answers to the latter's dispatches, pretending to misunderstand his instruc-

[1] Doyle's Steuben, 105, Trevelyan's American Revolution, Part 2, II, 45

tions, disputing his warnings of the gravity of the situation, and urging the greater advantages of some different line of action   He lingered from November 17th to December 2nd, debating whether to obey the commands of Washington and join in the retreat, or to await the arrival of reinforcements from the north   He at length decided to follow the army, crossing the Hudson at King's Ferry, and making a detour by way of Morristown in order to avoid the enemy, but, despite Washington's earnest appeals to hasten, he moved as slowly as possible, and did not arrive in the neighborhood of Chatham until the 8th of December   Continuing his leisurely progress, he reached Basking Ridge on the 12th, where he was taken prisoner the next morning by a party of British cavalry on a tour of observation from New Brunswick

Lee's force was made up of McDougall's brigade, including the Fourth Rhode Island, the Seventh Connecticut, the First and Third New York, and the First Maryland, and Nixon's brigade, consisting of the First, Second and Third Rhode Island, and the Second, Sixth and Twelfth Massachusetts [1]   They numbered somewhat less than 3,000 men, who are said to have been as good soldiers as any in the American army, but they had been exposed to the greatest hardships and privations, and some, unable to endure the fatigues of the march, had been left at Haverstraw, while those who remained fit for duty were so destitute of shoes that in some places their route might have been traced by bloody footprints upon the rough and frozen ground [2]   They marched in column of fours and in route step, each man carrying his gun as he pleased   Thirty men of Nixon's regiment constituted an advance guard, and flankers marched in single file upon either side, while Glover's regiment acted as a reserve, prepared to draw

[1] Gardner's The Rhode Island Line in the Continental Army, 4
[2] Heath's Memoirs, 96

out of the column in case of sudden attack, and to form one hundred yards in the rear. The soldiers wore no uniform, but were dressed in hunting-shirts and rough linsey-woolsey suits; their officers, as a rule, being distinguished only by a sash or a corded or cockaded hat. Each man possessed a powder-horn suspended from one shoulder, while a bullet-pouch hung from the other; but they observed no uniformity of weapons, which included muskets, rifles and fowling-pieces of various sizes and patterns.[1]

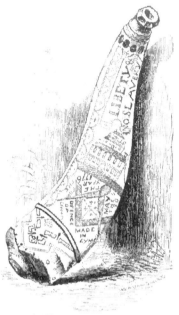

REVOLUTIONARY POWDER HORN

On the day of his arrival at Morristown, Lee indited a letter to the commander-in-chief, advocating in the following terms the establishing of a post at Chatham:

Morris-Town, December ye 8th, 1776.

Dear General:

Colonel Humpton will give you a return of the Militia already assembled, and of those (if it can be called a return) expected. The whole will, as it is said, make by tomorrow morning one thousand. My corps that passed the North River will amount (for we are considerably diminished) to seven and twenty hundred; in fact our Army may be estimated at four thousand. If I was not taught to think that your army was considerably reinforced, I should immediately join you; but as I am assured you are very strong, I should imagine we can

[1] Mellick's The Story of an Old Farm, 332, 340.

make a better impression by hanging on their rear, for which purpose, a good post at Chatham seems the best calculated It is at a
happy distance from Newark, Elizabeth Town Woodbridge, and
Boundbrook It will annoy, distract, and consequently weaken 'em
As to your Excellency's idea of surprising Brunswick, the post I propose taking offers the greatest probability of success But we are so
ill shod and destitute of light-horse that this desultory war is hard
upon the poor soldiers, but must do 'em the justice to say that they
have noble spirits and will, I have no doubt, render great service to
their country

     God bless you, General

                    Yours most sincerely,

                                   CHARLES LEE

To his Excellency, General Washington
        Trenton [1]

     A similar letter, practically a duplicate of the above,
was written at the same time to Congress [2]
     In accordance with the plan thus indicated, and in total
disregard of Washington's imperative commands to follow
and join him without loss of time, Lee took post at Chatham
on the same day It would be interesting to know where
he established his headquarters in the village, but no positive
information upon this point has been obtained It is highly
probable that he stopped at one of the commodious taverns,
where he could readily secure ample accommodation for his
retinue as well as suitable quarters for himself but, on the
other hand, he might have felt that, for a prolonged sojourn
in the village, lodgings in some private house would be more
comfortable and agreeable A history of Morris County
compiled by the Lewis Historical Publishing Company
in 1914 places Lee's headquarters at Day's tavern,
but gives no authority for the statement The only
contemporary reference to the subject which the writer of

[1] N Y Historical Society Collections Lee Papers, II, 336
[2] American Archives, Ser 5, III, 1121

these pages has found is contained in a letter written by Robert Morris to Silas Deane, announcing Lee's capture by the British, and erroneously giving Chatham, instead of Basking Ridge, as the scene of this misfortune[1] The general was betrayed, he wrote, while lodged at a farm house after passing a place called Chatham near Elizabeth Town—a mistake which may be explained by the assumption that Morris had heard from Lee while at Chatham, and thought that he had remained here up to the time of his capture. Lee was stopping at a tavern near Basking Ridge when he fell into the hands of the enemy, and from Morris's reference to a farm house, we may perhaps venture to assume that while at Chatham the general established himself in some private dwelling. Still, probability favors a hotel as his stopping-place.

Finding Lee so dilatory, Washington looked about for other troops who could be summoned to his support without too greatly weakening the posts at which they were stationed. There was a small detachment of the Massachusetts Continental line at Ticonderoga who had been engaged with the enemy under Carleton; but as the latter had now retired to Canada for winter quarters, their presence in that region was no longer needed,[2] and Washington directed them to march forward and join him on the Delaware River. This detachment was commanded by Lieutenant-Colonel Joseph Vose. On the day that Lee established himself at Chatham a letter was dispatched to him by General Heath at Peekskill, announcing that Vose had arrived from Albany on the preceding day, and that he (Heath) had advised him to follow Lee immediately. The latter was greatly pleased to learn of the approach of these reinforcements, and he

---

[1] American Archives, Ser 5, III, 1333; Diplomatic Correspondence, I, 171. A similar mistake was afterwards made by General Heath in his Memoirs, p 99

[2] Spark's Washington, 204

[3] American Archives, Ser 5, III, 1123

hastened to pen the following answer, the tone of which
indicates a disposition to attach the Ticonderoga troops to
his own command, although Washington had issued no
orders to that effect but, on the contrary, had directed these
regiments to hasten to his support

                              Chatham December ye 9th 1776
Dear General
    I am very much obliged to you for your welcome tidings and
have only to beg that you will direct the regiments you speak of to
march without loss of time to Morris Town   I sent an express to
you last night from the General, ordering your division over the
river, which, I confess for my own part, I am heartily sorry for, as
I think we shall be strong enough without you, and New England,
with your district, will be too bare of troops   I am in hopes here to
reconquer (if I may so express myself) the Jerseys   It was really in
the hands of the enemy before my arrival
    Adieu, dear sir

                                               CHARLES LEE
To Major-General Heath,
         Peekskill [1]

    We shall have occasion to mention the Ticonderoga
troops later on
    Scarcely had Lee completed his arrangements for post-
ing his command at Chatham, when he received a further
communication from Washington, repeating his instructions
to march forward   It read as follows

                              Trenton Falls December 10th 1776
Dear Sir
    I last night received your favor by Colonel Humpton, and were
it not for the weak and feeble state of the force I have, I should
highly approve of your hanging on the rear of the enemy and estab-

[1] American Archives, Ser 5, III, 1138

lishing the post you mention But when my situation is directly
opposite to what you suppose it to be, and when General Howe is
pressing forward with the whole of his army except the troops that
were lately embarked, and a few besides left at New York, to possess
himself of Philadelphia, I cannot but request and entreat you, and
this too by the advice of all the General officers with me, to march
and join me with all your whole force with all possible expedition
The utmost exertions that can be made will not be more than sufficient to save Philadelphia Without the aid of your force, I think
there is little, if any, prospect of doing it I refer you to the route
Major Hoops would inform you of The enemy are now extended
along the Delaware at several places By a prisoner who was taken
last night, I am told that at Pennytown there are two battalions of
Infantry, three of Grenadiers, the Hessian Grenadiers, forty second
Highlanders, and two others Their object, doubtless, is to pass the
river above us, or to prevent your joining me. I mention this that
you may avail yourself of the information Do come on Your
arrival may be happy, and if it can be effected without delay, may
be the means of preserving a city whose loss must prove of the most
fatal consequences to the cause of America

    I am, &c

                                      Go Washington

To Major General Lee

    P S

       Pray exert your influence and bring with you all the Jersey
Militia you possibly can Let them not suppose their State is lost,
or in any danger, because the enemy are pushing through it If you
think General St Clair or General Maxwell would be of service to
command 'em, I would send either [1]

    Lee, however, was most reluctant to abandon his post
at Chatham, and he dispatched a reply, in which he en
deavored to palliate his insubordination by disputing
Washington's conclusions as to the enemy's apparent purpose He wrote

<hr/>

[1] New York Historical Society Collections, Lee Papers, II, 341

Chatham, December ye 8th, 1776

Dear General

Major Hoops has just delivered to me your Excellency's letter I am certainly shocked to hear that your force is so inadequate to the necessity of your situation, as I had been taught to think you had been considerably reinforced   Your last letters proposing a plan of surprises and forced marches convinced me that there was no danger of your being obliged to pass the Delaware, in consequence of which proposals I have put myself in a position the most convenient to co-operate with you by attacking their rear

I cannot persuade myself that Philadelphia is their object at present, as it is almost certain that their whole troops late embarked have directed their course to the Eastern Provinces, for Spencer writes me word that half of it turned the southwestern end of Long Island and started Eastward I detached Colonel Warner and Mons Malmadie to take direction of the Rhode Island troops, who are without even the figure of a General   It will be difficult, I am afraid, to join you, but cannot I do you more service by attacking their rear? I shall look about me tomorrow and inform you further

I am, dear General, yours,

CHARLES LEE [1]

To his Excellency, General Washington

On the 11th Washington again wrote to Lee from Trenton Falls, acknowledging the receipt of the above letter, and stating that the occupation of Philadelphia was beyond all question the enemy's object, which nothing less than the utmost efforts of the Americans could prevent   He repeated his assertion that his own force was entirely inadequate, and entreated Lee to push forward with every possible succour   On the same day he wrote to the president of Congress

* * * * * *   I received another letter from General Lee last evening it was dated at Chatham, which I take to be near

[1] American Archives Ser 5, III 1122
[2] American Archives, Ser 5, III, 1166

Morristown, the 8th of this month   He had then received my letter
sent by Major Hoops but seemed still inclined to hang on the enemy's
rear, to which I should have no objection, had I sufficient force to
oppose them in front, but as I have not at present nor do I see much
probability of further reinforcement, I have wrote to him in the
most pressing terms to join me with all expedition [1]

Various reasons have been assigned for Lee's conduct
That he was intensely jealous of Washington, and considered himself far better qualified for the supreme command, is clearly indicated by the tone of his correspondence
of the period, much of which has been preserved, and by the
criticisms of his superior in which he freely indulged , but
this of itself would scarcely account for his disobedience   It
is conjectured that he sought to prolong his independent
command in hopes of finding an opportunity, by some brilliant achievement, to greatly increase his prestige and
popularity, and by this means to supplant Washington, and
it has even been suggested that he withheld his support in the
expectation that the latter would suffer an overwhelming
defeat, and that he himself would then be the choice of
Congress for the rank he coveted, for General Ward's
resignation had left him second in command, and there
is little doubt that Washington's death or capture would
have brought about the realization of his fond ambition
But aside from the fact that his force was so imperatively
needed on the Delaware, there can be no question that his
plan of taking post at Chatham, or in some neighboring
village, and harassing the enemy's rear, was a good one
The British line of communication, extending across the
entire State, was so long that it could not be effectually
guarded, and was particularly exposed to attack, and had
Lee carried out his plan of cutting it, Lord Howe would have

[1] American Archives Ser 5, III, 1166

[*] He once expressed the opinion that Washington was not fit to command
a sergeant's guard —Boudinot's Elias Boudinot, I, 145

found himself in a position of imminent danger   This fact
was thoroughly appreciated by the British general, and the
presence of so formidable a body of American troops in his
rear caused him much anxiety [1]

It was not long, however, before Lee decided to
abandon his post at Chatham, for the probable reason
that he dared not further disregard the commands of his
superior   His stay in this village was limited to three or
four days, and on December 11th we find him again in
Morristown, prepared to continue his march, and, notwithstanding Washington's explicit instructions as to the route to
be followed, writing to the latter that he had sent forward
two officers, one to ascertain where the Delaware could best
be crossed above Trenton, and the other to examine the road
toward Burlington, with a view of crossing the river by
the ferry below that town   He in a measure excused his
delay by stating that the 3,000 men of his command were so
ill shod that they had been obliged to wait two days for want
of shoes [2]

Upon the occupation of Elizabeth by the British in their
pursuit of Washington's retreating army, the patriots of that
city were obliged to leave their homes and seek safety in the
hilly region bordering the Passaic River above Chatham
Among them was Rev James Caldwell, pastor of the Presbyterian church at Elizabeth, who established a temporary
residence at Turkey, now New Providence   This gentleman,
as an army chaplain, was in close touch with the operations
of the troops, and kept himself well informed of the movements and apparent designs of the enemy   Having heard
from General Lee soon after the latter's departure from
Chatham, he sent him the following information, which he
felt sure would prove of value

[1] Abbotts Washington, 300, Fiske's American Revolution, I, 221,
Moore's The Treason of Charles Lee
[2] N Y Historical Society Collections, Lee Papers, II, 345

Turkey, December 12, 1776

Dear Sir

I thank you for your favour from Baskingridge, of this morning, and I intended to do myself the honour to wait upon you, and set out for the purpose, but found my horse would not perform the journey with sufficient expedition and cannot procure another horse. And indeed I find this the best place to observe the enemy's motions. From sundry persons who have been upon the road, between Brunswick and Princeton I learn the Army has very generally marched forward, indeed, all except guards of the several posts. Yesterday they sent a reinforcement to Elizabeth Town from Amboy, of near one thousand. Some say the whole at Elizabeth Town are about one thousand, others say fifteen hundred. They are carrying off the hay from Elizabeth Town to New York. I believe Elizabeth Town is their strongest post as they were afraid of our Militia, who have taken off many of the most active Tories, made some prisoners, and among others shot their English Foragemaster, so that he is mortally or very illy wounded. A company of our Militia went last night to Woodbridge, and brought off the drove of stock the enemy had collected there, consisting of about four hundred cattle and two hundred sheep. Most of these cattle are only fit for stock. Colonel Ford begs your directions what to do with them. I advised that those not fit to kill should be sold recording the marks, that whig owners might receive the money for which they sell respectively. It will cost more than the value of them to keep them in a flock. They are driven up the country to be out of the enemy's way, and the Colonel will follow your directions as to the disposition of them.

At a Council of the Field Officers this morning a majority of them advised to remove the brigade of Militia back again to Chatham for which they assign these reasons. Many of the Militia, rather fond of plunder and adventure, kept a continual scouting, which kept out so many detached parties, that the body was weakened, and the enemy being now stronger at Elizabeth Town than they are, they thought they would better serve the cause by lying at Chatham till the expected army approaches for their support.

Colonel Ford also desires your directions with respect to the arms, horses, and other property taken with any of the enemy. The parties who take them think themselves entitled to these things

I enclose you some examinations   Colonel Ford thinks, from the circumstances of the wagons taken up at Brunswick to go to Morristown and Trenton that the enemy intended to retreat   I hope their retreat will be guarded against   I have very much suspected as soon as our whole Army is over the river they will return and reduce this Province, leaving only part of their Army at the river to prevent ours returning, till they have plundered us at their pleasure

With every kind wish for your prosperity, dear sir, your unfeigned friend and most obedient humble servant,

JAMES CALDWELL

The Honourable General Lee

P S

I have sent you Jacob Vincent and two or three Light Horse in whom you can depend [1]

The militia referred to by Mr Caldwell was Colonel Ford's brigade, which had been stationed in the neighborhood of Springfield and Connecticut Farms   After their withdrawal to Chatham, a letter was written by Colonel Symmes to General Heath, which throws light upon their condition and circumstances   It reads

Chatham, December 16th 1776

Sir,

I beg leave to represent to your Honour the distressed situation we are in with respect to salt   The brigade at this place has been destitute of that article some days   The men suffer exceedingly and we have information of there being salt at Hackinsack, Second River, and Newark   As we understand your Honour takes that route, we beg the favour of a party's advancing from your Army on the road and gathering all the salt to be had   Wagons can be pressed on the road to bring it forward   Captain Harker waits upon your Honour with this   His orders are to await your pleasure, until we can be acquainted with the success of the undertaking   If salt can possibly

[1] N Y Historical Society Collections, Lee Papers, II, 346,

be sent to our relief, I beg your Honour will interest yourself in the affair

I have the honour to be, Sir,

your Honour's most obedient humble servant,

JOHN CLEVE SYMMES

Colonel of Sussex Militia

Major-General Heath, near Hackinsack [1]

This brigade of militia had rendered very efficient services, and had inflicted considerable injury upon the British in a series of skirmishes near Elizabeth and Woodbridge, attacking their convoys, and killing or capturing their foraging parties, and it is said that Lord Howe himself, while engaged in the pursuit of Washington, narrowly escaped capture by a scouting party at Piscataway I earning that the militia had their base at Chatham, that Lee had taken post here, and that Heath was moving in this direction, the British commander decided to attack the village, and terminate the operations of the Americans in this quarter Accordingly he detached Brigadier-General Leslie at Bonumtown, about the middle of December, to march upon Chatham and disperse the rebels who were gathered there Leslie proceeded to Elizabeth and approached Chatham by way of Springfield

A sudden activity among the English was observed and promptly reported by the scouts of General Heath, who wrote to Washington from Hackensack on December 15th that several thousand British troops had landed at Elizabeth on the preceding day [2] It was not long before the alarming intelligence of the enemy's advance reached Chatham This was the first experience that the people of the village had had in actual warfare, and we can readily imagine their excitement and terror upon learning of Leslie's

[1] American Archives, Ser 5, III 1247
[2] Hatfield s Elizabeth, 451

approach   Definite information as to his numerical strength
could not be obtained, and it was extremely uncertain
whether the New Jersey militia, who alone opposed him,
could succeed in overcoming the well-disciplined British
troops, for whose prowess our ancestors entertained a
wholesome regard

Leslie set out from Elizabeth on the 17th of December,
at the head of 800 troops   On that day Colonel Ford's
brigade was somewhat scattered   The Sussex battalion,
under Colonel Symmes, lay at Chatham, Colonel Spencer's
Essex battalion was posted at Springfield, and the Morris
County regiment was stationed about midway between them,
among the defiles of the Short Hills   The enemy's approach
was detected and reported by videts whom Spencer had
stationed on the main road about two miles east of Springfield, and a light horseman[1] was dispatched at full speed to
Chatham to warn the colonel commandant that the British
were in sight   The brigade was already under arms, and it
immediately marched to Spencer's support   The latter felt
that he was not strong enough to cope with so formidable a
body of the enemy, and he fell back from Springfield in the
direction of Chatham, meeting the brigade at Briant's tavern
A spirited fight with the British then ensued, which, commencing late in the afternoon, continued about an hour, and
was terminated by darkness [2]

This, the first engagement at Springfield, may be regarded as a drawn battle, neither party winning a decisive
victory   In fact, each side seemed to feel that they had
suffered a defeat   Although the strength of the combatants
appears to have been nearly equal, the Americans believed
themselves to be greatly outnumbered, and, despairing of
checking the enemy's advance, they fell back under cover of

[1] Nathaniel Crane of Captain Marsh's Light Horse —*Drake's Historical
Sketches of the Revolution and Civil War*, 20
[2] Hatfield's Elizabeth, 452

darkness to Chatham, while the British, amazed by the stubborn resistance of the raw and undisciplined militia, also withdrew during the night, abandoning all hope of penetrating the country lying beyond the Short Hills But this skirmish at Springfield, however insignificant in itself, was important in its results It was the first instance in this State when British troops were forced to turn and retire, and when the outcome of the fight became generally known and it was proven that the British soldiery was not invincible, the effect was to greatly stimulate and encourage the waning spirits of the patriots

The disheartened militia, however, had little conception of the success of their effort and of its far reaching effect when they fell back to Chatham, smarting under what they believed to be a defeat During the evening Ford wrote to Heath, who was still at Hackensack, urging the general to come to his support

> Chatham, 17th December, 1776,
> ten o'clock in the Evening, and
> twelve miles west of Elizabeth Town

Dear Sir

We have since sunset had a brush with the enemy, four miles below this, in which we have suffered, and our Militia much disheartened They are all retreated to this place and will in all probability be attacked by daybreak The enemy, we have reason to believe, are double our numbers General McDougall is with the northern battalions that were coming on with Colonel Vose, and intends marching directly to General Washington He is this night in Morris-Town, eight miles west of this, and we have no expectation of his assistance If in your wisdom you can assist us, we may possibly beat them yet, but without your aid we can't stand They are encamped (say one thousand British troops) at Springfield, and will be joined by four hundred and fifty Waldeckers from Elizabeth-Town by the next morning's light I know, sir, it is not for me, nor would I presume, to direct you, but if you can consistently, I beg and

pray you would come to our assistance If you think proper to come
to our assistance, the bearer will give you our situation and that of
the enemy, and be your guide, after which you will be a proper judge
whether to beat up their rear or to march in their front and join us,
or rather suffer us to join you, and march the whole down upon them

    Am your most obed servant,

                JACOB FORD JUN., Colonel

To the Hon General Heath, at Second River or Hackinsack [1]

    This letter was quickly followed by a second.

               Chatham, 18th December, 1776
                   5 o'clock.

Sir

    Since writing my last I have certain intelligence that the troops
we engaged last night were General Leslie's brigade who marched
some days since from Elizabeth Town to the southard They received an order to countermarch to the same place That brigade is
from twelve to thirteen hundred strong and the Waldeckers upwards
of four hundred At Spank-Town, six miles to the southard of Elizabeth Town, there is five hundred British troops That is all the
enemy you have to combat in this country at present We are
not certain whether the enemy who attacked us have or have not yet
returned to Elizabeth Town Lord Stirling is on this side the river
Delaware, with a small detachment joined to General Sullivan, with
orders not to recross the river, if my intelligence be good, and I be
lieve it is

    I am, your most obedient,

                JACOB FORD, JUN

To Major General Heath [2]

[1] American Archives, Ser 5, III, 1260

[2] American Archives, Ser 5, III, 1277 The engagement is thus re
ferred to in a certificate made by Colonel Symmes in support of an application of Captain Kirkendall for a pension It is copied from the court
records of Sussex County

               Sussex Courts, February Term, 1782

    Captain Samuel Kirkendall having presented to the Court a certificate
in words and figures following viz

    These may certify that on the Seventeenth day of December, in the year
of our Lord one thousand seven hundred and seventy-six, I, the subscriber,

Had the British general pushed forward on the following morning, he would undoubtedly have succeeded in reaching Chatham, or even Morristown, without encountering a very determined resistance, but, fortunately for the Americans, he apparently overestimated their strength, and dared not venture among the Short Hills During the night he quietly withdrew from Springfield, carrying his dead and wounded in wagons, and retreated with such expedition that, although he was pursued by the militia as far as Westfield, he was not overtaken

The 17th of December witnessed the arrival at Morristown of the Ticonderoga detachment, which, it will be recalled, had been ordered by Washington to join his army General Heath had written to the commander-in-chief from Hackensack as early as the 15th that this brigade had marched to the neighborhood of Chatham, where it would arrive, he thought, that night or the next morning[1]—information which was not strictly accurate, for the troops marched to Morristown in the first instance, and their subsequent detention at Chatham was quite unexpected This detachment formed a part of the Massachusetts Continental line, and consisted of Colonel Elisha Porter's regiment,

then having the command of the Militia from the County of Sussex in the State of New Jersey, lay at Chatham, in said State, with other battalions of Militia forming a brigade under the command of Colonel Jacob Ford, when Colonel Ford had advice that the British troops to the number of eight hundred men, under the command of General Leslie had advanced to Springfield within four miles of Chatham Colonel Ford thereupon ordered me to proceed to Springfield and check the approach of the enemy if possible According to orders I marched to Springfield with a detachment of the Brigade and attacked the enemy in Springfield that evening In the skirmish Capt Kirkendall of the Sussex Militia was wounded in the hand, his hand was split by a musket shot from his middle finger to his wrist, by which wound he has lost the use of his right hand

Given under my hand at Newton, in the State of New Jersey, this 6th day of May, 1780

To whom it may concern JOHN CLEVE SYMMES, Colonel

—*New Jersey Historical Society Proceedings*, Ser 2, V, 42

[1] American Archives, Ser 5, III, 1234

numbering approximately 170 men, the Twenty-fifth Continental infantry of about 100 men, known as Bond's regiment in honor of its colonel, William Bond, who had died a few weeks before, and the Twenty-fourth Continental infantry, numbering about 250, still called Greaton's regiment, although its former colonel, John Greaton, had recently been transferred to the Third Massachusetts, and had been succeeded by Lieutenant-Colonel Joseph Vose, who was in command of the brigade[1] As these troops had been recruited in Massachusetts, they were sometimes referred to in military correspondence and orders as the "Eastern" or "New England" detachment

On the following morning, when this brigade was preparing to leave Morristown, news was received of Ford's engagement at Springfield, and as a renewal of the conflict was anticipated, General McDougall, who had arrived at Morristown a few days before,[2] and whose rank entitled him to assume command of all the troops in this region, immediately ordered the Ticonderoga regiments to Chatham to support the militia, believing that the exigencies of the case necessitated this departure from the commands of Washington The brigade remained at Chatham until the next day; and then, finding that the enemy had retired, and thinking that there was no immediate prospect of a further engagement, Colonel Vose prepared to continue his march across the State, but the inhabitants protested so strongly against being left without any means of defence save that of the militia, whose condition was somewhat demoralized, that General McDougall decided to assume the responsibility of de-

[1] American Archives, Ser 5, III, 1296, Heitman's Register of Continental Officers, 110, 259, 561

[2] McDougall, who had been prevented by sickness from marching with his brigade, which formed part of Lee's division, followed the troops when sufficiently recovered, with the intention of overtaking and rejoining them, but upon reaching Morristown he learned of Lee's capture, and feared to proceed further without a bodyguard

taining him in this place   These facts are more particularly
stated in the following interesting letter from McDougall
to Washington

Chatham in East Jersey, 19 December, 1776

SIR

The rheumatism and other disorders detained me at Haverstraw, and separated me from my brigade   Eight days since I found
myself much better, and followed General Lee's division to Morris
Town, where I arrived the day after he was unfortunately taken
This catastrophe determined me, by the advice of friends, not to
proceed unless I had a guard   The three regiments from the northward, under Colonel Vose, were hourly expected in Morris Town
They did not arrive until the day before yesterday late in the evening
Provisions and other necessaries were prepared for their march next
morning to join you, but an express arrived at night with information that Colonel Ford's Militia had an engagement with the enemy
at Springfield and that he expected it would be renewed the next
morning, to gain the pass of the mountains   The country in general
being greatly discouraged and on the eve of making a surrender of
this State, I judged it my duty to order those regiments to march at
four a m to support Colonel Ford   The enemy early next morning retired towards Spank Town

When Colonel Vose this morning was preparing to march to
Morris Town, the Militia and principal gentlemen were much dejected, and assured me if those troops were not left here to countenance them, the Militia could not be collected to make any opposition to the enemy, and those who were imbodied would disband
which would eventually end in a submission of this State   Indeed,
some of the most important, sensible and zealous of the people declared they would provide for their own safety as they had no hopes
of being able to assemble the Militia if those continental troops were
removed   They asserted that General Lee gave them assurance that
those troops should be left here for their protection, which was countenanced in some measure in a letter of General Heath's to Colonel
Ford, and to remove them after so many of the troops passed through

the State, would be to abandon them to the enemy, which is the idea generally held by too many of the friends of the country, but if any troops stay, they were in no doubt of collecting a respectable number of the Militia   In this state of things, I feared if I advised Colonel Vose to proceed to the Delaware, I should be chargeable with all the bad consequences   These facts will be authenticated to you by the Committee of Morris Town

The submission of this State would draw after it consequences easier to conceive than to express, and are too obvious to render an enumeration necessary   To prevent an event so fatal to our common cause, I have ventured to advise Colonel Vose to remain in this State, and shall post his troops with the Militia, in the best manner to cover the country not in the hands of the enemy   It is the only chance we have for retaining it   Orders for him will readily find him by apply- ing to Colonel Remsen, at Morris Town   or Colonel Ford   I find by Colonel Vose that those troops are determined to go home at the expiration of their time, which would nearly be accomplished before they could reach you,[1] which was a consideration which induced me to advise his stay, and as their assistance to you would not bear any proportion to the prospect of their service here   I hope these con- siderations will justify me to your Excellency, as the service and the safety of our common cause were the only motives which determined my advice

I am greatly mortified that I have no reason to expect I shall be able to do duty in the course of the winter in the manner I could wish, from the complication of disorders that afflict me   If the time was not so critical to the country I would resign, as I do not wish to be a burthen to it   But as this might at this crisis be a prejudice to the cause, subject to the abuse of our enemies, I decline it, but wish to be favoured with the General's advice for my future con- duct   If I stay here, unless I am with a detachment of the Army, I shall be exposed to the like misfortune that befell General Lee   If I am with the Army, the houses are so necessary to them that I can- not be accommodated, I shall, however, endeavor to remain in this

[1] The Ticonderoga troops afterwards consented to extend their term of service, upon receipt of a liberal bounty with full pay —*Carrington's Wash- ington the Soldier,* 147

neighbourhood till General Heath arrives at Morris Town, which I have reason to expect will be in a few days

I am, with earnest wishes for your success and happiness,

your Excellency's very humble servant,

ALEX McDOUGALL

His Excellency General Washington.

P S

The enemy are changing their troops so often from Hamnsak to Elizabeth Town, that it is impossible to give a true state of their numbers in frontier towns of this State   Colonel Ford has had from eight hundred to one thousand of the Militia collected now about seven hundred   Greaton's regiment, about 250, Bond's do 100, Porter's do 170—520

I have taken the liberty to transmit to you a letter of General Heath's approving of my advice in detaining that corps [1]

The letter given below was dispatched to General Heath by William Malcolm (Malcom), colonel of a New York Continental regiment attached to General Scott's brigade which formed part of Heath's division   From the military correspondence of that period it appears that Malcolm was then engaged in waging a sort of guerilla warfare against the British and tories, with whom he had had several sharp skirmishes on the west side of the Hudson, notably in the vicinity of Tappan, Nyack, Hackensack and English Neighborhood

Chatham, December 19, 1776

Dear General

I got to this place this moment   General McDougall most providentially was before me   An order from Head Quarters for the Ticonderoga detachment to join the grand Army had almost lost this State   The Militia, who are numerous and brave in this quarter, finding themselves abandoned, came to a resolution to save themselves and families by dispersing   The principal people supposing themselves forsaken by the Army, were also dejected, and

[1] American Archives, Ser 5, III, 1296

would have retired To avert so capital a blow, General McDougall
hath detained Colonel Vose until further orders, but this leaves the
issue doubtful A repeated order may arrive next moment, and the
State lost For this weighty consideration surely it will be advisable
that you move this way Suppose Tappan and the vicinity is exposed,
the enemy cannot approach the forts by land (with artillery) but
through the pass of the Clove, and surely General Clinton's arm is
competent to defend that ground perhaps to do more

I am informed you can expect to be joined here by about one
thousand good Militia This will enable you to cover this valuable
country which abounds with forage and which must expect the
vengeance of the enemy From their attachment to their country and
their zeal they are remarkably obnoxious in proportion to their fears,
and therefore they ought to be supported This quarter is capable of
being easily defended and much benefit arise thereby I hope to
meet you on Saturday at Morris Town, or a shorter road which Mr
Sanford will show you Time is precious, I can only offer my respect
to General Parsons, General Clinton if with you, and your suite,
and that with much respect and esteem I am, dear General,

            your most obliged and very humble servant,
                              W MALCOLM
To Major General Heath, Pyramus

      The facts contained in this are true
                        .
                        ALEX McDOUGALL [1]

To the great relief of the officers in this quarter, an
order soon arrived from General Washington directing the
Ticonderoga troops to remain in the neighborhood of Morristown, "in order to inspirit the inhabitants and as far as
possible to cover that part of the country' [2] The commander-in-chief wrote to General McDougall

                  Head Quarters Bucks County 21st Decr 1776
Dear Sir
      I am this Evening favored with yours of the 19th from Chatham
I not only approve of the Disposition you made of the three Regiments

      [1] American Archives, Ser 5, III, 1297
      [2] Sherman's Historic Morristown, 202

under Colo Vose because I think it was a very judicious one, but I
had previous to the Receit of your Letter determined upon exactly
the same plan and had sent Orders to Colo Vose to halt at Morris
Town, that he might afford protection to the well affected in the
Neighbourhood and give Spirits to the Militia

If you find your Health such that you cannot take an active
part where you are, or stay there without further prejudice to it, I
would have you return to peekskill and there, in conjunction with
Genl Geo Clinton take charge of that department, as I have ordered
Genl Heath to join me with as many of the Connecticut and Massachusetts Militia as can be spared

I think with you, that tho' your State of Health may require a
Resignation that this is not a proper time to make it, our Enemies
would probably attribute it to the late unfavorable Aspect of our
Affairs, and therefore I would advise you to try, whether a little
Rest might not contribute to the Cure of a disorder, which is gener-
ally brought on by Colds and Fatigue [1]

GENERAL McDOUGALL TO GENERAL HEATH

Chatham, 20 December, 1776

My dear General

I was honoured by your favour of the 18th   It came very seas-
onable   I was happy to find you and the other General Officers
considered it advisable to detain Colonel Vose's corps   It was a
measure absolutely necessary to prop the drooping spirits of the Militia   This moment Colonel Vose received General Washington's
orders of the 18th   to tarry in this State which has relieved me from
many embarrassments

The enclosed is the last intelligence we have of the state of the
enemy   Whenever the service will permit your advancing to Morris-
Town it will be of great importance in protecting this distressed
State   As this is to accompany a letter to you, which we suppose to

[1] Washington Papers in the Library of Congress, B II, pt 1, 147

be from General Washington, and forwarded by express, time will
only permit me to add, that I am,

with great respect,

your very humble servant,

ALFX MCDOUGALL

To Major-General Heath, Pyramus

Intelligence by John Halstead, from Elizabeth-Town

John Halstead left Elizabeth-Town this morning about eight
o'clock Says there is no troops in Elizabeth-Town but Waldeckers,
the same that has been there for two weeks past Says the drums
beat this morning, about daybreak, and he understood they were
to have marched, but that they did not, and the reason why, as he
understood, was the badness of the weather Knows not which way
they were to march, but it was said they were to have a little march
out o' town, that he thinks six or seven hundred British troops went
through town the day before yesterday, near twelve o'clock, towards
New-Ark, and that they have not as yet returned
Chatham, 20th December, 1776.[1]

McDougall now received intelligence that the enemy,
with upwards of thirty-nine hundred men, was preparing to
march upon Morristown by three different routes one from
New Brunswick via Basking Ridge, another from Elizabeth
by way of Chatham, and a third from Newark, doubtless by
way of Hanover and Whippany, and, fearing lest his retreat
might be cut off, he decided to retire to Morristown in order
to keep open his communication with the country to the westward Accordingly, on the 22nd of December, he withdrew
from Chatham, taking with him Ford's militia and presumably the Ticonderoga brigade as well, for the latter seems
to have been stationed in Chatham up to this time Ford's
troops had become so scattered since the skirmish at Springfield during the preceding week that his command was
reduced to about two hundred, but even this depleted force

[1] American Archives, Ser 5, III, 1315

was now withdrawn from Chatham, and the village left without protection except that of a few soldiers who remained to keep watch The Essex militia, however, was directed to guard the passes of the Short Hills between Chatham and Springfield [1]

McDougall's information proved to be erroneous, the enemy hesitating to leave the shelter of the towns to the eastward A number of stragglers ventured out from time to time, some of whom were captured almost every day by the Americans, and escorted through Chatham to Morristown, where they were closely confined

About this time General Washington directed General William Maxwell to go to Morristown and take command of the Ticonderoga detachment and the local militia, having been informed that eight hundred of the latter troops were under arms at that place Maxwell's instructions were to collect as large a number of the militia as possible, and to harass the enemy on their front and rear, cutting off their convoys at every opportunity He arrived at Morristown on the 24th of December, and on the 30th McDougall turned over the command to him He found scarcely any of the militia under arms, except those who were guarding the different passes, the captains having allowed most of their men leave of absence for the ostensible purpose of recruiting, but he was assured by Colonel Ford that a full regiment could be soon made up [2]

The gallant Colonel Ford, however, was not destined to perform further services in the line of his duty In carrying on this skirmish warfare during the fall and winter he had been in constant service on the lines, marching and countermarching with his troops about Elizabeth, Springfield, Westfield and Chatham, in making what was called by

[1] American Archives, Ser 5, III, 1364, 1489
[2] Ibid, 1474, Upham's Washington, 1, 205

the soldiers the "mud rounds,"[1] and had been subjected to greater hardship and exposure than his constitution could bear. Within a few days after his return to Morristown he was stricken with an acute attack of pneumonia while still in active service, and died on the 10th of January, 1777, in the 39th year of his age.[2]

[1] The marches and countermarches of this campaign were called the "mud rounds" in reference to the condition of the roads, which were alternately frozen into ruts so deep as to render them almost impassable, and thawed into veritable quagmires. The veterans of the Revolution long recalled the "mud rounds" as a campaign of exceptional hardship and suffering.

[2] Sherman's Historic Morristown, 203; Historical Magazine, X, 92.

CHAPTER VIII

Opening of the Campaign of 1777—Maxwell's Activities—Washington at Morristown—Many of the Soldiers billeted in private Houses—Their Sufferings from Disease and Famine—Pennsylvania and Rhode Island Troops at Chatham—General Sullivan stationed here—His Discontent—His Correspondence—Captain Bauman commands the Artillery at Chatham—His Perplexity caused by conflicting Orders

"**I** BEG you will collect all the men you possibly can about Chatham, and, after gaining the proper intelligence, endeavor to strike a stroke upon Elizabeth-Town or that neighborhood, at any rate be ready to co-operate with me."

Thus wrote General Washington from Trenton on December 30, 1776, to "the commanding officer at Morristown" [1] and General Maxwell lost no time in carrying his instructions into effect At the head of Vose's Continentals, and with as large a body of militia as could be gathered, he attacked the enemy with so much spirit that he compelled them to evacuate both Elizabeth and Newark Then followed a series of engagements of greater or less importance lasting for six months, the object of the campaign being to drive the British out of New Jersey, and in this the Americans were ultimately successful A noteworthy skirmish occurred at Springfield on January 5th, in which the Americans, without the loss of a single man, overcame an equal force of Waldeckers, killing eight or ten, and capturing the remainder of the party, which numbered thirty-nine or forty The militia was led on this occasion by Lieutenant-Colonel Oliver Spencer, whose bravery was soon rewarded by pro-

[1] American Archives, 5th Ser, III, 1488

motion to the rank of colonel [1]   Another encounter took
place on February 1st, which was less satisfactory in its
results   It was thus reported in the *New York Gazette
and Weekly Mercury* of February 10th   The paper, being
published in a city which was occupied by the British, was
necessarily in sympathy with the crown, and due allowance
must be made for bias and exaggeration.   For example, the
number of Americans participating in this insignificant skirmish is alleged to have been greater than that of Washington's entire force at the time

On Saturday the 1st Instant, a smart Skirmish happened at
Springfield in New-Jersey, between a Party of near 4000 Rebels,
under the Command of Sullivan, and the 42d Regiment (the famous
and gallant Highlanders) under Sir William Erskine   The Rebels
were attempting to possess a Hill, which would have given them a
considerable Advantage   Sir William, perceiving their Design,
directed his Highlanders to dispute the Ground   They advanced
with their usual Ardor and Intrepidity upon the Enemy, notwithstanding the great Disparity of their Numbers, and came instantly
to close Quarters with them   The Spirit of these Heroes was not to
be matched by Rebels, and, accordingly, they soon gave up the Point,
and retired with the utmost Precipitation, leaving behind them above
Two hundred and Fifty Men killed upon the Spot   The Bravery
and Conduct of Sir William Erskine and this Regiment have only
been equalled by Col Mawhood and the gallant 17th   The Loss on
the part of the Troops, amounted only to 18 in killed and wounded

An American report of the affair is also given   It
differs so widely from the tory version that, were it not for
the date, the mention of Sir William Erskine, and the con-
ceded British victory, the engagement could hardly be identified as the one just described.

Extract of a letter from an officer of distinction, dated at

[1] Hatfield's Elizabeth, 455

Chatham (between Morristown and Elizabeth-town, New Jersey)
February 3, 1777

"We have hemmed the enemy in and begin to pinch them   On
the 23d ult we trimmed two regiments near to Woodbridge, killed
thirty privates, and several officers   Had Col ————, who commanded, behaved well, we should have destroyed one regiment   He
is now under an arrest   We lost no men that day

"On the first instant, three thousand of the enemy, under command of Sir William Erskine, came out of Brunswick to forage—
They had eight pieces of cannon—Several of our scouting parties
joined, to the amount of six hundred men, under command of Col
Scott, of the Fifth Virginia regiment   A disposition was made to
attack the enemy   Col Scott with ninety Virginians on the right,
attacked two hundred British grenadiers, and drove them to their
cannon   The other parties not marching so briskly up to the attack,
the Colonel was engaged ten minutes by himself, and, three hundred
fresh men being sent against him, he was obliged to give way, and
formed again within three hundred yards of the enemy   By this time
two other divisions had got up with the enemy, but superior numbers
at last prevailed   Our troops retreated about a quarter of a mile,
formed again, and looked the enemy in the face until they retreated
The enemy had thirty-six killed, that the country people saw, and
upwards of one hundred wounded   We have lost three officers and
twelve privates killed, and have about as many wounded   Lieut
Gregory, from Elizabeth City County, Virginia, a brave officer, and
Adjutant Kelly, of the 5th Virginia regiment, one of the bravest men
in the army, he was carried off the field with a flesh wound only,
and five more Virginians, but the enemy coming on that ground,
murdered them, by beating out their brains, with a barbarity exceeding that of the savages "[1]

With the opening of the year 1777 the tide turned in
favor of the Americans, and the cause of independence,
which had seemed almost lost in New Jersey during the preceding months, now appeared much more hopeful   Washington's brilliant victory at Trenton was quickly followed by

[1] Almon's Remembrancer, IV, 98

his success at Princeton, and he soon compelled the British
to abandon all their outposts beyond New Brunswick, their
full strength being required at that place for the protection
of their stores As a result of his operations, and of Maxwell's activities, the enemy, who were practically in possession of the State only a few weeks before, now retained only
their posts at New Brunswick and Perth Amboy[1] But the
country lying between those towns and Elizabeth was still
ravaged by their marauding parties, and encounters between
them and the Americans were of almost daily occurrence,
our troops constantly moving from Chatham and Springfield,
or from Westfield and Scotch Plains, to cut off the British
foraging parties, and to capture their spies[2] These disturb-
ances kept the inhabitants of the border in constant anxiety,
and it is probable that for them the winter of 1776-7 was as
exciting as any period of the war

Shortly after the battle of Princeton (on the 6th of
January to be exact), Washington led his army to Morristown, and went into winter quarters His force at that time
numbered about 3,000 men,[3] there being 43 regiments,
divided into 10 brigades under Brigadier-Generals Muhlen-
burg, Weedon, Woodford, Scott, Smallwood, Deborre,
Wayne, Dehass, Conway and Maxwell, and five divisions of
two brigades each under Major-Generals Greene, Stephen
Sullivan, Lincoln and Stirling The artillery was commanded
by Brigadier-General Knox[4] Many of the soldiers en-

[1] Sherman's Historic Morristown, 213

[2] Hatfield's Elizabeth, 459

[3] Sherman's Historic Morristown, 214

[4] Sparks' Writings of Washington, IV, 423 n Morristown was
selected for winter quarters by the advice of General Knox—*Schroeder's
Life and Times of Washington*, I, 536 Lossing, in his Washington
Biography, II, 398, says "Washington chose Morristown in 1777 only
as a temporary halting place for repose, but soon perceived it most secure
and eligible for the winter encampment A chain of hills running from
Pluckemin by way of Chatham and Springfield to the great falls of the
Passaic at Paterson made approach difficult for a hostile army, and at his
rear was a populous and fertile country full of provisions and forage"

camped in the Loantaka valley, about three miles southeast
of Morristown, where a number of rude huts was erected
for their shelter, while others were billeted in private houses,
not only in Morristown, but throughout the neighboring
villages; among the latter being the three regiments of
Colonel Vose, who, for the most part, were quartered in
private dwellings in the district afterwards known as Chatham Township [1]

We are indebted to the Brothers Tuttle for a valuable
description of the encampment, and an interesting record of
events occurring at that time   They thus describe the manner in which those troops who were not stationed in camp
were billeted·

A large part of the soldiers were quartered upon the inhabitants
in Hanover, Whippany, Chatham, Madison, and Morristown   This
was done by commissioners, of whom Aaron Kitchel, of Hanover, was
one [2]   Twelve men were quartered on Parson Green, sixteen on
Anna Kitchel's husband Uzal, a score on Aaron Kitchel, and so
throughout the farming district   To these families it was almost
ruinous, since all they had was eaten up in the service, so that when
the army marched off it left the region as bare as if it had been swept
by a plague of locusts [3]

Every house throughout this entire region was filled to its utmost
capacity with either officers or soldiers   Persons appointed by the
Commander-in-chief passed through the towns and examined the
houses, and, without much consultation with the owners, decided
how many, and who, should be quartered in each   Often, without
even going into the houses, these persons would ride up to the door
and write "Colonel Ogden's Head-quarters," "Major Eaton's Headquarters," "Twelve privates to be billeted here," "Six officers to be
quartered here," &c, and, generally without much regard to the convenience or wishes of the occupants, the arrangements of these Commissioners were carried out   In many cases the best rooms were

[1] Historical Magazine, Ser 2, IX, 208
[2] Harper's Magazine, XVIII, 293
[3] Annals of Morris County, 38

placed at the disposal of the troops, while the families owning them
retired to their kitchens and garrets Boards were set up on the
floor, across the end of the room opposite to the hearth, just far
enough from the wall to permit of a person lying down at full length
This space was then filled with good wholesome straw, and there, all
the soldiers billeted in a house, numbering sometimes six, sometimes
twelve, and sometimes even twenty, crowded in together, and, covering themselves each with a single blanket, while the fires were kept
burning, defended themselves as best they could from the severities
of those stern winter nights In some cases the soldiers had their
meals provided by the families with which they were quartered, while
in others they drew their rations and prepared them for themselves,
as is generally done in camp In the case of the officers, except when
their families were with them, the former course was generally
adopted

This method, though necessarily arbitrary, was met by a people
of "willing mind" Aaron Kitchel and his father, Joseph, of Hanover, had two houses, and gave up the larger one, on condition that
the old people might have the other, required only to take care of
three sick English prisoners, of whom there was no danger of their
catching the small pox   The Sayres Richards, Ely, Beach,
Kitchel, Smith, Tuttle, and other families were served in the same
way, making no complaints [1]

The winter of 1777 was an exceptionally cold one, but
the severity of the weather was by no means the least of
the hardships to which the soldiers were exposed. they also
suffered from the lack of food and clothing, and from
various diseases caused by their enfeebled vitality and un-
sanitary surroundings Early in January an epidemic of
smallpox broke out in Morristown, and spread with alarming rapidity throughout this entire region, carrying off
many of the soldiers, and great numbers of the civil population as well The patriotic inhabitants of the entire
countryside sought by every means in their power to alleviate
the sufferings of the troops, and supplied the army with

[1] Historical Magazine, Ser 2, IX, 208, 358

necessaries as far as their slender means would allow
"Provisions," says Dr Tuttle, "came in with hearty good
will from the farmers of Mendham, Chatham, Hanover,
and other rural places, together with stockings shoes, coats,
and blankets, while the women met together to sew for the
soldiery"[1] The shortcomings of the commissary department aroused the ire of General Washington, who, on
February 22nd, penned a sharp rebuke to General Irwin, in
charge of that branch of the service

> The Cry of want of Provisions comes to me from every Quar-
> ter—Genl. Maxwell writes word that his People are Starving—Genl
> Johnson of Maryland yesterday informd me, that his People could
> draw none—this difficulty I understand prevails also at Chatham[1]—
> What Sir is the meaning of this?—and why were you so desirous
> of excluding others from this business when you are unable to accom-
> plish it yourself?—Consider, I beseech you, the consequence of this
> neglect, and exert yourself to remove the Evil and Complaints which
> cannot be less fatal to the Army than
>
>   disagreeable to,
>
>   Sir,
>
>   Your most obedt humble Servant
>
>   Go Washington[2]

[1] Stockings, mittens leggings, blankets and all kinds of domestic fabric
employed those earnest women The Kitchells, Smiths and Greens, of Hanover, the Jacksons, Beaches and Winds, of Rockaway and Pequannock, the
Condits, Fords, Johns and Hathways, of Morristown, the Carters Piersons,
Sayres, Millers Thompsons and Browns, of Chatham, the Thompsons,
Drakes and Careys, of Mendham, were only a few, who, from the beginning of the war, counted all things as loss unless independence was won,
and the army was made the recipients of their bounty '—*Carrington's The
Strategic Relations of New Jersey to the Revolution*, 25

This was not the only occasion when the women of northern New
Jersey interested themselves in the welfare of the soldiery after the military hospital at Princeton was established, their benevolence was manifested
in gifts to its sick and wounded inmates We read in the *New Jersey
Gazette* of February 25, 1778, that the church at Hanover had sent a donation of clothing and linen to the hospital, and in the issue of April 8 1778,
that similar gifts had been received from the churches of Newark, Elizabeth Town, Connecticut Farms, Turky and South Hanover (now New Providence and Madison), Springfield, Morristown, Scotch Plains and Bound
Brook Chatham was included in the parishes of South Hanover and
Springfield

[2] Ford's *Writings of Washington*, V, 251 n

One of the soldiers of Washington's army participating in the campaign of 1777 in northern New Jersey was James McMichael of Pennsylvania, who recorded his adventures in a diary which has been preserved, and in which a few references to Chatham are found McMichael was at that time a sergeant in Captain John Marshall's company of the Pennsylvania Rifle Regiment, commanded by Colonel Samuel Miles We quote as follows from his journal

January 12 —We marched from Morristown at 3 P M , and arrived at Chatham at dark, in the suburbs of which we got very agreeable quarters The young ladies here are very fond of the soldiers, but much more so of officers

Apparently nothing occurred during McMichael's stay at Chatham which he considered worthy of note in his journal The next entry reads

January 23 —At 4 P M marched from Chatham for Springfield, where at   P M we got quarters

On the 24th he mentions a brush with the enemy at Quibble Town, and, after an interval, the narrative continues

January 31 —Yesterday we marched to Elizabethtown, and to-day, after passing through Connecticut Farms and Springfield, reached Chatham, where I secured my former lodgings

Here another gap occurs which is terminated on February 10th by the brief statement that, having obtained a furlough, the sergeant left Chatham at 7 A M [1]
A letter from John Marshall, the captain of Sergeant McMichael's company, is reprinted from the Pennsylvania

[1] Pennsylvania Magazine of History, XVI, 141

Archives Its signature as there given—J Harshall—is unquestionably a misprint

Chatham, Feby 1st 1777

Sir,

My so long defering writing to you was sometimes for want of an opportunity, and when that ofter d had not any paper I shall Just give you a brief acct of our proceedings since you left us A few days after we arriv'd at this place, a party of our Regt was ordered out on a scout with Col Weine, who met with a party of the plunderers, had a small skirmish with them, in which we lost Sergt Weaver Soon after a large party was ordered out, Messrs Robb, Sneider, & myself was in the number, the whole was commanded by Col B——r, from Virginia,[1] a man who has distinguish'd himself for, I was going to say cowardice but shall only impute it to his weakly constitution not agreeing with the smell of sulphur, but to give you a more particular acct of the matter, our body consisted of about 300 men (officers included,) who met with upwards of Double the number, near Bonum Town, we were posted in a very advantageous piece of ground, with a great plenty of Timber, the Enemy were in the open field with two field pieces, but were twice repuls'd as they attempted to gain the woods, after fighting near half an hour we were obliged to retreat, and to the great surprise of everyone, without the loss of either one man or blood, except one cowardly fellow who was much contus'd, in running off, ran into a briar bush which scratch'd his hand that the blood appear d Our Col however took care to make a safe retreat

It is said the Enemy had that day kill'd & wounded upwards of seventy, many of which were officers of distinction.

Mr Hufner is just arrived with seventeen men, which it like

---

[1] Col Mordecai Buckner, of the 6th Virginia Col Parker, writing to Gen Washington from Springfield on Jan 24, gave a detailed account of the fight on the road from Brunswick Landing to Woodbridge, and stated that his superior, Col Buckner, left on horseback as soon as the firing began, rode four miles to his quarters and announced that all was lost Consequently Parker was obliged to draw off his troops, two of whom were captured, though none was killed or wounded —*Calendar of Weedon Correspondence American Philosophical Society Proceedings, XXXIII*

Buckner was afterwards cashiered —*Maryland Historical Magazine, I, 132, Heitman's Register of Continental Officers, 130*

those heretofore, will he only an additional trouble to us, as they are much dissatisfied, some wanting money, &c

I shou'd be glad how soon some more of the officers, or the whole Regt was ordered here, or even called to Philada, many indeed has gone without my leave

You'l Please Sr give my compliments to Gentlemen, the officers of our Corps, except Mr Robb's & Soiergens Complimts

believe me to be Dear Si, your most Obed't H'ble serv't

J Harshall

[Directed]
To Major Emon Williams,
    in the Penna Rifle Reg't, Philadelphia [1]

A detachment of Rhode Island troops, which had formed part of General Lee's command during the preceding autumn, was stationed in Chatham about this time, as appears from the diary of Private John Howland of Captain Dexter's company in Colonel Lippett's regiment Describing his experiences subsequent to the battle of Princeton, Howland writes

> Our brigade, after our arrival at Morristown, was divided, and marched in different detachments towards the enemy's lines   Part of our regiment was quartered for a short time at Chatham, and the foraging parties of the enemy were kept in check by our patrols and piquets   In February, captain Dexter's company were discharged at Chatham   I shouldered my pack, and in company with others travelled to Peekskill, where we crossed the Hudson by the same ferry we had crossed on our march westward under general Lee   Our paper money wages, forty shillings per month, was never paid fully, and we received nothing to bear our expenses home.[2]

W J Mills, in his Historic Houses of New Jersey, mentions a letter written at Chatham by Private Caleb Miller of the Revolutionary army to his mother, telling of a

---

[1] Pennsylvania Archives, Ser 1, V, 211
[2] Stone's Howland, 65, 70, 78

longing to hear the Newark church-bells, which he says
'have a sweeter tone than any he has heard hereabouts,"
and expressing the hope that the day will soon come when he
"can feel the green covering of his native village." The
writer of the present volume has been unable to locate this
letter, which is probably in some private collection

While Washington's army was in winter quarters in
the early part of the year 1777, Major-General Sullivan, in
military parlance, "lay in front of Morristown," to oppose
any advance which might be attempted by the enemy, and
to give timely warning to the commander-in-chief   For this
duty he was stationed at Chatham, remaining here about
four months [1] His command at that time consisted of seven
Maryland regiments (being the full quota of Maryland),
the single Delaware regiment, and Colonel Moses Hazen's
regiment known as "the Congress Own"[2]   He also had a
detachment of artillery under Captain Sabastian Bauman,
of whom more will be said hereafter [3]

[1] Sullivan is thought to have taken post at Chatham early in January,
at the time of, or shortly after, the arrival of the army at Morristown   It
is not probable that he remained here continuously during the winter, for
the occasional movements against the enemy would require his presence elsewhere, but he maintained his headquarters at Chatham until the 15th of
May, when he was directed by Washington to take command of the troops
at Princeton —*Washington Papers in the Library of Congress*, B III, 157

Historical Magazine, Ser 2, VII, 85   Col Hazen commanded the
Second regiment of Canadian volunteers, numbering at one time nearly
500   After the withdrawal of the American troops from Canada the
regiment gradually decreased to about 100 men, and in order to refill
its depleted ranks it was agreed to enlist Americans from any of the
States   Recruiting was accordingly carried on by Col Hazen throughout New York, and by Lieut-Col Anthill in New Jersey, Pennsylvania,
Maryland and Virginia   Their success was indifferent, for the New England States were paying a higher bounty to recruits than they were authorized to offer   Thereafter the regiment was called 'the Congress Own"
because it was not attached to the quota of any State —*Griffin's Catholics in
the Revolution*, I, 119, *Griswold's Generals of the Revolution*, II, 291,
Sparks Writings of Washington, II, 267 n

[3] On January 14th, Col George Johnston, Jr, secretary and aide de
camp of Washington, wrote to his friend Levan Powell   The main body
of the Enemy (8,000) are at Brunswick, 10 miles from their Fleet, entrench-
ing   Gen'l Sullivan with about 2,000 at Chatham, about 6 miles from
them, Gen'l Maxwell with better than 2,000 (which number is increasing
hourly) lies at Elizabeth Town, which is 20 miles from Brunswick, S o E't,

General John Sullivan at this time was thirty-seven
years of age   He was born in Berwick, Maine, of Irish
parentage, his ancestors having been members of the historic
Clan O'Sullivan of the ancient kingdom of Munster   He
was a lawyer by profession, practising at Durham, New
Hampshire; and besides his military career, he served the
public at various times as delegate to the first Continental
Congress, member of Congress under the Constitution,
governor of New Hampshire, and judge of the Federal
district court in that State   He is described as dignified,
genial and amiable, possessing an erect and well-propor-
tioned (though somewhat corpulent) figure, five feet nine
inches in height   His features were animated and handsome, his eyes dark, and his hair black and curly, and he
possessed a powerful voice, which was deep but melodious [1]

Sullivan was a man of undoubted courage and patriotism,
the value of whose military services cannot be overestimated;
and it is said that, with the exception of Greene and Arnold,
he was trusted by the commander-in-chief beyond any other
general in the army   But despite his jovial good nature, he
was unfortunately possessed of a hasty temper and an im-
perious spirit, through which he was involved in frequent
difficulties, both during and after the war, and which excited
such animosity on the part of the other officers of the army
as to lead them in many cases to ridicule his achievements

there he has taken 200 prisoners and much baggage "—*Powell's Levan
Powell, 51*

Christopher Marshall, of Philadelphia, wrote in his diary under date
of January 18th "Sundry pieces of news today, but none to be depended
upon from the camp, except that Gen Washington had his headquarters
at Morristown, and Gen Sullivan with his advanced guard at Chatham,
about five miles distance, and that Gen Howe was at Amboy and the
heights of Brunswick with his army "—*Duane's Marshall's Diary, 113*

On March 11th, John Taylor wrote from Kingston to Gen Schuyler
'I left Morristown the 7th instant   General Sullivan, who was station'd
at Chatham is gone home to see his family "—*Schuyler Correspondence, Ban-
croft's MS Transcript, I 141, in New York Public Library*

[1] Murray's Sullivan and the Battle of Rhode Island, 2, 4, 27, Schroeder's
Life and Times of Washington, I, 523, Proceedings of the New York State
Historical Association, 1906, 17

and to question his reports [1] He was greatly dissatisfied
with his post at Chatham, which he felt to be far beneath
his dignity, and longed for a larger field for the exercise of
his abilities   His complaints of unjust discrimination were
vigorous and persistent, although little concerning them can
be learned, for his biographers, in emphasizing his engaging
qualities, have failed to some extent to record facts tending
to show that at times he was swayed by pique, envy, and
similar unworthy emotions   But the following conciliatory
letter, which was addressed to him from Morristown by the
commander-in-chief, in an effort to reconcile his mind to the
duties assigned him, is a clear indication of his discontent

Do not, my dear General Sullivan, torment yourself any longer
with imaginary slights and involve others in the perplexities you feel
on that score. No other officer of rank, in the whole army, has so
often conceived himself neglected, slighted, and ill treated, as you
have done, and none I am sure has had less cause than yourself to
entertain such Ideas   Mere accidents, things which have occurred
in the common course of service, have been considered by you as
designed affronts   But pray, Sir, in what respect did General
Greene's late command at Fort Lee differ from his present command
at Baskenridge, or from yours at Chatham? And what kind of
separate command had General Putnam at New York? I never
heard of any, except his commanding there ten days before my arrival
from Boston, and one day after I had left it for Haerlem Heights, as
senior officer   In like manner at Philadelphia, how did his command
there differ from the one he has at Princeton, and wherein does
either vary from yours at Chatham? Are there any particular emolu-
ments or honours to be reaped in the one case and not in the other?
No   Why then these unreasonable, these unjustifiable suspicions?
Suspicions which can answer no other end, than to poison your own
happiness, and add vexation to that of others   General Heath, it is
true, was ordered to Peekskill, so was General Spencer, by the mere
chapter of accidents (being almost in the country), to Providence,

[1] Sebring's The Character of General Sullivan, in Proceedings of the
New York State Historical Association, 1906, 16, 17

to watch the motions of the fleet then hovering in the Sound   What
followed after to either, or both, was more the effect of chance than
design

Your ideas and mine, respecting separate commands, have but
little analogy   I know of but one separate command, properly so
called, and that is in the Northern Department, and General Sullivan, General St Clair, and any other general officer at Ticonderoga
will be considered in no other light, whilst there is a superior officer
in the department, than if they were placed at Chatham, Baskenridge,
or Princeton

But I have not time to dwell upon subjects of this kind   In
quiting it, I shall do it with an earnest exhortation, that you will
not suffer yourself to be teased with evils, that only exist in the
imagination, and with slights, that have no existence at all, keeping
in mind, at the same time, that, if distant armies are to be formed,
there are several gentlemen before you in point of rank, who have a
right to claim a preference

I am, with regard, dear Sir,

your most obedient, &c [1]

Among the American manuscripts relating to the
Revolutionary War which are now in the Royal Institution
in London is a letter from General Sullivan to Sir William
Howe, dated at Chatham, February 8, 1777, enclosing, by
order of General Washington, a list of prisoners captured
by the British in New Jersey, and stating that if an exchange
is consented to, he will send to New York, Amboy or Brunswick as many soldiers, and at such time, as may be appointed   The prisoners named are   Caleb Potter, Zach
Seikell, James Lambert, John Haines and John Williams,
confined in New York, John Melick and William Brookfield, confined in Amboy, and Elias and Elihu Campbell,
taken at Springfield and supposed to be in New York [2]

[1] Ford's Writings of Washington, V, 289
[2] American MSS in the Royal Institution, Carleton Papers, I, 88

GENERAL SULLIVAN TO GENERAL WASHINGTON

Chatham Feby 9th 1777

Dear General

My Disorder has not ibated but has Really weakened me So much that I am totally unable to wait on Yr Excy to Day with Respect to the Small pox my opinion is that the only way to get Rid of it is Immediately to Send all Infected persons to Some Back Town where an hospital Should be Erected, to this place Should Every person be Sent if the Symptom of the Disorder appears on him at the place Innoculation Should be allowed & Such Detachments of the Army Sent there from time to time for Innoculation as the Service will allow of Dr Genl I am yours most Sincerely & affectionately,

JNO SULLIVAN

His Excy Gen'l Washington [1]

SAME TO THE SAME

Chatham Feby 13th 1777

Much Respected General

I Recollect once to have Read That on the Fatal Ides of March when Cesar was going to the Capitol Artemidorus presented him with a paper Containing Those words "Cesar Beware of Brutus 'Take Heed of Cassius come not near Casca have an Eye to Cinna "Trust not Trebonius, Brutus Loves thee not These men have all "but one mind and That is bent agt Cesar if Thou art not Immortal "Look about Thee Security give way to Conspiracy" The writing Artemidorus Desired him to read Instantly but he Delayed & was assassinated with this paper (by him unread) in his Pocket—the Reading of which might have Saved him I am as far from Superstition & have as Little faith in the Intrail of a Beast as any man Dreams have never Regulated my Conduct—yet for Some Reason I wish your Excellency would be prevailed upon not to go much to the Eastward of Morris Town, particularly about the Neighbourhood of Mr Saml Ogden The Eastern parts are Inhabited by Tories & no Troops of ours in that Quarter a plan to Entrap might

[1] Washington Papers in the Library of Congress, 13, 220

be Easily Laid & very Easily Carried into Execution I would not wish to make you Act Different from what your own Reason would Dictate if in my power but The people fear for you & they Seem to feel the Danger to which their Country would be Exposed Should Such an Event take place (which heaven forbid) I am not Credulous perhaps not Enough So & yet I fear Events believe me great Sir There is more weight in the unanimous voice & opinion of all The people than there could be in those Dreams and prodigies which Even Staggered Cesars Resolution & made him once Determine not to appear in the Senate forgive me Dear Sir when I say That Wisdom may Sometimes be Consumed in Confidence & The Noble Spirit which knows no fear may be the best assistant to its Enemies for Compleatg its Ruin for as Said the paper (which might have Saved Cesar) "Security gives way to Conspiracy" I can Scarcely Account for my fears nor can I prove What I Really believe which is that you have many Enemies Around you which if opportunity would permit would Readily assist to Entrap your Excy and Leave a wretched Army to Lament the Loss of That Leader who has been their only Support Dear General if I have gone too far Impute it to my zeal for my Country & regard for your Safety

I have the honor to be Dear General yours most affectionately,

JNO SULLIVAN

P. S

I wish not to Show Ingratitude to the Family of the ogdens by Suspicions they have Ever treated me in the most open Generous manner & I cant help believing the one with whom you Live is Sincere I doubt of Samuel I believe you will Soon have a Deposition proving that old Mr Ogden of New York was possessed of yr Proclamation before it was published here This will prove a Correspondence

Yr Excys most obedt Servt

J S[1]

The letter given below was written by Sullivan to Meshech Weare, a member of the Executive Council of New Hampshire The general's eulogy of the Yankee soldiers, and the comparisons he draws, remind us of the

---

[1] Washington Papers in the Library of Congress, 13, 246

jealousy which existed during the Revolution among the troops from different parts of the country, especially between the New England men and the Southerners, whose mutual aversion, however trivial its causes, sometimes led to quarrels which the presence of Washington himself was hardly sufficient to restrain [1]

Chatham, Feby 13th 1777

Hon & much respected Sir,—

Your favor of the 14th December never reached me till about a week past—since which I have had no time to answer it   All the Gentlemen officers appointed for the new army, are long since departed on the Recruiting Business, otherwise I should gladly have comply'd with your request to send them off & supplying them with money   There would have been no difficulty in supplying Col Scammel with the money, had he been on the spot when your letter arrived

Your Committee appointed four Captains at White Plains   They say they could enlist a number of men out of their old companies if they had the money   I, with some difficulty, borrowed the money as there was orders not for any to be drawn out of the Chest except by warrt from the Commander in chief who was then in Pennsylvania; however by advice of your Committee & by the assistance of General Lee, I obtained the money giving my Rect to be accountable   The whole amount was 2880 Dollars, viz 720 to each of the four Captains   I paid to Captains Scott Gilman & Robinson & took their Receipts in behalf of the State   The other Captain was absent   I desired Captain Gilman to take the money & convey to him, he thought best for him not to Risque it, but promised to send the other Captain to me, but our perpetual Hurry & constant marchings, I suppose prevented   My hurry at Morristown & sudden removal to the advance post prevented my attending to it while Captain Gilman was here, and the misfortune is that I have entirely forgot the man's name, so that it is out of my power to tell whether he is at home or here, or whether he is dead or alive   I am so far removed from the New Hampshire Troops and constantly employed, that I have as yet

[1] Mrs Warrens American Revolution I, 330, Irvings Washington, II, 124, 280

had no opportunity to forward it to your State whose property it is
Captain Dearborn is now here, I will endeavor to forward it by
him, with the Receipts, which you will be kind enough to keep for
my security and that of the State, he will set out in about a week

I hope, dear Sir, the Assembly of our State will pardon me for
not writing them oftener of the State of affairs in the Army,—of
our victories & defeats, advances & Retreats, but I have many things
to allege in excuse I do not recollect that I am a letter in debt to
the Assembly (or one of its members) as none of them except yourself have ever honored me with a line All of yours I think I have
punctually answered I have been so full of Business that I could
not find time to write, but still I have a more weighty reason, which
is, That I cannot give an account of a victory or defeat where I was
an actor without saying something for or against myself, & I have a
great aversion to writing against myself & to write in favor would
be evidence of a very suspicious kind Indeed, I always had an aversion to fighting upon paper, for I have never yet found a man well
versed in that kind of fighting, that would practice any other Perhaps you may want to know how your men (the Yankees) fight, I
tell you exceeding well when they have proper officers I have been
much pleased to see a day approaching to try the difference between
Yankee cowardice & southern valor The Day has or rather the days
have arrived and all the General officers allowed & do allow that
the Yankee cowardice assumes the shape of true valor in the field,
and the Southern valor appears to be a composition of boasting & conceit General Washington made no scruple to say publicly that the
remains of the Eastern Regiments were the strength of his army,
though then their numbers were comparatively speaking but small,
he calls them in front when the Enemy are there, he sends them to
the rear when the Enemy threatens that way, all the general officers
allow them to be the best of Troops The Southern officers and soldiers allow it in time of danger, but not at all other times Believe
me, Sir, the Yankees took Trentown before the other Troops knew
anything of the matter more than that there was an engagement,
and what will still surprise you more, the line that attacked the Town
consisted of eight hundred Yankees & there was 1600 Hessians to
oppose them At Princetown when the 17th Regt had thrown 3500

southern militia into the utmost confusion a Regiment of Yankees restored the day This General Mifflin confessed to me,—though the Philadelphia papers tell us a different story It seems to have been quite forgot, that while the 17th Regt was engaging those Troops that 600 Yankees had the Town to take agst the 40th & 55th Regts which they did without loss, owing to the manner of attack, but enough of this, I don't wish to reflect,—but beg leave to assure you that Newspapers & even Letters don't always speak the truth You may venture to assure your friends that no men fight better or write worse than the Yankees, of which this Letter will be good evidence

Dear Sir, I am with much esteem your most obedt servt

JNO SULLIVAN

Honble Meshech Weare, Esq [1]

GENERAL SULLIVAN TO JOHN ADAMS

Chatham, February 14th 1777

Dr Sir,

I hope you will pardon me for not writing to you oftener of the state of affairs in the way of our victories and defeats, advances and retreats, but I have many things to allege in excuse I don't recollect that I am a letter in debt to you as I think I have punctually answered yours I have ever been so full of business that I could find no time to write, but still I have a more weighty reason, which is that I cannot give an account of a victory or defeat where I was an actor, without saying something for or against myself, and to write in favor, would be evidence of a very suspicious kind Indeed, I always had an aversion for fighting upon paper, for I have never yet found a man well versed in that kind of fighting that would practice any other Perhaps you may want to know how your men (the Yankees) fight I tell you exceeding well, when they have proper officers I have been much pleased to see a day approaching to try the difference between Yankee cowardice and Southern valour, the day has, or rather the days have arrived, and all the General officers allowed, and do allow, that the Yankee cowardice assumes the shape of true valour in the field, and though the Southern appears to be a composition of boasting and conceit, Gen'l Washington made no scruple to say publicly that the remains of the Eastern Reg'ts were the strength of his army, though their numbers were comparatively speaking, but small   He calls them in front when the Enemy are there—he sends them to the rear when the Enemy threatens that way—All the General officers allow them to be the best troops—The Southern officers and soldiers allow it in time of danger, but not at other times   Believe me, Sir, although Yankees took Trenton before the other Troops knew anything of the matter—more than that there was an engagement, and what will still surprise you more, the line that attacked the Town consisted of but eight hundred Yankees and there were sixteen hundred Hessians to oppose them

At Princeton when the 17th Reg't had thrown 3500 Southern Militia into the utmost confusion a Reg't of Yankees restored the day   (This General Mifflin confessed to me) though Philadelphia papers tell a different story   It seems to have been quite forgot, that while the 17th Reg't was engaging those troops that six hundred Yankees had the town to take against the 40th and 55th Reg'ts, which they did without loss, owing to the manner of attack   But enough of this   I don't wish to reflect, but beg leave to assure you, that newspapers, and even letters do not always speak the truth   You may venture to assure your friends that no men fight better or write worse than the Yankees, of which this letter will be a good evidence

Dear Sir   I am, with much Esteem, Your most obedient servant,

JNO SULLIVAN

Hon'ble John Adams, Esq [1]

GENERAL SULLIVAN TO GENERAL WASHINGTON

Chatham Feby 14th 1777

Dear General

I am informed by Letter from the president of the Councill of New Hampshire Informing That that State Sensible of Colo Scammells merit appointed him Colo of one of their Regiments though he was from another State—I conclude therefore that This appointment was Accepted by him before your Exceys orders would have Reached him & as the (Infamous New England) Bounty will be an

Inducement to the Soldiers he will hold that appointment   Your Excy will therefore please to Supply officers to that Regiment of Such persons As your wisdom Shall Direct

I have the honor to be your Excellencys most obedient Servant

JNO SULLIVAN.

His Excellency General Washington [1]

The artillery attached to General Sullivan's division at Chatham consisted of six companies or parties commanded by captains and captain-lieutenants, and numbered in all about 150 men   Sabastian Bauman of Wallkill, N Y , as senior captain, was placed in command, and his correspondence indicates that while stationed at Chatham he was accompanied by his family

At the battle of Trenton the Americans had captured six Hessian field-pieces, two of which were subsequently sent to Morristown, while the remaining four were assigned to Bauman's artillery at Chatham   No record has been found to show where the guns were placed in this village, but the probabilities of the case strongly favor the supposition that they were planted near the main road, on the rising ground just west of the river, forming a battery which would command the bridge and the ford below it

During February, 1777, General Greene decided that these six field-pieces should be sent to Philadelphia, and the order was transmitted to Captain Bauman by Lieutenant Samuel Shaw, the regimental adjutant at Morristown, who promised to send three other cannon to Chatham to replace the Hessian guns, but General Sullivan, who relied largely upon the strength of his artillery to guard the bridge and to protect the stores at Chatham, was most unwilling to reduce the number of cannon at this place Bauman therefore found himself in the unpleasant position

[1] Washington Papers in the Library of Congress, 13, 253

of being peremptorily ordered by the military authorities at
Morristown to send the Hessian guns away, while the
general under whose immediate command he was insisted
that at least one of them should be retained   Some letters
relating to this embarrassing situation are given below
They are selected from a large collection of Captain Bauman's papers in the library of the New York Historical
Society

LIEUTENANT SHAW TO CAPTAIN BAUMAN

Morristown 17th Feby 1777

Sir,

Major General Greene having ordered that those Six Hessian
Pieces taken at Trenton should be sent to Philadelphia to be bored
out for Sixes, I shall be glad if you will have those four that are
on your command with the Ammunition &c got in readiness immediately, to be brought up here tomorrow morning ten o'Clock, when
I shall send you some other Pieces with Ammunition Suitable in
their stead   Pray don't fail of having them in readiness so that
they may come up as soon as the others get down

I am Sir

Yrs

S SHAW,
Adjt Arty

Capt Bauman
[Addressed]

To Capt Bauman, Commanding the Artillery at Chatham

SAME TO THE SAME

Morris Town 18 Feby 1777

Dear Sir,

I herewith send you three Brass three Pounders in lieu of the
four Hessian Pieces, concerning which I wrote you yesterday   I
hope you have got them together so that they may come up as soon
as these get down   There is one Ammunition Waggon, containing
the Ammunition for the two long Pieces, if you should want more

you can reserve it out of what you have for the Pieces that are to be sent up And the remainder you will forward with the Pieces to this Place immediately

My Regard to the Officers if you please and believe me to be

Yrs &c

S SHAW

Capt Bauman

[Addressed]

Capt Bauman, Commanding the Artillery at Chatham

SAME TO THE SAME

Morris Town, 19th Feby 1777

Sir,

The General having directed that *all* the Hessian Pieces which were taken at Trenton should be sent to Philadelphia for certain purposes, I am to acquaint you that your reserving one of them has been a means of preventing my sending the others off this morn'g agreeable to orders. Must beg you to Send the other up immediately If Gen'l Sullivan should object to its coming away without another being sent in its place please to inform him, that as we shall have six pieces of Cannon less than heretofore, what he now has with him is more than a proportionable part of the whole To say nothing of our want of men to supply even what Cannon he will there have left

I am Sir

Yrs

S SHAW,
Adjt Arty

Capt Bauman

[Addressed]

To Capt Bauman Commanding the Artillery at Chatham

CAPTAIN BAUMAN TO LIEUTENANT SHAW

Chatham Feby 19 1777

Sir

in my letter of yesterday I acquainted you with the Reason why all the Hessian Pieces were not sent to morristown according to the generals Direction

General Sulivan Absolutely Declared he would not Let one go,
How Could I act any other ways then to Obey his Command   General Sulivan and General Stephenson are gone out riding, as soon
as they Return I shall lay it a second time before them and in which
I can do no more then to act according to there Determination

Remain Sir

Your humble Servant

SABAST BAUMAN

Copi To Sam Shaw

adjutant of artillery at morristown

LIEUTENANT SHAW TO CAPTAIN BAUMAN

Morris Town 19 March 1777

Sir,

The Bearer of this, Lieut Adam Hope, is directed by the Commander in chief to deliver into your care a Serjeant & Seven men
lately enlisted, to do duty in the Artillery till such time as they may
be called for   You will see they are taught the Exercise, and dispose
of them in such a manner as you will judge best for the good of the
Service

I am Sir

Yrs

S SHAW,
Adjt Artily

Capt Bauman
[Addressed.]

To Capt Bauman Commanding the Artillery at Chatham

CAPTAIN BAUMAN TO GENERAL KNOX

Chatham, March 20th 1777

Sir,

Before I address you or enter upon public matters I shall beg
leave first to congratulate you on your safe arrival at Morris Town

Your are well acquainted with a detachment of artilly ordered
by you under the Command of Captn Allen to join Major General
Sullivan's division, now under command of Major General Stephens
You are likewise sensible that those pieces, and ammunition wagons

have been carried through hard and bad roads last summer, and part of the winter, which occasioned the whole to be at present much out of repair and incomplete for a new campaign

During your Absence, I had the honor to Command this detachment of Artillery at Chatham But found at my arrival a Vast deficiency, of Horses, Harnesses and all Kind of Tacklings so absolutely necessary in case of a Sudden movement which however is over in my humble opinion for the want of a good wagon master, and as the Service may Suffer thereby I would beg you to mediate with the wagon master, in order to appoint one for this detachment—this detachment is under the eye of a general whom nothing escapes, and he trusting all to my care, found however something insufficient on our march yesterday, things which arise from the same nature I have above related, and desired me to Write to you upon the Subject And in the mean time to apply for proper ammunition wagons and Drivers

And as nothing but the good of the Service lies to my heart, which you may perceive in an order I issued Some days ago And as I dread nothing more, but a neglect may be lay'd to my Charge, and the care of Artillery and stores at this place is not like the case of a Singall Company I would therefore beg the General most earnestly to assist me both with orders and advise Should I be continued for a time in this command

S BAUMAN,
Capt of Artilly

To General Knox

LIEUTENANT SHAW TO CAPTAIN BAUMAN

Morris 22 March 1777

Sir,

Capt Lieut Symonds being much indisposed, and standing in need of some person to look after him in quality of a Waiter, I must beg the favour of you to furnish him with a suitable one from the Detachment under your Command, to attend on him during his illness

I am Sir   Yrs &c   S SHAW
Adj Art

Capt Bauman

P S   Your Letter was delivered to the General, but he having some other business on his hands prevented his answering it—he will see into the matter you mentioned the beginning of next week

[Addressed ·]

S Bauman, Esqr Commanding the Artillery at Chatham

SAME TO THE SAME

Morris Town 25 April 1777

Sir,

General Knox desires you would collect the Abstracts of Pay to the Continental Artillery under your command, to the first of this month and forward them to him without loss of time   The present state of the Corps, necessarily consisting of many detachments, calls for the utmost attention & care in making up the Abstract for those men, and the General presumes neither will be wanting on your part   He would recommend it to the other Officers to be exceedingly careful in doing the same for their respective parties, as the men will be mustered and the Abstracts strickly examined, and no omission or mistake whatever be overlooked

I am Sir

Yr most obedt hum Servt

S SHAW,

Capt Bauman

[Addressed]

To the Commanding Officer of Artillery at Chatham

SAME TO THE SAME

Morris Town 1 May 1777

Sir,

Since I wrote you respecting the Abstracts of Pay to be made out for the Detachment under your Command there has been some alteration in the establishment, a copy whereof I send you as Settled this day, agreeable to which you must make up your Abstract

I am Sir

Yrs &c

S SHAW,

A Weekly Report of the Detachment of Artillery Commanded by Capn Bauman In General Stephens Devision

Chatham 24th May 1777	Captains	Capt Lieutenants	Lieutenants	Sergeants	Corporals	Bombadiers	Gunners	Drums & Fifes	Matrosses	Total Effective	Sick Present	Sick absent	Dead	On Furlough	Absent with o leave	Absent by leave	Total
Capt Bauman	"	3	3	1	2	1	2	12	25	5	5	"	1	"	"	"	4
Capt Jones	"	1	2	1	1	3	1	14	24	3	1	"	"	"	"	"	4
Capt Doughty	1	1	4	3	2	"	"	18	30	1	3	1	"	"	1	"	6
Capt Clarke	"	2	3	2	2	2	"	10	22	5	2	"	"	1	"	"	8
Capt Lieut Simonds	2	"	1	1	"	"	"	8	12	"	"	"	1	"	"	"	1
Capt Lieut Freeman	1	2	2	0	2	2	"	4	13	1	"	"	"	"	"	1	1
Total	4	9	15	8	9	8	3	66	126	15	11	1	2	1	1	1	31

Capt Bauman's Compy
Sergt McKinny on Furlough at Fishkills
Corpl Noustrant Sick at Fishkills

Corpl Kip
Abm Riokhow   Sick at Mendham
John Garrison   Hospital
Abm Willis

Sergt Cockran Sick at Chatham

Captn Clarke's Compy

John Mayne
Lot Little   Sick at Ellz: Town
Jerry Ring absent with° leave

Captn Lieut Simonds party
Sergt Fairbrother on Furlough

Captn Jones Compy
John Taylor Matross Sick
     at Princetown

Captn Doughty's Compy
Sergt Seely absent at the
Lines by Genl Knox's leave

Squire Harris
Robt Gilhespy   at Mendham
Danl Smith   Hospital

Establishment of Pay for a Company of Artillery in the Service
of the United States of America

Captain	50 Dollars per °
Captain Lieutenant	40
Four Lieutenants it	33⅓ each
Six Serjeants	10
Six Corporals ⎫	9
Six Bombardiers ⎭	
Six Gunners ⎫	
Drummers ⎬	8⅓d
Fifer ⎭	
Twenty eight Matrosses	8⅓d

Total sixty

Colonel 100   Lieutenant Colonel 75   Major 62½
Conductor of Stores 26 & ⅓d

Direction of letters

Address, Sir

To His Excellency General Washington—or to General Washington Esqr   Commander in chief of all the Forces of the United States of America

To the Honble Major General Green   To the Honble Brigadier General Knox

[Addressed]

To Sabastian Bauman Esq   Commanding the Artillery at Chatham

GENERAL KNOX TO CAPTAIN BAUMAN

Sir,

Morris Town 25th May 1777

Your are with the detachment of Artillery field pieces and ammunition to march to morrow morning for the Camp near Bound Brook

Your route will be by the way of Baskenridge

General Stevens will order a party of Infantry as an escort

If you have any Invalids you are to send them to Morris Town

I am Sir

Your Huble Servt

Capt Bauman   H Knox

[Addressed]

To Capt Bauman of the Artillery Chatham

CHAPTER IX

ALTHOUGH the post at Chatham was commanded by General Sullivan in the winter and spring of 1777, Major-General Adam Stephen of Virginia was also stationed here His stay in this village seems to have been contemporaneous with that of Sullivan, and after the latter's departure, he succeeded to the command of the post He was doubtless accompanied by his staff and bodyguard, and perhaps by a part of his division, but it is doubtful if a considerable number of Virginia troops were stationed in Chatham, as they are thought to have encamped during that winter near Middlebrook A sermon preached to these soldiers by one of their chaplains in the spring of 1777, which was printed in pamphlet form and is still extant, contains a dedication which is dated at Chatham, showing that it was prepared for the press at this place, but whether it was preached here is open to question It is entitled THE LOVE OF OUR COUNTRY, A SERMON PREACHED BEFORE THE VIRGINIA TROOPS IN NEW JERSEY, BY JOHN HURT, CHAPLAIN. The dedication reads as follows

To Major General Stephen, and the Officers and Soldiers of the Fourth, Fifth and Sixth Virginia Battalions
Gentlemen,
In compliance with your request, I have published the following discourse To your patronage it is humbly inscribed, not out of complaisance to your request of publishing it, but from the more

certain testimony of being an eyewitness that you approve its sentiments by your *actions*, For after all the definitions of patriotism that ever was, or ever will be, given, this is the quintessence of it, "The "opposing ourselves foremost in the field of battle against the enemies "of our country"

I am, Gentlemen, with all due respect,

Your fellow soldier and humble servant,

JOHN HURT,[1] *Chaplain*

Chatham, April 20th 1777

The following requisition for supplies required for the military hospital at Chatham is reminiscent of that period It is signed by Edward Duff, surgeon of the Fifth Virginia regiment, and is addressed to John Cochran, who, a few days later, was appointed surgeon-general of the Middle Department

Wanted for the Sick at Chatham.

Sugar one Barrel

Tea six Pounds

Chocolate 12 Pounds

Wine 15 Gallons { Port if to be had, if not to be had Midera

Butter one Furkin

Hogs Lard ~~10~~ 20

EDWARD DUFF

To Ass't Surgeon

Doctor Cochorn

Morris Town

Direct'r of the Hosp'l G l

N B

Please send these necessaries immediately, as the Sick are now in need of them

Indian Meal to Whippeny

To be sent to Chatham

[1] Rev John Hurt was chaplain of Scotts brigade —*Ford's Journals of the Continental Congress, VI, 850*

On the back appears the following in different handwriting.

Sir Please Send to Chatham to Doc'r Duff one Barell Shugar and Eavery other thing that you have thats Rote on this order and Chargue it to the Genrall Hospatell

    To the Com'r G'r 1 Bbl 262 lb Sugar

                FRED MING, D Q M G

Aprill 1, 1777

    I have Deli'r 12 lb Lard

        6 lb Tea

                  Addressed

                      Doctor Cochoin

                      Morris Town

Endorsed.

    Gen'l Hospital [1]

Another reference to the hospital at Chatham is found in the diary of Lieutenant Ebenezer Elmer, who, in May, 1777, served as surgeon's mate under Dr Lewis Holwell of Shreve's regiment Elmer at that time was stationed at Spanktown (Rahway), and was in sole charge of the sick at Westfield, whom he was accustomed to visit every day He writes in his journal

Sunday, May 25th This morning we were alarmed before day by the Pennsylvania troops, which were moving towards Westfield and leaving the lines below entirely bare About 8 o'clock I set out for Westfield to see the sick, but when I came there they were all moved off to Chatham, and the troops, stores & every thing gone off from here to Bound Brook [2]

Some wartime letters written at Chatham during Stephen's sojourn in the village are given below. The first consists of a communication to the *Virginia Gazette*

[1] New Jersey Historical Society Proceedings, Ser 3, VI, 12
[2] New Jersey Historical Society Proceedings, Ser 1, III, 99

Chatham (N Jersey) Feb 15, 1777

To Messrs Dixon and Hunter,

Gentlemen —

General Stephen's brigade has engaged the enemy's strong foraging parties three several times lately and, with sustaining but little loss, did them very considerable damage On the first inst. they treated some of our wounded, who had the misfortune to fall into their hands, with the most savage barbarity—in consequence of that, the General wrote a letter to Sir William Erskine, a copy of which, and Sir William's answer have done myself the pleasure to enclose you

We lost that day two gallant officers Adjutant Kelly, of the 5th Virginia regiment, and Lieutenant Gregory of the 6th   Our hickory hearts, as usual, behaved like heroes, ninety of them, under the command of the brave Colonel Scott, beat at fair cutting, 230 of their best troops

I am, very respectfully,

Your obedient servant,

ROBERT FORSYTHE,
B Maj to Gen Stephen [1]

A communication to the *Pennsylvania Journal* of March 26, 1777, is also quoted

Chatham (New Jersey) March 10, 1777

Messrs Bradfords

Moved by duty to my country, & from a grateful respect for merit, I desire to acquaint the public through your paper, that Col Potter and Major Robinson with the officers and men of the Northumberland militia, under their command, have distinguished themselves in the most assiduous and active service, during this winter's campaign, and that they have deservedly received the repeated thanks of General Sullivan, General Maxwell, and my self under whose more immediate command they have so faithfully served

I am your's, &c

ADAM STEPHEN, Major General

[1] Almon's Remembrancer, IV, 213

GENERAL STEPHEN TO MAJOR ANGUS McDONALD

Dear Col

His Excellency General Washington has appinted you Lieu Col. ot a regiment to be raised in Virginia and commanded by Col Thurston   I desire you will not decline it   it is more honerable than if you had been appointed by convention or Committee, as their appointments are influenced by party or private views too often   Your appointment comes entirely from your own merit   Your Highland pride may stare you in the face and hellow out   Shall I serve under a ***de*   it is incompatable with my mistaken honor, merit, services, &c &c &c   I desire you will only Remember that in *br'y ** I was nothing in a Military way : in less than a year I was a col—Brigadier —Major General   Had not my attachment to the Interests of America been superior to all Scrupolosity, I would have now been poking at home about the mill—the times require active men and the useful will be promoted and employed—it is Merit not sin**sity that will be attended to in the time of distress

As to your having engaged in the Sheriff's Business—This year's collections will be finished before the Regiments can be raised—and tor the next year's collection, the Doctor and you can put it on a different footing   While you **g*e about collecting you can be recruiting   I am desirous to have you and Col Thurston told me he would rather give a hundred guineas than you should decline & I am in hopes you will find it consistent with your interest   But should you be obstinate—G-d forbid   Write a polite letter to General Washington thanking his excellency for his notice and making the best excuse you can

I am Dear Col

Yours affectionately

ADAM STEPHEN

Chatham, March 15

P S

Fighting is now become so familiar that unless it is a very great affair we do not think it worth mentioning   I shall only mention that my Division is an excellent school for a young soldier   We only fight eight or ten times aw***—in short I have got my men in such spirits—that they only ask when the enemy come out and where

they are—without enquiring into their numbers and so tall on We
have killed Jack Hall—you remember him—he was an old Capt in
the 52d Regt [1]

GENERAL STEPHEN TO GENERAL WASHINGTON

Sir,

Inclosed I send Your Excellency a Return of the men of my
division, exclusive of General Maxwells Brigade, of which I have
got no return yet

I go on the Out posts to day and do not approve of the mens
being so dispersd as not to be Able to support one Another The
troops at Quibbletown were kept in awe by Appearances yesterday,
had they happily reinforced their pickets a little, or Show'd some
men dispersd behind them here & there, & marchd to the Rear to
Bound Brook—Their appearance would probably have occasioned a
precipitate Retreat of the Enemy.

There is a Certain Capt Russel who commanded a Company
raisd in Loudon County for a Year only—He is now come up to
this place, & has been in Binny Coty since we arrivd in October,
but never joined us before, nor has he done a days duty, these Six
months Has no Company The men have all gone home, except a
few which are inlisted into other Companies His Lt Mucklehanny
is likewise here—he has been all Winter wt the S [*illegible*] at Wil-
mington I would be glad to have your Excellency Orders about
them Col Johnston knows these GentMen They never applyd
for Orders to go Recruiting, & the time of their Companies Service
expird in February and I dare say many of them Stragled home
without being paid, Which hurts the recruiting greatly

I expect some intelligence from York—Paulus Hook, Bergen &
Staaten Island, & have the honour to be Sir,

Your most Obt Ser,

ADAM STEPHEN

Chatham 14th April '77

p s

Our people Catchd another of the Wretches in Cedar Swamp
If your Excellency has no particular Commands at present I think

[1] *Pennsylvania Magazine of History,* XV, 243

it best that General Mulhenberg should go on the Lines get acquainted with ye Country, & a habit of looking at the Enemy [1]

COLONEL JOHNSTON TO GENERAL STEPHEN

Headquarters Morris Town 14th April 1777.

Dear Sir

Your favour of this date was delivered to his Excellency this
Moment   I have it in Orders from him to inform you, that he
directs a Court of Inquiry may immediately examine into Capt
Russell's behaviour, of which Report must be made, to enable his
Excelly to form some Idea of the Measures proper to be adopted
respecting him

His Excellency thinks, That Genl Muhlenberg can & will be
of much greater advantage to the service by equipping & preparing
his Brigade for the Field, than getting acquainted with the Lines,
in which nothing will be done after the Enemy take the Field   Genl
Muhlenberg will therefore attend to the orders he received yesterday

The great difference in the state of Rawlings' Battalion between
the last Retn & that of about a Month past & which was the subject
of a letter to you some time since, His Excellency wishes to have
accounted for

Lieut Bradford of Capt Smith's Compy in the same Battn
has been here to excuse his absence from duty since December last
His Excelly will determine nothing 'till you (after making Inquiry)
by means of the same Court that examines Capt Russell—report how
the Affair stands

I am Dr Sir

Yr most obedt Servt

GEO JOHNSTON, A D C [2]

FINDINGS OF A COURT OF INQUIRY

A Court of inquiry held at Chatham the 17th April 1777 by
order of Major Genl Stephen for Several purposes therein containd

[1] Washington Papers in the Library of Congress, 14, 271
[2] Washington Papers in the Library of Congress, B III, pt 1, 69

Present

Colo Geo Mathews Pr

Lt Colo Parker	Capt Long
Capt Parramore &	Lt Waring

On Enquiry into the absence of Lt Bradford, the Court find that Mr Bradford was sick about the 8th of Decr 1776 & apply'd to Capt Long of his Regiment for leave to look for quarters, that Capt Long referred him to Genl Mercer who commanded the Brigade who gave him leave to find sick quarters in the Neighbourhood of Trenton ferry where his Brigade at that time layd

That Mr Bradford instead of getting quarters thereabout went off to Maryland where he remain'd untill the 27th of March 1777 at which time he joind his regiment at Chatham

Lt Bradford pleads sickness as an excuse for his Absence The Court find by the Regimental returns of Colo Rawlings Battn that Lt Bradford was returnd absent without leave

The Court then resumed the other part of Genl Stephens' order, with respect to Capt Russell As no particular charge is laid against that Gentleman the Court are at a loss in what manner to proceed on an enquiry into his Conduct

We find the difference of late in Colo Rawlings Regimental returns owing to the return of Lt Bradford—one seigt & 5 privates who was reported absent without leave in that Regiment

GEO MATHEWS Prd[1]

GENERAL STEPHEN TO GENERAL WASHINGTON

Chatham 20th April 1777

Sir,

Inclosed is an Acct of Capt Beals Expedition The firing heard when I expected Capt Bell was attacked, was their New Recruits exersising

The Enemy came out from Amboy yesterday Six miles took a light horse man belonging to the Jersies & Returned again with Impunity The mans horse was worth £120 I am told Genl Vaughan was out, & the Brave Capt Conways house & plantation was burnt under the Genl Eye G Maxwell & my Self had resolved on Retaliation as your Excellency will observe by a Copy of the pass

[1] Washington Papers in the Library of Congress, 15, 2

intended for Mrs Smith, However tho' perfectly Sensible of the Extensive influence it would have had, over Tories, Whigs & our Enemies, if any Spark of humanity Remains with them—yet, Suspecting that we might have been Accused of doing it wantonly, as we had not Consulted Your Excellency—We have hitherto let it alone

The reason I can possibly give for the Enemys returning with impunity, is our people not being Acquainted wt the County or their not Attending to their knowledge of it properly

I shall hear I expect from N York to morrow, & from Brunswick on Tuesday

I have the honour to be Sir

Your most oht Sert

ADAM SILPHEN

p s

Some Recruits are embodying for our Service about Hackensack. Shall I detail some men to join them, & beat up Col Beards Quarters at Hoebuck [1]

MILITARY PASS

Mrs Smith has been indulged in living happily at home, ever Since her husband deserted the Interests of America

Her house being now burnt, in retaliation for the loss of Capt Conways house & plantation burnt up this Afternoon, Under the Eye of Genl Vaughan—

Mrs Smith is permitted to go to the Same General for Accommodation [2]

GENERAL STEPHEN TO RICHARD HENRY LEE

Dear Sir—

I languished to hear from you, and at last received the pleasure of your letter yesterday .The sending Americans to their antipodes, was as wicked and extensive a plan, as the agents of the devil could form on earth I suppose the intended attack on our state, is a creature of the volatile Burgoyne, engendered on Lady Dunmore

---

[1] Washington Papers in the Library of Congress, 14, 311
[2] Washington Papers in the Library of Congress, 15, 1

or his Lordship, who doubtless will attend with his council, in order to add some more oderiferous beauties to his Ethiopian seraglios

Should they get the troops, which I reckon impossible, they may distress individuals, but can do nothing towards conquering our country   To prevent this attack, and obviate all difficulty, our present object ought to be the destruction of their army in the Jerseys Virtue is certainly wanting, or we should have had men enough to have effected it before this time   The Virginians, with a few Jersey men, and as few Pennsylvanians, are likely to bear the burden of the day, the myriads of the north, the great warriors, who were to do the business, if we found money, seem cloyed of fighting, and are wonderfully backward in turning out   I wish no attention had been given to the defense of the western frontier, further than having the militia supplied with ammunition and embodied   The clouds which threaten from Canada and the savages, and all other *petites*, would have dispersed yea, dissolved like meteors, upon the destruction of Howe's army

On Monday, the 14th, I resolved the enemy should make compensation for their excursion to Boundbrook, I went along the out posts of my division, with General Maxwell and planned the attack of their pickets, at Amboy and Bonum town   Captain Conway, of the first Jersey regiment, behaved to admiration, brought off three out sentries without disturbing the guard and got the countersign, in short he had nothing to do but kill or bring off fifty men of the picket, when he was unhappily abandoned by the men of the second Jersey regiment, and obliged to drop the affair

The attack at Bonum town, was more successful, the picket were all taken or killed except three

I am, with great esteem, dear sir,

Your most obedient humble servant,

ADAM STEPHEN
Chatham, April 22d 1777.

Colonel Richard Henry Lee,
in Congress Philadelphia [1]

[1] Lee's Richard Henry Lee II

GENERAL STEPHEN TO GENERAL WASHINGTON

Chatham, 23d April, 1777

Sir,

The next important Intelligence 1 rec'd from N York, was of a certain Conquest of America before October

Betts of 100 Guneas to 1, that Genl Howe would be in philadelphia the 1st of May

The Scarcity of timber & plank at York has prevented the finishings of the Bridge of Boats

Naval Stores So Scarce that they cannot fit out their transports for their Return home

Tar 5 Guneas p Barrel, Flour very plenty, & twelve months Salt provisions for 20,000 Men Sailors Scarce & Sickly aboard their Ships

On the 16th Between 40 & 50 Sail of Vessels saild, as was reported aboard the Ships, & in the City, for Halifax under Convoy of the Tarter   Uncertain whether there were troops aboard or not. It is said they went for Coal & forrage

Twelve large Ships arrivd at York from England on the 21st Uncertain what they had on board   The Number of Tory Regiments at Bergen Confirmd

The Preston Commodore Hotham has taken a privateer Brig of 16 Guns fitted out at Charleston S Carolina

It is said that Delancy Brigade has Orders to Embark for S Carolina

They Intend to Waggon their boats from Brunswick   These goes into Each other & all into a Waggon   Their Horse, Grenadiers & light Infantry, on the flanks of the Convoy   May Heaven blast their purposes! We cannot boast of the Arm of flesh, so many Arms are Weakly from Inoculation & otherwise

They say the Continental Army Consists of 5,000 men, & that no more Can be raisd for Continental Money

I have the honour to be Sir

Your most Obt

ADAM STEPHEN

P S

This will be deliverd to Your Excellency by Capt Mathews of

the 4th the fittest Officer I am acquainted with for a Major of a Regimt or Brigade

[Addressed]

To His Excellency General Washington [1]

GENERAL STEPHEN TO AN UNNAMED ADDRESSEE

Chatham 23d April 1777

Sir

By———— from B———k I have advice that Eight hundred men came in the Ships from England   There is a Report that Rhode Island is to be Evacuated, but no account of the Arrival of the troops   The 15th & 27th did duty at York & my friend was uncertain is to the names of the 36th & 4th mentioned from Newark yesterday

Ten Boats for the Bridges are arrived at Brunswick, $16\frac{1}{3}$ foot in length four feet wide & $2\frac{1}{2}$ deep, Waggons are fitting up for their Carriage

Genl Skinners force consists of about 1,000, to be joind by Some regular troops, & to proceed from Bergen through Sussex & the back posts of the Jerseys, when the troops march for Philadelphia

The Enemy have their provisions convoyd into the Delaware by Water.

The Sick Sent from the Jerseys to N York

Brunswick not to be Evacuated

Thomas Long, not an American, nicknamed Bunk Eye, from his prominent Eyes, height $5\frac{1}{2}$ feet, age upwards of forty, Wears Whitish Cloaths, rather fair Complexion, He was Schoolmaster Near Raway, distressed the Inhabitants on the passage of the B troops through the Jerseys   He is gone for Philadelphia as a Spy, two days ago   He Associates with Quakers   It would be of importance to seize him, as the Enemy is much in want of Intelligence from that City   He has been there three times

Other Matters in their former State

I have got a York paper of the 17th, nothing Material but the great Success of the B Brick Expedition

[1] Washington Papers in the Library of Congress, 152, IV, 107

I will forward it, after learning a prayer that is in it, & am with great Respect Sr

Your most Ob' hul Sv

ADAM STEPHEN

The Enemy attempted Retaliation the Night before last, but were beat back, pursued, & kept up all night   By a person from B town They had one Man killd & 2 wounded   We sufferd none Majr Crawford of ct troops behavd well

They Report in Brunswick, that they have killed 100 & taken 200 more, & that the highlanders have got ample satisfaction for the loss of their picket.

The Enemy Cannot be Ready to March this Week   They intend an Excursion for horses   All Should be orderd back from the Lines [1]

GENERAL STEPHEN TO GENERAL WASHINGTON

Chatham 12th May 1777.

Sir

I can now with propriety Congratulate your Excellency on a Certain and Considerable Advantage gaind over the Enemys best troops, by the Continental Troops of My Division

Col Cooks Prov Rgt begun the Attack, supported by the 1 Regt of that State, they behavd well, & the Captains Chambers & Par distinguished themselves

Capt Phelps of Col Wards Regimt behaved well & the few men that were with him did honour to the Corps

The Combatants in the first Onset were within 50 yards   Some of them nearer, & None further off than 100 yards

The Conflict continued half An hour, when the Enemy gave way, leaving three Officers & thirty Nine men dead on the ground our people took possession of

The Enemy were Reinforced, & the Continental troops Supported by 150 Virginians Compelld them to give way again, wt Considerable loss, but as the Action had by this time Continued upwards of an hour, & our Videt discovered about 2,000 men within a quarter of a Mile, on their way from Brunswick

[1] Washington Papers in the Library of Congress, CC 152, 4, 103

The troops were prudently withdrawn, in the very Nick of time

We have three killd, three officers & 12 privates Wounded a Leut of Capt Chambers Company [*illegible*] & 4 men taken We have lost Several Straglers taken plundering the Dead   I am Convinced the Enemy have at least 200 killd & Wounded

It was a Bold Enterprise   It was the time & Rapidity of the Attack that Secured us the Success we met with

I have the honour to be Si

your most Obt hubl Ser,

ADAM STEPHEN

[Addressed]

To His Excellency General Washington

[Indorsed]

From Genl Stephen with an Acct of the Attack upon Piscataway General Stephens May 12th 1777 relating to an attack upon Bonum Town [1]

GENERAL WASHINGTON TO GENERAL STEPHEN

Morris Town 12th May 1777

To M General Stephen

Dear Sir

Your account of the attempt upon the Enemy at Piscataway is favourable, but I am sorry to add, widely different from those I have had from others, (officers of distinction) who were of the party I cannot by them learn, that there is the least certainty of the Enemy's leaving half the slain upon the Field you speak of in your letter of this date, that instead of an orderly retreat, it was (with the greatest part of the detachment) a disorderly route, and, that the disadvantage was on our side, not the Enemy's, who had notice of your coming and was prepared for it, as I expected

I am &ca

Go WASHINGTON [2]

GENERAL STEPHEN TO GENERAL WASHINGTON

Chatham 14th May 1777

Sir,

I reced the honour of your Letter last night   Your Excellency

---

[1] Washington Papers in the Library of Congress, 15, 166
[2] Washington Papers in the Library of Congress, B III, 150

has not seen an Officer that was in the Action Saturday Night   They were of the party, but to their Staying at Such a distance from the Scene of Action The Surviving Highlanders owe their Existence.

I took delight in mentioning the Troops to your Excellency who distinguished themselves   The Reverse gives me pain, hoping that time, Attention, & habit, will improve us   Whether owing to the order in the field, or to what, I am uncertain, but one half of the troops were not Engaged, & never had the ground gaind from the Enemy

Time will discover the Loss of the Enemy a more Accurate Acct than I had, is Seldom Obtaind

The troops who Stayd a Quarter or near half a mile in the rear must needs have run damnd hard to retreat by the way the troops engaged did   But the fighting troops Were halted a Considerable time on a Rising ground untill they Had an Opportunity of Coming off

I can assure your Excellency from Intelligence that has never faild or disappointed me, that the Boats for the Bridge, are taken out of the Waggons, & put in the Water   The Expression of a Certain Officer of great Rank is "Sir Wm Howe has been pleasd to lay aside the Expedition of philadelphia at present, that Troops were daily expected on to fill all the Regiments, & 6000 of a Reinforcement   Then they should Work us"

They do intend an Attack on Bound Brook   they have had Spies out, Observing their Cannon, Encampment, and the first thing they do is to take possession of the [Moun]tain, with a Body of troops in one of these [illegible]   They have procured good Guides for the purpose

Genl Lord Cornwallis, the Genls Grant, Mathews, & Lessly Sir William Colier & Sir George Osburn, were Reconntrg the ground about Drakes farm on Munday

They have pulld down the fences, & thrown Cut [illegible] into the hollows for ¾ of a Mile round

They talk of bringing their troops into more Compact Order, that they may be more Capable of acting either on the defensive or Offensive for this purpose the destroying Raritan Bridge is in Agitation, & forming a Bridge of Boats at Brunswick

The above Intelligence I esteem Certain & of the Utmost importance

I am with great Respect Sr

Your most Obt hubl Serv

ADAM STEPHEN

P S

I beg your Excellency will not countenance the Story of Officers at M [*illegible*] town whose Regts were on the Lines, nor permit Officers to go home without ordering them of my division to Acquaint me Col Harkins had orders to move near to Bonum Town Sunday he sent me word that he was just Setting off for Virginia [Addressed]

To His Excellency General Washington [1]

SAME TO THE SAME

Sir

The General Court Martial yesterday seemd to hurry over Business without that Solemn Attention that is necessary to Command Respect & establish discipline

I orderd Doctor Griffith to be Summond to appear agt Capt Russel, Who had been frequently at philadelphia, & seen the Capt appearing abroad wt a healthy Countenance He was not Summond The Captain notwithstanding the Repeated orders for all Officers to join their Corps, passd Six months wtout seeing Us untill his Company had disappeard, we cant tell how or where, and Docr Griffith informs me that to get his Company & Secure Rank which he has not yet Merited by his Service, he Inlisted his Company for One Year only

The Court has clard Lt Gill for going to Virga wtout leave upon his Saying that he had leave from Capt Fox & although Fox could not give him leave, he never showd this Leave to the Court With what Countenance Can Soldiers be punishd for neglect of Duty, if the Officers escape wt impunity ? Gill had not done duty for Six months I had given him leave to go home for his health from Portsmouth

The Tory Regiment made an Excursion as far as Acquaquen-

[1] Washington Papers in the Library of Congress, 15, 185

nonk & two nights ago Commg Off Capt Marinus & Several others
I take a tour to day by Newark & Elisabethtown, for Intelligence &c
I have a great passion to wait upon the Tory Regiment, who are so
mischievous to that Neighbourhood

I should think it advisable that Genl Herd should move his
Quarters frequently, Taking post for a short time about Hackensack,
Then down on Barbados Neck, Then to his old post again   The
men will be more healthy, & the Enemy more puzzled

My Confidential Servant informd me that Several Captains &
Lieutenants in the British Army at Brunswick are going to Embark
for Britain, That officers & men are tired of the Service, That mixing
with the men at a game at Coits, he heard them say, there were
numbers of Rebels in England, that one half of the City of London,
was of the same way of thinking wt the Americans

I have the honour to be Sir,
your most Obt hubl Servt
ADAM STEPHEN

Chatham 15th May 1777
The Virginians laid in Ambuscade apprehended the Deserter &
we had him tryd yesterday   They impute the Discipline to Tryon
I have ordered all Sallies oft the Lines
[Addressed]
To His Excellency General Washington [1]

SAME TO THE SAME

Chatham 17th May 1777
Sir
This moment arrived   I have learnd that the Hessians em-
barked in the Boats mentioned in my last, amount to about 350
That the troops sent over to the Jerseys was not so much to Execute
any present Enterprise, as to guard agt one   As soon as the Enemy
understood that the Artillery & troops were moved from Newark,
They immediately gave orders for There troops to proceed to the
Jerseys   It was reported here that M G Tryon was dead   He
is neither dead nor wounded

There is not above 800 Effectives in N York   The Circum-

[1] Washington Papers in the Library of Congress, 15, 209

stance which gives the greatest pleasure & Discovers the situation of the Enemy more Clearly, is, that the people formerly Attachd to Governmt, are become our friends, & would willingly leave N York if they Could

On Tuesday last 40 of the Enemy most dangerously wounded on Saturday were Carryd into N York

Maji Fraser of the 2d Batt of the 71t & Capt Stewart of the Light Infantry were wounded

Bergen is in the same Situation as formerly It must be Attempted to morrow night, or the Tide will not Answer again for a Week Can so many men be spared from the Lines?

I have a deserter from Bergen here, but he is so drunk, I have ordered him to sleep

I hope a parcel of these deserters will be hangd one on Every Road leading to the Enemys posts

I have the honour to be Sr

your Excellency's Most obt hubl Serv
ADAM STEPHEN

[Addressed]

His Excellency General Washington [1]

GENERAL WASHINGTON TO GENERAL STEPHEN

Head Quarters Morris Town 17th May 1777.

Sir

Yours with the plan for the attack upon Bergen is this moment come to hand I see many difficulties to prevent the matters being carried effectually into execution The first and principal one is, the known disaffection of the Country, which is such, that the instant such a Body as one thousand Men began to assemble the Enemy would have notice of it, and the consequence would be, that were they strong enough they would prepare themselves to give you a Reception, and were they not, they would retreat from Bergen to Paulus Hook, and after they got beyond the Hills it would be impossible for you to follow them These have ever been my Sentiments upon this matter The thing must be effected by Surprise or not at all, and I have no conception that Boats sufficient for the purpose could be

[1] Washington Papers in the Library of Congress, W

collected, and such a Body of men embarked without the Enemy's having notice of it

In my opinion theretore, the Enterprise had better be laid aside, for I really think it would end in our being worsted, if the Enemy were prepared to receive us, or of their getting out of our way if they were not

I am Sir Yr most obt Servt

Go WASHINGTON

[Addressed]

Major Genl Stephen
        Chatham [1]

GENERAL STEPHEN TO GENERAL WASHINGTON

Chatham 24th May 1777

Sir,

I wrote Your Excellency last Night from Col Shrives's Quarters, where I was Concerting Measures for attacking the Enemys Camp near Amboy, before they had all left the Town, or could get the Camp fortifyd, when I was disconcerted, by receiving the enclosd from Genl Mullenberg, & advice of the same sort from Genl Maxwell

This Manoeuvre is of very extensive Consequence   It gives the Enemy Command of the Country

There is not a Sentry between the Pickets of this place and Amboy

Traitors have no interruption in Corresponding with, or Supplying the Enemy with provisions

They may make themselves masters of Westfield where we have Some Stores, of Springfield where we have an hospital of 25 Sick & wounded & Parrels troop of horse without arms

They will Certainly overrun Newark & Elisabethtown at the Latter I by the Address of Col Spencer had Settled a Certain Correspondence wt N York & Staaten Island   An Authentic Correspondence is of immense advantage

And the Enemy taking possession of these places again tho' of no great importance, Will make a figure in their pompus Announciations from St James's

[1] Washington Papers in the Library of Congress, B III, pt 1, 174

Unless the Enemy is immediately attack'd to Advantage I am apprehensive we shall lose Credit by this Movement

I forgot to mention last Night that a French Ship is taken & Carry'd into N York, the day before yisterday, with Seventy men on board   What they are, or what the transport had aboard we expect to hear in a few days

The Boats intended for the Bridge, ly below the New Bridge at Brunswick in the River

Not the least appearance of a Movement   They are employ'd in levelling the Streets of Brunswick

A new Redoubt, with Cannon, erected, about 1 mile N W of this Side of the End of the New Bridge

They are more Strict than formerly in admitting people   The Common Soldiers are damning the French for Supplying Us, & there is a Report amongst them, That the Duke of Richmond & Ld Camb-den are sent to the Tower

I have the honour to be Sr

> Your most Ob hu Ser
>
> ADAM STEPHEN

Chatham 24th May 1777
[Addressed]

His Excellency George Washington [1]

FROM THE *PENNSYLVANIA GAZETTE*, MAY 28th 1777

Extract of a letter from the Jersies dated Chatham, May 19

"Since my last, a considerable number of General Stephen's division, being hastily assembled from the different posts attacked the 42d, 2d battalion of the 71st and 33d, and six companies of light infantry, posted at Bonum-town, Piscataway, and in that neighbour-hood   It was a bold enterprize as the enemy might be easily rein-forced from Brunswick, the Landing, or Amboy   We had learned the hour of their dining, and gave them time to take a drink 'rd made a sudden attack upon them about half an hour after four Among their killed were Major M'Pherson 3 Subalterns 3 Ser-geants, and as we are informed by a person from Piscataway, 60 privates   Major Frazer of the 71st and Capt Stewart of the light

[1] Washington Papers in the Library of Congress, 15 298

intantry wounded   It is said 120 privates were wounded, 40 of them
dangerously, and carried to New York   We lost 2 killed, 1 Captain,
3 Subalterns, 11 privates wounded, 1 Subaltern dangerously wounded, and taken with about 12 of his division

'This great advantage gained over the best of the enemy, has
compelled them to send from New-York, one battalion of Hessian
Grenadiers the 10th and 55th British regiments, to reinforce those
posts "

We do not know how long General Stephen remained
at Chatham in the early part of 1777 but, although it is
unlikely that he stayed here continuously, he seems to have
made this place his headquarters until the latter part of
May That he was here as early as January—not long
after Washington established his winter quarters at Morristown—is indicated by the mention of his name in the
following order, which was directed to Brigadier-General
John Cadwalader, commanding a brigade of Pennsylvania
troops at Morristown

Sir
     March your Brigade from hence to Chatham or the Posts below
that   Consult Genls Sullivan and Stephen upon the Propriety of an
attempt upon any of the Enemy's Posts —or giving them a formidable
alarm—and, if you shd find a willingness in your officers and Men
to the undertaking of any practicable Scheme, do not omit, in conjunction with the Troops at the Posts of Chatham &co to prosecute
it   Genl Sullivan is already wrote to on this head
     From thence you are at liberty to March your Brigade to Phila-
delphia and when they are dismissed, communicate to them my
Sense (contain'd in an address to yourself) of the Important Services
they have rendered their Country at this severe & inclemant Season
                    Given at head Quarters,
                  Morris Town this 23d day of Jany, 1777
                          GO WASHINGTON [1]

[1] Pennsylvania Magazine of History, XXXII, 164

Cadwalader's brigade was styled "The Associators of the City and Liberties of Philadelphia " It was organized in that city when the news of the fight at Lexington was received, and originally consisted of three separate battalions, of which the third, numbering about 500 men, was commanded by Cadwalader who then held the rank of colonel This battalion was called the "Greens," in reference to the color of its uniform, but it was perhaps better known as the "Silk Stockings," a name suggested by its aristocratic connections, many of the leading families of Philadelphia being represented in its ranks Toward the end of July, 1776, the Associators joined Washington's army, and, at the suggestion of the commander-in-chief, they were reformed into a single brigade under Cadwalader, who was promoted to the rank of brigadier-general, Lieutenant-Colonel John Nixon succeeding him in command of the third battalion The Associators fought bravely at Princeton, and remained in winter quarters at Morristown for a few weeks, but they seem to have rendered no other services of importance except at Valley Forge during the winter of 1778 [1]

The movement of these troops from Morristown to Chatham, in compliance with the above order to General Cadwalader, is described in the diary of William Young, a sergeant of Captain Thomas Fitzsimmons's company in Colonel Nixon's battalion An excerpt, commencing at Morristown on January 22, 1777, is quoted While the brigade remained at Chatham, Sergeant Young, with others, was billeted in the house of Enos Ward, which is still standing on the northerly side of Main Street a short distance west of Elmwood Avenue

Wed 22 At twelve came orders to hold ourselves in Readiness to march to-morrow.

Thurs 23 All hands getting Ready for a march, being under orders to march at 9 o'clock Set out about 12 Reached

[1] Hart's Nixon, Wharton's Colonial Days and Dames 145, 185

Bottel town marched on to Chatam town   There halted and went
into Quarters   It is now snowing   Great firing heard at near Brunswick   This town is   miles from Morriston   The Mistress
of the house kindly Let me and son Lay in her Room by the fire-side
for which favor I Desire to be thankful   Mr Towers continues to
be very Bad   Our people are Buying Rum of a New England man
The man of the house is very friendly   Our people are very unruly
and almost beyond Shame   A great Deal of Swearing amongst them
all   The whole Brigade is very uneasy on account of our Route
Some Swear they will go home To-morrow by themselves   We are
now about 14 miles from Elizabethtown near forty from Princetown,
25 from Brunswick   Our road Leads within 8 or 9 miles from
Brunswick   I fear all our men are not honest   What a wretch is
man   Death that should effect a soldier more Immediately, yet he
must be doing Mischief with some of our company   There are some
that cannot let anything Lay that comes in their way   For in this
house one of them was Detected in taking a gammon out of the
Cellar   Great God make us Better men   Renew us by thy Holy
Spirit   Convince us of sin in all its shapes, and Bring us near thyself
In Mercy change our hearts, and then and not till then shall we do
as we would be done by   Grant this for Jesus Sake, Amen and Amen

Friday 24   Slept But Indifferently   Rose before day   It
Snowed all night   This Morning it turned to Rain and very Sloppy,
it being the day we were to March home   Our company are uneasy
to be home, but it being Sloppy agree to stay a day or two Longer
in hopes it will be clear weather.   One of our men had taken from
Mr Enos Ward, the Master of the house where we are Quartered, 2
Gammons out of the Cellar, and secreted a pair of Breeches, and
an under Jackets, all of which were proved on him (Joseph Crovat)
Mr Enos Ward appears to be a kind friendly man, a shoe Maker by
trade   Mr John Towers continues to be very Bad   The Doctor
has been with him   Breakfasted with [the] man of the house with
my son, for which I paid 1 / 8   News just came that our people yesterday near Brunswick attacked the Regulars, then made a hasty
Retreat which Drew them into an Ambush when our people surrounded them, Killed a good number, took 1500 prisoners   Our
people were under the command of General Sullivan   Praise be to
thee O God!   How many of our people are Lost I know not.   It

HOME OF CAPTAIN ENOS WARD
From a Recent Photograph.
Owned by the Ward Family until 1904, when it was sold by Raphael H. Ward the Captain's Great-Grandson

stills Rains, and like to Rain all Day It is now very Sloppy and like to be more so as the Snow melts As soon as it clears up we purpose to Set out for home if heaven permits [1]

Sergeant Young's company set out a little after 8 o'clock the next morning, marching by way of Pluckamin and Lamington

In April, 1777, the name of Henry Lee appears in connection with the history of Chatham This gallant young soldier was then a captain in Colonel Theodoric Bland's (the First) regiment of Continental light dragoons, and it was not until a later date that he was promoted to the rank of major, and won undying fame as "Light-Horse Harry," the commander of the celebrated partisan legion Two of his letters are reproduced They are addressed to Colonel Bland at Morristown, and allude to the latter's order that he should take post at Chatham

Boundbrook, April 18th 1777

Dear Colonel

Your favor by Lt Payton, I received yesterday, am much obliged to you for your favorable sentiments of me and mine I find my station is Chatham, you require that I march thro' Morristown How happy would I be, if it was possible for my men to be furnished with caps and boots, prior to my appearance at head quarters You know, dear colonel, that, justly, an officer's reputation depends not only on the discipline, but appearance of his men Could the articles mentioned be allowed my troop, their entrance into Morris would secure me from the imputation of carelessness, as their captain, and I have vanity to hope would assist in procuring some little credit to their colonel and regiment Pardon my solicitations on any head, respecting the conditions of my troop, my sole object is the credit of the regiment.

Yours, affec't etc

[1] Pennsylvania Magazine of History, VIII, 272

Bound Brook, April 25th 1777

Dear Col

I cannot but blush when your letter to Captain Harrison reminds me of my neglect in [not] sending up the pay roll of my troop for the present month I have no excuse to plead, but the incessant duty with which I have been occupied, by order of General Lincoln It is enclosed in this letter As it will arrive at the paymaster's quarters before Captain Dandridge's possibly can, the real damage will be none, but the example is injurious to order and unpardonable

On receiving the late regimental orders, by which my troop was ordered to Chatham, I acquainted General Lincoln of my removal. He required me to tarry a day or two till he could hear from Col Bland, to whom he intended to write The purport of his letter was to request my detention with him I thanked the general for his politeness, tho' did not require his intercession with you on that head, fearing lest I might be accused of local partiality, which I conceive improper in any officer On your answer's coming to hand, I sent out my quartermaster sergeant, with his supernumeries this morning, expecting to follow this day with my troop The general still detains me His reason, I believe, is an attempt meditated against the Hessian picquet It will be executed on Saturday night On Sunday I hope to arrive at my station

I have mentioned these matters to you, that you may know the real cause of my tarrying here, and not be induced to judge me as acting with impropriety

Your most obt servant and affectionate friend, etc [1]

During the following July Chatham was occupied for a few days by Colonel Daniel Morgan and his battalion of skirmishers—"Morgan's Rangers," as they are known in history—whose daring exploits and romantic adventures give them the pre-eminence of the various commands of the Revolutionary army Some uncertainty exists concerning Morgan's birthplace, though it is generally supposed that he was a native of New Jersey, and the assertion has been

[1] Campbell's The Bland Papers, I, 51, 53

made that he was born in or near Morristown;[1] but at an
early age he became a resident of Frederick (now Clarke)
County, Virginia, and he served in the militia of that State,
at first as a teamster and private, and finally as an ensign,
during the French and Indian War, having joined Brad-
dock's expedition at the age of seventeen He commenced
his Revolutionary career soon after the outbreak of hostilities as captain of a rifle company which he himself had
raised and later was commissioned by the Continental
Congress colonel of the Eleventh Virginia regiment In the
spring of 1777 a corps of sharp shooters was formed, consisting of five hundred picked men carefully selected from
the best regiments of the various States, and Morgan was
placed in command Washington directed this corps to act
as a body of light infantry, exempting it from the common
duties of the line [2] It was divided into eight companies, the
principal officers at the time of its formation being Lieutenant-Colonel Richard Butler of Pennsylvania and Major
Joseph Morris of New Jersey [3]

Not only was Morgan's battalion of the greatest service in general action, but it is declared to have formed a
better corps of skirmishers than had ever been attached to
any army, even in Europe Its value and efficiency were soon
recognized, and a system of independent rifle corps was
adopted by both British and Americans, especially in the
South

Morgan's Rangers played a conspicuous part in the
campaign of 1777 in eastern New Jersey, and were highly
commended in official reports On June 30th the British
withdrew to Staten Island, thus terminating the border
warfare which had continued in New Jersey since the first of
January, and it was after their departure that Morgan led

---

[1] Barber's New Jersey Historical Collections, 395
[2] Sparks' Writings of Washington, IV, 461
[3] Graham's Morgan, 122, Walton's U S Army and Navy, I, 54

his command to Chatham   Here he remained about a week,
awaiting orders to determine his further movements   These
orders, written by Washington's aides-de-camp, are given
below   The Lott farm, at which the first is dated, was near
Troy, N J

COLONEL TILGHMAN TO COLONEL DAYTON

Mr Lott's Farm, 11th July 1777

Dear Sir,

The Army marched from Morris Town this Morning with
intent to move towards the Clove, if therefore you obtain any
further intelligence, you are to send it after us   The Army will
halt this Evening near Rockaway Bridge[1] and will move forward
in the Morning except any fresh accounts should change the present
disposition   If the Enemy make any move either up the North or
East Rivers be pleased to send immediate intelligence to Col Morgan
who lays at Chatham, that he may govern himself accordingly   We
have [no] further accounts from Ticonderoga which [*illegible*] us
believe that the accounts of it having fallen into the Enemy's hands
are without foundation

I am Dear Sir

Yr most obt Servt

TENCH TILGHMAN

Col Dayton
Elizabeth Town [2]

ORDERS TO COLONEL MORGAN

Mr Lotts Farm 11th July 1777

Dear Sir

Upon a presumption that the Enemy intend to move either up
the North or East River our Army marched this Morning from

---

[1] During the Revolution the name "Rockaway Bridge" was applied to
the structure spanning the Rockaway River on the road from Troy Hills to
Lower Montville   It had no reference to the village of Rockaway, which
is several miles farther up the stream —*Erskine's Army Maps in Library of
the New York Historical Society*   Many other authorities might be cited

[2] From original in possession of a private collector in New York

Morris Town and will proceed leisurely towards the Clove, unless we have some certain intelligence that they intend Southward

Colo Dayton who is at Elizabeth Town watching the Motions of the Fleet will give you immediate information which way they go It up the East or North River, you will follow directly, keeping upon the right Flank of the main Army The Road is rather better than the one we march You need not harass your Men, but come on leisurely, if there is any occasion to hurry we will send an express to you

I am Dear Sir

Yr most obt Servt

TENCH TILGHMAN

[Addressed]

To Colo Morgan at Chatham [1]

Head Quarters near Clove,
19th July 9 o'clock

Dear Sir

We have received your Letter of this date from the Intelligence receiv'd this afternoon we have every reason to believe that the Enemy are about to move up the North River It is therefore his Excellency's Orders that upon receipt of this you March your Corps to the Bridge at the great Falls, from thence to Paramus, thence to Kakegate & thence to Haverstraw, there to observe the motions of the Enemy, & if they land on the West side of the river below the Highlands you are to take possession of the Road to the forrest of Dean Furnace, & oppose their penetrating that way—but if the Enemy push up the River you are to get over the Mountains to fort Montgomery & there wait for further Orders

Your Baggage (except what you think necessary for the Men to carry) is to be sent by the nearest Route towards this place & from hence to whatever place the Army is, under a small Guard

The Swivels &c which you mention, you are to send to the Commissary of Military Stores at Morris Town You will Observe to take as much cook'd provision with you as you conveniently can

[1] Morgan's Revolutionary Papers, Myers Collection, 1037, in New York Public Library

Inclos'd you have a Letter for Colo Bland, wch you will forward immediately to him by Express

    I am Dear Sir

              Yr mo Obed Servt

                    JOHN FITZGERALD

[Addressed]

    Colo Morgan [1]

A noteworthy incident which occurred here during August, 1777, was the departure of Sullivan's expedition to surprise and capture a force of about 1,000 refugees on Staten Island These "New Jersey Volunteers," as the tories styled themselves, were gathered from various parts of this State, forming a corps under the command of General Courtlandt Skinner, and had their base of operations on Staten Island, whence they made frequent raids upon the patriots in the vicinity of Elizabeth In order to check their activities, General Sullivan, who was then encamped at Hanover, planned a night attack upon Staten Island At the head of 1,000 men, selected from the brigades of Smallwood and De Borre, he started from Hanover on August 21st, and, marching by way of Chatham, where he halted for rest and refreshment, he reached Elizabeth in the evening There he was reinforced by the First and Third New Jersey Continental regiments, commanded respectively by Colonels Ogden and Dayton, together with 100 militia

The tories were found to be scattered in small detachments for a considerable distance along the shore of the island, thus necessitating a division of Sullivan's forces The operations of Ogden and Dayton were eminently successful, but Sullivan himself was not so fortunate He was unexpectedly confronted with a strong force of British regulars who came to the aid of the refugees, and as he had failed to provide a sufficient number of boats to secure his

[1] Morgan's Revolutionary Papers, Myers Collection, 847, in New York Public Library

retreat, his rear guard fell into the hands of the enemy
This misfortune overbalanced the success of Ogden and
Dayton, and the enterprise as a whole was regarded as a
failure.[1]

Captain Robert Kirkwood of the Delaware regiment
thus records in his journal his adventures in Sullivan's expedition:

Thirsday 21st   Our Brigade March'd at 11 O'Clock [from
Hanover] by the Way of Bottle Hill which is 5 miles from thence
to Chatham seven miles and there Refresh'd from thence we march'd
thr'o Spring field to Elizabeth Town point ten miles there our men
unloaded themselves of their knapsacks & Blankets & Crossed the
River in the Greatest Silence on to Staten Island all which we effected
By day Break, from thence we proceeded towards the East end of
the Island where coming near A Guard Consisting of About 100
Men of British Troops but upon first of us they Ran away at this
place We Destroyed near 3000£ of Stores Besides A Quantity brought
off, we traveled near 20 Miles on the Island but Could not see any
more of the Enemy   About 1 O'Clock Came to the Blazing Star
[Ferry] Where we all Cross'd but 100 men who were Detain'd about
Bringing over Stock these were attacked & most taken Prisoners
after they had fired all their Ammunition away that night the
Prisoners beat off the Guard & the greatest part of them got over
the River, the Prisoners that were taken from them were as follows
Viz 3 Cols, viz Barton, Lawrence, & Allen, 4 Captains 6 Subalterns & 150 Privates all of the greens[2]

[1] Hatfield's Elizabeth, 462, Irving's Washington, III, 195
[2] Delaware Historical Society Papers, LVI, 154

CHAPTER X

The Second Continental Light Dragoons in Winter Quarters at
Chatham—A Cavalry Sword unearthed on the Camp-ground—
Correspondence respecting the Cavalry—Letters of Governor
Livingston relating to the Overtures of the British Government

DURING the winter of 1777-8, although the main army
was encamped elsewhere, the military was well represented in this neighborhood Rev Dr Samuel L Tuttle
tells us that a considerable number of officers and privates,
chiefly New England troops, were stationed in Bottle Hill
(Madison) and vicinity, and, while it is probable that some
occupied the huts which had been built during the previous
winter in the Loantaka valley, most of them were billeted
in private houses, where, as before, the best rooms were set
apart for their use [1]

It was at this time that a detachment of the Second
Continental light dragoons (Colonel Elisha Sheldon's regiment) was ordered to Chatham for winter quarters, as we
learn from the memoirs of Major Benjamin Tallmadge, by
whom this detachment was commanded.[2] The major fails
to state the time of his arrival and departure, beyond saying
that he was ordered to Chatham at the close of the operations before Philadelphia, in January, 1778, and that
he was directed to leave in the early spring, but from war-
time correspondence it appears that he was in Trenton as
late as January 12th, so it was probably about the middle of
the month that his troops were removed to Chatham, and
from the same source we learn that the detachment left the
village to join the army under Gates at Fishkill on or about
the fourth of the following June

[1] Historical Magazine, Ser 2, IX, 329
[2] Johnston's Tallmadge's Memoirs, 38

Sheldon's regiment of Continental light dragoons was recruited mainly in Connecticut, but it numbered among its members some officers and men from New York and New Jersey The Fifth troop contained 41 Jerseymen in a total of 76 rank and file [1]

Tallmadge so expresses himself in his memoirs as to give the impression that Sheldon's entire regiment spent the winter in Chatham,[2] and the impression is confirmed by Washington, who, in a letter to Colonel Stephen Moylan, dated May 24, 1778, directing him to march to Valley Forge with his regiment of Continental cavalry and those of Colonels Bland and Baylor, adds "Sheldon's is to remain at Chatham "[3] As a matter of fact, however, Sheldon's dragoons were scattered in various detachments at that time, and only two troops were quartered here The entire regiment was never assembled as a unit under Colonel Sheldon until the following August [4] The cavalry at Chatham was under the immediate command of Tallmadge, for although Sheldon appears to have visited the encampment from time to time during the winter, he did not remain here continuously

While we know the approximate length of time during which the dragoons remained in the village, the location of their encampment cannot be ascertained No record relating to the subject has been found, and even tradition fails to point out the spot It is highly probable, however, that the troopers occupied the property used as a camp-ground by a portion of the Continental army in the summer of 1781, lying south of the turnpike and east of River Road on the Union County side of the Passaic—a situation which would have been eminently desirable and convenient for a detachment of cavalry, as the adjacent racetrack would afford ex-

[1] Walton's U S Army and Navy, I, 40 Connecticut Men in the Revolution

[2] Johnston's Tallmadge's Memoirs, 38

[3] American Catholic Historical Researches, New Series, V, 168

[4] Johnston's Tallmadge's Memoirs, 129

cellent facilities for drilling and exercising the horses, while
the tavern on the opposite side of the turnpike would furnish suitable and comfortable quarters for Major Tallmadge and the other officers

On October 9, 1885, a Revolutionary sword was found
which may have belonged to one of these troopers   The
camp-ground is bisected by a stream known as Spring Brook
which widens into a pond at this point, and the sword was
unearthed by William Phipps, Jr, of Chatham, who was
employed with others in enlarging and deepening the pond
to facilitate the harvesting of ice   The spot where the relic
lay, though now submerged when the pond is full, is near
the shore, and is believed to have been above high water
in Revolutionary times.   It was thought that the weapon
was buried with the remains of a deceased soldier, a surmise which was confirmed by a veteran of the Civil War,
who stated that the vicinity of a water-course was a favorite
place for war-time interments because moist earth is easy to
dig; and that it was not unusual, when interring a deceased
soldier, to bury his sword or musket with him, and the supposition was further strengthened by the fact that Mr
Phipps also found two pieces of board about fifteen inches
long by four inches wide, which, though decayed, retained
enough of their original shape to show that they had been
"halved" together, and which might have formed part of
a rude coffin

The sword, when new, was a very formidable weapon.
Some surprise was occasioned by its size and weight, which
were such that none but a muscular and powerful man could
wield it effectively   Its entire length is about 38 inches, but
was orginally greater, as the point of the blade is missing,
having apparently been broken off before the sword was
buried   Despite the corrosion of the metal, there is evidence
that the blade had been two-edged for a few inches near
the point   When the relic came to view, Mr Phipps broke

the blade, a short section of which was first exposed, believing it to be a root, and the blacksmith
who was employed to repair the fracture pronounced the weapon to be composed of the best
razor steel, of a quality far superior to that used
in the manufacture of swords at the present time

The hilt was covered with leather, bound with
a copper wire, but the leather was so greatly decayed that it fell to pieces soon after its exposure
to the air The scabbard, which presumably was
also of leather, had entirely disappeared with the
exception of the metal hook by which it was
suspended from the belt [1]

Upon the blade near the hilt the letters
U S -L D could be discerned, and a discussion
as to their significance at once arose among antiquarians, some of whom held the meaning to be
"United States, Light Dragoons," and others,
"United States, Lee's Dragoons", the latter believing that the sword had belonged to a trooper
in "Light-Horse Harry" Lee's Partisan Legion
The writer favors the first of these interpreta-
tions. In February, 1777, the weapons of the
Continental army were directed by Congress to
be properly marked for indentification, and it seems more
probable that the same inscription was adopted for the
swords of all the battalions and regiments of cavalry, rather
than that a different device was permitted for Pulaski's,

SWORD
UNEARTHED
ON THE
CAMP GROUND

[1] The Continental Congress, by resolution of March 2, 1778, advised
young gentlemen of the New England and Middle Atlantic States to form
troops of light cavalry to serve at their own expense, except as regards
provisions, and in a list of accoutrements included a sword, the description
of which closely agrees with that of the relic mentioned in the text, viz
"A well-tempered sword, the blade straight, and three feet long, with the
back sharpened up six inches from the point, an open guard about the hilt,
that will be light and yet defend the hand, with a scabbard of substantial
leather without wood "
—*Public Papers of Governor George Clinton, II, 829*

Lee's and Armand's battalions and for each of the four
regiments of Continental light dragoons in the army
Moreover, the supposition that the weapons were engraved
with the initial letter of the commandng officer's name is
open to the objection that a new device would be in order
with every change of leader, by death, promotion or resignation, or by the consolidation of two or more separate
commands And the fact that the horses of Sheldon's
cavalry were branded on the hoofs A L D—American
Light Dragoons[1]—is further evidence that the letters on the
sword had a similar meaning But aside from this, there
is greater likelihood that the weapon belonged to one of
Tallmadge's men than to a trooper of Lee's legion, because
Tallmadge was in winter quarters here for upwards of six
months, while Lee, though stationed at Chatham, and often
passing through the place in the course of the war, did not,
as far as we know, remain here so long

But the theory that the letters "L D" stood for Lee's
Dragoons found many advocates, one of whom was the
editor of the *Madison Eagle,* who, on October 31st, published the following article

AN HISTORICAL RELIC

From time to time many relics are dug up in the neighborhood
where stirring scenes were enacted during the struggle for liberty,
and on October 9, William Phipps and William Sayre while at
work near Spring Brook in the neighborhood of Chatham, dug up a
Cavalry sword, that from its incrustation by rust and dirt had evidently remained concealed from view for years, a liberal application
of kerosene enabled the letters U S-L D to be discerned, and
from the light of history it may be concluded that the weapon
belonged to a trooper in "Light Horse Harry's" command The
battle of Springfield occurred June 23, 1780, and the bridge on the
Vauxhall Road was guarded by Lee's horse who after an obstinate
resistance were driven back, several troopers being killed and
wounded, four of the latter were brought to Condit's Tavern, and

[1] Public Papers of Governor George Clinton, III, 90

died in the barn near by and were buried in the direction of the Mill Dam,[1] it is probably to one of these nameless heroes, the sabre belonged, and is now found long after his remains have mouldered away

Through the kindness of Mr George B Vanderpoel, on whose property the sword was found we are permitted to place it in our window where it will be exhibited for a short time

Among the papers of General Washington now preserved in the Library of Congress is the correspondence of the commander-in-chief with Major Tallmadge during the War of Independence, and a part of this correspondence is quoted below The letters which we have selected relate chiefly to the purchase of provisions, horses and equipment, and indicate the general condition of the cavalry while quartered at Chatham in the winter of 1778

MAJOR TALLMADGE TO GENERAL WASHINGTON

Chatham Febry 9th 1778

May it please your Excellency

The Regt having arrived at a place which will most probably be our Quarters for some time I have set down to report our situation to Genl Polaski, & having other matters to lay before your Excellency I can at the same time inform that the few men & horses which we have with us are in tolerably good Qrs & tho' the place is but small, I trust we shall not want for forage or provisions during our stay

Lieut Colo Blackden I conclude will provide Cloathing for the Regt in N England Boots & Leather Breeches excepted, which I was directed to ingage   I am happy to inform that I have already

---

[1] According to the official report of General Nathaniel Greene, who commanded at Springfield, Lee's loss amounted to 1 trooper killed and 4 wounded —*Barber & Howe's N J Historical Collections 195*   The reference in the *Madison Eagle* to Condit's tavern was taken from the writings of Dr Tuttle, who ascertained that four American soldiers wounded at Springfield were brought to this tavern, where they died —*Historical Magazine, Ser 2 IX, 333*   He does not state to what command they belonged, they may or may not have been Lee's men

better than 100 pairs of leather Breeches in store, & the remaining Complement for the Regt is ingaged, & will be ready for us shortly

With respect to Boots, by the assistance of Mr Caldwell, D Q M Genl for this Departmt, 250 pairs are ingaged near this place, & tho' in every other place where we have made inquiry none could be ingaged under 24, 26 & 30 Dolls pr pair, our whole Complement is ingaged & will shortly be compleated for 14 Dolls — the money to be paid on the Delivery of the Boots

With respect to the Breeches I have made no particular agreement, but they are to be apprised by indifferent Judges, the Magistrates &c &c   Those that I have on hand have been averaged at 16 Dolls apiece—which is more reasonable than I expected to obtain them, being several Dolls less than the Clothier Genl gave for Breeches of the same Quality at Lancaster & the back Counties several months ago

Much has been said about the augmentation of the Troops, if such a plan is determined on, could wish to know it as soon as possible that the recruiting business may be immediately undertaken

Your Excellency must be well assured that a number of horses are wanting for the Dragoon service   As Capt Sheldon is now in N England, where horses are perhaps cheaper than in any other part, any Directions in the above particular should be immediately attended to

I am confident that I need not remind your Excellency of the necessity of setting about the aforesaid business immediately as the Winter, which has already too far elapsed, will soon be over & we called into the field, with prospects of rendering our Country not that service, which might be expected from the Establishment

As much Depends on our having money to pay off our Contracts for the Regt, I am requested by Colo Caldwell to desire your Excellency to enable me to pay off the aforementioned bills punctually, & should any further supplys of boots be needed by the Clothier Genl as I think they will hardly be purchased so cheap in any other State, I doubt not but that they might be ingaged if application was soon made

I have just recd 149 horseman's Swords, taken with Genl Burgoyne, which are all that we may expect from that Qr   They are very strong & heavy having steel Scabbards

Hoping that your Excellency's Directions in the premises may be forwarded as speedily as possible to Genl Polaski or myself

I remain, with all respect, your Excellency's most obdt & very hble Servt,

BENJA TALLMADGE

Major Commdt 2d Regt L D

Genl Washington [1]

Major Tallmadge's mention of the swords taken with Burgoyne's army is worthy of note, as showing that some of the munitions of war captured at Saratoga were sent to Chatham for safe-keeping, while the date of the letter gives us the approximate time when the trophies arrived It appears, however, from the writings of Dr Joseph F Tuttle, that most of the captured articles were stored in Succasunna He states (Annals of Morris County, page 54)

An aged woman, Mrs Elizabeth Doland, died at Mount Hope, Morris County, in 1852, more than ninety-one years old, who once told me that, when eleven years old, she was living at Walmsy's Tavern at Pompton when the trophies of Burgoyne's surrender were passing through, on their way to Morris County, where they were to be stored She had been to a neighbor's house, and, on her return, found the house in a commotion In the bar-room was a heap of curious brass instruments which belonged to a German Band, captured with Burgoyne's army She says that, during the three days the Band remained, she had music enough and was glad when it was gone The artillery and stores were drawn by oxen, and Mrs Doland says that some of the cannon required three yokes The train passed from Pompton to Morristown, through Montville, Troy and Hanover It is an interesting fact that the Presbyterian Meeting House at Succasunna Plains, some twelve miles West of Morristown, was used as a place of storage for the muskets, cannon, and other articles taken at Saratoga There is now living—1854—a gentleman, in Morristown, the Hon Lewis Condict, who, when a child, saw these stores at that old church The larger cannon were ranged and

---

[1] Washington Papers in the Library of Congress, 21, 258

sheltered outside the building, and the entire church was filled with the captured munitions   On the road from Morristown to the Plains, just as you are descending the hill, was the house of a Mr James Young, the garret of which was filled with drums, band instruments, and other accutrements requiring shelter   Dr Condict says he has often, when visiting at Mr Young's house, amused himself with beating the drums there stored. And it may be surmised that the fact of these trophies of a British defeat being stored in Morris County, was one of the reasons why the enemy had such a desire to penetrate that region—a desire which was never gratified

GENERAL WASHINGTON TO MAJOR TALLMADGE

Head Quarters 20th Feby 1778

Sir,

I am glad to be informed by your Letter of the 9th Inst that you are established in quarter, where you are likely to have means of putting your men and horses into good Condition , As you have been so successful in contracting for boots and Leather Breeches, I would not have you confine your views in these articles, to the precise number that may be wanted by your Regiment, but wish that you would extend them in such a manner as to be useful to the other Regiments

The Sums which may be wanted to fulfil your agreements must be drawn from the Quarter master General in whose hands a fund is established for defraying all expenses of this kind

It gives me pain that there should be any delay in the important business of providing Remounts, this matter among others is under the consideration of the Committee of Congress, and nothing can be done in it 'till their determination is known

I am &c

Major Tallmadge
        Chatham [1]

MAJOR TALLMADGE TO GENERAL WASHINGTON

Chatham March 7th 1778

May it please Your Excellency

Having a Dragoon just riding to Camp, I am induced to trouble your Excellency with a line on matters respecting the Regt

[1] Washington Papers in the Library of Congress, B V, pt 1, 143

In my last I noted that Colo Sheldon & Lt Colo Blackden were both absent in N England Am now to inform that Lt Colo Blackden has procured Coats & Vests for the Regt Colo Sheldon has been for some time expecting orders to purchasing Horses for the Regt Of this I wrote largely in my last letter to your Excellency, & being again called on by some Officers of the Regt who are absent on furlough & could assist much in the aforesd Duty, am most pressingly to request Directions in this particular Genl Polaski has sent orders for recruiting men but no money has been forwarded for this purpose I have sent out several nonCommissd Officers on this service & furnished them with money but have it not in my power to advance what may be needed in this business By a letter just recd from Capt Belden of our Regt now in Connecticut, am informed that Recruits & Horses might be engaged, the former on the old terms, & the latter on reasonable Conditions, if money could but be sent on or an order forwarded to Colo Sheldon on the Loan Office in that State

In my last I made mention of the Boots & leather Breeches engaged for the Regt The former are engaged at 14 Dols pr pair, which are to be of good substantial work & approved of by two indifferent Persons This is on all hands agreed to be very reasonable

Colo Sheldon engaged one Mr Estey of this State to make 140 pair of leather Breeches, of good quality, for the Regt & promised him for sd Breeches the price current at the time of making the Contract Mr Estey accordingly engaged Stock & Workmen to fulfil the engagement at the price then current also Some time after this State regulated the prices of the necessaries of life &c &c, and tho' nothing in particular is mentioned about the articles in question still as the act is in general terms they are doubtless included But in the same act a particular exception is made declaring that the intention is not to alter or affect any bargain made previous to the existence of sd act Your Excellency will please to forgive my being lengthy on this Subject, as it most interestingly concerns Mr Estey as well as the Regt The price current, & for which hundreds of pairs were sold at the time the abovementioned Contract was made, was 30 Dols & rising Mr Estey engaged to deliver Breeches of firm, substantial leather & approved Work, for 26⅔ Dols pr pair or thereabouts I have examined the Breeches, & find that he has fulfilled his engagement in the amplest manner, having spared no pains to procure the best leather & giving them good strong, & sufficiently neat work   In fine if those Breeches of which I made mention in my last as apprized by the Magistrates at 16 Dols pr Pair, were worth ten, I can with the greatest sincerity declare that I think these are worth 30   The Breeches which we have heretofore drawn have been of so poor a nature, that they have not indured, the most of them, more than 4 months, & I am confident those made by Mr Estey will indure constant service for a Year

The reason why I have been so lengthy on this Subject is this Some Gentlemen have taken much pains to make Mr Estey uneasy with his Contract & present situation, (as he is but a young Trades-man, & has perhaps expended more than he is worth to oblige the Regt) insinuating that we intend to take the Breeches at our own price, which if much short of the 'forementioned, would make him a great looser   In fine Mr Estey has completely fulfilled his Engagemt & as the honour of the field Officers of this Regt is pledged, on the other hand, that he should be dealt with on honorable & equitable terms, am most humbly to ask your Excellency's Directions how to proceed   If the money can be forwarded, or if I may but be authorized to promise him the money on the aforementioned terms, the Breeches are ready to be delivd   Less than this I think Colo Sheldon, who was empowered to get Cloathing for his Regt as cheap as he could, cannot do, & I am confident as a Servt of the Publick, I think the Bargain highly advantageous, & what ought to be ful-filled.

I am bound to inform that all our supplies come with great difficulty & reluctance from the People, merely for want of money to pay off publick Arrearages   With respect to Cloathing in par-ticular the money must be deposited on the Rect of the articles   If we can be able to do this, I trust the Regt can be tolerably cloathed; if not, I know not what other steps to take

I have one thing more to mention & I will trouble your Ex-cellency no further   We have some Dragoons whose Famelies & Affairs suffer much by reason of their absence   Wish to know whether such men may be dismissed the Service, after procuring a Substitute approved of by the Commanding Officer

With much respect, I am your Excellency's most obt & very hble. Servt

BENJA. TALLMDGE
Major Commdt 2d Regt L Dr

Genl Washington [1]

GENERAL WASHINGTON TO MAJOR TALLMADGE

Head Quarters 10th March 1778

Sir

Annexed is a Copy of my last Letter to you, which from the tenor of yours of the 7th Inst I am inclined to think you never received it went by the return of the Dragoon who brought yours of the 9th Feby

The Legislature of N Jersey certainly never intended that the Law regulating the prices of necessaries should have a retrospective view, and affect any anterior Contracts You ought therefore to settle with Mr Estey according to the agreement which Col Sheldon made with him

As the Congress has called upon those States in which there is the best breed of Horses to supply the Cavalry I cannot take it upon me to put money into Col Sheldon's hands for purchasing Remounts for his Regiment in particular, which will be provided for among the rest—but if he will engage some good horses at a reasonable price upon Credit, I will undertake that they shall be paid for hereafter I have no doubt that he will be able to enlist a number of men for the established *continental bounty,* as the Service of the Cavalry is sought by many who are unwilling to enter into the Infantry

The debts which accrue from your Contracts must as I said before be paid off from the Fund which is established for that purpose in the hands of the Quarter M General

Major Tallmadge [2]

The *New Jersey Gazette* of April 23, 1778, contains this advertisement relating to the steps then being taken by the State to obtain remounts for the cavalry

[1] Washington Papers in the Library of Congress, 22, 121
[2] Washington Papers in the Library of Congress, B V, pt 1, 267

His Excellency the Governor desires the gentlemen employed by this state to purchase horses for the service to send them as soon as purchased to such of the following places as may be most convenient, with reference to those parts of the state in which they are bought, taking receipts for the same, with the proper descriptions, *to-wit* to Capt Harrison, at Pennington, to Col Sheldon, at Chatham, to Major Clough, at Trenton, or to Lieut-Col White, at Brunswick, or to the commanding officers at those places

Referring to the purchase of these horses, Colonel Stephen Moylan, who commanded the four regiments of Continental cavalry then in New Jersey, wrote to Washington from Trenton on May 5th

I have seen but five horses of those purchased by the State   They were sent to Major Clough, who rejected them as unfit for the service   I am told there are some tolerable good ones delivered to the regiments at Chatham, Brunswick and Pennington, I propose visiting them this week, and expect from the late accounts I have from each, to make a more favorable report of them than in my last to your Excellency [1]

MAJOR TALLMADGE TO GENERAL WASHINGTON

Chatham May 4th, 1778

May it please Your Excellency

As Colo Sheldon is about riding for Head Quarters to Day I think it my duty to inform your Excellency of the State of that Part of our Regt which is on the other side the North River, & of which I have had the more immediate Charge for these four Weeks past   Your Excellency need not be apprized that ⅓d of the Regt was detached from us & did duty in other Departments thro' the last Campaign, to regulate & superintend which has been my duty for the time beforementioned

I am to inform that the Troop Commanded by Capt Bull, which served in the middle Departmt the last Year, is in good Qrs & in tolerable good Condition   Tho' much worn down with hard service,

I must in justice to the Officers & Men declare, that with diligence & close attention their Horses are much recruited

The Troops Commanded by Capt Seymour, which served in the Northern Army, was so exceedingly reduced, & has been so short a time in Qrs, that their Condition is not so promising

With respect to arms both Troops are much in want (Swords excepted of which I believe they have nearly a supply) The Sadlery work has been rectified & repaired as much as possible I should be wanting in my Duty should I omit to mention that our Supplies of every kind have been much retarded for want of Money Capt Seymour's Troop has been supply'd wholly on Credit & in a Country where by means of the Regulating Laws necessaries are hard to be obtained even for money, it is but reasonable to suppose that a distant, & even (with some) a doubtful Paymt will be but a poor inducemt to part with those Commodities to the Publick for which they can have the ready Cash in any other Market

I am extremely unhappy to find by a letter lately recd from Your Excellency by Colo Sheldon that the Honour of the Officers as well as the Dignity of the Regt are so very low in your Excellency's opinion I formerly had the Vanity to think that we were Considered in a different light For me to apologize & answer to the Charges therein contained, is needless, since the Colo has wrote so largely on the Subject But it being Commy of Forage, Purchaser of Boots Cloathing &c for the Men, Superintendant to the Armourers & Sadlers Employments &c &c, entitles the Man who acts in these several Capacities to the Character of being indolent & inattentive to duty, I would acquiesce in the Charge I can add to this that never since I have been a Member of the Continental Army have I asked for, or enjoyed the benefit of a furlough to Visit my Friends I wish not to enlarge on so disagreeable a subject, but with as much reluctance as I should quit a service which from principle I wish to support, & a Genl whose Commands it has been my highest ambition to obey, whenever my Conduct shall be reprehensible by the latter or of no avail to the advancemt of the former Honour as well as Inclination would urge me to impose on the Publick no longer Tho not particularly pointed at in your letter, my Honour, as well as the Honour & Services of all my Brother Officers seem to have been so depreciated in your Excellency's opinion that unless a Change of

Sentiments is experienced, I am well convinced we can serve with but little Cr[edit] & no satisfaction hereafter

With much Respect I am, Your Excellency's most obdt Hble Servt.

BENJA TALLMADGE
Major 2d Regt L D

Genl Washington [1]

GENERAL WASHINGTON TO MAJOR TALLMADGE

Valley forge 13 May 1778

Sir

I received your favor of the 4th Instant by Colo Sheldon

I do not censure the conduct of Officers or hurt their feelings in the smallest degree thro choice   When I do it, I always regret the occasion, which compelled me to the measure   How far the conduct of the generality, or of Individual Officers in your Corps may have been reprehensible and deserving the reproof and charges contained in my Letter, I cannot determine upon my own knowledge I shall be happy if they were without foundation, However, my information was such that I could not disbelieve the facts   It came thro various channels, and it appeared that the Horses had been neglected and greatly harassed   Colo Moylan in his general report of the state of the Cavalry informed me "That the second Regiment had been most cruelly dealt with   Of 54 Horses which he had seen paraded, that he did not think Ten could be selected fit to go on any duty   That they had been really starved during the Winter and the blame thrown from the Officers on Mr Caldwell, who acted as a Commissary of forage, but that the true reason of their being in such condition, according to his believe, was that few or none of the Officers had been with the Regiment"   If this was the case,—If the Horses were neglected thro their absence or not attended to as well as circumstances would admit, the Officers certainly are reproacheable for not having done that duty they owed the public

I am Sir Your Most Obedt Servt

GO WASHINGTON

Major Tallmadge of
      Sheldon's Dragoons [2]

[1] Washington Papers in the Library of Congress, 23, 72
[2] Washington Papers in the Library of Congress, B V, pt 2, 203

The order of the commander-in-chief removing the cavalry from Chatham was couched in the following terms

> Head Quarters Valley Forge
> 29th May 1778

Sir,

An extent of Country between Gen Gates and the enemy make it necessary to employ horse in that quarter   I therefore desire you may proceed immediately to the North River and put yourself under the command of Genl Gates with all of your cavalry that are in a condition to march   With such as remain you will leave proper officers

> I am &c
>
> Go W

Col Sheldon
    Chatham [1]

From a letter of Lewis Pintard, an extract of which is given below, we learn that the cavalry left Chatham on the 4th of June   The letter is addressed to Colonel Samuel B Webb, a member of a prominent family of Connecticut, and one of Washington's aides de camp, and refers to his brother John, who was a captain in Sheldon's regiment   The letter is now in the library of the Connecticut Historical Society Its date, 1777, is clearly an error, as it alludes to events which occurred in the summer of 1778

> New York, 6th June, 1777

Dear Sir

On my return Home Saturday last I received a letter from Mr Boudinot, desiring me to meet him in the Jerseys

I set out Monday in the storm, and on my way to his house, at a little village called Chatham, about ten miles from Morristown, I

---

[1] Washington Papers in the Library of Congress, B V, pt 2, 353   Tallmadge wrote to Gates on June 1 that he would start from Chatham as soon as he could remount all his men, expressing pleasure at 'the agreeable prospect of seeing the Regt once together, which has not happened since we have been raised "—*Johnston's Tallmadge's Memoirs, 129*

had the pleasure to see and dine with your younger brother, Captain
of the Light Horse, who was very well, and in high spirits, glad to
hear so straight from you He set out Thursday last with his troop
of horse and many others to join General Gates at Fishkills [1]

* * * * * * * * *

Two letters are given below which were written at
Chatham in April, 1778, by Hon William Livingston, the
first governor of the State under the republic The Council
of Safety of New Jersey, of which the chief executive was
ex-officio a member, met in Morristown during the last days
of April and the first week of May in that year,[2] and this
accounts for Livingston's presence in the vicinity He was
a staunch and ardent patriot whose activities in the American cause led the enemy to offer a reward for his capture,
and repeated attempts to take him prisoner were made by
British troops and bands of tories Hence he was usually
attended by a detachment of soldiers, and seldom spent two
successive nights in the same building It happened more
than once that the tories made a descent upon the house
where he had passed the previous night, only to find that he
had eluded them [3] It was doubtless owing to these conditions that the governor came to Chatham at the period of
which we write, and probably lodged at times in various
other villages in the neighborhood, instead of remaining in
Morristown during the entire session of the Council of
Safety

Upon the surrender of Burgoyne at Saratoga, and the
ratification of a treaty of alliance between France and the
American republic, the British ministry realized the difficulties of the task they had undertaken, and began to doubt
the possibility of subjugating the colonies, hence commis-

[1] Webb's Samuel B Webb, 265
[2] Minutes of the Council, V, 268, in library of the New Jersey Historical
Society
[3] J F Tuttle's Annals of Morris County, 48

HON. WILLIAM LIVINGSTON

sioners were sent to offer the Americans all they had asked
if they would reassume their loyalty to the crown   This
conciliatory proposal, which would have been eagerly accepted at the commencement of the war, now came too late,
and was rejected by the Continental Congress   The following letters of Governor Livingston illustrate the opinion
generally held by the patriots regarding these overtures
The first is addressed to Henry Laurens, the President of
Congress, and its friendly and informal tone, despite the
fact that the two gentlemen were not personally acquainted,
is attributed by Livingston's leading biographer to their
similarity of views upon many points of public interest, and
their equal devotion to the cause of independence

Chatham, 27th April, 1778

To Henry Laurens, Pres't etc
Dear Sir,

I am under great obligations to you for your long and agreeable
letter of the 19th instant, which I received yesterday, and considering
my prompt pay, such as it is, I know you will make an abatement
in the price, that is to say in the length of my answer

I really pity you amid the multiplicity of business in which you
are immersed, but if it should be our good fortune to drive the devils
out of the country this summer, as I doubt not we shall, if we exert
our endeavors in an humble reliance on the Lord of Hosts, instead
of suffering ourselves to be gulled by the——of Lord North, it will
be a very pleasing reflection to us during the remainder of our lives,
that we have been instrumental in delivering one of the finest countries upon the globe from the tyranny which would have rendered it
like Babylon an habitation of owls and of dragons   You have my
hearty thanks for the loan of the London Evening Post, which I return you according to request   The extraordinary freedom which
these writers take in opposing the measure of the ministry, is a happy
symptom of the national discontent   North is certainly at his wits'
end, and as Huldibras says

> "He that was great as Julius Caesar,
>   Is now reduced like Nebuchadnezzar "

I hope we shall not be such blockheads as to accede to ridiculous terms, when we have so fair a prospect of obtaining peace upon almost any terms, tho' my good friends in New York have faithfully promised to cut my throat for writing, which they seem to resent more than fighting I have already begun to sound the alarm in our gazette, in a variety of short letters, as tho' everybody execrated the proposals of Britain Peace I most earnestly wish for, but for Heaven's sake let us have no badge of dependence upon that cruel nation, which so lately devoted us to destruction, and is so precipitately hastening her own

If whatever is is right, a fortiori, whatever is by act of Congress must unquestionably be right But in my private judgment, I should be totally against the plan of allowing the officers half-pay after the war It is a very pernicious precedent in republican States, will load us with an immense debt, and render the pensioners themselves in a great measure useless to their country If they must have a compensation, I think they had better have a sum certain to enable them to enter into business, and become serviceable to the community

I am, &c

WIL LIVINGSTON [1]

LIVINGSTON TO WASHINGTON

Chatham, 27th April, 1778

Dear Sir,

I had the honour yesterday of your Excellency's favours of the 15th. and 22d April

*   *   *   *   *   *   *   *

I am obliged to your Excellency for the enclosures in your favour of the 22d of April I entertain exactly the same sentiments with you concerning the design and tendency of the bill and instructions— but I hope in this they will be (as in every thing else they have been) disappointed by that Providence which appears evidently to confound all their devices I should have been very happy to have received Lord North's speech only two days sooner, to have contributed my mite towards some observations upon it, to be inserted in the West New Jersey Gazette, but it coming too late for that purpose, I must

<hr>

[1] Sedgwick's Livingston, 279

defer it to the succeeding week; though I could wish it was undertaken by an abler hand, and one of greater leisure. To provide,
however, some antidote to prevent meanwhile the operation of his
lordship's poison, I have sent Collins[1] a number of letters, as if by
different hands, not even excluding the tribe of petticoats, all calculated to caution America against isiduous acts of enemies. This
mode of rendering a measure unpopular, I have frequently experienced in my political days to be of surprising efficacy, as the common
people collect from it that everybody is against it, and for that
reason those who are really for it grow discouraged, from magnifying
in their own imagination the strength of their adversaries beyond its
true amount.

*   *   *   *   *   *   *

I have the honour to be, With the highest esteem, Dear Sir, &c.

WIL LIVINGSTON.[2]

[1] Isaac Collins, the editor of the *New Jersey Gazette*.
[2] Sedgwick's Livingston, 281.

CHAPTER XI

Shepard Kollock and the *New Jersey Journal*

THE most noteworthy event occurring in Chatham during the year 1779 was the establishment in this village of the *New Jersey Journal*—a newspaper which contributed very materially to the successful outcome of the Revolutionary War

In colonial and Revolutionary days newspapers were scarce None was regularly published in New Jersey until December, 1777, when Isaac Collins founded the *New Jersey Gazette*—issued at first in Burlington and later in Trenton—which circulated chiefly in the southern parts of the State The inhabitants of the northern and northeastern portions, while they read the *Gazette* to some extent, depended more generally upon the newspapers of New York, which, after the occupation of that city by the British, necessarily supported the home government, and tried to discourage the cause of American independence

In the winter of 1778-9 someone conceived the idea that if a newspaper strongly in sympathy with the patriot cause were published and circulated in northern New Jersey, it would serve a most useful purpose in encouraging the people, and counteracting the pernicious influence of the tory press of New York The *New Jersey Gazette*, owing to the fact that its editor was a Quaker, was not particularly bellicose, and there was need for a patriotic newspaper which should be more zealous and aggressive Some historians attribute the plan to General Henry Knox of the Continental artillery, while others ascribe it to Alexander Hamilton The project was duly carried into effect, the publication being

intrusted to a young officer of artillery named Shepard
Kollock, who was a printer by trade

This distinguished patriot was born in Lewes, Delaware, in September, 1750, the son of Shepard and Mary
(Goddard) Kollock   He learned the art of printing in the
office of his uncle, William Goddard, editor of the *Pennsylvania Chronicle*, in Philadelphia   In 1770, owing to failing
health, he went to the island of St Croix, West Indies,
where he found employment in a newspaper office, and where
he made the acquaintance of Alexander Hamilton, then a
boy of fourteen, who had attracted attention by writing a
vivid and interesting description of a West Indian hurricane,
which was printed in Kollock's paper   Soon after the outbreak of the Revolution the young journalist returned to his
native country, filled with a desire to participate in the
struggle for freedom, and in 1776 became a lieutenant in a
company of New York artillery of which the captain was
Alexander Hamilton, his former friend of St Croix   On
January 1 1777, he was commissioned first lieutenant under
Captain Thomas Theodore Bliss in Colonel John Lamb's
(the Second) regiment of Continental artillery, and served
as brevet captain   He resigned his commission January 3,
1779 [1]

[1] Mary Kollock in *The Spirit of 76*, January, 1898, William P Tuttle
in *The Madison Eagle*, March 12 1897   Heitman's Historical Register of
Continental Officers, 336, Stryker's Officers and Men of New Jersey in the
Revolution 90

The muster roll of this regiment, in August, 1779, contained the names
of two residents of Chatham   They were Bazaliel Ackley and Stephen
Carter, who were matrosses in Captain John Doughty's company —*Calendar
of Historical MSS of the Revolution in Office of the Secretary of State of
New York II, 339*

The following recommendation was written for Kollock by Isaac Collins, editor of the *New Jersey Gazette*   The language of the postscript is
explained by the fact that the writer was a Quaker

Burlington, 12 mo 27 1775

The bearer, Sheppard Kollock is a candidate for a Captain or Lieutenant's Commission in the Continental service, and would willingly serve
in one of those Regiments to be raised in this Province   From a long
acquaintance I believe him to be a young fellow of good principles and
resolution, and he appears to be hearty in the American Cause   As such

Shepard Kollock was united in marriage with Susannah, daughter of Isaac and Hannah Arnett, of Elizabeth, N J, and he probably made that place his home as far as his military activities would permit   When the approach of the enemy imperiled the safety of the city, the Arnett and Kollock families removed to New Providence, consequently the captain was not a stranger in this vicinity when he founded the *New Jersey Journal* at Chatham [1]

Whether the plan of publishing this newspaper was evolved by Knox or by Hamilton, there can be little doubt that it was the latter who advised the selection of Shepard Kollock to carry out the undertaking   The theory has been advanced that Kollock wearied of the hardships of army life, and resumed his former occupation for pecuniary profit, but this is extremely doubtful, for the success of the undertaking was problematical, and such a venture could hardly

---

I recommend him to thy particular notice   If thou canst serve him, the obligation will be as gratefully acknowledged as tho' it was immediately conferred upon

Thy very respectful friend,
ISAAC COLLINS

P S—This is the first time, perhaps, that ever a person of my Profession recommended a man for such an office   But such is the idea I have of Public Justice and Self-Defense

I C

To John Pope, merch't, Mansfield

—*Penna, Magazine of History, XLIII, 260*

[1] Hatfield's Elizabeth, 607   Isaac Arnett seems to have kept a store at New Providence in the winter of 1779-80 —*The New Jersey Journal, Nos 44, 51*

Children of Shepard and Susannah Kollock

HENRIETTA, m, Feb 5 1805, Rev John McDowell, D D, of Elizabeth, N J

HENRY Presbyterian clergyman b New Providence, N J, Dec 14, 1778 d Savannah, Ga, Dec 29, 1819 m, Jun 1, 1804, Mahetable, widow of Alexander Campbell of Richmond, Va, and daughter of William Hylton of Jamaica, W I

SHEPARD KOSCIUSKO, Presbyterian Clergyman b Elizabeth, N J, Jun 25, 1795, d Philadelphia, Pa, Apr 7, 1865, m Sarah H——

MARY, m Mr Nash

SUSAN DAVIS, m Mr Witherspoon

JANE, m Rev William Anderson McDowell, D D, of Morristown, N J

LYDIA, m Mr Holdrick

ISAAC ARNETT

—*Seller's Kollock Genealogy, 28, Kollock's Memoir of Henry Kollock, Hatfield's Elizabeth, 667.*

be expected to pay in that time of general depression   It
is much more likely that he was directed by his superiors to
publish the paper, and regarded the work as a military duty
Quoting from the writings of the late William Nelson:

That it (the *Journal*) was started as a "war measure" with
official backing, further appears from sundry receipts (the original
are in my collection) of the Army Commissary at Morristown during
1780, showing that on February 2, he furnished Kollock with "Nine
Hundred Wt of old Tent Unfitt for service," also the same day
"one Ream letter Paper three Ream Common Paper"   A week later
"one Ream of Common Paper" was furnished for the use of "Shepard
Kollock Printer at Chatham," and three days later "Fourteen quire
common & four quire large Post Paper" receipted for by Shelly
Arnett, who was an apprentice and a few years later a partner of
Kollock   On March 29 "One ream Common paper" was furnished
to Kollock "for printing returns"   On May 21, he was given "Eight
Hundred Three Quarters & Twelve pound old Tent Cloath," presumably to be manufactured into paper   On June 4, the Commissary
delivered for his use 'Two Bundles Old Tent Rags wt Two Hundred One Quarter Also Six Ream Paper for Printing returns for
Adjt Genl   Also One Other Bagg wt Two Hundred One Quarter
old tent Rags"   The furnishing of a newspaper printer with supplies from the very scanty army stores is, I think, rather a unique
incident of the Revolution [1]

The *New Jersey Journal* first appeared on February
16, 1779, and was continued until the close of the Revolution   It was a weekly paper, issued every Tuesday until
January 25, 1780, and on Wednesdays thereafter   Its
publication ceased in the autumn of 1783, but the exact date
of its discontinuance is not known, for many numbers of the
paper have been lost, and we cannot be certain that the latest
issue now extant was the last one printed.   Toward the
close of the war Kollock announced his intention of moving

[1] Nelson's New Jersey Printers of the 18th Century, 19

from Chatham to New York as soon as the departure of
the enemy would permit   The city was evacuated by the
British on November 25, 1783, and it is believed that the
publication of the *New Jersey Journal* ceased at that time

In addition to its news columns, the *Journal* contained
essays, communications, poems, etc, written in a tone
heartily in sympathy with the cause of freedom, and it
undoubtedly exercised a most potent influence   The British
recognized its power and effect, and often threatened
vengeance against its proprietor; but never succeeded in
penetrating this region

Captain Kollock doubtless would have preferred to
publish his paper in Elizabeth, but this was prevented by the
frequency with which that city was raided by the enemy
Why Chatham was selected as the seat of publication, instead of the more populous and important village of Morristown, is a matter of conjecture   Possibly the editor
thought that Chatham, being nearer the enemy's lines,
afforded better facilities for gathering news, or that the
moral effect of the *Journal* would be strengthened by the
fact that it was printed as close to the British outposts as
was consistent with safety   The ease with which the enemy
reached Springfield in 1776 and 1780 shows that Chatham
was as near the danger zone as he could safely approach

The patriot printer moved his establishment two or
three times during his stay in Chatham, but the scene of his
labors cannot be accurately fixed   The paper itself does not
state the exact location of the printing office at any time, nor
does it refer to removals, except upon the occasion of the
battle of Springfield, which occurred June 23, 1780   The
people of Chatham were greatly terrified by the intelligence
that a large and powerful British force was approaching,
and, fearing that the enemy's advance could not be checked,
many of them sought safety in flight   During the week of

the battle the *Journal* failed to appear, and in the next issue the omission was explained by the fact that the printing office had been removed in the late alarm This statement, however, may not indicate a change of location it may simply mean that the editor left Chatham in company with many of his neighbors, taking his printing outfit with him and that upon his return when the danger was past, he resumed business at the old stand

We are able to determine approximately the various locations where the paper was published by the discovery, in after years, of broken and worn-out type, but we are obliged to rely upon tradition, or the probabilities of the case, to arrive at the order in which the several quarters were successively occupied Samuel Condit the last proprietor of the tavern which stood near Mrs Mary C Allen's present home, on the north side of the turnpike east of the river and was kept during the Revolution by Timothy Day, used to say that he had often found type in the garden on the west side of the hotel from which he argued that the *Journal* had been printed in one of the west rooms of the house, and that the discarded type had been thrown from the windows [1] But although it is very likely that Captain Kollock occupied a room in the tavern, it is not an absolute certainty, for a building which in later years was a store, standing at the opposite end of the garden, may have been used as the printing office The type found by Mr Condit might have been thrown from the windows of either house

Still, it is probable that the printing office was in the tavern, and that this was the first home of the *New Jersey Journal* That Captain Kollock upon his arrival at Chatham, should first secure the necessary accommodations in a public house, while seeking more suitable and permanent quarters elsewhere, is much more likely than that he resorted

[1] Historical Magazine Ser 2 IX, 330 Tuttle's Bottle Hill and Madison, 77

to the hotel at a subsequent date   Moreover, the tavern's location, standing as it did near the mouth of the road to New Providence, would add to its convenience, if we assume, which is by no means improbable, that Kollock continued to live in New Providence for a short time after founding his paper, before he and his family moved to Chatham

At another period, says tradition, the *Journal* was housed in a building which stood upon the property now owned by George M Decker, on the northerly side of Main Street between the river and the mill-race,[1] which, upon its demolition, was found to contain scattered type beneath the floors, the type apparently having been lost by dropping through the crevices between the boards

It further appears that the paper was published for a time in a house which stood upon the land owned until recently by the Chatham Presbyterian church, on the north side of Main Street, about thirty rods west of the Passaic In later years this building was occupied as a general store by William R McDougall and Mahlon Minton   It was torn down in 1832 when a church was built upon its site, and Mr McDougall used to say that type was then found beneath the floors[2]   Certain advertisements which appeared in the *Journal* in April, August and December, 1780, describe the location of the printing office as "near the liberty pole," and from information derived from various sources it is possible to locate the Revolutionary liberty pole on or near the land now owned by Clark C Cyphers, which adjoins the above property on the east   We may therefore assume that during 1780, and perhaps the following year, the paper was printed in the building referred to above

The home of the *Journal* was changed for the last time in 1782   In April of that year the editor purchased from Rev Ebenezer Bradford, pastor of the Presbyterian church

[1] Lewis Publishing Company's *Morris County*, I, 289
[2] William P Tuttle in *The Madison Eagle*, March 12, 1897

at Bottle Hill (Madison), a small schoolhouse which the latter had erected during the earlier years of the Revolution, and in which he taught a classical school It was built where the former passenger station of the Lackawanna Railroad in Madison used to stand[1] Captain Kollock moved it to Chatham, and placed it upon or near the site of Mrs George T Parrot's present residence, on the south side of Main Street opposite Mr Cyphers' property This building he used as a printing office and general store during the remainder of his stay in Chatham, and it was probably his residence It was destroyed by fire in 1870, at which time is was occupied as a bakery by George Linabery.

"The Chatham paper," as it was familiarly called by both Americans and British, was printed upon a sheet measuring about 15 by 19 inches, folded to make four pages, each of which was divided into three columns 3¾ inches wide, but without column rules The following imprint extends across the bottom of the fourth page "CHATHAM, Printed by SHEPARD KOLLOCK, by whom essays, articles of intelligence, advertisements, &c, are thankfully received and carefully inserted Subscriptions taken at 3/9 per quarter "

Although many numbers of the *Journal* are still in existence, there is no complete file covering the entire period of its publication A few bound volumes of the paper are preserved by antiquarians and antiquarian societies, of which the collection owned by the New York Historical Society is said to be the largest and most complete, but in each of these volumes several numbers are wanting

From the fact that the editor frequently advertised for rags, and on one occasion for a boy to learn the art of paper making, we infer that the paper he used was manufactured in Chatham Compared with modern newspapers,

[1] Tuttle's Bottle Hill and Madison 78, William P Tuttle in *The Madison Eagle*, March 12, 1897

the appearance of the *Journal* is crude and unattractive, with
its coarse, rough paper, its blurred print, and its irregular
lines, yet we cannot doubt that its subscribers regarded it as
the perfection of journalistic achievement, it being fully
equal, in respect to literary composition, presswork, and
quality of paper, to the contemporary newspapers of New
York, Boston and Philadelphia

The subscription price per quarter was fixed at "three
shillings in produce or the value thereof in money", the
value, in April, 1780, being twenty-five dollars in paper or
five shillings in specie In 1781 the price was "half a dollar
in specie or the value thereof in produce", and this, it was
explained, meant "half a dollar hard money, and not half a
state dollar, as some have mistakenly supposed " The publication could hardly have been a financial success, judging
by the printer's frequent appeals to delinquent subscribers
He seems to have had the same difficulty in collecting subscriptions that the editors of rural newspapers experience
at the present day, and at times to have almost despaired of
continuing the business In the issue of September 6, 1780,
he writes

The last number of this paper terminates the second quarter of
the current year The Editor presumes his subscribers must be sensible of the great expence he is at in publishing a news-paper at this
time of general difficulty, and the necessity there is for punctual payments—He is therefore surprised, that though he has so often requested payment of those in arrears, so little notice has been taken
of it, many of whom have not yet paid off their last year's subscription, which, by the depreciation of the money, if now paid is of so
small value that it is hardly worth receiving —Those subscribers in
the vicinage of Chatham, the Printer expects will pay him in produce at the old rate, those at a distance, who pay cash, he hopes, in
future, will be punctual in their payments quarterly

Again, on August 15, 1781, he writes as follows

This day's paper finishing the second quarter of the current year, the Editor returns his warmest acknowledgments to those gentlemen who have paid him with the same cheerfulness that they became subscribers, but at the same time, cannot help regretting that there are so few of this class of men on his list, which occasions so many embarrassments and difficulties that at the expiration of the present quarter (unless greater attention is paid to supplying him with the needful) the publication of the *New Jersey Journal* will be suspended, if not totally dropped It is hoped those who are in arrears will take the earliest opportunity, either by the post, or through their friends, to pay the same, which request, if complied with, will enable the Printer to go on with his business, and make such improvements in his paper as to render it worthy of their patronage

The next notice, which appeared November 14, of the same year, is rather more peremptory

This day's paper finishes the third quarter of the current year Those who are in arrear are seriously requested to pay the same by the 31st instant, or they may depend upon being————

At the end of the third year of the *Journal's* history (February 13, 1782), the editor, while acknowledging "the high sense he has of the favours of those gentlemen who, by their punctual payments, have enabled him to keep in the field of literature and politics," gives warning to "a number of contrary principles, who have been callous to every gentle invitation to come and discharge their arrearages,   that self preservation dictates the absolute necessity of shortly balancing his books, and hopes they will not, by their neglect of payment, compel him to do what is repugnant to his inclination "

The patriot printer encountered other difficulties besides those caused by the delinquency of his subscribers During the month of February in the "hard winter" of 1780, scarcity of paper compelled him to reduce the size of the

Journal to a sheet measuring approximately 10 by 18 inches, each page containing only two columns instead of three "The inclemency of the weather," he wrote, "which has stopped all the paper mills, obliges us, for the present, to reduce the size of our paper, but as soon as it moderates, so that the mills can go again, it will be printed on paper of the usual size " The issue of October 3, 1781, consisted of a half sheet only (two pages instead of four), and a card in the news columns attributed the abridgment to the editor's illness

In examining the files of the *New Jersey Journal* one is impressed with its lack of local news The editor, of course, could not describe the movements of the army without betraying his country's secrets, but we cannot so easily explain his failure to report more incidents of a non-military character which could have been published without jeopardizing public interests The historian, having in mind the wealth of information contained in public prints of modern times, would expect to find in this Revolutionary newspaper a mine of historical data relating to Chatham, but in this respect the *Journal* is very disappointing At that period almost all journalists seemed to consider local news of but little interest or importance, and as even the weekly or semi-weekly papers then printed in New York generally confined such matter to a few sentences, we cannot wonder at the shortcomings of a newspaper published in a country village In almost every issue of the *New Jersey Journal* is a news article headed CHATHAM, but this caption simply indicates that the news therein contained was compiled or edited at Chatham —it seldom relates to local occurrences [1] In common with

[1] This caption was technically called the "Chatham head" It was a feature which was not peculiar to the *New Jersey Journal* news articles under the Chatham head also appeared at irregular intervals in the *New Jersey Gazette,* of Trenton, and in some of the papers of New York, Philadelphia, and other places As a rule they contained general news compiled at Chatham by someone who, in the case of the patriot papers, was probably

other papers of the period, the *Journal* was mainly filled with
tidings gathered from all sections of the American colonies
and various parts of Great Britain, considerable space being
allotted to Parliamentary debates and other intelligence
from London, and even an uprising of the Sepoys in India
received more attention than happenings in Chatham   Local
events seem to have been noticed only when the incident
itself was considered remarkable, or when public interest had
been aroused to an unusual extent   Some of these items
read as follows.

On Friday last arrived at Camp, from Philadelphia, his Excellency Mons Gerard, Ambassador from the Court of France, to
review the army, where he was received with the honours due to his
high station, and on Saturday last he set out to return again

No. 12, May 4, 1779

On Saturday last was executed for desertion, at camp, a soldier
belonging to the Jersey brigade, and on Monday three spies shared
the same fate

No 71, June 21, 1780

Mrs Washington passed through this place, since our last, on
her way to philadelphia

No 72, July 5, 1780

General Washington, we are told, put the army in motion last
Sunday, and moved towards King's Bridge, and as a very heavy
cannonade was heard most of last Sunday night and Monday morning, it is supposed Fort Washington was attacked

No 126, July 18, 1781

Last Wednesday morning Solomon Brant terminated his life by
cutting his throat   He got up very early in the morning and walked

Captain Kollock himself or one of his employees   It is quite unusual to
find under the Chatham head in these distant publications any mention of
events which occurred in Chatham

out, but not coming to breakfast as usual, his wife sent his daughter to look in the cornfield if he was not there, when, to her astonishment, she found him a corse

No 128, August 1, 1781

Last Friday, Benjamin Rogers, a simpleton, was drowned in Pesaic river, near the Old Mill[1] He went to bathe, as was usual, and was seen to dive off of a tree, but never more appeared until he was taken up

No 130, August 15, 1781

Just as this paper was going to press, the following copy of a letter from Col Miles, D Q M G at Philadelphia, to Col Neilson, at Trenton, was received

"Philadelphia, Oct. 22, 1781

"SIR,

"I have the pleasure of Congratulating you on the capture of Cornwallis and his whole army on the 17th instant The particulars are not come to hand The President of Congress has just received a copy of Count de Grasse's letter to the Governor of Maryland, sent by water to Annapolis, so that there is not a doubt of the Fact The Count has taken his troops on board and gone out to meet Mr Digby That they may meet is the hearty prayer of, Sir,

"Your most obedient servant,
"SAMUEL MILES, D Q M "

Col Neilson

A Philadelphia paper of Monday last has the following paragraph —"With the most unbounded pleasure we can assure the public that dispatches have this moment arrived, giving an account of the unconditional surrender of Lord Cornwallis on the 17th instant, to our magnanimous General Washington "

No 140 October 24, 1781

---

[1] Reference is occasionally found in the *Journal* to the old mill located on Passaic River about a mile from Chatham This was probably the structure built near the Watchung Avenue crossing by William Broadwell, who settled here in 1737 A deed evidencing the sale of a neighboring tract of land in 1824 contains a reference to "the old mill now called Franklin Mill"—*Morris County records, 1-3, 412* The Franklin mill stood on the south side of Watchung Avenue between the river and the race, and was demolished in March, 1909

On receiving confirmation of the capture of Cornwallis, twenty gentlemen of this place and the neighbourhood, met on Monday evening last at Mr Day's tavern, where they supped, and spent a few hours in convivial mirth and jocund festivity Illuminations and bon-fires were exhibited on the occasion

Nothing could exceed the joy that was visible in every countenance on the news of Cornwallis' capture, bonfires and illuminations were exhibited in almost every town and village in this State

No 141 October 31, 1781

Friday passed through this place under guard, seven tatterdemalions, taken the preceeding day on Bergen by a party under the command of Captain Hendricks

No 174, June 12 1782

Last Friday one Cook, a soldier in the second Jersey regiment, was hung at camp for the reiterated crimes of desertion and theft

No 179 July 17, 1782

Further items are quoted in other parts of this volume in connection with the historical events to which they refer.

The dearth of Chatham news in the columns of the *Journal* naturally leads to a perusal of the advertisements [1] Some of these possess considerable local interest, but a large number of them were sent from distant parts of the State, owing to the scarcity of newspapers at that time, and throw no light upon the history of Chatham Much attention was given to the breeding of horses, indicating the value of these animals in newly settled districts at a time when almost all land travel was on horseback, John Leary, Jr, Nathaniel

---

[1] A few advertisements relating to Chatham were inserted in the *Gazette* before the *Journal* was established During February, 1778, Eunice and Foster Horton advertised dry goods, etc, for sale at their store, and on June 3, 1778, John Hunt offered for sale a farm of 108 acres "pleasantly situated in a village of great resort called Chatham" In the *Pennsylvania Packet*, of July 15 1777, at which time no newspapers were published in New Jersey, Jacob Morrell advertised for the return of a light bay horse strayed or stolen from his home in Chatham

Seabury and John Blanchard of Chatham being among the
numerous advertisers of this business   The crime of horse-
stealing seems to have been prevalent, for many rewards
were advertised for the return of stolen animals   Rewards
were also offered for the apprehension of runaway slaves
and apprentices of both sexes, most of the latter advertisements having been received by the editor from distant places
Legal notices are also found, referring to sheriffs' sales and
sales of forfeited estates   Official notices were inserted
from time to time by the civil and military authorities, relating to such matters as the value of the currency, standard
of weights and measures, contracts for furnishing supplies
for the army, and rewards for the arrest of deserters   A
few of these notices, which have reference to Chatham, are
quoted in illustration

TO BE SOLD (for CASH) At the house of William Darling, Chatham, Thirty Cast HORSES, on Saturday the 4th of
November, by AARON FORMAN Q[uarter] M[aster]   Morristown, October 31 1780

No 89 November 1 1780

The Committee of Essex County Associators request the Whig
inhabitants of Morris county to meet them at the house of Matthias
Woodruff, in Chatham, on Tuesday the 24th instant, precisely at
one o'clock, on business of the greatest importance.

Vaux Hall, April 17, 1781
No 113, April 18, 1781

As there is great reason to believe that a considerable number of
muskets, the property of the United States, have been left with some
of the inhabitants of this state, All persons who have any such
muskets, or know where they are secreted, are requested to give immediate information to some continental officer that they may be
recovered for the use of the states   Any person convicted of pur-

chasing from a soldier either arms or ammunition, must expect to be prosecuted agreeable to the laws of this state

Elias Dayton, Col Com Jersey Brigade

Chatham, June 26 1781

No 122, June 20, 1781

PUBLIC Notice is hereby given to all who belonged to the brigade of wagons, in the service of the United States, conducted by Daniel Day, deceased, to meet the Executors of the said Daniel Day at the house of the subscriber, on Saturday next, at 2 o'clock in the afternoon, with their evidences to prove their right to the certificates taken by said Day for said brigade

Timothy Day

N B All who are indebted to said estate, are requested to settle the same immediately, to prevent trouble.

April 2 1782

No 164, April 3, 1782

Of greater interest are the quaint business cards and similar advertisements of the residents of Chatham, which, in the absence of more voluminous local news, give some conception of everyday occurrences at that early period We seem brought into closer touch with the Revolutionary village when we read that John Stevens supplies fresh beef in season on Tuesday and Friday evenings, for hard cash only, and that he gives cash and the highest prices for fat cattle, that Timothy Day has some household mahogany furniture for sale, and will supply any kind of furniture of any quality; that John Donohue is conducting the weaving business at his shop near Nathaniel Bonnel's, and that Nathaniel Bonnel is erecting a fulling mill at Chatham, in Morris County, which will be ready to go in ten or fifteen days Groceries, drygoods, hardware, &c, are advertised with some degree of regularity, to be sold for cash, work, or country produce, by the village storekeepers, Foster Horton, the editor himself, Jacob Morrell, and the latter's successor, Samuel Alling West India rum and French brandy are offered by Sylvanus Seely, Joseph Fordin and

Jacob Hallett, iron wire, copper rivets and teakettle bottoms by Samuel Van Horn, and books by Peter Smith and the editor of the *Journal*.

Domestic articles, household goods, &c, at public vendue (such auctions sometimes indicating a change of residence) are advertised by William Darling, Timothy Day, John Donohue, Jacob Hallett, William Leary, Jacob Morrell and Matthias Woodruff, as well as by Azariah and Foster Horton, executors of Eunice Horton, deceased Real estate at public and private sale is also offered the editor advertises a house and lot, Ezekiel Gillam, a house and shop near the printing office, John Leary, George Townley and Andrew Stockholm, a farm, and a house and shop near the old mill, Peter Smith, a farm, Stephen Day, a lot of grass belonging to the widow Miller at the new bridge, John Blanchard of Chatham, land known as Great Piece, at Horse Neck, and Thomas Randall of Chatham, a house with garden and pasture to be let at Connecticut Farms

Elias Dayton, George Everson, Matthias Winans and Matthias Woodruff request a speedy settlement by their respective debtors, David Vanderpool forewarns the public to desist from trespassing upon his meadow, under penalty of prosecution, Captain Elijah Squier of Cheapside advertises for a school teacher for the ensuing summer, Joseph Meeker announces a reward of two dollars for a lost saddle, Thaddeus Day will give thirty dollars for information leading to the recovery of a red bull, Elihu Linley offers fifty dollars for the return of a black mare strayed or stolen, and Christopher Beekman of Griggstown, a reward of two hundred dollars for a horse stolen at Chatham David Baldwin of Chatham advertises for a mare strayed or stolen at Pequanack, and Cornelius Osborne of Hanover Township, near Chatham, offers one hundred and fifty dollars for a black horse stolen from the stable of Mr Mercereau on Staten Island, while Moses Cory, Thaddeus Day, Timothy

Day, Paul Day, Joseph Grummon and Samuel Searing describe estrays which have come to their respective plantations, and call upon the owners of such animals to appear and remove their property

Stockholm and Leary intimate that all persons having demands against them should present the same to William Leary of Chatham,[1] John Donohue, announcing a vendue of

[1] Andrew Stockholm and John Leary were partners in trade in the spring and summer of 1781, as is shown by a letter addressed to them by one of their correspondents The post rider having been captured by the enemy, and the mail-bag carried to New York, the letters it contained, including the one given below, were published in Rivington's *Royal Gazette* of June 9

Boston, May 23, 1781

Gentlemen —Your favor 11th instant I received this day I wrote you two letters within those seven days, giving an account of our friend Dickson's business and shipments, &c &c which I hope is come to hand I think it absolutely necessary that Leary goes immediately to Philadelphia, that he may give me an exact account of every kind of business there, particularly exchange, which, to our concern, will be of an amazing service I also think it high time for Stockholm to go immediately to the Cape, as an amazing deal of business may be carried on with a very small capital, if he will come this way, I shall be able to supply him with some money, and in a little time, if we are not very unfortunate, with more I shall write to Dickson, as you desire, not to ship any goods to Philadelphia, but what is entirely covered by ensurance, as the risk of getting safe is much greater than coming here I shall have an opportunity next Sunday, at which time I shall send him 1500 livres—I believe I could send him more, but French bills are not now selling, so that if you have any hard money by you, by all means purchase in Philadelphia, where I am informed they may be bought at 4s 6d the dollar The brig Sally is not yet arrived, am in great hopes she will in a few days, especially as the English fleet have now left Rhode Island, where, no one can tell, but the French are going out to protect their convoy, which consists of 15 transports, two frigates, and a 50 gun ship, so that in a few days we shall, I imagine, hear something new, at any rate it will give an opportunity for our property to come safe I sincerely hope some of the vessels bound to Philadelphia are arrived, as the first shipments to us are of very great consequence

We have nothing further worth your attention, should anything turn up, let me know, and depend you shall be made acquainted with everything this way

I remain, with esteem, gentlemen,

Your most obedient servant,

JOHN R LIVINGSTON, & Co

P S Dickson has shipp'd to Philadelphia in the Marquis le Fayette, of 42 guns, 400£ sterling in tea,—in Capt Josiah, 200 in do and linens,—in Capt Bell, 200 in do do—in ship Franklin, 12614 livres, what article unknown,—in the brig Sally, to Providence, 12614 livres, unknown,—in the ship Aurora, arrived, livres 5000, chintzes and callicoes

I wrote you this, as you may not have received my two former letters mentioning it

Mess Stockholm and Leary, Chatham

his house, household goods, shop and garden, one mile from Chatham near the old mill, wants two apprentices in the carpenter and joiner business (house- or ship-carpenter) to go to Philadelphia till New York is in our possession, the editor advertises for one or two boys of good characters, willing to learn the beautiful and genteel business of printing, for a boy of twelve or fourteen years old as apprentice to the art of paper making, for a schoolmaster, for two post riders, one for Morris County, the other for the lower route, for an experienced book binder; for good untainted sheepskins, with or without wool, and for clean linen rags, for which latter commodity he offers two sheets of writing paper or the highest price in money per pound—the highest price varying, with the fluctuation of the currency, from three pence to two shillings

From time to time references to the United States lottery are found, this being a matter in which Rev James Caldwell seems to have taken an active interest   It is announced in the *Journal* of February 2, 1780, that lottery tickets of the third class are to be had of Mr Caldwell at Springfield, or Mr Aaron Ogden at Newark   The issue of October 4th, of the same year, contains a card inserted by the parson which reads

A list of fortunate numbers in the third class of the United States lottery to be seen at Mr William Darling's in Chatham, Mr Woodruft's, Springfield, Mr Aaron Ogden's Newark, and Mr Winans's, Elizabeth Town

Those who have drawn blanks are to preserve their tickets for renewal

And on March 7, 1781, the reverend gentleman advertises that those who purchased from him lottery tickets in the third class may renew them in the fourth, by applying at his house in New Providence with tickets and cash

Occasionally the *Journal* contained the echo of a domestic tragedy—a card stating that the subscriber's wife has left him without just cause or excuse, and that he will assume no responsibility for any debts which she may contract in his name, sometimes followed in the next issue by a spirited reply from the indignant spouse, containing denials and recriminations In cases where such notices were continued through successive numbers of the paper, the husband's accusations and the wife's countercharges were generally printed in immediate sequence The advertisement of Ebenezer Searls may be regarded as typical of these warnings

WHEREAS RUTH, the wife of the subscriber, having destroyed my interest, and behaved herself in a very unbecoming manner, This is therefore to forewarn all persons not to trust her on my account, as I am determined not to pay any debts of her contracting after this date

Oct 10, 1780　　　　　　　　　EBENEZER SEARLS

WHEREAS an advertisement appeared in the last Chatham paper, forewarning all persons not to trust the subscriber on her husband's account This is therefore to acquaint the public, that I will not pay any debts of his contracting from the date hereof As to his interest which he says I have destroyed, I know of none he has, without it is what he claims of my estate, in which he has no right, there being a contract between us previous to our marriage which cuts him off of any claim

Oct 17, 1780　　　　　　　　　　RUTH SEARLS

In answer to a notice of similar import inserted by William Crawford, his wife replied

Whereas William Crawford, my husband, has been so lost to every principle of honour, friendship, truth and common humanity, as to advertise me as having eloped from him These are to let the

public know that what he has asserted is without the least colour of
truth, as he refused letting me enter the house on any account, for
no other reason than making a visit to a neighbour in the afternoon,
and, by reason of a hard shower, was detained until the next morning   If this is the way women are to be treated by husbands, we
are more wretched than slaves
June 6, 1781   MARY CRAWFORD

One of those who published a notice of this character
was Levy Gardner, whose wife in her answer not only
denied his accusations, but offered a reward of thirty
dollars and all reasonable charges to "any person that will
take up said Gardner, and secure him in any gaol, so that his
wife may have restitution made her "
Two cases are noted in which the husband embellished
the conventional disclaimer of responsibility with poetic
lines   John Scott thus concluded his advertisement

THE INJURED HUSBAND
What friendly ray, in pity drest,
    O say, can hope bestow,
To give distraction sight or rest,
    Or sooth eternal woe?
Life's little lamp, one tender beam
    To grief no more can spare,
But faintly turns a dying gleam
    On anguish and despair
Look down unending source of fate,
    From your obedient skies,
And Oh! instruct a wretch to hate
    The fair he must despise
Whatever tortures rend his breast,
    Whatever conflicts roll,
Teach him to tear her from his breast,
    And root her from his soul
Once, pure as winter's whitest snow,
    She gave her sacred vow!

Once, pure as innocence, but Oh,
 Just heaven what is she now ?
Then grant a wife, indulgent fate,
 On which my heart is set,
Or if I must not think to hate,
 O let me but forget

William Willis expressed his sorrow in like manner

Since it was my fortune to be join'd
 To such a wretched mate,
I've strove to reconcile my mind
 To my unhappy fate
I've born insults and threats likewise,
 I've strove for to persuade,
But them that's hardened so in vice
 Regard not what is said
Without a cause she left my bed,
 And broke her marriage vow,
So basely from me she has fled,
 Who then can blame me now ?
Then pity my unhappy fate,
 Beware of woman's arts,
For oft within a snowy breast
 Lurks a deceitful heart

Shepard Kollock did not confine his operations in the
printing business to the publication of a newspaper he also
printed almanacs, sermons, poems, &c , in pamphlet form:
and from his advertisement in the *New Jersey Journal* for a
book binder, to whom he offered constant employment and
good wages, we infer that these pamphlets were substantially bound   They were advertised in the paper from
time to time when ready for sale   Many of them are still
extant, and contain the Chatham imprint, and the advertisements imply that some of those which have been lost were
also printed, as well as sold, by the editor   At one time he

announced through the medium of his paper that he proposed to issue a weekly magazine of science and amusement
to be called the *Political Intelligencer,* provided the necessary support and encouragement were assured, but apparently the desired encouragement did not materialize, for no
record remains of such periodical having been published
here

CHATHAM IMPRINTS

1779   Rev Uzal Ogden A Sermon on Practical Religion (No 1)
       Rev Jacob Green A Fast Day Sermon
       Rev Wheeler Case A Book of Eight Poems on Several
                        Occurrences in the Present Grand
                        Struggle for American Liberty
       United States Almanac for 1780

1780   Rev Uzal Ogden A Sermon on Practical Religion (No 2)
       Rev Jacob Green A Sermon on Persons Possessing the
                        Iniquities of their Youth in After Life
       Rev Jacob Green A Sermon Designed for Instruction and
                        Warning of Youth of Both Sexes
       United States Almanac for 1781

1781   Associated Presbytery of Morris County   A View of the
                        Christian Church and Church Govern-
                        ment
       Rev Uzal Ogden A Sermon Delivered at Roxbury at the
                        Funeral of Mrs Elizabeth Hackett
       United States Almanac for 1782

1782   Poems on the Capture of General Burgoyne
       Isaac Watts. Divine Songs for the Use of Children
       United States Almanac for 1783

1783   Isaac Watts Psalms of David
       Rev Ebenezer Elmer Elogy on Francis Barber
       Rev Amzi Lewis   The Covenant Interest of the Children
                        of Believers

As a storekeeper, Kollock dealt in a limited variety of groceries and drygoods, but was a rather extensive book-seller, and it is thought that some of the school-books which he advertised for sale, notably the spelling-books and primers, were printed by himself

Captain Kollock ceased the publication of the *New Jersey Journal,* and moved to New York, shortly after the evacuation of that city by the British The last number of the *Journal* which has been located is dated November 12, 1783, and contains the announcement that the paper would be discontinued "at the evacuation of New York," to be succeeded by the *New York Gazette and Country Journal*[1] There could not have been more than one or two subsequent issues, since the evacuation took place on November 25th.

Upon taking up his residence in New York, Captain Kollock opened a book store at No 22 Hanover Square, and had a printing office at the corner of Wall and Water Streets, where he printed the *New York Gazeteer,* a tri-weekly publication which was the first newspaper issued at such frequent intervals in the metropolis He also printed the first city directory.

About a month before his departure from Chatham, namely, on the 14th of October, 1783, Captain Kollock founded a newspaper at New Brunswick called the *Political Intelligencer and New Jersey Advertiser,* which he published in partnership with his brother-in-law, Shelly Arnett, who had served an apprenticeship in the printing office at Chatham This New Brunswick paper was subsequently moved to Elizabeth, where it first appeared April 20, 1785 About a year later Kollock changed its name to the *New Jersey Journal and Political Intelligencer*—a title reminiscent of his sojourn at Chatham, combining the name of the periodical which he had hoped to publish in this village with that of the

---

[1] American Antiquarian Society Proceedings, XXVI, 418

one which actually existed here—and finally adopted the name of the *Elizabeth Daily Journal*, which has been retained to the present day.

Captain Kollock became a permanent resident of Elizabeth about the year 1788, and continued in the printing business until September 1, 1818, when he sold his interest in the *Journal*. He held the office of postmaster of Elizabeth until 1829, and served as a lay judge of the Court of Common Pleas of Essex County for thirty-six years. He was appointed aide-de-camp to Governor Bloomfield with the rank of brevet captain, and was reappointed by his successor; and was one of the original members of the New Jersey Society of the Cincinnati. He died at the home of his son-in-law in Philadelphia on July 28, 1839, at the age of eighty-eight, and was buried in the churchyard of the First Presbyterian church of Elizabeth.[1]

[1] *Newark Daily Advertiser*, July 30, 1839.

The following announcements are taken from the *New York Gazetteer* of December 10 and 24, 1783:

The Editor, while a publisher of the New Jersey Journal at Chatham, exerted every faculty to stimulate his countrymen to oppose the galling yoke we were threatened with; and to maintain the cause of freedom and the rights of mankind even at the risk of his personal safety.

TO BE SOLD. THE HOUSE and LOT where the subscriber formerly lived, beautifully situated in the pleasant village of Chatham, and an exceedingly good stand for a merchant, physician or tradesman. Any person desirous of purchasing will be allowed a reasonable time for payment.

S. KOLLOCK.

CHAPTER XII

THE most distinguished prisoners of war who were detained in Chatham during the Revolution were Major-General William Phillips and Major-General Friedrich Adolph Baron de Reidesel, two of the chief officers of Burgoyne's army in the disastrous campaign which terminated with the surrender at Saratoga

The terms of surrender, which were entitled ARTICLES OF CONVENTION, in deference to the wishes of General Burgoyne, who preferred the word "convention" to the more humiliating "capitulation,"[1] provided among other things that he and his entire army should be permitted to return to England, on condition that they would not again serve in America during the war This was a most unfortunate stipulation, to which General Gates never should have consented, for it is clear that if the captives, who numbered between four and five thousand, were allowed to return home, they would release an equal number of British troops then serving in Europe, who could be immediately sent to America without violating the terms of the conven-

---

[1] Windsor's Handbook of the American Revolution, 149

tion, thus completely nullifying the victory   Moreover, the patriots hoped that the friendly attitude of the French would ripen into active assistance, since war between France and England was anticipated, and if Burgoyne's troops, instead of being held captive, were permitted to return to Europe, and should be employed there in fighting against the French, the friendship between France and America would be seriously menaced

Soon after the removal of the captured army from Saratoga to Cambridge, Mass, whence they were to take ship for England, Burgoyne petitioned that they might be allowed to embark in Rhode Island in order to facilitate and expedite their departure, and he took occasion, in a letter to Gates, to protest against an alleged violation of the terms of surrender, which provided that the officers and men should be separately confined, stating that they were all imprisoned in the same enclosure, and insisting that "the public faith had been broken" As a matter of fact, some of the articles were violated by both parties   The British failed to give up certain equipments as agreed, and to surrender the colors of their various regiments   The Americans were assured that the flags had been destroyed, but it was afterwards learned that they had been hidden, and later smuggled out of the country   There was a good deal of wrangling on both sides, and the Continental Congress at length decided to detain the captured army until assured that the articles of convention would be fully lived up to   Congress feared that if Burgoyne believed, or pretended to believe, that the Americans had committed a breach of faith, as charged in his letter to Gates, he would not hesitate to entirely disregard all the terms of surrender as soon as he and his troops were afloat and although they permitted him and his staff to sail for England on parole, they refused to allow the departure of his army until the articles of con-

vention had been ratified by the British government This
the British government did not do, and the captives were
accordingly held in this country until the close of the war [1]

In November, 1778, they were removed from
Cambridge to a detention camp at Charlottesville, Va, remaining there until 1780, when the operations of Cornwallis
in that vicinity imperilled their safe keeping They were
then conveyed to the Shenandoah valley, later to Frederick,
Md, and finally to Lancaster, Pa During the years of their
captivity occasional attempts were made by some of the
British prisoners to escape and to rejoin their army, and a
few of them were successful The Germans who seem to
have been guarded with much less care, deserted in large
numbers upon the march from Cambridge to the South, and
established permanent homes among their countrymen who
had previously settled in America A few of the prisoners
enlisted in the American army,[2] and others were exchanged
from time to time, but a large number remained in captivity
until peace was declared in 1783

The artillery in Burgoyne's force was commanded by
General Phillips, while Baron Reidesel led the German
mercenaries The latter was accompanied by his wife and
children during the campaign, and Madam Reidesel's journal, which has been printed both in German and English,
contains a very interesting record of its writer's exciting and
perilous experiences Upon Burgoyne's departure for England, Phillips, by virtue of his rank, declared himself the
commanding officer of the "convention troops," as the captured army was called in reference to the articles of

[1] Avery's United States, VI, 130.

[2] On September 27, 1780, an advertisement appeared in the *New Jersey Gazette* inviting Germans who had deserted from the British army to join the Royal Regiment of Deux Ponts and that of the Duke of Lauzun's Hussars, both of which were then serving in America under Rochambeau

[3] Avery's United States, VI, 132, Green's American Revolution, 128

convention under which they had surrendered;[1] and "in this trying situation," says his biographer, "he at times exhibited evidences of a cholerick and impatient temper"[2] The phraseology is probably milder than the circumstances warranted, for Phillips was a man of singularly irritable disposition and ungovernable passion, who held the Americans in the utmost contempt and detestation[3]

Phillips was a personal friend of Lord Cornwallis, and the latter took an active interest in an endeavor to bring about his exchange, which was ultimately effected In the autumn of 1779, while Phillips and Reidesel were confined in the South, they received the welcome intelligence that they with their adjutants were to be permitted to go to New York on parole, and they immediately started on the journey northward At York, Pa, Reidesel was joined by his wife and children after a temporary separation, and the party traveled together to Bethlehem, and thence to Elizabeth, N J, but at the latter place, while almost in sight of their destination, they were bitterly disappointed to learn that they would not be allowed to proceed, Congress having decided to detain them pending the adjustment and payment of certain accounts against the convention army They were, therefore, obliged to return to Bethlehem, through which they had already passed twice in the course of their journeys in captivity, and while on their way from Elizabeth to that place the party stopped, from about the 1st until the 7th of October, at Chatham They remained at Bethlehem about six weeks, and were then permitted to continue their journey to New York[4]

[1] Windsor's Handbook of the American Revolution 149
[2] O'Callaghan s Burgoyne's Orderly Book, Munsell's Hist Ser VII, 60 n
[3] Drake's Dictionary of American Biography, 714
[4] Stone's Madam Reidesel's Journal, 163, Stone's Von Elking's Reidesel, II, 71, Ford's Journals of the Continental Congress, XV, 114 n

EXTRACT OF THE JOURNAL OF MADAM REIDESEL

We came to a very pretty place, opposite Staten Island, called Elizabeth-town, where we found many royalists who welcomed us joyfully and treated us with hospitality We were now so near New York and counted so surely on the exchange of my husband and the actual fulfilment of our dearest wishes, that, as we sat together at dinner, we confidently believed that we should cross over immediately to New York and be restored to freedom that same evening But suddenly the door opened and an officer, sent by General Washington, stepped inside and handed to General Phillips a letter with an order to return again, as the congress had refused to ratify the exchange The eyes of General Phillips, who was by nature very passionate, fairly scintillated with rage He struck the table with his fist, and said, "This is pleasant! but we should have expected it from these people who are all rascals!" I was like one petrified, and could not utter a single word He seized me by the hand, and said to me, "Now, my friend, do not allow your courage to fail you Follow my example! See how collected I am!" "Everyone" answered I to him, "shows his sorrow in his own fashion I keep mine in my heart, and you manifest yours with passion But it is my opinion that you would do better not to allow these people to see you in such a passion, who will only make sport of you, and may perhaps make you still more trouble ' He acknowledged that I was right, thanked me, and assured me that he like myself, would bear his sufferings with resignation From this time he conducted himself perfectly quietly

ORDER OF BRIGADIER-GENERAL WILLIAM WOODFORD

To Joshua Mesereau, Deputy Commissary of Prisoners

Elizabeth Town September 30, 1779

Sir,

You will remove Major General Phillips and the Officers of the Convention Troops under your care with their families and attendants to Chatham, where you will have proper quarters provided for them till you receive further orders for their destination [1]

[1] American MSS in the Royal Institution, Carleton Papers, II, 44.

From Gaine's *New York Weekly Mercury*, October 4, 1779.

The Generals Philips, Reidesel, &c, advanced on their Parole from the Convention army in Virginia, as far as Elizabeth Town in Jersey, on their Way to this City, were, as we are informed, yesterday prevented from proceeding by an Express from the Congress, which occasioned their being removed to the Village of Chatham, in that Province

From the same paper of October 11th

CHATHAM, October 5 — On Thursday last arrived here Major General Philips, of the convention troops, and his suit, and on Saturday, Major General Reidesel, of the Brunswick troops, with his Lady and suit   They were as far as Elizabeth-Town, on their way to New-York, on parole, but were stopped by order of Congress, and ordered here until further orders

MAJOR GENERAL PATTISON, OF THE BRITISH FORCES IN NEW YORK, TO VISCOUNT TOWNSHEND

New York, Octr 8th, 1779

My Lord

* * * * * * * *

Leave having been granted by the American Congress for Major Generals Philips & Reidesel to come from Virginia to New York on Parole, they arrived at Elizabeth Town in the Jerseys on the 30th Sepr, from whence Captain Campbell, Dy Qr. Mr General, was immediately dispatch'd hither with a Flag of Truce, and on the same Evening I sent hither [thither] proper Vessels for conveying those Officers & their Families, but to my great surprise and Disappointment I received advice from General Philips the Day following that an Order came the Evening before from Congress, to stop their proceeding to New York, and to remove them to Chatham, without assigning Reason for their Detention, since which they have been

sent further into the Country, to Easton   General Washington has
been wrote to upon the Subject, but his Answer is not yet arrived "[1]

*   *   *   *   *   *   *

A few of Phillips's letters dating from this period are
preserved among the American manuscripts relating to the
Revolutionary War in the Royal Institution in London   On
October 5th he writes to Sir Henry Clinton from Chatham
in New Jersey, refers to two previous letters announcing
his arrival and detention at Elizabeth Town; Major
Skinner has just informed him of an order that Reidesel and
himself with their respective families should proceed back
to Easton, Bethlehem, or Reading in Pennsylvania;[2] Major
Skinner has given permission for Lieutenant Bibby to carry
this letter to New York, enquires if it might not be well to
detain the flag ready to sail to Virginia until something is
determined, as they would require to send every material for
living if they are to return there, having sold off all their
furniture, not conceiving it possible that any obstructions
could be made, the Resolves of Congress upon which they
are detained are of the 27th and 28th September, is entirely ignorant of the motives; is sorry for Reidesel as he has
need of medical advice, proposed to request an explanation
and suggests if it would not be more proper to return to
Virginia than to linger for the decision of the American
Congress who so often alter their way of thinking upon the
subject of his situation, awaits the return of Lieut Bibby
with his Excellency's commands to set out from this place

In a second letter of the same date from Chatham in
New Jersey, he requests Clinton to give orders that two

<hr/>

[1] New York Historical Society Collections, VIII, 129

[2] The Board of War directed that Phillips and Reidesel should be
detained either at Laston, Bethlehem, or Reading   Washington considered
Bethlehem preferable, and issued orders accordingly —*Washington to Skinner, October 2, 1779, Washington Papers in Library of Congress, B.X, pt
I, 235*

hundred guineas may be sent out by Lieut Bibby for his use

On the following day he writes again to Clinton from Chatham in New Jersey, stating that Major Skinner accompanied Lieut Bibby to Elizabeth Town to assist him in getting permission to go to New York, but on their arrival at Elizabeth Town, Major Hay, the Commandant, judged proper not to allow it   Had proposed to send in his baggage that it might be sent to Virginia in a flag if necessary, this, also, refused unless submitted to a strict search Requests permission for an enclosed list of articles required by Madame de Reidesel to be sent to Elizabeth Town where an officer will remain to receive them.   Should the flag sail immediately he begs only £400 may be sent and requests him to order Mr Smith the Secretary to write an account of their situation to Virginia   Major General de Reidesel and himself set out for Easton to-morrow morning

He also penned the following letter to General Washington

Chatham October 6th 1779

SIR

I shall answer the letter you have, Sir, been pleased to send me by Major Skinner from *Easton* for which place I am going to set out

I writ to you, Sir, from *Elizabeth Town* in consequence of the detention of Major General de Riedesel and myself, but to that letter I have not received any answer

I will not wound General Washington's feelings with a description of my sentiments of the unkind treatment of the American Congress, they are such as I believe every Man of sense and honor must approve

I am greatly obliged for much politeness shewn me by Major Skinner.

I have the honor to be, Sir, with due respect Your Excellency's most Obedient and most humble Servant   W PHILLIPS

His Excellency General Washington.[1]

[1] Washington Papers in Library of Congress, 34, 97

SIR HENRY CLINTON TO GENERAL PHILLIPS

H[ead] Q[uarters] N[ew] Y[ork]
October 11 1779

My dear Sir,

I have your letter from Chatham & as you may well imagine am no less surprised than chagrined at your disappointment I trust yet that as you were exposed to this very troublesome journey & allowed yourself to be elated with the pleasing hopes from Genl Washington's immediate orders, he will by his interposition on the occasion prevent your having any ground for complaint against *him*

I have given directions for your being supplied with the articles you ask for

You will from public report become acquainted with the measures which this and other circumstances have made me take with respect to prisoners

I am, with every wish for your welfare, &c

I shall be much obliged to you if you will recommend Capt Featherstone to succeed to Capt Craig's Compy in the 47th I mean to interfere as little as possible in the promotions of the Convention Army, but I think he is entitled to a Company & I cannot give one any where else, he is besides an older Capt Lt than the gentn of that rank in the Regt [1]

On November 1st Baron de Reidesel wrote from Bethlehem to William Fitzhugh, after describing the journey from Virginia, which, owing to poor health, he found very fatiguing

You will easily imagine what was my astonishment at seeing two Hours after my arrival at Elizabeth Town a Resolve of Congress, that we should not be admitted into New York for the present, but wait further Orders, adding that we should be removed immediately to Chatham, and from thence have been ordered to Bethlehem, where we now are [2]

[1] American MSS in the Royal Institution, Carleton Papers, II, 49
[2] Ford's Correspondence of Samuel B Webb, II, 216

The suit of Phillips and Reidesel consisted of sixteen persons, four house servants and twenty horses[1] Their expenses at Bethlehem amounted to \$32,000 in paper money, or about £400 specie   A traveler who bought silver coin consented to exchange some of their paper currency for specie at the rate of 80 to 1, and thus enabled them to discharge their indebtedness[2]

Phillips and Reidesel remained at Bethlehem about six weeks, and were then permitted to go to New York on parole   By order of the Board of War, their journey to that city was commenced under the escort of Colonel Hooper, a deputy commissary of prisoners stationed at Easton, who was instructed to deliver them to Major Skinner, commissary of prisoners at Elizabeth, while the latter was directed to proceed towards Easton until he met the captives and to conduct them to their destination   The party did not pass through Chatham on this occasion, but followed another route, in order to prevent the prisoners from observing the activities of the army in this vicinity

WASHINGTON'S INSTRUCTIONS TO HOOPER

Head Quarters West point 22d Novr 1779

SIR.

By a letter from the Board of War I am informed that they have directed you to conduct Major General Phillips and Riedhesil and their families to Eliza Town   As I would not wish them to see the Ground near our new encampment, you are to avoid the Chatham Road and conduct them by the way of Bound Brook to Elizabeth Town   You are not to communicate your reasons to them for this change of the Route

I am Sir Yr most obt Servt

Colo Hooper or Officer conducting Generals Phillips and Riedhesil to Eliza Town[3]

[1] Stone's Madam Reidesel's Journal
[2] Mrs Ellet's The Women of the Revolution, I, 137
[3] Washington Papers in Library of Congress, B X, pt 2, 217

WASHINGTON'S INSTRUCTIONS TO SKINNER.

West point Novr. 22: 1779.

SIR:

By direction of His Excellency the Commander in Chief, I transmit you the inclosed by Express. It was intended for Colo. Beatty, but the General was informed on inquiry that he was not in Camp. You will perceive by the Copy of the Letter to you from the Board of War No. 4, that they originally intended you should conduct the business of sending Genls. Phillips & Riedesel & their families in. It is the Commander in Chief's wish that those Gentlemen should not proceed on the route by Chatham, but by Bound Brook. The Two officers who came on with a view of going to Canada by Water, are to be permitted to go to New York on parole. His Excellency desired me to mention this, least there should be any difficulties about their going in as they may not come within the description of either of the Generals families.

I am Sir

Yr Most Obt St

ROBT H: HARRISON

secy.

To Abraham Skinner, Esq
 Deputy Commissary of prisoners
  by John DeCamp Express.[1]

[1] Washington Papers in Library of Congress, B.X., pt. 2, 225.

CHAPTER XIII

The 'Hard Winter" of 1779-80—Choice of eligible Sites for the
Army's Winter Quarters—Localities near Chatham considered
—A Position near Morristown selected—Passage of the Troops
through Chatham—Their Hardships and Sufferings in Camp—
Lord Stirling's Expedition against Staten Island—Attempt to
capture Washington—Courtship and Marriage of Ensign
d'Anterroches

AT the close of the campaign of 1779 Washington was
again confronted with the necessity of selecting a suitable place for his army's winter quarters—a problem which
on this occasion seems to have been the subject of much
doubt and uncertainty As late as November 30th, General
Nathaniel Greene wrote to one of the quartermasters "We
are yet like the wandering Jews in search of a Jerusalem,
not having fixed upon a position for hutting the army " He
suggested to Washington two sites for the winter encampment Acquackanonck (Passaic) and Morristown, regarding
the former as more desirable, but the commander-in-chief
preferred the latter, and sent Greene to Morristown to look
over the ground [1] Knowing that Washington had not been
fully satisfied with that location when encamped there in
1777,[2] Greene directed Lord Stirling and Colonel James
Abeel to explore the surrounding country in the hope of
finding a more favorable site, the result of which investigation is thus set forth in a letter written by Stirling to Greene,
now in the library of the American Philosophical Society of
Philadelphia

[1] Sherman's Historic Morristown, 279
[2] Spark's Writings of Washington, IV, 264

Baskingridge Novr 9th 1779

DEAR SIR

In Consequence of Seeing your letter to Colonel Abeel of the 4th which I meet in My way to Kakiate, I immediately went in order [to] fulfill your Wishes towards Boon Town and traced the Country from thence to Chatham, in all that Course I could not find a Spot that would answer, the purpose, where there is water, there is no wood, and where there is wood there is no water, besides the General possition will by no means Coincide with what I believe to be the Wishes of General Washington or yourself, we then proceeded by Springfield to the Scotch plains, and this morning along the foot of the Mountains to the Quibble Town Gap, there are several Scituations below the mountains might do as to wood and water and plenty of good houses, but upon the whole they are all too much Exposed, to an att[ack] from the Enemy, there is nothing to Cover the front [illegible] either flanks the Quarters of all General Officers [illegible] be in front of the Line, in Short the whole will be [illegible] air without the least defense against an enterpr [illegible] Genius, in my opinion it will not do below the hills We proceeded on thro' the Quibble Town Gap to a Certain Tingle's and turned to the left between the Mountains and in going on for about four or five miles we found Several Scituations which think are preferable to any in New Jersey, the whole ground is very Similar to our Encampment at Middle Brook in 1777, three Gaps thro' the Mountain in front and three or four Roads in the Rear, one on the Right towards Pluckemin and another on the left towards Springfield & Chatham, yet on the whole it is not a [illegible] miles to the Sound between [paper torn] Check the in [illegible] Enemy either to the Northward or Southward better than any possition we have had in this State As to the particular Scituation Corps, each division by being placed about a Mile from each other and nearly opposite the Gaps will have plenty of Wood and Water, and on Grounds Exposed to the South Eastry sun, warm and Comfortable In short I do not think there is any Scituation so eligable on this Side of the Hudsons River It is true there are not many Comfortable Houses for the Quarters of Genl Officers, five or six pretty good, & 8 or 10 more so so, but we can make Shift if we begin early with makeing Huts of Convenience Some of the Roads &

Bridges in flanks & Rear will want repair, and attention should be paid to them before bad weather Comes on I did intend to proceed immediately to my division, [*illegible*] and a little fatigued with five days traveling, and [*illegible*] are my horses, I will set out again in a day or [s]o and join them, unless his Excellency should think I may be more usefull in this part of the Country I therefore must desire you will Communicate this letter to him, and I should be Glad to have his Sentiments as soon as possible

I have this Evening received Intelligence that [Ca]pt Prince has received a letter from Capt Dennis [*illegible*] Monmouth telling him that a fleet was Sailed from New York, with Eight thousand troops on board said to be for the West Indies I was at Genl Maxwells Quarters yesterday Evening, he had no such Intelligence but all the Intelligence from N York agree that every [pre]paration is making there for an Embarkation.

With Great Affection & Sincereity

I am ever yours

[Signature missing][1]

Colonel Abeel's report was embodied in a somewhat crude map showing the territory which may be roughly described as extending from Millburn to Basking Ridge, and from Springfield to Morristown, though dealing chiefly with the country lying on the east side of the Passaic River above Chatham An explanatory note was appended which reads as follows

REMARKS

As no Proper Ground was to be found between Chatham and Boon Town, his Lordship & myself proceeded from Chatham down to Van Arsdall's Tavern near Springfield[2] and proceeded along the foot of the mountain to Quibble Town Gap, & found many good places for the Army to encamp, but as the encampment would be too much exposed, we crossed the mountain thro' Quibble Town Gap in between the first & second mountain where we find a most

[1] Greene MSS, II, 60

[2] Shown at the corner of the road to Westfield, opposite the present hotel in Springfield

Beautiful place for the whole Army to encamp Wood & Water being plenty the Ground dry, roads leading through the mountain to Morris Town, Basken Ridge and Middlebrook, a Number of houses are in between the mountains some pretty good, on the left lays Chatham where many houses are that would do for head Quarters, but in that Case it will be necessary to Station a Brigade on the mountain marked A [1] there is plenty of Room in between those mountains for six or eight divisions & a large space may be left between them, a fine country for Forrage is in front of the first mountain towards Elizabeth Town & over the Second Mountain is a most Beautiful rich Vale between that and Long Hill, abounding with fine meadows and Plenty of Forrage the mountain in the Rear of the 2d mountain has scarcely any Wood as his Lordship & myself traversed it for many miles, in Short it far exceeds the encampment at Middle Brook the Road between the two mountains is very good and never Deep as it is hard Gravel and not very Rockey, many more Roads then are Pointed out in this Sketch lead from the Intended Incampment to Morris Town, Turkey, Baskenridge, Quibble Town, Middle & Bound Brook & Raritan, Elizabeth Town, Rahway, Woodbridge, &c a fine Road leads to Bryant's between Chatham and Springfield,[2] as it was very cold when I made this draft I hope the Genl will excuse its not being done better

James Abeel
D. Q M G

Morris Town, Novr 1779

It will be necessary to Build three or four Block Houses at each Gap in the first mountain & Station a Regt or Company at each, they will overlook all the Country round about & prevent a surprise, the Bridges on Pissaick will want repairing a Little and also some part of the Road, this may be soon done

The map was accompanied by the following letter

Sir
Morris Town Thursday 10th Novr 1779

According to your desire I have been & reviewed the Ground

---

[1] The mountain near Millburn

[2] Bryant's tavern shown at the corner of the Morris Turnpike and the lane which now forms the eastern boundary of Summit

between Bounton and Baskin Ridge but cou'd find no proper Ground for an Incampment at Long Hill and so on to Chatham but find in between the first & second Mountain as you will find described in the Rough Sketch here inclosed a most Beautifull Place for an Incampment abounding with Wood Water and every other necessary to make it agreeable his Lordship & myself think it preferable to the last Incampment at Middle Brook as I have made my remarks on the Sketch inclosed I need not say more his Lordship I dare say has been very Particular in his Letter as he knows the Country well I am preparing everything necessary as fast as possible & hope to have everything ready to be on the Ground when called for I shall make use of every exertion in my power

I am with esteem, Sr,

Yr Most Hble Servt

JAS ABEEL, D Q M G

N B I will send out & Provide some Fowls Turkeys Potatoes &c for the Genl in time

Major Genl Greene [1]

The locality finally decided upon lay about four miles southwest of Morristown on the road to Basking Ridge, and early in December the troops arrived and encamped there The army at that time consisted of Maxwell's New Jersey brigade, Stark's New Hampshire brigade, Clinton's New York brigade, Hand's brigade, two brigades of Connecticut, two of Pennsylvania and two of Maryland, together with Knox's brigade composed of two regiments of artillery and one of artificers, having besides the light mounted field pieces several larger and heavier guns for siege purposes.[2] A few of the northern regiments approached Morristown by way of Pompton and Whippany, but the greater part of the army marched over the Short Hills and through Chatham and Madison on their way to camp The latter division was

[1] Greene MSS, III, 1, in library of the American Philosophical Society
[2] Sherman's Historic Morristown, Chapters XV, XVI

unfortunately preceded by a rumor that the entire army had
been defeated in a recent battle, and was in precipitate
retreat, with the enemy in close pursuit [1] The consternation
of the people of Chatham upon hearing this report was only
equalled by their relief upon ascertaining its falsity

Dr Samuel L. Tuttle gives a realistic description of the
passage of these troops: the companies of armed pioneers
with their axes and other implements for preparing the
way for the army, the squads of officers on horseback, the
companies and battalions of soldiers on foot, the artillery,
and the long trains of baggage wagons, drawn by horses
and oxen with drums beating, flags flying, and the earth at
times shaking under the heavy roll of the artillery and
wagons and the tramp of horses The army reached Madison at dusk and encamped there for the night Their tents
were pitched close together on both sides of King's Road,
forming a double line which extended from the Presbyterian cemetery to the present corner of Seaman Street
The camp-fires were kept burning throughout the night,
and in the morning after an early breakfast, the troops
marched on to Morristown [2]

The winter of 1779-80 was one of exceptional severity,
and the sufferings of the soldiers at Morristown, who were
destitute of sufficient food and clothing, equalled the privations they had borne during the memorable winter at Valley
Forge Beginning early in November and continuing until
March, snowstorms of great violence occurred in rapid succession The waters surrounding the city of New York, and
even the lower bay, were covered by a solid and unbroken
sheet of ice, upon which the British cavalry and artillery
were able to cross to Staten Island and New Jersey with
greater facility than they could travel on land The worst
storm of the entire Revolutionary period was experienced on

[1] William P Tuttle in *The Spirit of '76*, March, 1900
[2] Historical Magazine, Ser 2, IX, 330

January 3rd, when the snow fell in great quantities, and in many places was blown by the wind into drifts ten and twelve feet in height [1]

So greatly were the roads obstructed by the heavy fall of snow that, for several days, access to the encampment, even from Morristown and Menham, was practically impossible,[2] provisions for the army could not be obtained, and the troops were brought face to face with starvation At one time the soldiers ate every kind of horse-food except hay,—buckwheat, common wheat, rye and corn composing the meal from which they made their bread Washington was obliged to call upon the magistrates in the several counties of the State to gather provisions for the troops, allotting to each county a certain proportion of flour and grain, and a certain number of cattle, to be delivered to the army at stated periods, and intimating that if the supplies were not forthcoming, they would be forcibly requisitioned But a resort to extreme measures proved unnecessary, for as soon as the plight of the soldiers became generally known, the sympathies of the people were aroused, and they responded promptly and cheerfully to Washington's demands, many counties furnishing supplies in excess of the quantity specified [3] One of the magistrates to whom the commander-in-chief applied in this emergency was Stephen Day of Chatham, who himself donated an entire beef to the army [4]

Dr James Thatcher, in his Military Journal, thus describes the hardships of the troops

The weather for several days has been remarkably cold and

---

[1] Hatfield's Elizabeth, 478, Mellick's The Story of an Old Farm, 514 A British spy, upon his return to New York from Morristown, reported ' The snow road from Morris Town to Elizabeth Town well beaten—very deep out of it, some places drifted to the height of four feet "—*New York Colonial Documents, VIII, 785*

[2] Harper's Magazine, XVIII, 300.

[3] Barber's New Jersey Historical Collections, 389 n

[4] Lewis Hist Pub Company's Morris County, 1, 295

stormy On the 3d instant, we experienced one of the most tremendous snow storms ever remembered, no man could endure its violence many minutes without danger of his life Several marquees
were torn asunder and blown down over the officers' heads in the
night, and some of the soldiers were actually covered while in their
tents, and buried like sheep under the snow   The snow
is now from four to six feet deep, which so obstructs the roads as
to prevent our receiving a supply of provisions For the last ten
days we have received but two pounds of meat a man, and we are
frequently for six or eight days entirely destitute of meat and then
as long without bread The consequence is, the soldiers are so
enfeebled from hunger and cold, as to be almost unable to perform
their military duty, or labor in constructing their huts

His Excellency, it is understood, despairing of supplies from the
Commissary General, has made application to the magistrates of the
state of New Jersey for assistance in procuring provisions This
expedient has been attended with the happiest success It is honorable to the magistrates and people of Jersey that they have cheerfully complied with the requisition, and furnished for the present
an ample supply, and have thus probably saved the army from destruction

Again, in March, he writes

The present winter is the most severe and distressing which we
have ever experienced An immense body of snow remains on the
ground Our soldiers are in a wretched condition for the want of
clothes, blankets, and shoes, and these calamitous circumstances are
accompanied by a want of provisions It has several times happened
that the troops were reduced to one-half, or to one-quarter allowance, and some days have passed without any meat or bread being
delivered out

It was discovered by investigation at Philadelphia that
the frost had penetrated the ground to a depth of three feet
seven and a half inches [1] On March 18th, Washington
wrote to Lafayette from Morristown

Pennsylvania Magazine of History, XXVII, 50

The oldest people now living in this country do not remember so hard a winter as the one we are now emerging from In a word, the severity of the frost exceeded anything of the kind that had ever been experienced in this climate before [1]

During the winter of 1779-80 the advance guard of the army was posted at Springfield, instead of being placed at Chatham as was done in 1777 The latter village, therefore, was comparatively bare of troops, though it continued to be a station of the local militia, and in all probability a guard was constantly maintained at the bridge

In January the people of Chatham witnessed the setting out of Lord Stirling's expedition against Staten Island, but as his plan was guarded with the greatest secrecy, they probably were not aware of the significance of the movement The ease with which Staten Island could be reached by means of the ice in the sound, which formed a natural bridge from shore to shore, and was amply strong enough to bear a large body of troops, determined Washington, notwithstanding the depleted condition of his forces, to attempt a surprise attack upon the enemy's outposts A large number of sleighs—said to have been about 500— were collected for the transportation of the troops with their ammunition, tools, rations, &c , and on the 14th of January Lord Stirling set out from Morristown with approximately 1500 men, both infantry and artillery Every effort was made to conceal his design, as he depended for success upon surprising the enemy The expedition passed through Chatham during the afternoon

At Elizabeth Stirling was joined by General William Irvine with his detachment, who had been sent on the 9th of January to reconnoiter the enemy's position and by Colonel Dayton's regiment of New Jersey troops, thus increasing his force to about 2500 men Soon after midnight on the 15th

[1] Baker's Itinerary of Washington, I, 174

he crossed to Staten Island but, despite the caution which had been observed, the British had received warning of the raid, and were found to be on the alert   Perceiving that they were strongly fortified and intrenched behind an abattis of snow, Stirling did not risk an attack, but retired about daybreak, having captured a few prisoners and received several deserters   The casualties on each side were trifling, but about 500 of the Americans were frostbitten, and all suffered severely from the cold   The expedition not only proved a failure, but was the cause of retaliatory raids by the British upon Newark and Elizabeth [1]

Barber and Howe, in their Historical Collections of New Jersey, record the tradition that when Washington and his army lay at Morristown in the "hard winter" of 1780, a party of British cavalry left New York for the purpose of taking him prisoner   They proceeded by way of Elizabeth During the night they were overtaken by a violent storm of hail, snow and rain, that froze as it fell, covering the ground with a thick crust which cut their horses' ankles, and so impeded their progress that at dawn they had advanced no farther than Bottle Hill, now Madison, and as their object could not be successfully carried out in broad day-light, they were forced to abandon the enterprise and return to New York   Mistrusting the loyalty of the guide, who was an American spy, they placed him in the centre of a hollow square, and rode with drawn sabres

The mention of Elizabeth and Bottle Hill indicates that the party passed through Chatham   It is not claimed by Barber and Howe that this anecdote is more than a tradition, but Dr Samuel L Tuttle, writing at a later date, gives it as an authentic fact, and says that when the circumstance became generally known, it created a great sensation,

Stryker's N J Volunteers (Loyalists) in the Revolution, 18, Hatfield's Elizabeth, 478-9, Sherman's Historic Morristown, 346, Thatcher's Military Journal, 134

not only among the troops, but throughout the entire
countryside [1]

It is probable that some such attempt was actually
made, for it is referred to by various writers, among them
being Thomas Jones, a tory resident of New York during
the War of Independence, who mentions the incident in his
History of New York in the Revolution   Though he writes
from the loyalist point of view, Judge Jones takes frequent
occasion to criticize the shortcomings of the British commanders, and to comment unfavorably upon the lack of success which often marked their efforts, and he describes the
attempt to capture Washington in his usual caustic style

> In the winter of this year [he writes] information was received
> at New York, that Washington's quarters were in a house at Mor-
> ristown at some distance from the huts occupied by the rebel army
> The snow was very deep, the winter prodigiously cold, and as no
> danger was apprehended, his guards were trifling   Clinton thought
> the capture of Washington would put an end to the rebellion   I
> believe it would, as no other person could have kept such a hetero-
> geneous army, as the rebel one then consisted of, together   Four hun-
> dred horse were dispatched for that purpose   This alert turned out
> as all others did   It failed   The guides got frightened, the party
> bewildered, they lost the road, and after a cold, tedious and fatiguing
> excursion of 24 hours, without ever seeing a rebel, returned to New
> York all frost bitten   This manœvre was laughed at by the rebel
> army, derided by the militia, and cursed by the Loyalists.   Thus
> ended this famous alert an alert which was to have ended the war,
> (as Clinton supposed)   But God knows, through the stupidity or
> wickedness of our Commanders in Chief, all our alerts, battles and
> seiges, during the whole war, (a very few excepted) met with the
> same fate, and ended in the same manner [2]

The letter which follows, written by Colonel James
Abeel to one of Washington's aides-de-camp, gives some

[1] Historical Magazine, Ser 2, IX, 331
[2] Jones's New York in the Revolution, I, 318

particulars of an attempt by the British to capture the commander-in-chief on February 10, 1780, and the statement that the advance of the enemy was impeded by snow, leads us to think that this was the enterprise referred to by Barber and Howe Colonel Abeel does not intimate, however, that the invaders succeeded in reaching Bottle Hill, or in penetrating any part of Morris County

The following Intelligence was given me this day by a Person from Elisabeth Town & I believe may be depended on as fact, Vizt —

That a Party of between 4 & 500 Horse and three thousand foot under the Command of Genl Gray crossed Powls Hook on Thursday last and marched as far as the West end of Coll Schuylers Swamp and intended to march on to Morris Town by Way of the Notch, the light Horse were to endeavour to bring off his Excellency, & the foot to take the Rout towards Chatham to support the horse if they succeeded in their enterprize and to bring off a Number of Cattle belonging to the Publick in their Rout which are at Horse Neck Genl Skinner & Coll Sterling to cross with about 2000 Men at Elizabeth Town & Coll Simcoe with 300 Horse & some foot to cross at Raway to draw our attention that way, but the Snow being so deep in the Swamp that Genl Gray cou'd not advance a Signal by 5 Rockets was given to Genl Skinner that it was not possible to advance & by Skinner with 5 Rockets from the Bridge at Elizth Town to Simco, which occasioned their return to Staten Island & the other Places they crossed 10 or 12 P of Artilry lay in readiness at Deckers Ferry to be transported to De Harts Ferry That all the Inhabitants on York & a part from Long Island were embodied & had recd Ammunition & Cloathing & were to guard the City that 87 Sleds had Crossed from New York this day Week to Staten Island with Amunition & Provision that the River was passable on the Ice from Powls Hook to Long Island that all or most of the British Troops were come from Long Island to New York & Staten Island, that 3000 Men were on Staten Island he brought me three Papers but one has been taken away and the other two you will herewith receive I make no doubt but his Excellency has

long ago had the Intelligence but [if] he shou'd not I now send it
& am with respect Sr

                              Your Most Hble Servt
                              JAS. ABEEL, D. Q. M. G.
Sunday 13th Feby 1780[1]

    Shortly after the arrival of the army in this region,
during the winter of 1779-80, occurred the romantic marriage of the Chevalier (afterwards Count) d'Anterroches,
a prisoner of war in the hands of the Americans, and Miss
Mary Vanderpool of Chatham.[2]

    Joseph Louis d'Anterroches was a scion of a
noble family in the south of France, the genealogical
records of which are said to extend back to the twelfth
century, revealing in each generation men who took a leading
part (chiefly in the line of military service) in many of the
great events of French his-
tory. The seat of the
family was the Chateau de
l'Audubertie at Bas Limou-
sin, near Tulle, in the Department of La Correze,
and there Joseph Louis
was born on August 25,
1753, the son of Jean
Pierre Count d'Anterroches
and Lady Jeanne Francoise
Teissier de Charnac Count-
ess d'Anterroches; the latter a near relative (probably a cousin) of Madame

COUNT D'ANTERROCHES'S DAUGHTER
(MRS. ROGERS)

[1] Washington Papers in Library of Congress, 35, 370.

[2] This international love story is delightfully told by Mrs. Emeline G.
Pierson in Leslie's Monthly Magazine for August, 1893, from data supplied by Count d'Anterroches's daughter, Mrs. Warren Rogers. The facts
contained in the text have been freely drawn from that article; and the
author further acknowledges his indebtedness to Warren R. Dix, of Elizabeth, N. J., a great-grandson of Count d'Anterroches, for additional information of more than passing interest.

de Lafayette. The young chevalier naturally inherited the martial spirit of his soldier-ancestors, and his fondest ambition was to enter the army; but, being a younger son, his father designed him for the church, and insisted that his studies should be directed to that end. Upon attaining the proper age, he was accordingly sent to the home of his uncle, Alexander Cæsar d'Anterroches, Bishop of Condon, under whose tutelage he was prepared for a clerical life; but he was firmly impressed with the belief that he had no fitness nor calling for the priesthood; and in 1776, before his studies were concluded, he ran away, went to England, and enlisted as a "gentleman volunteer" in the Sixty-second regiment of infantry; his choice of a foreign country as a field for his military career probably indicating his apprehension that if he were found in the army of France, his family would possess sufficient influence to bring about his discharge. His aristocratic father, upon ascertaining his whereabouts, would not suffer him to serve as a private, but bought him a commission as ensign, corresponding to second lieutenant in our service, at a cost which is said to have approximated £400. As he signed the roll with his surname only, according to the

THE BISHOP-UNCLE.

usual custom of the European nobility, his Christian name does not appear on the British army lists, and he was known simply as "Mr." d'Anterroches.

In 1777 the Sixty-second regiment was ordered to America, where it formed a part of Burgoyne's army which surrendered at Saratoga. After his capture by the Americans,

JOSEPH ALEXANDER, COUNT D'ANTERROCHES.

HEAD OF THE FAMILY, 1776

D'Anterroches obtained permission to write to Lafayette, informing his distinguished relative of his unfortunate plight; and through the interest and influence of the marquis he was released on parole. Nothing is known concerning the terms of his parole, or of his movements between the surrender at Saratoga in 1777 and his appearance at Chatham in 1780; but as it is probable that considerable time elapsed before he was given an opportunity of writing to his kinsman, and that a further delay occurred before his release could be effected, there can be little doubt that a large part of the interval was spent in captivity with the convention troops at Charlestown, Mass., and later at Charlottesville, Va.[1]

Family tradition is that after his release he became an

[1] Among the papers of General Gates in the library of the New York Historical Society we find a letter from Lafayette to Gates, written at Camp near Valley Forge, April 10, 1778, and containing the following paragraph which may possibly refer to D'Anterroches:

"There is also at York a gentleman of my family who had been left sick in Carolina, and by the neglect of some I need not to mention was never sent for till this time. he has been excepted from the general rule of [illegible] the French officers sent by Mr. Deane as he has been considered as one in my family what in fact he is. he was to be a captain eighteen months ago, and I do not ask from Congress any particular thing for him but what they will judge proper."—*Gates Papers, Box 9.*

On December 23, 1779, Washington wrote from Morristown to John Beatty, Commissary General of Prisoners: "Your letter of this date to Mr. Harrison has been laid before me. On account of the very distressed situation of Mons. d'Antroche as represented by you, I have no objection to your permitting him to go *to New York on parole* to return when called for. If he can effect his absolute exchange for the Officer entitled in regular course, It will be agreeable to me."—*Washington Papers in Library of Congress, B.X., pt. 2, 491.*

aide-de-camp on the staff of Lafayette, but it is inconceivable
that an officer of the British army would tender his services
to England's enemies and fight against his erstwhile comrades   As a stranger in a strange land, however, he would
naturally attach himself to his relative's official family, and
while riding about with the marquis he might easily be mistaken for a staff officer, but he was not so occupied at the
time of his arrival at Chatham, for Lafayette spent the
winter of 1780 in France   His name remained on the
British army lists until 1787, but this fact does not prove
his continuance in the service   it may simply indicate his
neglect to tender his resignation at an earlier date

Referring again to family tradition, we learn that the
chevalier first met Miss Mary Vanderpool on or near the
bridge over the Passaic River, while he was riding through
Chatham with a party of American officers   Captivated by
her beauty, he immediately lost his heart, and was not long
in ascertaining her name and residence, and presenting himself as a suitor.

"Polly," as she was invariably called, was the daughter
of David Vanderpool, a tanner and currier by trade, and a
soldier in the New Jersey militia, whose great-great-grand-
father had come from Holland   She was born August 7,
1758, the eldest of a family of six children   Her father was
the owner of a large old-fashioned farm-house, standing
upon the property still owned by his descendants, on the
south side of the turnpike just east of the river, the house occupying the approximate site of the present dwelling, though
somewhat nearer the road   It was a frame building, two
stories in height, with two windows on each side of the front
door, and a covered porch with a seat on either side   A
flight of sixteen or eighteen steps led from the door-yard
down to the roadway, which, at that place, is much lower
than the adjacent land   About a hundred years after the
time of which we write, the remains of his tan-vats were

discovered a short distance below the surface of the ground, on the easterly side of the brook which crosses the property, and a few rods from the turnpike.

As a matter of convenience when signing his name, David often shortened it to V D Pool—a custom which obtains to this day in Holland—and in the course of time even this abbreviation was abandoned for the simple "Pool " He was enrolled for military duty in the name of David Pool, and during his declining years he was familiarly known as "Old Pop Pool" throughout the village

David Vanderpool is said to have been a captain in the Revolutionary army, but the assertion cannot be proven by the military records   No official mention of his having served as an officer has come to light, and in Stryker's Officers and Men of New Jersey in the Revolution he appears simply as a private of Essex County militia, although General Stryker, when consulted upon this point, said that such omission is not conclusive, because the New Jersey records relating to the Revolutionary War are extremely imperfect   The only documentary evidence of David's military rank consists of the certificate of Polly's marriage at the French Legation in New York, which refers to her father as formerly captain in the service of the United States, and as the certificate was prepared with great care as to details, containing a full recital of all the circumstances of the marriage, and was sent to France for filing in order to make title to lands, it was evidently regarded as a document of great importance, and would not be likely to contain a false statement   David's grandchildren, in conversation with him and his wife, were often told that he had been a captain in the Revolution, and had held that rank in the battle of Springfield, and the fact that he had a sword which was preserved in the family for many years after his death, and which was said to have been presented to him by the men of his company, adds weight to the assertion that he

held a commission The sword was described as a very
elegant and costly weapon, set off with ornamentations of
elaborate design, and it may have been one of the swords
taken from the captured British army at Saratoga, which
were delivered in charge to Major Tallmadge while he was
stationed at Chatham in 1778

Captain Vanderpool strongly objected to the proposed
alliance between his daughter and the young chevalier He
positively forbade Polly to marry "that d——d French-
man," and assumed so uncompromising an attitude that the
heart-broken lover took to his bed, turned his face to the
wall, and vowed he would die Family tradition assigns the
chevalier's nationality as the sole reason for this opposition,
but it is far more probable that his connection with the
British army was the cause of the difficulty Party feeling
at that period ran very high The country was overrun with
spies, by whom information of the most vital importance
was often conveyed to the enemy, and everyone whose ante-
cedents were not known to be above criticism was under suspicion It is by no means improbable that D'Anterroches
was regarded by the patriots in general with distrust and
aversion, and the opinion held that, notwithstanding his
endorsement by Lafayette, he should be more closely confined It may readily be surmised that to David Vanderpool, who was engaged in fighting his country's battles in
company with his friends and neighbors, whose respect and
esteem he desired to retain, the thought of a marriage between a member of his family and one of the enemies of
his country was extremely repugnant It is more than likely
that Polly was twitted by her acquaintances about her affection for a British officer, and that for these reasons she
and her family endeavored to gloss over the fact that the
chevalier was a prisoner of war, and to emphasize his relationship to Lafayette, allowing the impression to be
formed that he was an aide-de-camp of the marquis, and that

her parent's disapproval of the marriage was grounded solely upon the bridegroom's foreign birth

Whether the stern father's prejudice was eventually overcome is perhaps doubtful, but it is certain that if the parental consent was wanting, the young couple managed without it, and on the 30th of January, 1780, they were united in marriage at the parsonage in Madison by the Rev Ebenezer Bradford, pastor of the Presbyterian church at that place, whose parish included Chatham   Polly often visited the old parsonage in after years, saying that she was greatly attached to the house by reason of its pleasant associations   The wedding ceremony was quiet and simple the festive gathering common to such occasions was precluded by the severity of the weather and the unsettled condition of the country, and a fine wedding gown for the bride was lacking, for New York was in the hands of the enemy, and materials for its manufacture could not be obtained. But an elegant trousseau was afterwards sent to Polly by her husband's parents, which compensated for the want of a more elaborate costume on the occasion of the wedding

The simple ceremony at Madison was not considered a sufficient compliance with the marriage laws of France, and seven years later a second ceremony was performed, according to the rites of the Roman Catholic church, in the chapel of the French Legation at New York

The chevalier and his bride first established a home in Easton, Pa   Why that town was selected as a place of residence does not appear, but it is probable that when D'Anterroches expressed a wish to cease traveling about with the army as a paroled prisoner, and to retire to civil life, the military authorities gave him permission to reside in Easton as a place far removed from the scene of conflict, where, if he were secretly disposed to render assistance to the British, he would find difficulty in gathering information or in communicating it to the enemy

In 1784, when the Revolution was ended and peace was restored, he removed with his family to Elizabeth, where a number of his countrymen resided, and became in the course of time the head of the French colony in that city. In later years he served in the United States army, taking a prominent part in suppressing the Whiskey Insurrection in Pennsylvania; and before leaving the service had been advanced to the rank of major of cavalry.

HOME OF PIERRE AND JEANNE D'ANTERROCHES, ELIZABETH, N. J.
(Courtesy of *Leslie's Monthly*.)

CHILDREN OF JOSEPH & MARY D'ANTERROCHES.

JEAN PIERRE: born July 14, 1781, died December 24, 1854; married, November 20, 1800, Abigail Marsh of Rahway, N. J., who was born August 18, 1779, died April 14, 1825.

JEANNE FRANCOISE: born January 31, 1783, died June 10, 1862; married, April 5, 1801, John De Hart.

MARIE ALEXANDRINE: born August 29, 1785; married ——— Cook.

PAUL JOSEPH (Lafayette's namesake): born October 5, 1787, went to France in 1806, and the next year married his cousin, Marie

Judith Josephine, daughter of Jean Blaize Viscount d'Anterroches Resided at Puydarnac, Department of La Correze

MARIE ADRILNNL FRANCOISE born July 12, 1789, died October 12, 1800   She was named Adrienne for Mme Lafayette

MARIE ERNESTE HENRIFTIL born September 24, 1791, died January 4, 1873, married, May 26, 1817, Joseph Lyon, of London, England, who was born in 1779 and died December 16, 1839

JULIE FRANCOISE GABRIELLL born March 15, 1794, died June 22, 1888, married, (1) April 28, 1811, Edward Griffith, a native of Newcastle-under-Lyme, Staffordshire, England, who died January 20, 1820; (2) August 29, 1821, Warren Rogers, of New York, who died in 1843

FRANCOIS DE LOYAC born May 6, 1796, died in 1874, married, (1) Mary Lewis, (2) Amelia ———, (3) Dora Broome, (4) Annie Hines

JOSLPH LOUIS born July 15, 1799, died September 18, 1819 in New Orleans, La

ALEXANDRI born in December 13, 1801

In 1789, while the chevalier was visiting his parents in France, his little son Pierre was presented at the court of Louis XVI, and the boy's costume, patterned after the dress uniform of a French officer, is preserved in the family as an heirloom

Upon the death of his father and elder brother, the chevalier succeeded to the title of Count d'Anterroches, but did not live long to enjoy the honor   He was then in France on a second visit to his parents   After his father's decease, and before he could arrange his affairs and return to America, he himself fell sick and died in his native land on January 17, 1814, at the age of sixty-one

Polly Vanderpool d'Anterroches lived in Elizabeth and New York to the advanced age of eighty-six   When Lafayette visited this country in 1824 he received her and

her children at a private interview, and embraced them with
the affection of a relative   She died in New York July 31,
1844, and was buried in St   John's churchyard at Elizabeth

CHAPTER XIV

Insubordination of the Troops at Morristown—Knyphausen invades
New Jersey—Washington moves from Morristown to Chatham
—He occupies the Short Hills before Knyphausen's Arrival—
The British reach Springfield—They burn the Village of Connecticut Farms—They retreat to Elizabethtown Point—Clinton
attempts to reach Morristown—Encounters a stubborn Resistance at Springfield—Abandons the Enterprise—Wayne moves
to Chatham—Court-martial of Doctor Shippen

THE severity of the winter of 1779-80 proved a great
hindrance to the movements of both armies, and the
operations of the British at New York against the State of
New Jersey were limited to an occasional marauding expedition in the direction of Newark and Elizabeth, but with
the approach of spring, and the coming of milder weather,
it was anticipated that the enemy would resume their former
activities, and that their raids would be succeeded by inroads
of a more determined and serious character   For this
reason the New Jersey brigade under General Maxwell was
detached from the army at Morristown on the 14th of May,
and ordered to take post at Elizabeth to protect that city
and its immediate neighborhood   The passage of these
troops through Chatham was thus commented upon by the
New Jersey Journal:

CHATHAM, May 17   Last Sunday passed through this place the
Jersey Brigade on their way to Elizabeth Town where they are to
be stationed   They made a martial appearance, and we were agreeably surprised to find them so very strong

The privations of the troops encamped at Morristown
did not terminate with the breaking up of the winter, but

continued far into the spring and the patriot soldiers, who had endured with the most heroic fortitude the sufferings of the preceding months, now found their patience giving way   Mutterings of discontent were followed by signs of insubordination, until, on May 25th, the Connecticut troops mutinied, and declared their intention of returning to their homes, or of "gaining subsistence at the point of the bayonet" Their chief ground of complaint, aside from the universal one of lack of provisions, was that their pay was long overdue, and that, owing to the great depreciation of the Continental currency, their money, when received, was of little value   With some difficulty the mutiny was put down, a few of the ringleaders being placed under arrest, but the affair caused General Washington the greatest anxiety and annoyance.[1]

The tories and British spies lost no time in carrying news of the revolt to New York   Lieutenant-General Baron von Knyphausen, who commanded the troops in that city during Sir Henry Clinton's absence in the South, was given a greatly exaggerated account of the mutiny, being assured that the whole Continental army at Morristown was insubordinate, and that practically the entire population of northern New Jersey had become so weary of the struggle for independence that great numbers of civilians would eagerly join the British if offered adequate protection   Completely misled by these representations, Knyphausen believed that an excellent opportunity was now afforded, by a sudden and vigorous attack, to gain possession of Morristown, to destroy the stores and powder-mill at that place, and to annihilate, or at least to disperse, the American army—a masterstroke which in his opinion could have no other effect than to terminate the resistance of the patriots and re-establish British sovereignty in this region   On the night of June 6, 1780, at the head of a large force of British and

[1] Lossing's Washington, II, 669, Irving's Washington, IV 42

Hessian troops—infantry, cavalry and artillery—he crossed to Staten Island and thence to Elizabethtown Point, his plan being to surprise Maxwell's brigade, which was known to be in that neighborhood and, by a rapid march, to gain possession of the passes of the Short Hills, in which the strength of this part of the country lay. With the key of the situation thus securely in his hands, he would await the arrival of reinforcements, and then push on to Morristown.

The landing of the invaders was promptly discovered by the American outposts, who at once gave warning of the enemy's approach. The watchful sentinels on the crest of Hobart Hill between Springfield and Chatham quickly fired the beacon and discharged the alarm-gun, arousing the entire countryside. The farmer-soldiers seized their weapons and hastened to the repulse of the enemy, and Knyphausen was obliged to relinquish his plan of surprising Maxwell and gaining the Short Hills before the militia could assemble to aid in opposing his progress.

CAPTAIN DAYTON TO GENERAL WASHINGTON

SIR

I am directed by Colo Dayton to inform your excellency that the enemy landed this night at 12 oClock, from the best intelligence four or five thousand men & Twelve field pieces. & it is his conjecture they intend to penetrate into the country

I am your excellys most hum Servt

JONA DAYTON *Capt*
3rd J Regt

Near Eliza Town
past 1 oClock Wednesday morn [1]

The news of this sudden invasion brought Washington's sojourn at Morristown to an abrupt conclusion. Drums beat to arms, the troops turned out and formed, and regiment after regiment marched away toward the field of battle. Washington wrote to Lord Stirling that the British were

[1] Washington Papers in the Library of Congress, 38, 53

advancing rapidly in considerable force, and that the alarm
should be given and the militia collected, adding in a postscript "The enemy were on the road from E Town
to Springfield—We shall move towards Chatham "[1] At the
same time Colonel Alexander Hamilton, one of Washington's aides, wrote to Baron Steuben

DR BARON

I am commanded by The General to inform you that the enemy
are out in considerable force and by the last advice were advancing
this way We are going to meet them The General is just setting
out for Chatham and will be happy to see you there

Yrs Respect'y
A HAMILTON,
A D C

Hd Qrs
June 7 80 [2]

GENERAL WASHINGTON TO MAJOR TALBOT

Headqrs Morris Town June 7th, 1780
½ after 8 A M

SIR

I have this morning been informed that the Enemy landed
last night in force at De Hart's point, near Elizabeth Town, and
are advancing rapidly on the road to Springfield I wish you to communicate this intelligence to the Militia Officers in the vicinity of
your post immediately that they may alarm the Country, and that
You will march as expeditiously as You can, consistently with the
Men's healths with the Detachment under your command & with
all the Militia that will join You, for *Chatham*, keeping the Mountains below you on your left You will send on some of the Militia
Light Horse, or Messengers from time [to time] to Chatham in order
to inform yourself of the advance and situation of the Enemy & also
to advise me how far you are on your march

I am Sir Yr Most Obed St

G W

Major Talbot
or Officer commandg the Detachmt at Paramus [3]

[1] Magazine of American History, III, 499
[2] Steuben Papers in Library of the New York Historical Society
[3] Washington Papers in the Library of Congress, B XI, pt 2, 399

The order books of the period indicate that the troops
left Morristown about 7 A.M. on Wednesday, the 7th of
June, and advancing without a pause arrived at the Short
Hills on the same day but Washington himself halted for a
limited time when Chatham was reached   This is proven,
first, by the letters quoted above, which show his intention to
make Chatham a place of rendezvous, and possibly the base
of his contemplated operations, second, by the fact that Sir
Henry Clinton, when writing to Lord Germain of Knyphausen's incursion, stated that Washington's army at the
time was at Chatham with an advanced corps at Connecticut
Farms;[1] and third, by an itinerary of Washington, contained
in Volume III of the Magazine of American History, giving
his whereabouts on almost every day during the war, as
indicated by his orders, correspondence, &c, which places
him on June 7, 1780, "at Headquarters, Chatham"—an
assertion doubtless based upon some order or letter having
that caption   The same statement is made in a similar
itinerary of Washington compiled by the late Hugh Hast-
ings, who for many years held the office of State Historian
of New York, and published by him in Volume VIII of the
Public Papers of Governor George Clinton [2]

The probabilities of the case favor the supposition that
while the commander-in-chief stopped at Chatham to confer
with other generals and to issue some necessary orders, the
army marched on to the hilly region east of the village, so
that the defiles of the Short Hills were occupied before
Knyphausen succeeded in reaching Springfield   Washington's stay at Chatham was quite brief, however, for his presence was urgently required nearer the scene of conflict, and
it is doubtful if he remained here over night   In one of his

[1] Ford's Writings of Washington, VIII, 321, n

The *Pennsylvania Evening Post* of June 9, stated 'His Excellency gen
Washington's head quarters, it is said, are removed from Morristown to
Chatham "

Paul Day

Stephen Day Esq

Mr Vanhorn

Chatham Inn

Papaic River

Days Tavern

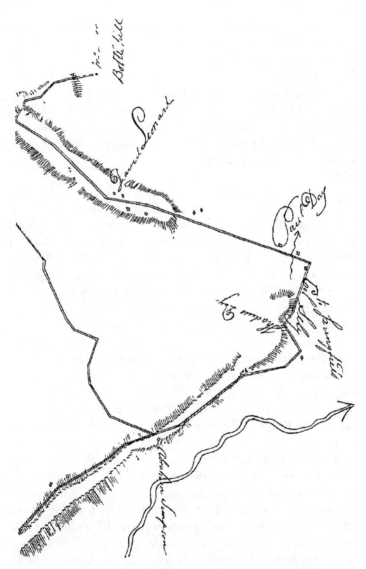

Bottle hill

Samuel Leonard

Paul Day

Springfield

Short hills

Hobart Gap

Colonels Simpson

REVOLUTIONARY MAP OF CHATHAM
By Robert Erskine Geographer of the Continental Army
From Original in Library of the New York Historical Society

letters he stated that upon receiving the news of the enemy's advance, he put the army in motion, and it reached the heights in the rear of Springfield on Wednesday afternoon [1] He did not say that he himself arrived there on the same day, but that was perhaps implied His headquarters on the Short Hills could not have been far from Chatham, if we may judge by a correction in the draft of a letter written by him to General Howe, the caption of which reads "Hd Qrs Short-Hills-Near-Chat Heights above Springfield June 10 1780 "[2]

General Knyphausen pressed steadily forward to the village of Connecticut Farms, or Union as it is now called He was assailed along his entire line of march by Colonel Dayton's regiment of the New Jersey brigade, and such of the militia as had time to gather, who, while unable to repulse him, so impeded his progress that, although he started from Elizabethtown Point before daybreak, he did not reach the neighborhood of Springfield—a distance of about eight miles—until late in the afternoon

At Connecticut Farms, where Dayton effected a junction with the remainder of the brigade under General Maxwell, the advance of the enemy was checked for over two hours, but the arrival of British reinforcements compelled the Americans to fall back, and they slowly retreated to a position on the Rahway River at Springfield, where they offered a still more determined resistance, the action being declared by Maxwell to be the closest he had seen in the war The patriots were at length driven across the river into Springfield, but Knyphausen perceived that he would not be able to enter the village before nightfall, and learning from American prisoners and deserters that Washington had reached the Short Hills, and could not be dislodged without great sacrifices, he decided to advance no farther The

[1] Sparks's Writings of Washington, VII, 75
[2] Washington Papers in the Library of Congress, B, XI, pt 2, 411

village of Connecticut Farms was sacked and burned, and
during the hours of darkness the enemy retreated to Elizabethtown Point, where 500 of their number intrenched themselves while the remainder crossed the sound to Staten
Island [1]

It is difficult to account for Knyphausen's conduct in
thus weakly abandoning his design without venturing an
engagement with the main American army   He left New
York for the avowed purpose of attacking Washington, of
capturing the military stores at Morristown, and of dispersing the Continental forces   His command, according to
both American and English reports, consisted of 6,000 men,
and greatly outnumbered any force which could be collected
to oppose him   He suffered no reverse, and encountered no
resistance except that offered by the New Jersey troops in
what would be considered at the present time but little more
than a series of skirmishes   Yet upon learning that Washington was marching against him, and was prepared to offer
him the opportunity he sought of measuring his strength
with that of the American commander, his courage seemed
to fail, and as soon as darkness concealed his movements, he
beat a hasty and ignoble retreat

He was of course surprised and disappointed to learn
the falsity of the information he had received concerning the
alleged insubordination of the Continental troops, and the
wavering patriotism of the people   but this circumstance
alone is not sufficient to account for his irresolution   The
probable explanation is that he considered the success of the
expedition to depend entirely upon his occupation of, and
unopposed passage through, the hilly region between Springfield and Chatham, for the knowledge that Washington had
reached that point before him seems to have been the means
of deterring him from further efforts   He was doubtless

[1] Hatfield's Elizabeth, Chap XXII

told that if he attacked the Americans among the hills his
troops would be at a great disadvantage even though his
enemy were far inferior in number and equipment, and it is
very possible that the dangers and difficulties of an advance
were magnified by the prisoners and deserters whom he questioned, and even by the guides he employed.

Dr James Thatcher, who spent the winter in camp at
Morristown, alludes in his Military Journal to the fact that
on June 7th his brigade was ordered to Chatham in consequence of the enemy's movements, and he briefly describes
the engagement at Connecticut Farms Lieutenant John
Shreve of the Second regiment New Jersey Continental line,
also refers to the invasion in his Personal Narrative He
writes

> They [the British] returned to Elizabethtown losing many men
> killed and wounded, and a sergeant corporal and twelve men taken
> prisoners I had the Camp Guard with twelve tories confined and
> Gen Maxwell sent me to Chatham, a village three miles west of
> Springfield, with the tories and the English prisoners where I
> remained about a week, and then took them to Morristown, put
> them in jail and joined the regiment on the lines near where Gen-
> eral Knyphausen lay at Elizabethtown [1]

Washington did not return to Morristown after the
enemy retired, but remained encamped at the Short Hills as
though awaiting a renewal of hostilities Perceiving that
a body of horse could be employed to good advantage in
reconnoitring, and in checking the activity of the British
cavalry in the neighborhood of Elizabeth, he caused his
command to be reinforced about this time by ' Light-Horse
Harry Lee's famous partisan legion Dr Thatcher, under
date of June 15th mentions in his Military Journal the
arrival of this beautiful corps of light dragoons the men
in complete uniform and the horses very elegant and finely

---

[1] Magazine of American History, III, 571

disciplined   The doctor adds that Major Lee was said to
be a man of great spirit and enterprise, and that much
important service was expected of him   Upon reporting
his arrival to the commander-in-chief, Lee received a
friendly reply, which was dated at headquarters near Springfield the 11th of June, and read as follows

Dear Sir,
      I have received your favor of this date.   The spirit which
has been exhibited by your corps gives me pleasure, and be
assured, meets with my thanks and approbation   As your rapid
progress must have fatigued the cavalry in some degree, I wish you
for the present to take post somewhere in our rear   Perhaps Chatham, or its vicinity, is as well calculated to afford you forage as
any other place   You will, however, when you have fixed upon the
spot, be pleased by a line to point it out to me   I shall be glad to
see you at my quarters tomorrow morning
                              I am, etc etc
                                             Go Washington
      To Major Henry Lee [1]

      Shortly after Knyphausen's incursion Sir Henry Clinton
returned to New York from his successful campaign in South
Carolina   Learning of his subordinate's humiliating failure
to penetrate the country beyond the Short Hills, he at once
decided that another attempt to reach Morristown should be
made, and, to guard against a second fiasco, that he would
lead the expedition in person   As a preliminary step, in
order to draw Washington and his army away from the
Short Hills, he embarked some soldiers in transports upon
the Hudson River, as though preparing to attack West
Point—a step which he had had under consideration, and
which Washington had been led to expect   The American
commander was deceived by this ruse, and, on June 21st, he

[1] Sparks's Writings of Washington, VII, 77

broke camp, again passed through Chatham, and commenced a leisurely march northward, intending to keep pace with the enemy as they ascended the Hudson. He left Major-General Greene at the Short Hills to guard the road to Morristown, with a force of about 2,500 men, consisting of Maxwell's brigade, Stark's brigade, Lee's dragoons, and a small body of local militia [1]

With Washington and the greater part of his army safely out of the way, Clinton landed at Elizabethtown Point before daybreak on the 23rd of June, with 5,000 infantry, a large body of cavalry, and from 15 to 20 pieces of artillery, and commenced his march toward Morristown. Again the alarm-gun and beacon-light upon Hobart Hill gave forth their warning, to be promptly repeated by corresponding signals upon the more distant peaks, while the militia gathered from every farm and village, formed companies at their various places of rendezvous, and marched to meet the foe. The latter, in the meantime, was advancing rapidly and in perfect order. Leaving Elizabeth at five in the morning, and marching by way of Connecticut Farms, Clinton soon reached Springfield, where Greene engaged him in a vigorous battle. Up to that point the enemy seems to have encountered little, if any, opposition; and their advance was so rapid that the Morris County militia, despite the alacrity of their movements, did not arrive at Springfield until the most serious part of the conflict was over [2]

In a work of this kind, the scope of which is purely local, a detailed account of an engagement occurring in another town would be out of place; and the full descriptions of the battle of Springfield which are contained in the county histories and in the biographies of General Greene make

[1] Sparks's Writings of Washington, VII, 83, Johnson's Nathaniel Greene, 191, Lossing's Field Book of the Revolution I, 323

[2] Irving's Washington, IV, 67, Barber's New Jersey Historical Collections, 193, Jones's Ashbel Green, 118

further repetition unnecessary. Suffice it to say that the Americans offered a most stubborn resistance, which, in view of the disparity of numbers, was highly creditable to the generalship of the commander and the courage of the men The principal action took place at the Rahway River, just east of Springfield, where Colonel Angell with about 200 Rhode Island troops engaged the main column of the enemy for thirty or forty minutes, and when a flank movement compelled him to retire, he did so in good order, carrying his wounded with him Superior numbers then enabled the British to press forward They drove back the Americans, who made a stand in the center of the village, and followed them as far as the rising ground which was about half a mile west of the Revolutionary settlement, though within the limits of the present town of Springfield [1]

At this point, however, Clinton seemed to lose courage Either because he was told that Washington had returned, and was trying to encircle his force, or because he was dismayed by the forbidding appearance of the Short Hills which now loomed before him, he did not pursue his advantage, but, following Knyphausen's example, he consigned the village to the flames, and hastily retreated to Elizabeth He was pursued the entire distance by large parties of militia, who kept up a continuous and galling fire, but so precipitate was his flight that he completely outdistanced Stark's brigade which was immediately dispatched in pursuit [2]

Clinton's failure to follow up his success at Springfield is even more inexplicable than the conduct of Knyphausen in the preceding incursion It may be urged in excuse of the latter that, after fighting a determined and elusive enemy all the way from Elizabeth, and losing many of his best troops

---

[1] Hatfield's Elizabeth, 497, Trial of Lt -Col Thomas of the 1st Foot Guards, 10, 11

[2] Hatfield s Elizabeth, 498, 499, Lossing's Field Book of the Revolution, I, 324

SPRINGFIELD BATTLE MONUMENT

at Connecticut Farms, it was disheartening to find his further progress barred by Washington and his army, in a position from which they could not be readily dislodged Clinton, however, was called upon to face no such formidable opponent He was confronted only by Greene, whose force was so small, as compared with the strength of the invaders, that the resistance offered is really astonishing It is true that Clinton engaged in a pitched battle, which was a much more serious and important action than that which terminated Knyphausen's raid, but Clinton succeeded in defeating his adversary, and, although his casualties were disproportionately large, his abandonment of the enterprise in the flush of victory is not easily explained Stedman, the English historian, accounts for his change of plan by suggesting that a further advance would have compelled him to fight his way through a country naturally difficult and abounding in strong passes, where his progress would be disputed with an obstinacy well illustrated by the resistance encountered at Springfield, that the expedition, even if successful, might prove too costly, and that the expected arrival of a powerful French fleet on the American coast precluded him from engaging in any enterprise which would require much time, or carry him a considerable distance from New York [1] This explanation, however, is by no means satisfactory Clinton must have been aware of the rumored proximity of the French fleet before he left New York, he undertook the march to Morristown with full knowledge of the topography of the intervening country, the distance he would have to travel, and the opposition he would be likely to meet He was informed of all the circumstances of Knyphausen's incursion, and was prepared to profit by any errors of judgment which might have contributed to the latter's failure Even the knowledge that reinforcements

[1] Stedman's American War, II, 244

were marching to Greene's support could hardly have dismayed the leader of so powerful a force, and we can only account for the relinquishment of his design by assuming that, upon viewing the steeps of the Short Hills, he overestimated the difficulty of penetrating such a region

General Washington received news of the battle late in the afternoon of the same day, while at Rockaway bridge, on the road from Troy to Lower Montville, about eleven miles north of Morristown He at once detached a brigade under Anthony Wayne to aid Greene by attacking the enemy's right flank, and at the same time fell back to Whippany, to be within supporting distance[1] Wayne pressed forward with all possible speed, but, upon reaching Chatham, he learned that the enemy had retreated, and that his presence in Springfield was not required He accordingly halted at Chatham for the night, and on the following morning rejoined the commander-in-chief

WAYNE TO WASHINGTON

Chatham, 23d June, 1780
8 o'clock P M

DEAR GENERAL—
You no doubt have heard that the enemy, after burning Springfield, are retired to their former posts on Elizabethtown Point Their number, from the best observation, did not exceed 4,000 They brought out three days' provisions, which probably is to serve them until they reach the vicinity of West Point I have not yet seen Gen Green, but from good intelligence, the grenadiers and light infantry, composing two battalions, together with all the other troops lately arrived from Charlestown, except the legion Embarked last evening, but had not sailed this morning May they not wait the return of those who marched from the point this morning, and proceed in conjunction up the river, in full confidence that this manœuvre has drawn your excellency's attention to this quarter?

[1] Irving's Washington, IV, 67

I shall in consequence move along the mountain towards Passaic falls, in the morning, unless countermanded by your excellency or General Green

Most respectfully, your obedient servant,

ANTHONY WAYNE

General Washington

WASHINGTON'S REPLY

Whippany, 11 o'clock P M
23d June 1780

DEAR SIR—

Some time before the receipt of your favor, I was informed that the enemy had returned to their station at Elizabeth town Point It is certainly difficult, if not impossible, to ascertain their views I, however, all things considered, wish to keep our force as compact as possible, and therefore wish you, if you find in the morning that the enemy are quiet or gone over to Staten Island, to return by the same route you marched to-day.

I am, dear sir, your most obedient servant,

General Wayne [1]   GO WASHINGTON

The American casualties at Springfield were light, for the fire of the British artillery was providentially too high to do much execution. Greene's losses were 13 killed, 49 wounded and 9 missing, while of the militia none was killed, and but 12 wounded. The British loss was much greater it was stated by Lieutenant Matthew of the Coldstream Guards to be not less than 500 killed, wounded and missing, besides officers, though this estimate probably included Knyphausen's incursion as well as that of Clinton [2]

As a precautionary measure, while the result of the battle was in doubt, a number of the American wounded were removed to a considerable distance from the village; and Dr Ashbel Green of the Morris County militia states

[1] Moore's Wayne, 109, 110
[2] Hatfield's Elizabeth, 499, Historical Magazine, Ser 1, I, 105

that the road by which his company marched to Springfield
was in places literally sprinkled with the blood of wounded
soldiers who had been carried along it[1] Four of the latter
were brought to Day's hotel near Chatham for surgical
treatment, and were placed in the barn of the tavern, where
they died a few days later[2] The interments were made a
short distance up the river (in Summit), on a plot of ground
now owned by George B Vanderpoel, lying between the
River Road and the mill-pond The graves were not marked
with monuments, and their exact location has been lost
but the late Stephen H Ward, an aged resident of Chatham, used to say that he recalled having seen in his boyhood some graves there, which, he was told, were the resting places of Revolutionary soldiers They were then
indicated by mounds, perhaps half a dozen in number, on
the high ground about 150 feet southeast of the mill-dam

The action at Springfield was the last attempt of the
British to penetrate this part of the State It was by far the
most important engagement of the war which occurred in
the vicinity of Chatham, and occasioned a more general
turning out of the men enrolled for militia duty throughout
this region than any other event of the struggle for liberty
Consequently its details were distinctly remembered by the
veterans of the Revolution, and were related by them to
their children and their children's children long after other
war-time incidents had been forgotten Not only did every
man who was qualified for military service hasten to the
repulse of the enemy, but a number who, by reason of their
vocation, or physical infirmity, were exempt from militia
duty, made their way to Springfield to witness the combat
from the slopes of the neighboring hills The suspense of
the people of Chatham while the battle was in progress can
be neither realized nor portrayed The distance of five

[1] Jones's Ashbel Green, 118
Historical Magazine, Ser 2, IX, 333

miles which separated them from the scene of conflict was
not sufficient to deaden the frightful thunder of the artillery, and their terror was increased a hundred fold when
dense clouds of smoke rising above the intervening hills
apprized them that Springfield was in flames With their
anxiety from the peril of their loved ones at the post of
danger were mingled the gravest fears for their own safety,
since the possibility of defeating so formidable a body of
British troops was considered by no means certain, and at
almost every house the families of the patriot soldiers could
be seen loading their most cherished possessions into wagons
to which oxen were attached (all the horses having been
commandeered), in readiness to seek a place of safety up
the Passaic valley, or among the Morris County hills

"The worst of consequences was anticipated," writes Dr Samuel L Tuttle, "but at length, the suspense of the whole community
was at an end when an express rider came dashing up the road, swift
as the wind, crying at the top of his voice, 'The British are flying
the British are flying,' and when our victorious troops were seen returning from the scene of the strife it was impossible for them to
restrain their joy Their long and repeated hurras, as they came
through the place the waving of handkerchiefs from every dwelling
along the lines of the march, and the tears of joy that were stream-
ing down the faces of persons of all ages and all conditions in the
community, showed very clearly what a deliverance God had wrought
out for them on that day Though there were many wounded and
some killed in the vicinity, never, on the whole, did the national flag
float more exultingly, and never did a heartier tribute of gratitude
arise from the dwellings and the hearts of this region, than those
with which that day was marked [1]

The perplexities and dangers to which the patriots were
exposed by the activities of the enemy, at the time of, and

[1] Historical Magazine, Ser 2 IX, 333

for a few weeks after, the battle of Springfield, are thus
alluded to in a letter of Rev James Caldwell

Chatham July 3d 1780

SIR,

Our situation here is exceedingly distressing Parties out continually after ever active Whig, and not a Centinel between us
and the enemy During the Alarm the farmers below cou'd not
work their fields, & now they dare not in safety. Corn and grass
suffer And no decency can be observed at Elizabeth Town about
Flags I know your Excellency must attend to your grand object—
from this we do not wish to divert you But if you can grant the
3d , or rather the first & third Jersey Regiments, You will add inexpressible joy to the Country, & add to the many favours granted.

Your excellency's most obed & very huml sevt.

JAMES CALDWELL.

His Excellency Genl Washington

[Addressed]
    Public Service
His Excellency
    General Washington[1]

The fact that the following letter, written by Colonel
Dayton of the Third New Jersey, is dated at Chatham, indicates that Mr Caldwell's request for the presence of that
regiment in the neighborhood was granted

Chatham July 7th 1780

SIR

There is not the least doubt that the British in New
York have certain accounts of the Approch of a French fleet, as a
number of large ships are now moored between the east and west
bank for the purpose of sinking to stop the passage or render it as
difficult as possible I have a boat laying up North River I propose
to direct a man to run away with her to New York and get into the

---

[1] Washington Papers in the Library of Congress, 39, 20

service or to follow fishing to Sandy hook until he gets a through knowledge of every obstruction in the narrows and then return to Eliz Town, if your Excellency Approves of this plan I have not the least doubt but I can procure a proper person to carry it into execution

By the best accounts I can get the number of the enemies Vessels mentioned in my last was nearly right, but it cannot be exactly ascertained as two or three are continually kept cruising twenty leagues off the Hook

Tuesday night last four men were taken out of their beds and carried to S[t]aten Island by eight or ten refugees, the men taken lives about one mile west of Eliz Town and are as good men as any in this country

I am your Excellencys most Obedient Hbl servant

ELIAS DAYTON [1]

During the interval between Knyphausen's raid and the battle of Springfield, Chatham witnessed a sitting of the court-martial appointed for the trial of Dr William Shippen, Jr, Director-General of Military Hospitals, on charges of official misconduct This was a celebrated case it attracted wide attention, caused the civil and military authorities much trouble and perplexity,[2] subjected them to severe criticism, and gave rise to bitter animosity between the doctor's adherents and his adversaries. As the court was composed of officers in active service, it was obliged to follow the army, holding its sittings at irregular intervals and in many different places The proceeding was commenced at Morristown in January, continued through the following summer, and terminated in Philadelphia A session was held in Springfield on June 15th,[3] and another in Chatham a few days later

[1] Washington Papers in the Library of Congress, 39, 56
[2] Balch's The Maryland Line in the Revolution, 115
[3] Washington's Orderly Book, March 23, to July 23, 1780

FROM THE ORDERLY BOOK OF THE FIRST PENNSYLVANIA REGIMENT

Head Qrs Short Hills, *June 21st* 1780

* * * * * * * * *

The Court Martial, of which Gen'l Hand is President, is to sit at Chatam to-morrow morning at 10 o'clock, at Darling tavern, and proceed on the trial of Dr Shiping The will sit from Day to Day till the business is finished, unless a movement of the enemy should make it necessary the should join their respactave Corps, in which cases the are to Do it without further orders [1]

William Shippen, Jr , was one of the most eminent and successful physicians of Philadelphia He was born in that city in 1736, the son of William Shippen, Sr , who was also a member of the medical profession He graduated from the College of New Jersey in 1754, studied medicine with his father, and afterwards in Great Britain, and received the degree of M D from the University of Edinburgh in 1761 Returning to Philadelphia, he commenced the practice of medicine and surgery, and also established a school of anatomy, his lectures being the first on that subject which had ever been delivered in America Through his efforts midwifery was first recognized as a science, to be studied as a regular branch of medical education His ability and success as a teacher led to his election, a few years later, to the chair of Anatomy and Surgery in the medical school of the College of Philadelphia, and subsequently to a corresponding office in the University of Pennsylvania [2]

Soon after the outbreak of the Revolution, Dr Shippen was appointed chief physician of the Flying Camp, and in April, 1777, was elected director-general of all military hospitals for the armies of the United States, being, in fact, the author of the plan upon which the hospital department

[1] Linn & Egle's The Pennsylvania Line in the Revolution, II, 534
[2] Appleton's Cyclopædia of American Biography, V, 512, Wicke's History of Medicine in New Jersey, 59

was organized As early as 1778, charges of dereliction of duty and misappropriation of hospital stores were made against him by Dr Benjamin Rush, physician-general of the Middle Department, but no action was taken at that time In 1780, however, the accusations were repeated in a form more explicit and positive, and the matter assumed so serious an aspect that he was placed under arrest, and a court-martial was appointed for his trial The charges are set forth in the following order

Morris Town, Jany 5th 1780

Sir

You are hereby ordered in Arrest on the following Charges, preferred against you at the Instance of Doctor John Morgan

First—Fraud, in selling Hospital Stores as your own property, & in making use of Continental Waggons for the Transportation of the Same

Second—Speculation in, & selling Hospital Stores, whilst the Sick were perishing for the want of them, accompanied with peculation, & Adulteration of Hospital Wines at Bethlehem

Third—Keeping no Regular Books of Accts with proper Checks and Vouchers for the Expenditure of Public Money & Hospital Stores And neglecting and refusing to pay just & reasonable Hospital Accts and insulting the person who applied for Settlement

Fourth—Neglect of Hospital duty, from which many of the Sick suffered in a Shameful and Shocking Manner, and making false Reports to the President of Congress of the State of ye Hospitals & of the Sick

Fifth—Scandalous and infamous practices such as are unbecoming the Character of an officer & Gentleman, in aspersing and calumniating the Reputation and Conduct of your Superior Officers to the Members of Congress in order to vilify, degrade and supplant them

By order of his Excellency

OTHO WILLIAMS A GL—

To Doctor William Shippen Jun Director General of the Hospitals of the United States of America [1]

EXTRACT OF GENERAL ORDERS

Head Quarters Morristown
March 13th 1780

A General Court Martial of the line to sit Tomorrow tin OClock at the new house in Morristown for the trial of Doctor William Shippen and such others as may be brought before them Brigadier General Hand is appointed President, Colonel Hazen Proctor Lieut Colonels DeHart & North & Majors Thever & Greer are appointed Members A Capt from each Brigade in Camp except the 2d Maryland and 1st Penna will also attend as members [2]

Shippen's principal accuser at this time was Dr John Morgan, who had previously held the office of director-general and chief physician of hospitals, and who acted as prosecutor at the trial, in the absence of the judge advocate general   The proceeding lasted several months, a number of witnesses being examined and a great mass of evidence considered: but the prisoner was at length acquitted upon the ground of insufficiency of evidence, although the court pronounced his speculations in hospital stores to have been highly improper and justly reprehensible   Then followed a protracted and most acrimonious correspondence in the Philadelphia newspapers between Shippen's friends and his opponents, the latter being led by Morgan whose letters (which often filled two and even three columns of print) charged that the court had been unduly prejudiced in the prisoner's favor, that the proceedings had been irregular in many respects, and that Shippen, instead of being exonerated by the decision, as he and his friends claimed, had been dishonorably acquitted   since the language employed by the

[1] From original in possession of the Washington Association of New Jersey
[2] Ibid

court in denouncing his conduct would be
disciplined armies as a sentence of guilt an
 After the conclusion of the trial, Cor
majority, reappointed Shippen to his for
action which caused much criticism of the
and renewed attacks upon the doctor's
thought to have been in consequence of th
sion of disapproval that he resigned hi
January, 1781.[1]

[1] Morgan's letters in the *Pennsylvania Packet*, N

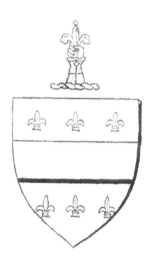

CHAPTER XV

THE opening of the year 1781 witnessed a serious insurrection of the Pennsylvania Continental troops who
were in winter quarters at Morristown   A feeling of discontent had been steadily increasing among these soldiers
since the preceding autumn, caused by a variety of trying
circumstances, chief of which were that the men had received
no pay for twelve months, and were destitute of proper food
and clothing, and that a misunderstanding had arisen concerning their term of enlistment   This the officers claimed
was for three years or during the war, but while a few of
the rank and file concurred in this opinion, the great majority
insisted that they were enrolled for three years only, and
were entitled to a discharge at the end of that period,
whether the war was concluded or not   At length the troops
were goaded into open rebellion by the offer, on the part of
the State of Pennsylvania, of a bounty of three "half-Joes"[1]
to any man who would enlist for the remainder of the war
To the veterans who had long endured the hardships and
perils of camp and battlefield, without pay and often without
rations, only to have their demands for money parried with
empty promises or totally ignored, this liberal offer to raw
recruits was particularly exasperating   They made it their

---

[1] A half-Johannes is meant   A Johannes, according to the standard of
New Jersey and Pennsylvania, was equivalent to £6 —*Almon's Remembrancer, 1776, III, 279*

principal ground of complaint, and declared their intention of marching in a body to Philadelphia, and demanding redress of the Continental Congress

On the evening of January 1st, about 1300 Pennsylvanians (comprising the entire line with the exception of portions of three regiments) turned out under arms, provided themselves with food and ammunition, seized a number of horses belonging to their officers, together with six pieces of artillery, and marched in the direction of Philadelphia Their departure was preceded by much disorder and even rioting, in the course of which at least one officer was killed, and General Anthony Wayne, who commanded them, was threatened with instant death if he attempted by force to oppose their progress [1] These troops formed the chief part of the force at Morristown, and the revolt caused the greatest anxiety, for it was feared that the mutineers in their anger and excitement would commit many acts of violence, and that the British, upon learning of the insurrection, would embrace the opportunity to advance from New York, the latter apprehension being increased by a report that a party of the enemy had actually landed at Elizabethtown Point [2]

The next morning General Wayne directed the New Jersey brigade, then encamped at Pompton, to march to Morristown to assist in quelling the mutiny and preventing disorder Colonel Israel Shreve, who commanded at Pompton, could not send the entire brigade, as some of the men were urgently needed for other duties, and some were unable to leave camp owing to insufficient clothing and equipment, but he detached a battalion of 250, being about half of his total force, and ordered them to Morristown under command of Lieutenant-Colonel Francis Bar-

[1] Sherman's Historic Morristown, 370 et seq , Hervey's Washington, 119, Lossing's Field Book of the Revolution, I, 312
[2] Boudinot's Llias Boudinot, I, 207

ber[1] Upon their arrival, the Jerseymen expressed sympathy
for the mutineers, saying that the latter had real grievances
which ought to be redressed, and in fact showed such un-
mistakable signs of insubordination that it was not considered prudent to oppose them to the Pennsylvanians[2] Instead, General Wayne ordered them to Chatham, to serve
the double purpose of preventing the insurgents from marching that way to join the British, and of opposing any advance which the latter might make   He wrote to Washing-
ton·

I have ordered the Jersey brigade to Chatham, where the militia
are also assembling, lest the enemy should take advantage of this
alarming crisis   Indeed, the alarm-guns have been fired, and the
beacons kindled towards Elizabethtown, perhaps occasioned by our
unhappy affair.[3]

COLONEL BARBER TO COLONEL SHREVE

Morristown Jany 6th 1781

Dr Sir,

I received yours inclosing General Wayne's to you, yesterday
morning   It was undoubtedly bad policy to send the Jersey troops
from their encampment, unless with an evident design against the
enemy   The cause of the Pennsylvanians is I fear too much considered as a just and common cause   The situation of the battalion
I have the command of is delicate, and I have the greatest reason
to be apprehensive of consequences   Some men of the 1st regiment
have been trying to foment an insurrection they as yet have been
altogether unsuccessful in the 2d and 3d   The other officers and
myself were up almost all last night expecting an attempt, but I now
enjoy the happiness to think that the party was small originally and
could procure very few adherents   In order to create a diversion from
this unhappy affair, I have been advised, and indeed it was

[1] Letter of Shreve to Washington, Washington Papers in Library of
Congress, 45, 67
[2] Hall's Parsons, 321
[3] Ford's Writings of Washington, IX, 90

my own opinion, to march the battalion to Chatham   Their attention will more likely be fixed on the enemy   I march today and will
quarter there this night   I think you had best avoid Morristown
unless you are bound by orders   Nothing from Gen Wayne on the
insurgents

    I am, Sir, yours &c

F BARBER
Lieut Col

    Since closing my letter I am informed that the Pennsylvanians
are stopped & are come to terms
Col Shreve [1]

Finding that he was unable to quell the mutiny, Wayne
decided to accompany the insurgents to Philadelphia,
promising to do all in his power to aid them in obtaining the
desired relief   When Princeton was reached they presented
to him, at his suggestion, a written enumeration of their
demands   These were

    1   A discharge for all those, without exception, who had served
three years under their original engagements, and had not received the
increased bounty and re-enlisted for the war
    2   An immediate payment of all their arrears of pay and cloth-
ing, both to those who should be discharged, and those who should be
retained
    3   The residue of their bounty, to put them on an equal foot-
ing with those recently enlisted, and future substantial pay to those
who should remain in the service

    Reasonable as these demands were, the general doubted
his authority to accede to them   He therefore referred the
negotiation to a committee of Congress, who, after con-

---

[1] Washington Papers in Library of Congress, 45, 71   On January 8,
Colonel Shreve, writing to Washington from Pompton regarding the unsettled condition of the New Jersey troops, said "I shall immediately set out
for Chatham to learn more particularly the situation of affairs in that quarter and finally settle the arrangement of the Brigade with Colonel Dayton,
who is at that place —*Ibid*, 45, 67

ferring with the Executive Council of Pennsylvania, effected
a satisfactory settlement of the soldiers' grievances, and thus
restored order in the brigade [1]

Sir Henry Clinton was soon apprized of the revolt, and
was led to believe the dissatisfaction of the mutineers to be
so great that they might readily be persuaded to join his
army He accordingly sent out two emissaries, John Mason
of New York and James Ogden of South River, N J, who
promised the Pennsylvanians a liberal reward in money and
clothing if they would lay down their arms, march to New
York, and accept the protection of the British government;
assuring them that no military services would be required
unless voluntarily offered. At the same time Clinton passed
over to Staten Island with a large body of troops, prepared
to welcome and protect the insurgents if they should accept
his offer The Pennsylvanians, however, merely demanded
the recognition by the government of a just claim—they had
no thought of treason, and not only was Sir Henry's proposal indignantly rejected, but his emissaries were tried as
spies, convicted, and executed [2]

A few excerpts are given from letters written in and
near Morristown at the time of this crisis On January 7th
the Marquis de Lafayette writes to the Chevalier de la
Lucerne, French Minister to the United States, concerning
the revolt·

Some men still remain in the huts, we are trying to assemble
them under the officers and to send them some miles [away] The
cannon which remains and a part of the the munitions will be sent
to Chatham, where there is a Jersay detachment. The other munitions will be sent elsewhere There has been a disturbance in the
Jersay detachment which is in front of us, caused by some English
and Irish soldiers, but the others have kept them quiet It is said
that a Connecticut Brigade is marching here, while waiting we have

[1] Barber's New Jersey Historical Collections, 393, 394
[2] Pennsylvania Archives, Ser 2, II, 665

behind us Princetown on our right approximately two hundred Pennsilvanians scattered about, in front of us three hundred militia and three hundred Continental troops of Jersay, who, joined to the enemy, who have nevertheless not yet come out, render our position a little precarious [1]

General Arthur St Clair, in a letter of the same date to Governor Joseph Reed of Pennsylvania, writes in part as follows

The Enemy have made no Movement yet in consequence of this affair and it may be that they are so much weakened by their late Detachments as not to be able to spare a sufficient Body, but I am persuaded that if they were in Jersey great Numbers would desert to them, as it is certain that british Emmissarys have set this Matter a going, and many of them have confessed to us that it was proposed to them to lead them all there   This however they nobly refused

The General is not yet arrived, and some appearance of similar disposition in the Jersey Troops induced Colonell Barber who commands them to move them to Chatham so that we are here in a very awkward situation and have this moment heard that they have sent some Person to bring off the remaining few —perhaps a hundred and all the stores, and we have not a soul to prevent it—the Militia being all out already   This may not be true, but if it is attempted it must be prevented at all Hazards [2]

The letter-books of Enos Reeves,[3] then a first lieutenant in the Seventh Pennsylvania regiment, contain references to mutiny   A letter dated Mount Kemble, January 2nd, 1781, concludes as follows

The militia are called out, they are to assemble at Chatham, in order to oppose the enemy if they come out, or the mutineers if they attempt going to them

[1] American Hist Review, XX, 581
[2] Pennsylvania Magazine of History, XXII, 244, from original in possession of the Washington Association of New Jersey
[3] Pennsylvania Magazine of History, XXI, 72-79.

Writing from Dr. Liddel's at "Mendem," under date of January 14th, he says:

The militia of this and neighboring counties are called out and ordered to rendezvous at Chatham, as well to defend the lines from any attempt of the enemy to penetrate the country at this time as to hinder any of the mutineers from taking that route, should they attempt it   We have certain intelligence that the enemy have reinforced Saten Island with a large body of men to be ready for any movement that may offer

In another letter written at the same time and place he says:

Col Humpton has arrived at Trentown and has sent up for his baggage—for the purpose of sending which, I have this day been to Squire Dailey who promised to send me a wagon to morrow

On January 17th he again writes:

Squire Dailey disappointed me in a wagon, and I wrote to Squire Stiles for one for the Colonel's baggage.

On the morning of the 16th breakfasted at Col Spencer's and got an order on Squire Stiles for three wagons, but on my arrival at his house found a prior order from the Deputy Q M from Morristown had deprived me of what he could furnish. I then proceeded to Squire Dailey's at Chatham, who promised me three, which he was to send the following morning   You must know that the mutineers stole my horse and I now have a borrowed one   The 17th I procured a wagon for the Colonel's baggage and gave orders for its setting off the next morning   I awaited the arrival of the teams from Chatham with great impatience, but to my great mortification found myself again disappointed   The teams for twelve miles round this place have been so harrassed since our arrival in quarters, with assisting in drawing the timber for building, drawing forage, provisions and timber for the redoubts, with what the mutineers impressed and what we have employed to move our stores, that a

person might almost as well attempt to make a wagon and horses as
to procure them otherwise

About this time a committee of officers of the New
Jersey line conferred with the State Assembly in an effort
to improve the intolerable condition of the troops   The
salary of the soldiers was long in arrear, they had received
it only in small amounts and at irregular intervals, and,
owing to the depreciation of the currency, the money paid
them was of little use   While these negotiations were in
progress the Pennsylvania mutiny occurred, and the officers'
committee took advantage of the consternation it caused
to demand payment for the troops at rate of "75 for 1,"
i e , seventy-five dollars of paper money for one of specie
The Assembly, dreading further disorder, at once complied,
directing all moneys then in the treasury to be sent to the
soldiers, and appointing commissioners to examine the terms
of their enlistments, and to honorably discharge those whose
period of service should be found to have expired [1]
The mutiny of the Pennsylvanians was followed by a
similar revolt of the New Jersey Continental troops which
bears more directly upon the Revolutionary history of
Chatham   The portion of the Jersey line which Colonel
Shreve commanded was in camp at Pompton, while the battalion which Wayne had ordered to Chatham at the time
of the Pennsylvania mutiny still remained here under Colonel
Dayton, the brigade commandant, there being, according to
the estimate of British spies, about 250 men at each place
These soldiers, whose sufferings were fully equal to those of
the Pennsylvanians, and whose terms of enlistment were
also in dispute, had been considerably demoralized by the
mutiny at Morristown and its successful outcome, and during the month of January a spirit of insubordination

[1] Magazine of American History, X, 338

gradually spread through the camp at Pompton which eventually ripened into open revolt

Late in the afternoon of Saturday, January 20th, Colonel Shreve was informed that the men were about to mutiny He immediately ordered them to fall in, meaning to scatter them in small detachments, but only a few obeyed During the evening about 160 suddenly rose in arms, making the same demands which had been yielded to the Pennsylvanians, and marched to Chatham with the intention of inciting their comrades at this place to join in the revolt The uprising was chiefly instigated by David Gilmour (Gilmore) of Somerset County a sergeant in the Second regiment, and John Tuttle of Morris County, a private in the First [1] The mutineers chose three leaders from among their number first, George Grant, a sergeant-major of the Third regiment, and a deserter from the British, second, Jonathan Nichols, a sergeant in Captain Mitchell's company of the First regiment, and third, John Minthorn, sergeant-major of the latter regiment [2]

COLONEL SHREVE TO GENERAL WASHINGTON

Pompton, 20 January, 1781

Sir,

It is with pain I inform your Excellency, that the troops at this place revolted this evening and marched towards Trenton Their behavior and demands are similar to those of the Pennsylvania line, though no blood has been spilt I was informed by a woman of their intention late this afternoon, and immediately ordered all the men off duty to be paraded, with design to detach them in different parties for the night, but found very few that would turn out I was amongst them for some time, but could not prevail upon them to desist They have lately received a part of the deprecia-

[1] Magazine of American History, X, 417 n , Stryker's Officers and Men of New Jersey in the Revolution, 607, 791, New Jersey Journal, No 102

[2] Magazine of American History, X, 417 n , Stryker's Officers and Men of New Jersey in the Revolution, 108, 121

tion of their pay, and most of them are much disguised with liquor
Colonel Frelinghuysen, one of the commissioners of the State, is now
here We mean to follow them in the morning, and endeavor to
bring them to reason I apprehend the detachment at Chatham
will join them If the other detachments should leave their posts,
I shall direct Major Throop to send to Dobb's Ferry, and to cover
the stores at Ringwood and at this place Colonel Dayton, I make
no doubt, will be able to do duty,[1] and will exert himself to com-
promise matters with those at Chatham

    I am, Sir, &c &c

                          I SHRIVE -

    History does not state whether the troops at Chatham
joined in the insurrection, but apparently they did not
Colonel Dayton, upon hearing of the approach of the
mutineers, diminished the force at this place by granting
furloughs to some of the men, and ordering others to Springfield, thus removing a large part of his command from the
influence of the insurgents The latter remained at Chatham
over Sunday, endeavoring to spread the seeds of insubordination, and doubtless causing the worthy citizens of the village
a good deal of anxiety. Learning that the Legislature had
appointed commissioners to examine into, and as far as
possible to relieve, the conditions of which they complained,
they agreed to select two representatives of their own, and
to submit the matters in dispute to arbitration, Colonel
Dayton being one of those chosen On Monday two of the
legislative commissioners, Rev James Caldwell and Colonel
Frederick Frelinghuysen, arrived at Chatham, and, with the
assistance of Dayton and Shreve, succeeded in pacifying the
excited troops Though they refused to treat with the
soldiers while in a state of insubordination, they assured
them that if they returned to camp and again yielded to
discipline, every grievance would be redressed, promising
discharges with full pay to the three-year men, who included

---

[1] Colonel Dayton was in poor health at that time
[2] Sparks's Writings of Washington, VII, 561

the whole line except about 150 who acknowledged that they had enlisted for the war   The mutineers then insisted that the three-year men should be discharged upon the unsupported evidence of their own affidavits (a privilege which had been granted to the Pennsylvanians) , but this the commissioners refused to promise, even in cases where the original muster rolls were missing, and after a protracted discussion the men abandoned their contention, professing satisfaction with the assurances they had received [1] Colonel Dayton, in view of their apparent contrition, and of the fact that they were previously unaware of the legislative action on their behalf, promised them a full pardon if they would immediately return to their duty, and he drew up a form of pardon, which, upon being read to them, was received with three cheers of approbation and acceptance [2] On Wednesday the troops started on their return to Pompton, but their penitence, unfortunately, was short-lived   On the march they again became insubordinate, and after their arrival at camp the ringleaders had little difficulty in once more arousing them to mutiny

COLONEL DAYTON TO GENERAL WASHINGTON

Chatham, Jana 24th 1781

Sir,

On Sunday morning I was alarmed with an account that the Jersey brigade had revolted, were directing their march this way and were in the neighborhood of this place   I immediately desired the officers of the detachment upon this station to sound the sentiments of the men under their immediate command, who soon disproved that they had no inclination to join with the seditious part of the brigade, but rather chose to avoid them   I gave permission to the major part of these to retire to their own homes and such of the

---

[1] Magazine of American History, X, 337, 340, Hatch's Administration of the Revolutionary Army, 138

[2] Sparks's Writings of Washington, VII, 561

remainder as were not prevailed upon to join them, were directed
to lay at Springfield until further orders

When the revolters were collected, the commissioners appointed
by the assembly to enquire into & redress the grievances of the brigade with myself acquainted them with what powers we were vested
and at the same time assured them that when they returned to their
duty & not till then, we would hear and treat with them   A point
which they strongly contested was that their own oaths should be
admissible in determining the term of their enlistments as with the
Pennsylvanians, this we did not think proper by any means to grant
them and they finally gave it up   They marched this day on their
return to the tents with Colo Shreve only, where they have
promised again to put themselves under the command of their officers   As soon as the men who were permitted to go out of the way
are collected, I shall detach a guard with the cannon to Morris town
and send on the others to the huts   As I am not without my fears,
that, when they discover they are not discharged agreeable to their
wishes by the commissioners, they may again become seditious and
not consider themselves amenable to the orders of their officers, I
would wish to be instructed by your excellency, whether in that
case it would not be advisable to call in the militia, who, I am of
the opinion can be at any time collected for that purpose, and make
up of more vigorous measures to humble them

I am happy to acquaint your Excellency that I am greatly recovered, altho my health and strength are not yet sufficiently established to warrant my continuance in camp at this season of the year

The enemy are now putting on board vessels, quantities of
military ordinance stores, in which 'tis also said that troops are to
be embarked, their destination is entirely unknown   May not the
British have in expectation a general revolt of the army, and from
these preparations, have their eye upon that point?

I am Sir your Excellency's most obedient and Hble servent,

ELIAS DAYTON

P S   Enclosed is a copy of the pardon granted the mutineers,
several of which did not comply with it, who are proper objects, of
whom I would wish to be made examples of [1]

---

[1] Washington Papers in Library of Congress, 45, 271

FORM OF A PARDON

Chatham, 23 January, 1781.

The commandant of the Jersey brigade, in answer to the petition of the sergeants for a general pardon, observes that, in consideration of the brigade having revolted before they were made acquainted with the resolution of the legislature directing an inquiry into their enlistments and of their agreeing immediately upon their being informed of the said resolution to return to the duty, and of their having neither shed blood nor done violence to the person of any officer or inhabitant, he hereby promises a pardon to all such as immediately without hesitation shall return to their duty and conduct themselves in a soldierly manner   Those who shall, notwithstanding this unmerited proffer of clemency, refuse obedience, must expect the reward due to such obstinate villainy [1]

General Washington, who felt that the Pennsylvanians had been dealt with too leniently, determined that drastic action was now necessary, for bad as was the condition of the Pennsylvania and New Jersey troops, it was no worse than that of the soldiers of the other States, and he realized that the entire army would soon be disrupted were the spirit of mutiny permitted to spread   At his direction, therefore, the following order was issued to General Heath

Head Quarters, 10 o'clock p m
Janry 21st 1781.

Dear Sir

His Excellency has just heard of the revolt of the Jersey troops, and directs me to inform you that he is determined at all hazards to put a stop to such proceedings, which must otherwise prove the inevitable dissolution of the army   He requests therefore you will be pleased to order a detachment to be made out from the garrison and other troops under your command, of five or six hundred of the most robust and best cloathed men, properly officered and provided for the purpose   The General expects the detachment

[1] Sparks's Writings of Washington, VII, 561

will be immediately compleated and equipped   And altho it should leave the posts very weak, he thinks there will be no risque, as the command of Major General Parsons will be returned before the enemy can take advantage of the movement   His Excellency will be at the Point in the morning

I have the honor to be, dear Sir,

Your most obedt and very hble servant,

D HUMPHRYS, A D Camp

Maj Gen Heath[1]

In compliance with these instructions, a detachment of 500 men was made up from the Continental troops of New Hampshire, Massachusetts and Connecticut, and marched on January 23rd from West Point to re-establish order and discipline in the Jersey line   The detachment was led by Major-General Robert Howe, who was directed to make no terms with the mutineers while in a state of resistance, and, after they had surrendered, to make an example of a few of the ringleaders by executing them on the spot   Lieutenant-Colonel Ebenezer Sprout was second in command of the detachment, and the other field officers were Lieutenant-Colonel Mellen and Major Oliver[2]   Dr James Thatcher, then a surgeon in the Ninth Massachusetts, accompanied the expedition, and he gives a graphic account of it in his Military Journal

At Ringwood they were joined by a detachment from the Second Continental artillery under Captain Stewart, with three 3-pounders   Here it was learned that Dayton and Shreve had failed in their efforts to settle the difficulty by negotiation, and that, while some of the revolters seemed disposed to accept the terms of surrender and pardon which Dayton had prepared, a majority had refused,[3] and Howe

[1] Mass Historical Society Collections, Ser. 7, V, 165

[2] Thatcher's Military Journal, 244.

[3] Atkinson's Newark, 122

[4] Magazine of American History, X, 331 n

perceived that an encounter with them could not be avoided
Marching from Ringwood at one o'clock in the morning of
the 27th, he reached Pompton at daybreak, found the insurgents asleep in their huts, and succeeded in surrounding
the camp before his presence was discovered   It was an
anxious moment for Howe and his officers, for they feared
that their men were at heart in sympathy with the mutineers,
and might refuse to obey an order to fire upon them, but
this apprehension proved to be unfounded   The insurgents
were awakened and peremptorily ordered to parade un-
armed in front of their huts   Upon their refusal, the
general sent Lieutenant-Colonel Barber to warn them that
if they did not obey within five minutes, he would put them
all to death, and by this threat he promptly brought them
to terms   Three of the ringleaders Gilmour, Tuttle and
Grant, were then tried by a court-martial of which Lieutenant-Colonel Sprout acted as president, standing in the
snow.   They were found guilty and sentenced to death,
though Grant was pardoned through the intercession of his
commanding officer, who represented to Howe that he had
acted as a leader with reluctance, and had tried to dissuade
the men from insurrection   The other two culprits were
immediately shot, twelve of the most guilty mutineers being
selected to act as executioners [1]

"This," wrote Thatcher in his Journal, 'was a most painful
task, being themselves guilty, they were greatly distressed with the
duty imposed upon them, and when ordered to load, some of them
shed tears   The wretched victims, overwhelmed by the terrors of
death, had neither time nor power to implore the mercy and for-
giveness of their God, and such was their agonizing condition, that
no heart could refrain from emotions of sympathy and compassion
The first that suffered was a sergeant and an old offender, he was
led a few yards distance and placed on his knees—six of the

[1] Thatcher's Military Journal, 244, Atkinson's Newark, 122, Magazine
of American History, X, 331 n

executioners, at the signal given by an officer, fired, three aiming at
the head and three at the breast, the other six reserving their fire in
order to dispatch the victim should the first fire fail it so happened
in this instance, the remaining six then fired and life was instantly
extinguished   The second criminal was by the first fire sent into
eternity in an instant   The third being less criminal by the recommendation of his officers, to his unspeakable joy, received a pardon   This tragical scene produced a dreadful shock, and a salutary
effect on the minds of the guilty soldiers   Never were men more
completely humbled and penitent tears of sorrow, and of joy, rushed
from their eyes, and each one appeared to congratulate himself, that
his forfeited life had been spared   The executions being finished,
General Howe ordered the former officers to take their stations, and
resume their respective commands, he then, in a very pathetic and
affecting manner, addressed the whole line by platoons, endeavouring
to impress their minds with a sense of the enormity of their crime,
and the dreadful consequences that might have resulted   He then
commanded them to ask pardon of their officers, and promise to
devote themselves to the faithful discharge of their duty as soldiers
in future "

A report of the insurrection as given in the *New Jersey
Journal* is here reproduced, the interest of which is en-
hanced by the fact that it was written and published in
Chatham, where the disturbance in part occurred

CHATHAM, January 31
On Saturday evening, the 20th instant, about one hundred and
sixty soldiers of the Jersey brigade, following the example of the
Pennsylvanians, left their huts and proceeded to this place, under
the direction of their sergeants   They were unacquainted with a
late resolution of the legislature, appointing commissioners to inquire
into their inlistments, but as soon as the commissioners, who met
them here the Monday following, had read and explained that resolution to them, they immediately agreed to return to their duty
The commandant of the brigade, in consideration of their great
penitence, and of their being unacquainted with the measures adopted

for settling the disputes respecting their inlistments, promised full
pardon to all who immediately returned to and continued in their
duty   But upon the way to, and after their arrival at the huts, a
few of the ringleaders, encouraged by emissaries from Sir Harry,
and perhaps by the too great clemency of granting them a general
pardon, again became insolent and mutinous   A detachment from
the main army, under the command of General Howe, which had
been sent on to quell the mutineers, arrived about this time, when
those who had forfeited the pardon, by not performing the conditions were apprehended by order of the General, and David Gilmore,
sergeant in the 2d regiment, and John Tuttle, private in the 1st,
were tried, found guilty, and immediately executed   Every mark
of penitence and respect for order was manifested by the others who
had offended, and entire order and subordination took place in the
brigade

The *New Jersey Gazette* thus describes the mutiny

TRENTON January 31
     On Saturday evening the 20th instant, about 150 privates of
the New-Jersey brigade, which were quartered at Pompton, left
their huts, and, under conduct of some of their sergeants, marched
towards Chatham   The proceedings of the Legislature at their last
sitting constituting commissioners to enquire into the claims of such
soldiers of the brigade as considered themselves entitled to a discharge on account of the expiration of their enlistments, had not then
been communicated to them   The commissioners went to Chatham
on Monday, and having read and explained to them the resolutions
of the Legislature, they immediately agreed to return to their duty
The commandant of the brigade, in consideration of their being
unacquainted with the measures taken in their behalf, and of their
acknowledgments of the offence, granted their request for a general
pardon   The commissioners having appointed a time for settling
their claims, they returned to the orders of their officers   A small
part only of the brigade were engaged in this matter, the greater
part disapproved of it, and all regret that it happened   To the
honour however of these brave men we mention it with pleasure,

that when they left their quarters they adopted a solemn resolution
to put to death anyone who should attempt or even propose to go
to the enemy's lines, and hang up without ceremony every tory who
should presume to say a word tending to induce any of them so
to do

The optimistic tone of this report indicates a desire to
belittle the gravity of the insurrection, and suggests that the
article was designed for British consumption, rather than for
general information The affair appears in a different light
when described from the tory point of view in Rivington's
Royal Gazette of New York, a few excerpts from which are
given below

NEW YORK, January 13
* * * * - * * *

These determined men [the Pennsylvania mutineers] provoked
to a separation from Mr Washington's army, by want of food, pay
in efficient money and cloathing, at present occupy the college and
houses in Prince Town an advantageous and elevated position,
where the country people amply supply them with all kinds of subsistence, the New Jersey brigade, reserved and silent spectators of
the event of this revolt, and amounting to about four hundred, are
at Chatham, all the Militia of the Province that can be forced out
are in arms, and hovering around the Pennsylvanians, they have
hitherto behaved to the Dissidents with an obsequious complaisance,
the necessity of which had been suggested to them by their dema-
gogues.

NEW YORK, January 17
* * * * * * * *

When the Jersey line, consisting of 400 men was paraded last
Sunday, at Chatham, Col Dayton offered to advance each man forty
pounds of the newly issued paper bills, to induce them to support
the militia in their hostile intentions against the revolters, but these
soldiers, *high in oath*, exclaimed, *The new is of equal value with the
old,—both worth nothing*

NEW YORK, January 27
* * * * * * * *

In this Gazette, dated the 17th instant, an account was given of the refractory behavior of the Jersey Brigade to their officers, their disaffection to the rebel service has at last broke out into an absolute revolt On the 19th inst (after the example of the Pennsylvania line) they declared themselves independent of their officers, and seized on everything necessary for their support in a state of separation on their march from Chatham they were attacked at Springfield Bridge, by a body of about 500 militia commanded by Colonels Seely and Freelinghausen when some blood was shed, and the militia defeated, the roads are bad, their movements very slow, and their destination not yet known, but on Wednesday evening they were within Seven Miles of Elizabeth Town

NEW YORK, Jan 31
* * * * * * * *

The Jersey troop, who had been some time as much dissatisfied as the Pennsylvanians, hearing the terms granted to the others, immediately revolted in like manner, chose their officers, and that part which lay at Pompton joined the rest at Chatham They received, without difficulty, a promise that they should be satisfied, and were returning to Pompton —Some, who had been straggling, were taken up, under pretense of their not having agreed to the terms proposed, and sent to Morristown gaol, a sufficient proof to the others, that it is only the power they have in their own hands they can procure the smallest justice from Congress and their tools

The New York public library possesses in its collection of manuscripts an orderly book of the Jersey line covering the period from December, 1780, to June, 1781 In this volume we find two orders of local interest, the second of which relates indirectly to the Jersey mutiny They read as follows

Brigade Orders, January 11 1781
* * * * * * * *

Major Hollingshead will join the detachment at Chatham under the command of Lieut Col Barber

Brigade Orders, March 3rd 1781

Adjutant Tomorrow, Bishop

At a Court martial held at Chatham the 28th February, 1781, whereof Captain Mead was president Lt Seely Lt Parrot Ensign Gary & Ensign Bishop members

William Jones was tryed for threatening the Commissioners lives

The Court have acquited him   Lieut Col D'Hart is sorry to observe from the proceeding of the Court Martial presented to him it by no means corresponds with his oppinion, he is therefore under the necesity of disapproving of the judgment & orders the prisoner to be sent to Morristown Gaol, with the Charge of endeavoring to excite Mutiny

Sir Henry Clinton was not discouraged by the failure of his negotiations with the Pennsylvania mutineers and upon learning of the New Jersey revolt, he repeated his offers, holding out similar inducements to join the British He employed as an emissary for this purpose a spy named Woodruff,[1] who was a cousin of Jonathan Nichols, one of the leaders of the insurgents, but Woodruff proved to be in sympathy with the American cause (or else was detected, and pretended to be a friend of liberty in order to escape) and he gave up his papers to Colonel Dayton Other papers, promising tempting rewards to any soldier who would join the enemy, were circulated among the mutineers, but the revolt was crushed so suddenly that no opportunity to accept these offers was afforded [2]

[1] The editor of the Magazine of American History thinks this was Uzal Woodruff of Essex County, a private in Captain Cranes company of the First regiment —Vol X, 417

[2] Gordon's Rise of American Independence, IV, 22, Marshall s Washington, IV, 367

It is said that Antony Gerlang and Tim Sharp, of Elizabeth, were also hired by Clinton to carry his proposals to the Jersey mutineers —Public Papers of Governor George Clinton, I II, 493

GENERAL WASHINGTON TO COLONEL DAYTON

Head Quarters New Windsor, Feby 7th 1781

Dear Sir

I find by the Arrangement of the Jersey Brigade, which has just come to hand, that Colo Shreve has retired from Service—this makes your presence extremely necessary with the Troops, and the more so at this time, as some dispute about rank is said to exist between Lt Col Barber & Lt Col Ic Hart, which, while there is no superior Officer, both of them may produce parties and cabals, to the great detriment of the service

Altho' your health should not be perfectly established, I cannot but hope you will have so far recovered as to be able to join and continue with the Brigade, I would not wish you to expose yourself, or attempt impossibilities, but I am certain you will be persuaded of the necessity of being with your Troops at such a critical and interesting period   Even if you are but in a convalescent state, I should suppose you might obtain such comfortable accommodations abroad, as would promote your recovery as effectually as at home—especially since you will find the Brigade at so small a distance from Morristown

I am, Dear Sir, With great esteem, Your most Obedt Hble Servt

Go WASHINGTON

Col Dayton [1]

COLONEL DAYTON TO GENERAL WASHINGTON

Chatham Feby 17th 1781

Sir

I had the honour to receive your Excellencys letter of the 7th instant four days since   I am sorry to acquaint your excellency that my health is not yet as well established as I could wish, being at present exceedingly troubled with a swelling on my thigh, which has confined me closely for a fortnight past, it however bears a favourable appearance & I expect to be able to join the troops in a few days   This your excellency may rely upon my doing, as soon

[1] Magazine of American History, XX 139

as I am able to sit on horseback. It has been intimated to me that General Washington disapproved of the measures adopted & pursued with the Jersey mutineers, and my not hearing anything from the General in answer to my letter on that subject increased my suspicion that my conduct had not been approved. As nothing can give me greater pain than your excellency's displeasure I could wish to be informed what part of my conduct was conceived to be reprehensible, that I might clear it up as I am convinced I could to the satisfaction of every one. I never wished for lenient steps with the insurgents but would gladly have been concerned in cutting a number of their throats if the officers, Commissioners and Militia whom I consulted had agreed in the propriety of such a Measure.

I am your excellency most Obedient & Humble Servant

ELIAS DAYTON

P S 20th

A vessel from General Arnold has arrived at New York in a short passage & brought accounts of his being in a hobble, as they term it themselves, one french ship of the line and two frigates are anchored opposite him in such a manner as to prevent his getting off without assistance from New York.

The enclosed is a letter from an Old correspondent in New York.

ELIAS DAYTON [1]

An interesting source of information concerning the details of the Jersey mutiny is a manuscript volume containing the reports of British spies. The original, which is known as Sir Henry Clinton's Record of Secret Daily Intelligence, is contained in the Emmet collection of manuscripts in the New York public library, and has been published in Volume X of the Magazine of American History. The reports were inscribed by several different hands, but most of the writing is thought to be that of Sir George Beckwith. The references to the insurrection which are given below, commence with an entry dated January 21st.

[1] Washington Papers in Library of Congress, 46, 238

Gould came in this Morning at 10 o'Clock from Elizabeth-town On Sunday Morning the Jersey Brigade, part of which lay at Pompton, mutinied & seized two field pieces & joined the rest of the Brigade at Chatham He saw some of them, whose complaints were about pay &c They told him they were determined, unless they got redress, to join the british One Grant, a Sergeant Major & a deserter from the british Army, commands them

They say'd they would come to Elizabethtown The Militia are turned out to oppose them, and this morning he heard a very heavy firing and some cannon, and afterwards passing Shots towards Elizabethtown by Springfield A violent Storm prevented his com-ing in before

Woodruff says the same

A Cousin of his, one Nicholls, is sworn to command

Information of Cap'n G of one of the Massachusetts Regiments 20th January   The Jersey brigade consists of 500 men, half at Chatham the rest at Pompton

Letter from Majr McKenzie to Maji DeLancey at Staten Isl-and, dated N York, Janry 26th 1781

Dr Major

One Jonas Crane came from Newark, left that on Wednesday, and was sent from Bergen Point, at 3 o'Clock yesterday, but did not arrive here till 12 last night, and only came to the office this morning at ½ past 10 The account he brings is, that on wednes-day while he was at a tavern at Newark, a Coll Courtland came in to desire the Major of militia, who kept the House, to call out the Militia, but very soon after a Major Cummins and Lieut Ray of the 2d N Jersey Reg came in & said he need not order them out, as the affair was settled That it was agreed to appoint Commis-sioners on both sides to settle matters in the same manner as had been done with the Pennsylvanians, they were to meet on Monday or tuesday at Chatham, for the troops there, and again at Pompton for the others who had marched back Coll Dayton was chosen by the troops, for one on their part Their demands the same as the Pennsyl-vanians—There was no person killed or wounded—There was some firing but the officers say'd it was when the two divisions joined

The above Man is gone to Newark and intends to return this Evening with two men to Bergen Point   I have desired him to take them immediately to you at Bankers

Y^{rs}

T Mc

Extract of a letter from Jersey   Jany 26   (To Peter Dubois)

A Committee of Officers from the Jersey Brigade, were with the Assembly endeavouring to adjust matters so as to pacify the soldiers as well as officers, The former not having received any pay for a considerable time, & the depreciated state of the money such, that they could do nothing with it in case they got it   This was the situation of matters when the revolution took place with the Pennsylvania line, The Officers committee catched the opportunity and insisted to be paid at 75 for one   The Assembly took fright and instantly complied, and likewise order'd all the Money then in the treasury to be sent up to the Men, with other promises, to quiet them, such as a redress of any grievances they might labour under discharges for those whose terms were expired, &c &c   After waiting some days and finding nothing but promises without performance, and the New Money they had received would purchase nothing but Rum, they on Sunday came to the resolution of quitting their huts at Pompton, and marched off to join their brethren at Chatham Some of the officers who had made themselves obnoxious to them they whip'd, some of the others remain with them   A Sergt Majr they chose for their commander, and the rest of the Officers from among themselves   They remain at Chatham and methods are taken by the Officers, who they suffer among them to reconcile matters   Such of them as are entitled to discharges will get them, and the remainder bought off with a little rum, fair promises, & some more money   I cannot learn that their intentions at present are farther than having redress, which they will obtain, as far as it is in the power of Congress to grant it

27th Janry   Intelligence by Mr J—

The Jersey Brigade are gone back to their huts at Pompton on thursday last about 3 o'Clock   The three Years Men are promised their discharges   These include the whole except about one hundred & fifty who acknowledge their enlistments for the War

All those who cannot produce their certificates their Oaths are taken   The Officers who commanded them were one Grant the second Nicholls, & the third Jno Minthorn   They permit Dayton Spencer & Ogden to command them in future   All the rest they reject   The Offis they refused to serve under declare their sentiments that Examples ought to be made of them, but the three above mentioned oppose it.   Those discharged are also to be paid off

On their first turning out they surrounded the house of an Officer (whose name he does not recollect) broke it open and forced him with threats of immediate death to give up the muster Rolls

Janry 18th [28th] 1781

A person sent out says that Genl Howe with a party of about one thousand of the N England troops, marched down the night before last to Pompton & met the Jersey Brigade; That he seized upon near sixty who were lodged in Morristown gaol   That about 100 escaped & took the road to Sussex and as is supposed intend joining the Indians   A Proclamation was issued offering pardon to all who should come in   About 200 came in in consequence of it   He saw the party putting the prisoners into gaol   The officers were at Chatham disputing among themselves about the conduct of the Men, some saying they were right, and ought to be discharged, others the contrary   20 or 30 said they would resign   The Dragoons were sent after the 100 that escaped

Copy of a letter from Mr J at Elizabethtown   rec'd Feb'ry 7th 1781

Sir,

I rec'd your two notes by Gould & Woodroff on thursday last I informed you in my last letter that the N Jersey troops had revolted about four hundred from Pompton joined those at Chatham on Sunday week   On Monday Mr Caldwell and Coll Frelinhausen commissioners from the legislature of New Jersey, with Coll Dayton and Shrive, persuaded them to return to Pompton with a promise that every grievance should be redressed   they accordingly returned on Wednesday under that expectation, but Washington foreseeing the consequence that would inevitably attend these mutineers, unless supressed, detached Genl Howe from N Windsor with one thousand Connecticut troops who surprised the Jersey troops in their huts on Saturday last   They immediately disarmed them and on Sunday shot David Gilmom & J Tuttle as principals in the mutiny

You may be assured the J troops knew of the terms offered by you to the Pennsylvanians, but I don't think they had it in view to come to you   They are so connected by relationship in this Country, that nothing but a total despair of redress of grievances would induce them to come over to you   1

[1] Some further items are quoted from Clinton's Record of Secret Intelligence which are of interest in connection with the history of Chatham

Extract of a letter from Capn Beckwith, dated 16th May 1781
Dear Sir,
Capin Hatheld informes me, that he had recd information from Jersey, that above one hundred of the detachment of the Jersey troops, sent with Fayette to the Southward, had deserted to us somewhere near Petersburgh, & nearly in one body, this was mentioned by an Officer of the Jersey troops quartered near Chatham   He likewise tells me, that the twelve Months men are under orders to March towards the frontiers, the Indians being very troublesome in that Quarter
                                    Yrs   G B

From Capin Beckwith, 5th July, 1781
          They report that the Jersey brigade are to march this Morning from Pompton and Chatham, to join Genl Washington   They are supposed to be about 500   They cannot tell where they are to cross the North River

Intelligence by J— S— M— 6th July, 1781
          A few days ago I received information by one that acts as an Aide to Col D— that they were to march on Thursday Morning towards King's Ferry   I thought it might be premature   They have marched   He told me that Col D— believed that General W— expected a French fleet to act in Conjunction to attack N Y
                              From F
                    favoured by J T J July 6th 1781
          From Col Robinson, 12th July, 1781   Intelligence by Moses Ogden, 11th July, 6 in the morning
          The Jersey brigade under Dayton, about 200 or 250 men, marched last Sunday for King's Ferry
          The Jersey Assembly have agreed to call the 16th part of the militia into 3 months' service, to be commanded by a Mr Hoagland   Likewise ordered 400 men to the Jersey brigade during the War   To give a bounty of 12 pounds hard cash pr man, and to raise the money immediately by tax &c
          [Subsequent reports of spies raised the number of New Jersey troops to 600, and later to 800]

This book of Sir Henry Clinton's is accompanied in the New York public library by a companion volume, also in manuscript, containing information brought to him by deserters from the American army   The following quo-

The uprising of the Pennsylvania and New Jersey lines, though regarded as a most unfortunate calamity at the time, was not without a beneficial effect. Public attention was directed more strongly to the imperative needs of the army, and the authorities realized that something must be done to alleviate the sufferings of the troops   They soon raised a sum equivalent to three months' pay in specie, which they sent to the soldiers, either as a gift, or on account of the depreciation of their salaries   This money, though falling far short of the amount due, was thankfully received by the men as evidence of a bona fide effort to improve their condition, and by this and other means the government succeeded in checking the further progress of insubordination [1]

The village of Chatham is mentioned in connection with the hostilities between the "Back Shad" and the "Inhabitants of Newark,' in the latter part of May, 1781   "Back shad" was a term used in those days to describe the thin, weak shad returning to the sea after spawning in April and May   The name was derisively applied to a number of people living near Newark Mountains, as Orange was then called, who appear to have been whigs, while the "inhabitants of Newark" were tories   The following report of the matter was published in Rivington's *Royal Gazette* of

tation which is selected because of its mention of Chatham, is a fair example of the whole

Novemr 21st 1780

George Hazell, a Waggoner in the Rebel Army left Chatham last Saturday   by Cheapside, Squier Town, Newark &c   Gen' Washington's Quarters are at Colo Dyers near the Falls   Provisions a pound of fresh Beef and ditto Flour   The Army is better clothed than ever he saw them   .   The Pennsylvanians are ordered to the Southward   Maryland Regiment went a Week ago to Lebanon &c   The heavy Baggage is moved off to New Windsor   The Ground for Huts is marked out, New Germantown between Morristown and Pluckemin   The reason for their sending away the heavy Baggage is that they intend attacking Staten Island

[1] Marshalls Washington, IV, 369   Money was also raised for the soldiers by popular subscription   General Lafayette donated 100 guineas — *Parsons' Washington*, 74

New York under date of June 21st, and was considered by Frank Moore of sufficient interest to be copied in his Diary of the Revolution.

JUNE 1. We hear from Newark in New Jersey, that a few days since a number of persons who live in the mountains, and from their wickedness and poverty have properly acquired the appellation of the BACK SHAD, in consequence of a resolution of the pious Reverend Commissary Caldwell, and his associates, who were lately convened at Chatham, repaired to the learned and revered Justice Campbell, and there agreeably to the directions of a late law made by the *humane* William Livingston, swore that a number of the inhabitants of the township of Newark, were dangerous to the liberties of the State, and ought to be removed back into the country, whereupon this great Magistrate issued his warrant for their removal; and gave them till this day to prepare for their departure; this will probably create some disturbance, as our informant tells us that the obnoxious inhabitants refuse to go unless compelled by force.

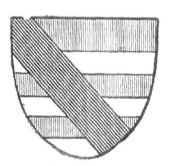

CHAPTER XVI

Movements of the Northern Army during the Yorktown Campaign—Washington threatens an Attack upon New York to
cover his March to Virginia—A permanent Encampment
established at Chatham—Bake-Ovens constructed by Roch-
beau's Commissary—Great quantities of Stores collected—
The American Troops halt at Chatham and Springfield, the
French at Whippany—Washington's Headquarters at Chatham
—Newspaper Comments and Military Correspondence—The
March toward the South suddenly and unexpectedly resumed—Success of Washington's Stratagem

IN the summer of 1781, while the Americans led by
Lafayette were confronting the British under Cornwallis in the Virginia campaign which terminated with the
surrender at Yorktown, Washington was engaged with Sir
Henry Clinton at New York. The American commander
was well informed of the situation in the South, and upon
learning that the French fleet of Count de Grasse had sailed
from the West Indies for Chesapeake Bay to co-operate
with Lafayette, he concluded that if the forces in Virginia
could be sufficiently strengthened before the arrival of
British reinforcements from New York, the defeat of Cornwallis was quite within the bounds of probability. The
stratagem which suggested itself to his mind was to march
rapidly southward and join the army before Yorktown, at
the same time causing the enemy to believe that an attack
upon New York was the object of his manoeuvre, so that it
would not occur to Clinton to move to the support of Cornwallis until too late. The manner in which he accomplished
this *ruse de guerre,* and completely outwitted his adversary,
despite the activities of the British spies by whom the country

was infested, was one of the most brilliant and masterful achievements of his military career [1]

For a period of two months the commander-in-chief, by his constant marches and countermarches in the territory lying north of New York, convinced Sir Henry Clinton that an attack upon that city was momentarily to be expected Early in July the latter was informed that Washington, who was then at Dobbs' Ferry, had been joined by the Count de Rochambeau with a strong detachment of French troops from Newport, and his anxiety was heightened by the intelligence that on the 22nd of the month the Allies had approached the heights of Harlem, and were reconnoitring in the neighborhood of his outposts So threatening indeed was the attitude of his opponents, that, despite the strength of his garrison and the proximity of a powerful British fleet, he dared not weaken his position by dispatching reinforcements to the support of the army which had been sent to the South

Toward the end of August, Washington decided that the time had come for carrying his project into effect He crossed the Hudson at King's Ferry, and commenced a southerly march through New Jersey, but, in order that Clinton might have no suspicion of the truth, he caused a rumor to be circulated among the patriots, through whom it reached the ears of the tories and was by them communicated

---

[1] There has been much dispute among historians as to whether or not Washington really intended to attack New York   The statements in the text are based upon a letter written by him to Noah Webster after the close of the war, in which he said "It never was in contemplation to attack New York, unless the garrison should first have been so far degarnished to carry on the southern operations, as to render our success in the siege of that place as infallible as any future military event can ever be made
That much trouble was taken and finesse used to misguide and bewilder Sir Henry Clinton in regard to the real object, by fictitious communications as well as by making a deceptive provision of ovens, forage, and boats in his neighborhood, is certain "—*Ford's Writings of Washington, XI 294* On the other hand, there is strong evidence that the southern movement was the conception of the Chevalier de la Luzerne, French Minister to the United States, and that the plan was at first rejected by Washington, who declared his intention of laying siege to New York, from which project he was dissuaded, with some difficulty, by Rochambeau

to the British, that he was preparing to attack New York
by way of Staten Island, in co-operation with the French
fleet, which, it was announced, was to enter the harbor and
bombard the city. He wrote fictitious dispatches alluding
to this proposed plan which were cleverly allowed to fall
into the hands of British spies,[1] and was equally careful to
mislead his own officers and those of Rochambeau, believing,
as he wrote in a subsequent letter, that "where the imposition
does not completely take place at home, it would never
sufficiently succeed abroad "[2]

As a further means to insure the success of his artifice,
Washington decided to pause for a few days on his march
to Virginia, and to concentrate his forces in the vicinity of
Chatham,[3] within striking distance of Staten Island, as
though gathering strength for the onslaught; and elaborate
preparations for what was generally believed to be a permanent encampment were accordingly made in this village,
including the building of a bakery, and possibly the erection
of storehouses and similar buildings as well   This work
was intrusted to the Chevalier de Villemanzy, a commissary
of war under Rochambeau, who, with fourteen or fifteen
French artificers, was sent to Chatham in advance of the
army to superintend the construction of the ovens, and to
make a demonstration of collecting great quantities of stores,
in order to confirm the popular belief that this point was to
form the base of operations against Staten Island and New
York[4] Mention is made of the erection of storehouses,
but the reference is not sufficiently definite and reliable to

[1] Headley's Lafayette, 192, Tower's Lafayette in the Am Rev, I, 267, n
[2] Ford's Writings of Washington, XI 294
[3] Sir Henry Clinton, writing to Lord Cornwallis, on August 27, that the
enemy had foraged within six miles of his lines, continues "This small
movement was made on the 18th, they fell back on the 19th, and passed
the Croton, afterwards crossed the Hudson at King's-Ferry, and are now
encamped in the neighbourhood of Chatham"—*Clinton-Cornwallis Controversy, II, 142*
[4] Balch's The French in America, I, 172

PART OF THE CAMP GROUND.

Spruck Brook appears in the foreground, and the Morris Turnpike is across in the distance. The bakery stood near the turnpike, opposite the house at the right of the picture.

enable us to state with certainty whether the provisions were stored in buildings especially erected for the purpose, rather than in the neighboring houses and barns [1] General Stryker, however, is quite positive that magazines for military stores were built [2] Ten days are said to have been devoted to these preparations [3] The satisfactory manner in which De Villemanzy discharged this commission seems to have been regarded as the most important service of his American campaign, as it is particularly mentioned in the short biographical notes contained in Balch's history of the French troops in the Revolutionary War The biographer adds that the chevalier "got himself cannonaded," and kept the garrison at New York constantly on the alert He died a peer of France in the reign of Charles X [4]

[1] Count Jean Axel de Fersen, one of Rochambeau's aides-de-camp, wrote to his father in Sweden "Everything seemed to announce a siege of New York The establishment of a bakery and other storehouses at Chatham, 4 miles distant from Staten Island our passage of the North River, and march toward Morristown seemed to indicate that we intended to attack Sandy Hook to facilitate the entrance of our vessels We were not long in seeing that our views were not turned upon New York, but General Clinton was entirely deceived, that was precisely what we wished "—*Magazine of American History, III, 438*

Washington feignit de ganger Staten-Island et Paulus Hook, et Rochambeau, pour accrediter l'erreur dit a M de Villemanzy, commissaire des guerres, d'aller construire des fours pres de Chatham—*Chotteau's La Guerre de l'Independance, 280*

On descend ensuite la rive droit jusqu'aupres de Staten Island, a Chatam, ou M de Villemanzy avait fort judicieusement etabli des fours et concentre des approvisionnemcntes, en vue de l'attaque de New York—*Noailles's Marins & Soldats Francais en Amerique, 233*

M de Rochambeau leur avait fait croire que son projet etait d'attaquer New-York, avant envoye un commissaire des guerres intelligent avec une forte escorte etablir des fours et des magasins a Chatam, pres New-York—*Luzerne's Memoirs, 347*

[2] The New Jersey Continental Line at Yorktown, 11

[3] Moore's Diary of the Revolution, 466

[4] Claude Blanchet, a commissary of the French army in America, set out on the first of September to follow and overtake the troops on their march to Virginia Describing the journey in his diary, he writes in part "On the same day I came to spend the night at Bullion's Tavern, after having passed through Chatham, a village where our ovens had been set up, which I was well pleased to visit, which caused me to go five miles farther and prevented my passing through Morristown, where General Washington had his quarters for a long time and where the Americans have some iron works as at Peekskill, I also lost the opportunity of visiting the country house of Lord Stirling, that American general whose nobility is somewhat contested "—*Balch's Blanchet's Journal, (Duane's Trans) 133*

The following war-time letter relates to Villemanzy's operations at Chatham, and indicates that while in this village he and his men were billeted in private houses·

                                        Morristown, Aug 13, 81
Dear Sir
     These Gentlemen will call on you for Billots for fifteen artificers of the French Army which I must beg you to grant them likewise every other assistance and direction that you can give them, both to facilitate their Business and ease the inhabitants
     These men tell me that the whole of the French Army are on the march to this State, that 20 ships have arrived at the Hook and that New York will very soon be invested
     I am, Sir,
                         Yr. hum Sevt,
                              CHA FARMAN, Q M V.
To Benjamin Day, Esq,
               Chatham [1]

     No record has been found in which the exact size of the ovens is given   They are described by Elias Boudinot as "very large",· and we can have no doubt that the bakery was built on an extensive scale, for it said to have been capable of supplying bread rations daily for 3,000 men [3]
     Owing to the erection of the ovens, which remained standing and were the subject of remark for several years, the location of the camp-ground was not lost sight of, like many other points of interest in the village   Dr Samuel L Tuttle, while gathering material for a history of Madison in 1855, conversed with Enos Bonnel, an aged resident of this neighborhood, who pointed out to him the spot where the ovens had stood, and said that he clearly remembered them   The encampment covered the fields at present owned by

[1] Morristown Daily Record, August 3, 1917
[2] Boudinot's Elias Boudinot, I, 231
[3] Carrington's Washington the Soldier, 336.

George B Vanderpoel and by the Prospect Hill Land Company, lying south of the turnpike and east of River Road on the Union County side of the Passaic the bakery standing on the property now belonging to Mr. Vanderpoel

The ovens were contained in a shed about four rods in length running parallel with the turnpike and a short distance from it, nearly opposite the present residence of Mrs Mary C Allen [1] and as they were solidly built of brick they remained long after the shed had disappeared but their site was marked until a much later period by the luxurience of the crops, the soil at that place having been fertilized by the deposit of ashes Tradition fails to indicate the time when the ovens were destroyed The late William C Wallace, who owned the property for many years during the middle of the last century and who came to Chatham in 1829, used to say that they had been demolished before his arrival, but he did not know at what date Neither can it be stated whether they were overthrown by human agency or by the action of the elements For a long time the bricks lay scattered over that portion of the field, but during the past twenty-five years they have been gradually removed in the process of clearing the land of loose stones to facilitate cultivation A few copper coins have been found from time to time on the site of the encampment which are thought to have been lost by the soldiers Though considerably worn and corroded they have been recognized as English halfpennies of the reign of George II

On August 19th, Washington detached Colonel Moses Hazen's regiment and two regiments of the New Jersey line under Colonel Elias Dayton and ordered them to Chatham to guard the bakery until the arrival of the army [2] He wrote to Dayton

[1] Historical Magazine, Ser 2, IV, 336
[2] Johnston's The Yorktown Campaign, 88

Head Quarters 19th Augt 1781.

Sir

You will march immediately with the Jersey Line and Hazens Regt to the Heights between Chatham and Springfield You will take the most eligible position and encamp there You will give Coll Seely orders to remain at Dobb's Ferry untill Wednesday when he is to march and join you You will order him, in a very particular manner, to keep scouts and patroles towards Bergen and to take every precaution against a surprise

There will be a French Bakery established at Chatham You are to furnish a small Guard for it and give them any assistance they may want [1]

From the 20th to the 25th of August the commander-in-chief was busily employed in transporting the allied armies across the Hudson at King's Ferry He took with him on the march to Virginia all of Rochambeau's forces and most of the American troops, leaving General Heath with 3,000 militia at Verplank's Point to guard the Highlands After crossing the Hudson the army formed in four divisions— two American and two French General Lincoln, with the First New York regiment and Scammel's corps of light infantry, which latter had lain in camp at Kakeat since the night of August 19th, advanced by way of Paramus, Acquackanack (Passaic) and Second River (Belleville) to Springfield, where they arrived and encamped on the 27th of August [2] The American main column included the park of artillery under Colonel Lamb, Colonel Olney's Rhode Island regiment part of the Second New York regiment (the full quota of which had not arrived from Albany when the army left the Hudson), two light companies of New York and two of Connecticut, a small corps of engineers, sappers and miners, Washington's baggage, the baggage of

[1] Washington Papers in Library of Congress, B, XIV, pt 1, 399.

[2] Magazine of American History, V, 7, Thatcher's Military Journal, 259, 323

the artillery ammunition, stores of all kinds, and thirty flat-
boats each capable of holding forty men, which had been
mounted on carriages, and were thought to be designed for
the passage of Staten Island Sound, though they were really
intended for use in Virginia[1] This division marched by
way of Pompton, Montville Troy, Whippany, Florham
Park and Madison to Chatham, and pitched their tents on
the camp-ground where Dayton's troops had preceded
them   The impression was made upon the entire community, and shared by the soldiers themselves, that not only
these regiments, but possibly the entire army, was to be
stationed at Chatham for a long time   Dr Tuttle in his
History of Madison states that Azariah Carter recalled
having seen the troops pass through that village on the way
to Chatham, and that he, together with Ichabod Bruen,
Captain Luke Carter and others, had a distinct recollection
of the impression made upon every mind that the army was
to be permanently quartered here   The number of these
troops cannot be stated with accuracy   The total American
force in Washington's army is variously given as 2,000 and
3,000, of whom by far the greater number encamped at
Chatham

The forces of Rochambeau, who followed the Americans from the Hudson, also formed in two divisions, both
taking the same route, the first column marching twenty-
four hours in advance of the second   The course from the
Hudson to the Delaware which Washington had mapped
out for them was by way of Suffern, Pompton, Whippany,
Bullion's Tavern, Somerset Court House, Princeton and
Trenton[4] On the 27th the first division, consisting of the
legion of Lauzun and the regiments of Bourbonnais and

[1] Magazine of American History V, 7, VII, 125

[2] Historical Magazine, Ser 2, IX, 336

[3] Johnston's The Yorktown Campaign 87, Marshall's Washington,
IV, 429

[4] Ford's Writings of Washington, IX, 343, n

Deux Ponts, with the park of heavy artillery, reached Whippany and encamped between that village and Hanover, where they were soon joined by the second column, which included the regiments of Soissonais and Saintogne.[1]   About

Bourbon Royal Standard

this time it was whispered among the French officers by those professing to have received authoritative information that their objective point was Yorktown, and not Staten Island; but so impenetrable was the veil of secrecy which concealed Washington's design, that the Duke of Deux Ponts, who commanded the regiment which bore his name, confessed in his diary as late as the 26th that he was totally in the dark as to the object of the march.[2]   The soldiers were soon enlightened, however, for upon leaving Whippany the French column, instead of advancing upon New York, turned about and marched through Morristown toward the south, thus solving the mystery which had puzzled them so long.

Dr. James Thatcher, who was then surgeon of Scammel's light infantry, thus described the situation by entries made contemporaneously in his Military Journal:

The real object of the allied armies [in] the present campaign has become a subject of much speculation. Ostensibly an investment of the city of New York is in contemplation—preparations in all quarters for some months past, indicate this to be the object of

[1] Magazine of American History, V, 7.
[2] Forbach (Count de Deux Ponts) My Campaigns in America (Green's Trans.), 124.

our combined operations   .   The success of a siege must depend
entirely on the arrival and co-operation of a superior French fleet
The enemy have a garrison on Staten Island, which is separated from
Long Island only by a strait two miles wide.   The capture of this
garrison would be a brilliant affair, and would essentially facilitate
our operations against New York   General Washington and Count
Rochambeau have crossed the North river and it is supposed for the
purpose of reconnoitering the enemy's posts from the Jersey shore
A field for an extensive encampment has been marked out on the
Jersey side, and a number of ovens have been erected and fuel provided for the purpose of baking bread for the army   From these
combined circumstances we are led to conclude, that a part of our
beseiging force is to occupy that ground

Our situation reminds me of some theatrical exhibition where
the interest and expectations of the spectators are continually increasing, and where curiosity is wrought to the highest point   Our
destination has been for some time [a] matter of perplexing doubt
and uncertainty , bets have run high on one side, that we were to
occupy the ground marked out on the Jersey shore, to aid in the
siege of New York, and on the other, that we are stealing a march
on the enemy, and are actually destined to Virginia, in pursuit of
the army under Lord Cornwallis

The passage given below is a quotation from the
autobiography of Brigadier-General Philip Van Courtlandt
of the New York Continental line

All my regiment having joined at and near Schenectady, I
marched and encamped on the Patroon's Flats   I had then the
largest and most healthy regiment in America, not excepting French,
English or German, and a fine band of music   Here I had to
remain for the completing of thirty-four boats, now building there
for the purpose, as reported, of taking our army from Elizabethtown
to Staten Island as soon as the French fleet would appear off Sandy
Hook in order to take New York

Count Rochambeau, having marched from Rhode Island with
the French forces, had advanced to the lines in Westchester County
near King's Bridge, some part of our army already in New Jersey,

and all things ready, the French fleet daily expected, I received orders
to take the boats, regiment and baggage, &c and proceed down the
Hudson to Stony Point   Landed and encamped, remained there
while the French passed, and some time after, until information
came that General Washington himself was at the ferry and wished
to see me   Upon approaching him he took me by the arm and went
some distance on the road, and gave me his orders both written and
verbal, which was to march to Chatham in New Jersey, take all the
boats, intrenching tools, &c and proceed with deliberation, informing him daily of my progress, for which purpose he sent a dragoon
every day, as my command was of great importance, being the rear
guard of the army   Upon my arrival at Pompton Plains he altered
my route, but at my request permitted me to take a more circuitous
one through Parcipany—the road being better passing Mr Lott's
and Beaverhout[1]—but not to pass the junction of the Morristown
road with the Chatham road until the next morning, then, instead
of going to the latter, I must pass through Morris and make an
expeditious march to Trenton, and enjoined secrecy for three days[2]

WASHINGTON'S INSTRUCTIONS
TO VAN COURTLANDT

Sir,

  You will take charge of the Cloathing, the Boats, Intrenching
Tools—and such other Stores as shall be committed to your care by
the Quarter Masr General, with these you are to proceed (in
the order they are mentioned) to Springfield by the way of Sufterans,
Pompton, the two Bridges and Chatham

  When you arrive at Springfield you will put yourself under the
order of Major Genl Lincoln or any other your superior officer
commanding at that place   You will also if occasion should require
it alter the above route agreeably to orders from either Majr Genl
Lincoln or the Qr Mr General   You will be particularly careful

---

[1] The farms of Abraham Lott and Lucas Beaverhout lay near the
intersection of the Parsippany turnpike and the road leading from Troy
Hills to Lower Montville
[2] Magazine of American History, II, 278

to collect all your men that are in a proper condition to march and will use your best endeavors to prevent desertion

Given at King's Ferry this 25 day of Augt 1781

Go Washington

To Colonel Cortland [1]

Respecting the time of the arrival and departure of the troops at Chatham there is some uncertainty Washington states in his journal that the two American columns reached the places assigned them (meaning Chatham and Spring-field) on August 28th, and that the army resumed its march on the 30th,[2] but his correspondence indicates that they arrived on the 27th and left on the 29th His letter of instructions to Lincoln at Springfield, directing the further movement of the latter's division is dated August 28th, and orders him to march at four o'clock the next morning, and there seems to be no doubt that the entire army started on the same day We learn from the following news-item published in the *New Jersey Journal* that the general and his staff arrived at Chatham on Sunday the 26th, at least one day in advance of the troops

CHATHAM, August 29 Last Sunday his Excellency General Washington, with his suit, arrived here, and remained until this morning when putting the army in motion, he took his departure

The movement of the troops was mentioned in other newspapers, from which a few excerpts are given

NEW YORK, Aug 27 The Rebel Army under the Command of General Washington, left their encampment at the White Plains last Monday, and we hear some of the Continental Troops are gone up the North River, the French Army crossed the Hudson on the 23d Instant, and proceeded on their March for Chatham, eight

---

[1] Magazine of American History, IV, 142

[2] *Ibid*, VII, 125

miles from Elizabeth Town, where their Artificers have been building Ovens, &c for more than ten days   Part of Dayton's Brigade
are also at Chatham, and a York Provincial Regiment is now stationed at a place called Fox-Hall [Vauxhall] 4 Miles from Newark,
and 7 from Elizabeth Town, so that the Number of Troops now
in that Neighborhood amount to at least six thousand, and their
greatest Distance from Staten Island is not more than nine Miles
                    —Gaines's *New York Mercury*, No 1558

   TRENTON, August 29   We hear the Allied Army have
crossed the North River, and that Head-Quarters are now at Chatham
                    —*The New Jersey Gazette* No 192

   NEW YORK   September 3   Our last Paper left Mr
Washington and his Army at Chatham, Fox Hall, &c since which
we have learnt, That on Tuesday the 28th ult it was resolved the
whole Body should move, that next Day being Wednesday the 29th
they struck their Tents, and the Army consisting of about six thousand in Number, Marched in three Divisions, that on Thursday
Evening the Thirtieth the Rear of the whole was at the Hills near
Bound Brook, and the first Division advanced towards Kingston,
their Artillery consisted of about 20 pieces of Cannon, 4 large Mor-
tars, and several Howitzers   Some of their Officers said that the
French Fleet were arrived at Sandy Hook, and that their Intentions
were to march to Black Point, and tacilitate their Landing, and second their Operations against their common Enemy the English.
   The Inhabitants of Elizabeth Town, Chatham, &c on General Washington's passing through them Places, said, What is to be
our Fate now !   In the Winter we were told we should be in New
York in the Spring, in the Spring we should certainly walk the
Streets of that Place in September, and now instead of attacking that
City, supported by a powerful French Navy, our whole Army is
leaving us to the Mercy of our Enemies
                    —Gaines's *New York Mercury*, No 1559

   On September 1st Constant Cooper, a post rider from
Morristown to Fishkill, was captured by a party of tories

and taken to New York   Some of the letters contained in his mail-bag were published in a newspaper, among them being a note written by Major Sabastin Bauman of the Second Continental artillery to his wife, announcing his arrival at Chatham   He wrote·

Chatham, 28th August, 1781

My Dear,

I have just time to inform you that we arrived here late last night, and march again this afternoon for Brunswick, and from thence I imagine for Philadelphia, and likely from there to Virginia   However this is only present conjecters of mine, probably from this reason, either to take Lord Cornwallis, or to lay ourselves in such a situation, to prevent his getting into New-York by land, which it seems from his present situation and movement he means to accomplish, as his communication by water or sea to New-York is broke off, and which appears to me his intend, and our present rapid movement   However all is guess work, and a few days will reveal the whole, as the French fleet with fifteen thousand land forces is expected hourly

I sent this by way of Post to Fish Kill, thinking it the surest way for you to get it, and if you write to me, send your letters by Post, directed to headquarters, grand army

Michal is well, and so am I, except a little cold I have which plagues me a good deal, my love and respect to all, and remain your husband,

S BAUMAN.

P S

Mrs Vandyke compliment to you   I had a very good breakfast there this morning

Mrs Bauman, Wall Kill

Good Will Meeting House

N B

You must send Conrad to follow the army [1]

While General Washington remained in Chatham on

[1] Rivington's *Royal Gazette*, September 8, 1781

this occasion he is believed to have had his headquarters in
the house of Jacob Morrell, now the residence of Frederick
S Tallmadge, on the southerly side of Main Street about
300 yards west of the river   Tradition has always designated this house as the local "Headquarters," and as such
it is mentioned in Barber and Howe's Historical Collections
of New Jersey, but details are entirely lacking as to the
length of time, or the period of the war, during which it was
occupied by the commander-in-chief. We may safely assume,
however, that it was in August, 1781, when the army encamped here for two or three days, because at no other time,
as far as we can learn, did the general remain in Chatham so
long   Dr Samuel L Tuttle in his History of Madison, and
Dr Ashbel Green in his Autobiography, assure us that
Washington, while staying at Morristown, often rode
through Madison and Chatham to the signal station at the
Short Hills for the purpose of observation, but there is no
evidence that he stopped in Chatham at such times, and
although he passed through the village at the head of his
army on June 7, 1780, halting there for a few hours, he
probably did not then remain over night   But as there can
be no question that the Morrell mansion was occupied by
him at some time during the Revolution, we have no hesitancy in declaring the occasion to have been in 1871, while
he was leading his troops on the memorable march to Yorktown

Jacob Bonnel, one of the early residents of Chatham, a
jeweler and clock-maker by trade, used to say that in his
boyhood he had seen Washington pacing to and fro in Mr
Morrell's door-yard, and a similar recollection was cherished
by Mrs Sallie Crane   These reminiscences, with the brief
mention in Barber's Historical Collections, are our only
authority upon the location of the headquarters, for Washington's journal does not refer to the subject, and the part
of his diary which describes the march to Yorktown makes

MORRILL MANSION—WASHINGTON'S HEADQUARTERS AT CHATHAM

From a Recent Photograph.

no mention of Chatham His presence here is proven by his correspondence, but although his letters of that period are dated at Chatham, they unfortunately do not indicate the house in which he lodged

Some of these letters are reproduced from contemporaneous copies now in the Library of Congress They were doubtless written in one of the rooms of the Morrell mansion

TO LAFAYETTE

New Jersey
Chatham 27th. Augt 1781

My dear Marquis

Your favr of the 11th did not reach me till yesterday morning I so soon expect to see you that I shall defer entering into a particular answer to the Contents, part of which is of a very disagreeable nature and must be handled delicately.

The whole force intended for the southward will be assembled in this neighbourhood today and tomorrow and will proceed to Trenton as soon as Craft can be collected there to transport them down the Delaware to Christiana The celerity of their further movement will depend upon the arrival of the Count de Grasse and the means of transportation which it may be in his power to furnish

Supposing the enemy to be held blockaded in certain positions, it will be necessary for me to know, beforehand, what will be the proper place of debarkation for the French and American Troops, that we may steer immediately to that point, and at which there should be a collection of draught Horses and Cattle and some Waggons to move the Artillery and stores which may be necessary for the immediate commencement of operations I am endeavoring to send round (but I doubt whether I shall be able to effect it) a small supply of salt provisions Should I fail, the troops will have occasion for Fresh the instant of their arrival in Virginia I would therefore wish, to avoid disappointment, that some Cattle might be prepared at the most probable place of debarkation, and I should also wish to know what are the chances or prospects of our supply while in Virginia

Your answer to these points will meet me at the Head of Elk or upon my way thither, and as there is a possibility that I may be upon the Bay, you may, if the Navigation is in our possession, send a Copy of your dispatches to the Head of Elk by Water

Let me know what position you intend to take after you have formed a junction with the Troops with Mr de Grasse, and whether you do not think that James Town will be a proper place of debarkation for us supposing the enemy remain in their present position of York and Gloucester?

I am my dear Marquis sincerely & Affecty Yrs[1]

P S   What number of intrenching tools have you and of what kinds[2]

TO COLONEL MILES, D Q M G

Head Quarters Chatham Augst 27th 1781

Sir

In consequence of a total alteration in our Plans, & the movement of a large Body of Troops to the Southward, I have dispatched a Messenger for the sole purpose of having provision made at Trenton, for the transportation of them to Christian by water   You will therefore be pleased to have the greatest possible number of Sloops Shallops & river Craft of all kinds, fit for the transportation of Men Artillery & Baggage collected from every quarter where they can be found & brought to Trenton by the 31st Inst, at which time the head of the Column is expected to arrive   Let others be procured & ordered to follow to the same place, as fast as may be, untill Orders are received to the contrary   You will use every exertion to have this business carried into execution without loss of time   I have also written to Mr Morris on the subject with whom I wish you to converse & advise respecting the Places Mode &c of obtaining the Craft—and I am persuaded he will afford you any assistance in his power

I have delayed having these preparation made untill this moment, because I wished to deceive the Enemy with regard to our real object as long as possible—our Movements have been calculated for

---

[1] Many of these letters are not signed, as they are copies contained in the general's letter-books

[2] Washington Papers, B XIV, pt 1, 433

that purpose, and I am still anxious the deception should be kept up a few days longer untill our intentions are announced by the Army's filing off—towards the Delaware These arrangements would have been made through the Quarter Master General but he having been left at King's Ferry to execute some business in his Department & the time of his arrival being uncertain I have thought proper to write to you myself on the subject, and to desire in the most earnest manner, that neither labour or expense may be wanting in the performance of the important business now committed to you

I am Sir &c

P S Be so good as to obtain Quarters for Myself & family (half a dozen Gentlemen) at some convenient Private Lodgings without mentioning particularly who they are if one house will not accommodate the whole, the nearer the lodgings are the better Also be pleased to forward the Letters to the Southward by Express.
Col Miles D Q M G [1]

TO ROBERT MORRIS

To the Honble Robert Morris Esqr &c

Dr Sir Chatham 27th August 1781

Accounts brought by several Vessels to Philadelphia and to the Eastward leave little doubt but that the Count de Grasse must have already arrived in the Chesipeak, or that he must be very soon there The Count de Rochambeau and myself have therefore determined, that no time ought to be lost in making preparations for our transportation from Trenton to Christiana and from the head of Elk down the Chesapeak I have written by this opportunity to Colo Miles and have directed him immediately to engage all the proper kind of Craft for the Navigation of the Delaware, which can be found in Philadelphia or in the Creeks above and below it, and as your advice may be useful to him, more especially so far as respects procuring the Vessels at a distance from Philadelphia, I have desired him to wait upon you for that purpose

I shall also be obliged to you for using your influence with the Gentlemen of Baltimore, to permit any Vessels which may be in that port to come up to Elk to assist us in transportation I have

[1] Washington Papers, B XIV, pt 1, 439

little doubt, from the cheerfulness with which they furnished the
Marquis last Winter, but they will comply with your requisition
on the present occasion   But lest there should be a necessity for the
interference of the Executive of the State, I have written to Governor Lee upon that and upon other matters   I enclose the letter
under flying seal for your information, and you will be good enough
to forward it by a Chain of Expresses which is established   Any
Vessel which may be procured in Chesapeak should rendezvous as
soon as possible at Elk River

You will be pleased to make the deposit of Flour, Rum and
Salt at the Head of Elk, which I requested in a former Letter

I am very fearful that about 1500 barrels of Salt Provisions
and 30 Hogsheads of Rum, which I directed to be sent from Connecticut and Rhode Island under Convoy of the Count de Barras
would not have been ready when the Fleet sailed from New Port
Should that have been the case, the disappointment will be great
I would wish you to see whether a like quantity of those Articles
can be procured in Philadelphia or in Maryland, if we should find
that they have not gone round from the Eastward

I must entreat you, if possible, to procure one months pay in
specie for the detachment which I have under my Command, part
of those troops have not been paid any thing for a long time past, and
have upon several occasions shewn marks of great discontent   The
service they are going upon, is disagreeable to the Northern Regiments, but I make no doubt that a douceur of a little hard money
would put them in proper temper   If the whole sum cannot be
obtained, a part of it will be better than none, as it may be distrib-
uted in proportion to the respective wants and Claims of the men

The American detachment will assemble in this neighbourhood
to day   The French Army to morrow

I have the honour to be &c

G WASHINGTON [1]

TO ROCHAMBEAU

Sir   Chatham 27th Augst 1781

By intelligence which I have received since my arrival at this

[1] Washington Papers, A VI pt 1, 241

place, I find that the enemy have been throwing Troops upon Staten
Island   This circumstance, and a desire of bringing up the rear
of the two armies will induce me to halt the American Troops one
day at Springfield, as I pray your Excellency to do those of the
French at Whippany

This Halt will Occasion no delay, as I could not, before this
period, take measures to assemble the Vessels of Delaware, at Trenton, without announcing the object in view, but an Express being
now gone for that purpose, I shall expect to have at least a part of
them at that place by Friday next, to commence the embarkation

I shall set out the day after tomorrow for Philadelphia, and
should be glad to know your Excellency's determination respecting
your journey thither—if to proceed with your Army, we will appoint
a rendezvous

With the greatest respect & personal attachment I have the
honor to be

Yr Excellencys Most Obedt & Hbl Servt

Go Washington -

His Excelly. Genl Rochambeau.

COLONEL TILGHMAN TO COLONEL
VAN COURTLANDT

Chatham 27th Augt 1781

Dear Sir

His Excellency desires me to inform you that he found the
Road by Ogdens Iron Works difficult for the Boats he therefore
wishes you to keep upon the Road from Pompton to Morris Town
untill you come to a place known by the name of Dodds Tavern you
there turn to the left and proceed to the Fork of the Passaic—from
thence you will take the same Road upon which the Artillery moved
to this place—it is by the way of Colo Cook's

I am Dear Sir Yr most obt servt

T Tilghman

Colo Courtland [1]

[1] Washington Papers, B XIV, pt 1, 439

WASHINGTON TO THOMAS McKEAN

Head Qurs Chatham 27th Augst 1781

Sir

I have the honour to inform Congress, that my expectation of the Arrival of the Fleet of Monsr De Grasse in the Chesapeak Bay, with some other circumstances, of which they have been informed in my letter of the 2d Augst and in which very little alterations have since taken place, have induced me to make an alteration of the concerted operations of this Campaign I am now on my March, with a very considerable detachment of the American Army, and the whole of the French Troops, for Virginia

As I expect to be in Philadelphia in a few days, I shall then have the honour to open my motives and intentions to Congress more fully, than it may be prudent to do by Letter at this distance

I have the honour to be &c

G WASHINGTON

To His Excelly Thomas McKean Esqr.
President of Congress [1]

TO LIEUTENANT COLFAX

Chatham 28th Augst 1781

Sir,

The inclosed are the Instructions which I meant to deliver verbally, with some explanation—but—your absence has prevented it[!] When business or Inclination (especially on a March) calls your from your command I should be glad to know it, that I may regulate myself, and orders accordingly

Your rout, & every thing relative to the inclosed order, is to be kept secret till the nature of the movement discloses itself

I am Your Obedt Servt

Go WASHINGTON

P S From Trenton you will contrive to forward Mrs Thompson to New town, or such other place as she wishes to go to -

[1] Washington Papers, A VI pt 1, 241
[2] Washington Papers, B XIV, pt 1, 455

TO MAJOR-GENERAL LINCOLN

Sir,

The Troops composing the Detachment under your Command may, till they are united with the force in Virginia, be formed into three Brigades—viz—the light Infantry to be commanded by Colo Scammel on the Right   The two York Regiments under Brigadr Sert. Clinton on the left, & Hazen's Jersey and Rhode Isld in the Centre

You will march tomorrow at four Oclock in the morning, in two columns, for Trenton   The left column is to consist of the three Brigades above (if Courtlands Regemt should join in time) the Baggage belonging to them, & 6 field pieces (two to each Brigade)   The right column will consist of the remaining artillery, Boats, Baggage, & those of every kind, to be escorted by the Corps of Sappers & Miners

The left column is to march through Westfield & Samptown to Raritan landing (above Brunswick)—

30th   To Princeton

31th   To Trenton

The right column is to proceed thro' Scotch plains and Quibble town to Bound Brooke

30th to Princeton

31th to Trenton

The junction of these two columns will be at Kingston (three miles short of Princeton) from whence the right column is to proceed, and be covered by the left

I have not, as yet, made precise arrangements with Qr Mr General respecting the number of Waggon's & Teams which are to go on from Trenton to the head of Elk, & from thence to Virginia. and it is possible, as he is yet behind, & I shall set [out] early in the Morning for Philadelphia, that I shall not—for which reason I commit the matter to you giving it as my opinion, that all the covered Waggons—if no more—will certainly be wanted in Virga

I foresee difficulty which will arise from the deficiency of Water transportation from Trenton to Christiana bridge—and that is, how to aportion the Craft equally between the french army & ours, without occasioning delay, as the Vessels will come up as they are engaged,

and the American Troops ought to be the advance. Some delicacy
must be used in effecting the latter, without the appearance of sel-
fishness, & giving umbrage to our allies by taking more care of ourselves then them

Perhaps one mean of doing it, may be, to let the contents of the
covered Waggons go on in them, and the Troops least suspected of
desertion and best able to march by land to the head of Elk   The
prospect of procuring Craft in time, & other circumstances, must
govern in this case

The Columns should be provided with guides—for want of
these the artillery yesterday came along a road which was sufficient
to destroy half the carriages that passed over it

Given at Chatham this 28th day of Augt 1781

G W——n [1]

TO COLONEL VAN COURTLANDT

Head Quarters Chatham Augt 28th 1781

Sir

As the Army will march tomorrow Morning before you will
probably have arrived, you will be pleased when you reach Col
Cook's to make yourself acquainted with the best Road leading above
the Mountains towards Trenton, this you will pursue at least to
Bound Brook, & from thence will continue the most direct Route to
Trenton, with your Regiment & all the Stores & other Articles which
have been committed to your charge   You will keep your destination a perfect secret for one or two days at least

I am Sir

Col Courtland [2]

TO CAPTAIN DOBBS

Chatham 28th Augst 1781

Sir

some particular Circumstances having produced an Alteration
in my Plan of Operations, there will be no Occasion for the Services
of the Pilots at present—they may therefore be directed to return
to their several Homes as soon as they please

[1] Washington Papers, B XIV, pt 1, 443
[2] Washington Papers, B XIV, pt 1, 449

You will make a Return to me of the Expense incurred by your & the Other Pilots Attendance on this Call & I will endeavor to procure you Payment as soon as may be

    I am &c   G W

To Capt Dobbs, Baskenridge [1]

TO GENERAL FORMAN

Chatham 28th Augst, 1781 7 oClock

Sir

I am this Moment favored with yours of this Day

Some particular Business calls me for a few Days to Phila whither I shall sett off To morrow Morng I shall be anxious to know further Particulars of the Fleet you mention—whatever Intelligence you can obtain, you will be pleased to forward to me in Phila with all the Expedition in your Power—the more minute your Discoveries the Better

The Position of Admiral Graves Fleet I shall be glad to know, whether he still remains at the Hook, or whether any Movements have taken place, & what

    I am &c   G W

If it is possible to get a Letter to Trenton any Time Tomorrow Night, I shall be there, & glad to hear from you before I leave it Genl Forman [2]

TO ROCHAMBEAU

Chatham 28th August 1781

Sir,

I do not find that the force upon Staten Island is large, or thrown over for any other purpose than that of defence—for which reason it is submitted to your Excellency's judgment to March your Troops in one or two divisions as shall be most easy & convenient to them—there moving in two divisions succeeding days, will occasion no delay, as the Second will be up by the time the first will have embarked

As I propose to go the lower Road I shall not have the honr of

[1] Washington Papers, B XIV, pt 1, 453
[2] Washington Papers, B XIV pt 1, 447

joining your Excellency till we arrive at Princeton where I will order
dinner to be ready at three oClock that we may lodge at Trenton
(12 Miles further)   As this will be a journey of 54 Miles from
Whippany I would suggest to you the expediency of making part of
it this Afternn   Colo Smith, one of my aids, who is well acquainted
with the Roads will have the honour of attending You to the rendezvous at Princeton

      With great esteem & regard & much personal attachment, I
have the honr to be

                       Yr Excellencys Most Obt Servt
                              Go Washington

His Excelly   Count de Rochambeau [1]

TO ABRAHAM SKINNER

                              Chatham 28th August 1781
Sir

      Having been authorized by Congress to proceed upon the Ex-
change proposed by Mr Loring at your last meeting, you will as
soon as convenient inform that Gentleman that the prisoners taken
at the Cedars will be allowed provided a proper allowance is made
on his part for the Canadian Officers taken at St Johns in 1775 and
sent in in 1776   You will be pleased to observe that a dispute hath
long subsisted respecting the actual Ranks of those Officers, the enemy
alledging that they were not of so high grades as they were called
Congress have now put the matter on the most generous and unex-
ceptional footing—"that their Ranks shall be adjusted according to
those specified in their Paroles except the enemy produce sufficient
proof to the Contrary"   I know of no more valid proof than a Certificate under the hand of the British Commander in Chief   You
will remark that the allowance of the Cedar prisoners is made to
depend upon a proper allowance for the Canadian Officers

      General Burgoyne as you will see by the Resolve of Congress of
which the inclosed is a Copy has been offered for the Honble Henry
Laurens Esq and the proposal may have been acceded to, but an
assurance is given in the same resolve that should such Exchange
have taken place, Credit shall be given for the Officers which may be

      [1] Washington Papers, D 1, pt 2, 325

received for him and payment made as soon as the matter is ascertained

Should the enemy reject the foregoing offer and chuse to wave the Exchange of Genl Burgoyne untill the fate of the proposal made by Congress shall be known, you will nevertheless proceed upon the other matter contained in Mr Lorings last proposal, but you will endeavour as much as possible to include Genl Burgoyne now

As we have not yet received any Returns from the Dy Commy of Prisoners to the southward, you are not to agree to the Exchange of any Characters taken in that Quarter When the Returns are obtained preference will be given to those who have been longest in Captivity except Congress should be pleased to order to the Contrary in any particular instances

I am &c

Abraham Skinner Esqr

Commy Genl prisoners [1]

TO THE QUARTERMASTER GENERAL

To the Quarter Master General,
or Deputy Qr M Gl with the Army

In all cases on the present March where the Draught Horses or Cattle of the Army shall fail, or where an additional number shall be absolutely necessary & cannot be procured by hire or in any other way except by Military force, You are hereby authorized & directed to impress such numbers of Horses or Oxen as shall be required to perform the public Service, taking care to have it done in such a manner as to secure the property of the owners as well, & with as little damage & inconvenience as the circumstances will admit

Given under my hand at Chatham this 28th day of Aug 1781 -

COLONEL VAN COURTLANDT TO GENERAL WASHINGTON

Pompton Augt 28 1781

Dear General

I have just received your Excellencys Orders of this Date, and

[1] Washington Papers B XIV pt I, 45
[2] Washington Papers, B XIV, pt I, 451

shall march on the road you are pleased to direct, but from the Information I have, the best rout is by the way of Troy, to the turn of by Bulls Tavern and then the road is Very direct to Chatham the Distance 24 or 25 Miles.

The Regiment is encamped near the yellow House (Curtis's Tavern) some of the Boats are Three Miles in the rear, so that it will take them Two days before they can arrive and perhaps it will be tryday Morning about Nine o Clock before they will all be in If your Excellency should think proper to direct my rout through Troy an Express may meet me where the Road turns of at Dodds Tavern tomorrow morning at Nine oClock

I am with most Esteem Your Excellencys Hume Sert

P CORTLANDT

His Excellency General Washington [1]

The troops took their departure from Chatham secretly by night, in order that their movements and the direction of their march might not be generally known, the object being to conceal their design upon Yorktown as long as possible Dr. Tuttle tells us that on the preceding evening not the slightest intimation of their contemplated departure was given   The camp appeared as usual   fires were lighted, sentries were posted, and the men retired to rest within their tents, but before the next morning they had all mysteriously disappeared, leaving nothing but the long shed filled with ovens, and that no one knew when they had started, nor whither they had gone [2]   It appears, however, from the following letter of Baron Viomenil, and Washington's reply, that the bakery continued in operation for two or three days longer, and that a small guard remained to protect it

Whipany's Camp the 28th of August 1781
At 8 oClok in the Night

Sir

the General Count de Rochambeau Setting out to follow the

[1] Washington Papers, 52, 3

[2] Historical Magazine, Ser 2, IX, 336

orders of your Excellency and having assur'd me of your favourable disposition to protect our Bakers in Chatam till we could be done with them the Intendant told me to day that it is a strong necessitée to keep them till the Second of September on purpose for to be able of giving bread to the army which would not be able to get any I have the honour to beg your Excellency to give the orders that She use Necessary to protect our etablissement in Chatham till the day Mentioned

I am with greatest respect from your Excellency Sir Your most humble Servant

VIOMLNIL [1]

REPLY

Chatham 29th Augst 1781 4 oClock

Sir

I am just now honored with your Favr of last Evening A Detachment of Militia consisting of a Sub[altern] & 25 Men, are already Ordered for the Protection of your Bakery—about 400 More men will lye near this Place which I think will be full Security so long as you mention

With &c I am
Baron Veomlnil [2]

G W

Washington wrote a similar letter to Rochambeau

Chatham Augt 28th 1781

Sir

I have just been honor'd with yours of this date, and will agreeable to your request, order a Detachment of Troops for the purpose of covering your Bake house in this place

I have ye honor &c.
Count de Rochambeau [3]

Instead of pursuing an easterly course toward Staten Island upon their departure from Chatham, as many of the

[1] Washington Papers in Library of Congress, 52, 4
Washington Papers in Library of Congress, D I, pt 2, 329
[3] Washington Papers in Library of Congress, D I, pt 2, 327

soldiers confidently expected, the army moved westward
by way of Main Street and King's Road to the present
borough limits, and through Madison, along the streets now
known as Division Avenue,[1] High Street, and Garfield
Avenue, toward Green Village,[2] reaching Bound Brook at
the end of the first day's march[3]

Washington records in his journal the hope that his
plans might be withheld from the British during the first
day's march from Chatham[4] Thereafter all attempt at con-
cealment was abandoned, but Clinton was so completely
deceived by the false despatches which had been permitted to
fall into his hands, that he believed the movement toward
the South to be a mere feint to distract his attention from
New York, and it is said that he was not aware of Washington's real design until the Americans had crossed the Delaware[5] It would seem that his spies were so far misled by
the appearance of a permanent encampment at Chatham as
to relax their vigilance, or that they are somewhat tardy in
sending in their reports, for although the march to Yorktown was resumed before daylight on the morning of
August 29th, we find Clinton writing to Cornwallis on the
30th—"Mr Washinton's force still remains in the neighbourhood of Chatham, and I do not hear that he has yet
detached to the southward"[6]

After their departure from Chatham the formation of
the American troops was changed General Lincoln's com
mand was formed into three brigades the light infantry

---

[1] The section of Division Avenue south of King's Road was closed when
the line of the railroad was altered in 1916 Prior to that time Division
Avenue crossed King's Road and continued to the eastern extremity of
High Street

[2] Tuttle's Bottle Hill and Madison 84

[3] Mellick's The Story of an Old Farm, 535

[4] Magazine of American History, VII, 125

[5] Lendrum's American Revolution, 374, Schroeder's Life and Times
of Washington, II, 248

[6] Clinton-Cornwallis Controversy, II, 145

under Colonel Scammel on the right, the New York troops of Brigadier-General James Clinton on the left, and the New Jersey and Rhode Island troops, forming a brigade under Colonel Dayton, in the center, two field pieces being added to the New Jersey brigade [1] The army advanced in three columns the right, consisting of the French troops of Rochambeau, followed by the Second New York regiment which thus formed the rear guard of the army, marched from Whippany by way of Morristown, Somerset Court House (now Millstone), and Princeton, the middle column, led by Brigadier-General Hazen, proceeded from Chatham through Bound Brook to Somerset Court House, and the left, being Lincoln's command, upon leaving Springfield followed the road through New Brunswick to Trenton, where the three columns crossed the Delaware [2] Dr Thatcher states that the line of march of the American troops, after the junction of the left and middle columns, was nearly two miles in length

Sir Henry Clinton's mortification upon being thus out-generaled was intensified by the inevitable criticism to which he was subjected in England, and in his Narrative of his Conduct in America he defends the course he pursued, describing the situation of the contending armies at New York, and pointing out that no efforts on his part could have prevented the success of Washington's strategy

Had my correspondence been produced [he continues] it would have appeared from it, and the returns accompanying it, that instead of seventeen, twenty, nay twenty-four thousand men, which it has been reported I had at New York (after the very ample reinforcements as the Ministry acknowledges which I had sent to the South ward) I had not 12,000 effectives, and of these not above 9,300 fit for duty, regulars and provincials But had I twice that number,

[1] Magazine of American History, V, 7, Feltman's Journal, 15
[2] Magazine of American History, VII, 125
[3] Military Journal, 326

I do not know that, leaving sufficient garrisons in the islands and posts depending (what is admitted by all would take 6,000) I could, as has been insinuated, have prevented the junction between Mons. Rochambeau and General Washington, which was made in the highlands, at least 50 miles from me; or that I could have made any direct move against their army when joined, (consisting then of at least 11,000 men, exclusive of militia, assembled on each side the Hudson) with any prospect of solid advantage from it. Or if I had as many reasons to believe that Mr. Washington would move his army into Virginia without a covering French fleet as I had to think he would not; I could not have prevented his passing the Hudson under cover of his forts at Verplanks and Stoney Points. Nor (supposing I had boats properly manned) would it have been advisable to have landed at Elizabeth town, in the face of works which he might easily have occupied (as they were only seven miles from his *camp* at Chatham) without subjecting my army to be beat, en detail. Nor could I, when informed of his march towards the Delaware, have passed an army in time to have made an impression upon him before he crossed that river.

And, speaking of the encampment at Chatham, he adds in a foot-note to the above: "Strong Camp behind Pisaick River within a few miles of his middlebrook Camp, which S. W. H. [Sir William Howe] with 15,000 thought too respectable to attack in '77."

CHAPTER XVII

Proposed Execution of Captain Asgill in Retaliation for the Murder of Captain Huddy—Circumstances of Huddy's Death—Washington is appealed to—He demands the Surrender of the Murderer—His Demand refused—He directs a British Prisoner to be selected by Lot for Retaliation—The Lots are drawn—Asgill the Victim

IN the summer of 1782 intense interest was aroused, not only in this country but throughout Europe, by the proposed execution of Captain Charles Asgill of the British guards, a prisoner of the Americans, to retaliate for the death of Captain Joshua Huddy of the New Jersey State troops who was murdered by the enemy while a captive in their hands. Many who heard of Asgill's unhappy situation could trace a resemblance between his case and that of Major André, whose death was still fresh in the minds of the people. Asgill, like André, was a young gentleman of wealth, culture and excellent prospects, belonging to a family of distinction. He was younger than André, being only nineteen years of age, and his lot was even more hard, as he had committed no military offense to merit such untimely fate. His case far exceeded that of André in the popular excitement it occasioned, for his execution was so long delayed that the matter was kept before the public during the entire summer, and it promised to parallel the André affair in its tragic conclusion. But from a military standpoint the incident was regarded as of comparatively little importance, and as Asgill finally escaped the ignominious death which threatened him, although by the merest chance, the entire case has been forgotten to a great extent.

The prisoner was under sentence of death for a period

of seven months, while Washington was negotiating with
the British commanders for the surrender of Huddy's
slayer, and during the greater part of that time he was
admitted to his parole and resided at Chatham   Never in
its history has Chatham figured so prominently in the public
eye· as the place of Asgill's confinement the village attained
a distinction on both sides of the Atlantic which it has never
since enjoyed, and, in view of this fact, no history of Chatham would be complete which did not review the circumstances of this dramatic occurrence in considerable detail [1]

The Revolutionary War was conducted with great
severity   History is replete with accounts of barbarities
committed by the enemy from time to time, and Washington
was often obliged to protest to the British generals
against the many acts of wanton cruelty which were per-
petrated upon the Americans who had been so unfortunate
as to fall into their hands   Perhaps in no part of the country were the patriots called upon to incur greater dangers
and to endure more severe hardships than in Monmouth
County, New Jersey   The inhabitants of that region were
subjected not only to the misfortunes and privations necessarily incident to war, but were obliged to contend with a
large number of malignant tories, who were guilty of
atrocities even more shocking than those of the British and
Hessian soldiery   A sort of civil war, separate and distinct
from the operations of the two armies, was carried on be-

---

[1] The history of the Asgill case, if written in full, would be very voluminous, a great wealth of material relating to it being contained in Revolutionary correspondence, newspapers and official records   To publish in the
present volume the whole of this data would serve no useful purpose, and
would weary the reader with frequent repetition and prolix discussions of
unimportant details   In selecting material from so prolific a source, it has
been difficult to decide which documents to make use of and which to ignore
An effort is made to present a concise statement of the Asgill affair, containing all the salient facts, and while letters are quoted which bear directly upon the subject, and depict or explain the various phases of the
case, we have avoided, as far as possible, the reproduction of those which
reiterate facts already noticed, or recount collateral incidents not essential to
a clear understanding of the narrative

tween the patriots and tories of Monmouth during the later
years of the Revolution, in which former friends and neighbors were pitted against each other, and the struggle was not
infrequently marked by murders committed on either side,
usually in retaliation for some previous outrage of similar
character.

Among the patriots of Monmouth County one of the
most energetic was Joshua Huddy of Colt's Neck, a captain
of artillery in the State troops,[1] a brave and efficient
soldier, and an indefatigable worker in the cause of freedom.
He waged a relentless warfare against the tory guerillas by
whom the county was repeatedly ravaged, and was so successful in circumventing and defeating them in their successive raids that he excited their bitterest animosity, and
caused them to strive again and again to accomplish his
death. He was finally captured by them in a battle at the
mouth of Toms River on March 24, 1782, and conveyed a
prisoner of war to New York, where he was detained in
various military prisons, and at length confined in the guardship *Britannia* anchored off Sandy Hook.[2]

At that time the affairs of the tories were managed and
to some extent controlled by an organization in New York
known as the Board of Associated Loyalists, a corporation
independent of the army, which had been organized upon an
application of their own by Sir George Germain, Secretary
of State for the American Department. This society, or
some of its members individually, decided that Huddy
should be hung to expiate the death of one Philip White,
who, it was claimed, had been tortured and murdered by
Huddy while he (White) was a prisoner. White was a
militant tory of Monmouth County, who had been captured
while Huddy was confined in New York, and had been shot

---

[1] Stryker's Officers and Men of New Jersey in the Revolution, 395.
Lee's New Jersey as a Colony and as a State, II. 246.
[2] Jones's New York in the Revolution, II, 227.

while attempting to escape   The patriots indignantly denied
that he had been murdered in cold blood, though it is not
probable that they treated him with tenderness, for one of
his captors was the son of a man whom he had murdered
a short time before[1]   But whatever the circumstances of
White's death may have been, it is clear that Huddy could
have been in no way responsible, since it occurred during the
latter's imprisonment   Nevertheless Huddy was removed
from the guardship on April 12 by a party of refugees
commanded by a renegade Jerseyman named Richard Lippincott (a brother-in-law of Philip White[2]), taken to the
Monmouth shore, and hanged on the heights near Middletown, upon a gallows improvised of fence-rails and pla-
carded with the following notice

We, the Refugees, having long with grief beheld the cruel
murders of our Brethren, and finding nothing but such measures
daily carrying into execution, we therefore determine not to suffer
without taking vengeance for the numerous cruelties   and thus begin
(and I say may those lose their liberty who do not follow on) and
I have made use of Captain Huddy as the first object to present to
your view, and further determine to hang man for man while there
is a Refugee existing

Up goes Huddy for Philip White [3]

This murder of an officer in the American service,
charged with an offense of which he was obviously innocent,
and without the pretense of a trial, excited the deepest indignation   Although the crime was by no means unprecedented, the circumstances surrounding Huddy's death
were considered particularly atrocious   He was regarded
not merely as a captive of the refugees, but as a prisoner of
the British army in New York, and it was consequently felt

Barber's New Jersey Historical Collections 365, Mellick's The Story
of an Old Farm, 543

[2] Sabine's Loyalists, II 19

[3] New Jersey Gazette, April 24, 1782

that this murder was directly chargeable to the British authorities

The patriots of Monmouth County believed that drastic steps should be taken to put a stop to such atrocities Captain David Forman, one of their leaders, prepared an accurate statement of the facts, supported by affidavits, and drew up a petition, which was approved by a large number of respectable and influential citizens, and signed by several of them, calling upon General Washington to endeavor by all means in his power to bring the guilty parties to justice, or, if that should prove impossible, to execute a British prisoner in retaliation, in order to deter the enemy from the perpetration of further crimes

These being a state of indubitable facts, fully proven, [continued the petition] we do as of right we may look up to your Excellency as the Person in whom the sole power of avenging our wrongs is lodged, and who has full and ample Authority to bring a British Officer of the same Rank to a similar End—for what man, after this instance of the most unjust and cruel murder, will presume to say that any Officer or Citizen, whom the chance of War may put into the hands of the Enemy, will not suffer the same ignominious death, under some such groundless & similar pretense

Retaliation was urged as the only means of preventing the repetition of such crimes, and of affording relief to the dangerous wrath of the people, and a resolution of Congress was quoted by which the policy of retaliation was expressly authorized in cases of this kind [1]

These papers, together with the placard which set forth the excuse for the murder, were intrusted to two line officers, Colonel Holmes and Captain Forman, who laid them before the American commissioners, General Knox and Goveneur Morris, at Elizabeth, who were then negotiating with

[1] Papers of the Continental Congress in Library of Congress, 152, V 10, 479

General O'Hara and Colonel Abercrombie of the British army for an exchange of prisoners, but Knox and Morris considered the matter to be beyond their jurisdiction, and advised that it be referred directly to Washington, which was accordingly done [1]

The commander-in-chief was then at Newburgh, N Y, where he had recently arrived after a short visit to the troops at Morristown He had had occasion to consider the expediency of retaliation at previous times during the war, but the execution of an innocent man in order to punish the crime of another was so abhorent that he had ever shrunk from carrying it into effect, and in letters which he had written at various times to the generals of his army, he strongly deprecated the plan of endeavoring to check the barbarities of the enemy by resorting to a measure equally barbarous Now, however, a crisis had arisen The circumstances of the case, the high standing and military rank of the murdered man, and the possible continuance of such outrages, required decisive action on his part He realized, too, that the people of Monmouth County were so greatly incensed that if their petition were denied, they would in all probability take the matter into their own hands, and resort to measures which would bring about a condition even more deplorable than that already existing

The general did not act, however, without his usual caution and forethought He knew that to have recourse to the stern measure of retaliation would expose him to a storm of adverse criticism, that although the sacrifice of innocent life in such cases had been authorized by Congress, and was now demanded by the people, yet he alone would have to bear the odium of the act, and that great pressure would be exerted to induce him to forego his purpose He was unwilling to adopt a course from which he might be compelled

[1] *New Jersey Gazette,* March 13, 1782, Ford's *Writings of Washington,* IX, 472, n

to recede, and he determined that he must be assured of the approval and support of the army before taking the step which the people of Monmouth County demanded He accordingly addressed to his officers a letter which read as follows

Head Quarters, April 19, 1782
To the General and Field Officers of the Army

The Commander-in-Chief submits the papers accompanying this, containing the case of Capt Joshua Huddy, lately hanged within the County of Monmouth in N Jersey State by a party of the Enemy to the Consideration of the Genl Officers and Command'g Officers of Brigades and Regiments, And thereupon requests from them, separately and in Writing a direct and laconic Reply to the following Queries, Viz

1st Upon the State of Facts in the above Case, is Retaliation justifiable and expedient?

2d If justifiable, Ought it to take place immediately? Or should a previous Representation be made to Sir Hy Clinton, and Satisfaction be demanded from him?

3d In case of Representation and Demand who should be the person or persons to be required?

4th In case of Refusal and Retaliation becoming necessary of what Description shall the officer be on whom it is to take place, and how shall he be designated for the purpose?[1]

The officers assembled at the headquarters of General Heath, who propounded the questions to them In order to secure the unbiased opinion of each, entirely uninfluenced by the views of his comrades they were forbidden to converse on the subject Each was required to write his answers on a piece of paper, fold and seal it, and address it to the commander-in-chief Colonel Humphreys and Colonel Trumbull of the general's official family attended the meeting, and were careful to see that his directions were strictly obeyed[2]

---

[1] Washington Papers in Library of Congress BXV, pt 1, 187
[2] Heath's Memoirs, 350

Twenty-five officers replied to the questions　Twenty-two agreed that satisfaction should first be demanded of Sir Henry Clinton, commanding the British forces at New York, while the other three held that the laws of war and the enormity of the offense justified the immediate execution of a British prisoner in retaliation, without previous notice They were unanimously of opinion that retaliation was justifiable and expedient, that the leader of the party who murdered Huddy was the person who ought to suffer, that in case he could not be obtained, a British prisoner equal in rank to Captain Huddy should be sacrificed, and that such victim should be selected by lot from among the unconditional prisoners that is, the prisoners who had surrendered at discretion, and not those who were protected by the terms of a capitulation or convention [1]

The views of the army having been thus obtained, Washington lost no time in writing to Clinton, demanding the surrender of Lippincott

Head Quarters, April 21st 1782

Sir,

The inclosed Representation from the inhabitants of the County of Monmouth, with testimonials to the facts (which can he coroborated by other unquestionable Evidence,) will bring before your Excellency the most wanton, unprecedented, and inhuman murder that ever disgraced the Arms of a civilized people

I shall not, because I conceive it to be altogether unnecessary, trouble your Excell with any Animadversions upon this transaction　Candor obliges me to be explicit　To save the innocent, I demand the guilty　Capt Lippincot, therefore, or the officer who commanded at the Execution of Capt Huddy, must be given up, or if that officer was of interior Rank to him, so many of the perpetrators as will, according to the tariff of Exchange, be an Equivalent

To do this, will mark the Justice of your Excell's Character

[1] Heath's Memoirs, 350, Ford's Writings of Washington, IX, 472, n

In Failure of it, I shall hold myself justifiable in the Eyes of God and Man, for the Measure to which I shall resort

I beg your Exy to be persuaded that it cannot be more disagreeable to you to be addressed in this Language than it is to me to offer it, but the subject requires frankness and decision

I have to request your speedy determination, as my Resolution is suspended but for your Answer

I have the honor to be [1]

CLINTON'S REPLY

New York April 25th 1782

Sir —

Your letter of the 21st Instant with the enclosed Testimonials of Captain Huddy's Execution was delivered to me Yesterday, and tho I am extremely concerned for the Cause, I cannot conceal my surprise and Displeasure at the very improper Language You have made Use of, which You could not but be sensible was totally unnecessary

The Mildness of the British Government does not admit Acts of Cruelty or persecuting Violence, and as they are notoriously contrary to the Tenor of my own Conduct and Disposition (having never yet stained my Hands with innocent Blood,) I must claim the Justice of having it believed that if any such have been committed by any Person under my Command, they could not have been warranted by my Authority, nor can they ever have the Sanction of my Approbation My personal Feelings, therefore, required no such Incitement to urge me to take every proper Notice of the barbarous Outrage against Humanity which You have represented to me the Moment it came to my knowledge, and accordingly, when I heard of Captain Huddy's Death, (which was only four Days before I received Your Letter,) I instantly ordered a strict enquiry to be made into all its Circumstances, and shall bring the Perpetrators of it to an immediate Trial.

To sacrifice Innocence under the Notion of preventing Guilt, in place of repressing would be adopting Barbarity and raising it to the greatest Height, Whereas if the Violators of the Laws of War

_____
[1] Washington Papers in Library of Congress, E, 469

were punished by the Generals under whose Power they act, the Horrors which those Laws were formed to prevent will be avoided, and every Degree of Humanity War is capable of maintained

Could Violations of Humanity be justified by Example, many from the parts where your Power prevails, that exceed and probably gave Rise to this in Question, could be produced

In hope that the Mode I mean to pursue will be adopted by You, and prevent all future Enormities, I remain Sir,

Your Excellency's &c &c

H CLINTON [1]

The position of Sir Henry Clinton was unquestionably delicate and embarrassing   His natural impulse was to disclaim all responsibility for Huddy's death, since the Associated Loyalists had acted without his knowledge and possibly contrary to his instructions, yet he hesitated to let it appear that he was unable to maintain discipline in the city of his headquarters, and he shrank from antagonizing the tories by yielding to Washington's demand   He and his successor, Sir Guy Carleton, who, a few days later, followed him in command of the British forces in America, endeavored to temporize   They both expressed the deepest indignation at Huddy's murder, insisted that the crime had been committed without the knowledge and sanction of the British authorities, and assured the American commander that the perpetrators should be brought to an immediate trial in which full justice would be done; at the same time attempting to distract Washington's attention by pointing out similar crimes said to have been committed by the Americans, and to persuade him to abandon his plan of retaliation   But they steadfastly refused to surrender Lippincott

Clinton laid the matter before the Associated Loyalists, who were filled with consternation at the serious consequences of the crime, and sought to exculpate themselves by throwing all blame upon Lippincott   A court-martial was

[1] Washington Papers in Library of Congress, 56, 78

ordered for the trial of the latter, in the course of which it appeared that William Franklin, president of the Associated Loyalists, had given him verbal orders for Huddy's execution, and that such orders were known and approved of by several members of the Board without being opposed by any The court decided that, although Lippincott had acted without proper authority, he had not been actuated by malice or ill will, but believed it to be his duty to implicitly obey the commands of the Board, and did not doubt their authority to issue such orders He was accordingly acquitted

Sir Guy Carleton, who had now succeeded Clinton in command at New York, sent a report of the trial to General Washington, and, realizing that the Americans would not be satisfied with the result of the proceeding, he promised, in an accompanying letter, to prosecute a further inquiry Soon afterwards he dissolved the Board of Associated Loyalists, in order to avoid further difficulties, and possibly with the view of appeasing the anger of the patriots [1]

While these proceedings were taking place in New York, Washington had not been idle Foreseeing the reluctance of the British commanders to surrender the murderer, and having but little hope that justice would be done as a result of their inquiry, he did not await the decision of the court-martial, but wrote on the 2nd of May to Brigadier-General Moses Hazen, commanding the prison camps at York and Lancaster, Penn, where many of the British troops captured at Yorktown were confined, directing him to select by lot a victim for retaliation His letter follows:

Head Qrs, 2d May, 1782

Sir,

The Enemy persisting in that barbarous line of conduct, they have pursued during the course of this war, have lately most inhumanly Executed Capt Joshua Huddy, of the Jersy State troops, taken

[1] Gordon s Rise of American Independence, IV, 287, 291

Prisoner by them at the Port on Toms River, and in consequence, I have written to the British Ambassador-in-Chief, that, unless the Perpetrators of that horrid deed were delivered up, I should be under the disagreeable necessity of Retaliating, as the only means left to put a stop to such inhuman proceedings

You will, therefore, immediately on recet of this, designate by lot for the above purpose a British Captain, who is an unconditional Prisoner, if such a one is in our possession, it not, a Lieutenant under the same circumstances, from among the Prisoners at any of the Posts, either in Pennsylvania or Maryland

So soon as you have fixed on the Person, you will lead him under a safe guard to Philadelphia, where the Minister of War will order a proper Guard to receive and conduct him to the place of his Destination

For your information respecting the Officers, who are Prisoners in our possession, I have ordered the Commissioner of Prisoners to furnish you with a List of them, it will be forwarded with this

I need not mention to you, that every possible tenderness, that is consistent with the security of him, should be shown to the person whose unfortunate lot it may be to suffer [1]

At the same time he addressed a letter to General Benjamin Lincoln, Secretary of War, directing that the prisoner should be sent to the cantonments of the Jersey line, which was the place assigned for execution As Captain Huddy had been an officer of the New Jersey troops, it was thought fitting that his murder should be avenged by the soldiers of his own State. The general wrote.

Head Quarters, Newburgh May 4th 1782

Dear Sir,

By the letter to Brigdr General Hazen, which I have enclosed to you under a flying seal, for your inspection, you will observe the distressing alternative to which we are at last reduced, I must request you will give that Letter a safe and speedy conveyance   .

As soon as the British Officer, whose unfortunate lot it is to be

[1] Washington Papers in Library of Congress, BXV pt I, 237

designated as the object of Retaliation, shall arrive in Philadelphia, it will be necessary to have a sufficient Escort, under the command of a very discreet and vigilant officer, in readiness to receive and conduct him to the Cantonment of the Troops of New Jersey, I pray you will be pleased to give the Orders proper for the occasion, and direct the officer Commanding the Party to apply to the Commandant of the Jersey Line, who will have final instructions respecting the matter

Keenly wounded as my feelings will be, at the destiny of the unhappy Victim, no gleam of hope can arise to him but from the conduct of the Enemy themselves. This he may be permitted to communicate to the British Commander-in-Chief, in whose power alone it rests to avert the impending vengeance from the innocent by executing it on the guilty—at the same time it may be announced, that I will receive no application nor answer any Letter on the subject, which does not inform me that ample satisfaction is made for the death of Capt Huddy on the perpetrators of that horrid deed [1]

By some error General Lincoln informed the commander-in-chief that there was no unconditional prisoner available, despite the fact that there were two British officers in the hands of the Americans who answered that description,[2] and Washington, feeling that the matter had progressed so far that it could not be dropped, wrote a second letter to Hazen directing him to make the selection from among the prisoners who were under capitulation

Head Quarters, 18th May, 1782

Sir,

It was my Wish to have taken for the purpose of retaliation an officer who was an unconditional prisoner of War I am just informed by the Secy at War, that no one of that description is in our power I am therefore under the disagreeable necessity to Direct, that you immediately select, in the manner before prescribed, from among all the British Captains who are prisoners either under

[1] Washington Papers in Library of Congress, A VI, pt 2, 113
[2] Ford's Writings of Washington, X, 5, n, 23

Capitulation or Convention One who is to be sent in as soon as possible, under the Regulations and Restrictions contained in my former Instructions to you

I am, Sir, &c &c

GO. WASHINGTON [1]

The senior captain among the British prisoners at York and Lancaster was Samuel Graham of the Seventy-sixth regiment of foot, who in after years became the lieutenant-governor of Stirling castle in Scotland Graham wrote a narrative of his experiences in the American Revolution, and to him we are indebted for a full account of the manner in which the victim was chosen for the purpose of retaliation [2]

In his description of their life in the prison camps, Graham alludes to a feeling of uneasiness which arose among the captives upon reading in the newspapers which occasionally reached them of atrocities committed by the tories, and the resultant appeals to Washington for retaliation, their disquietude increasing when the correspondence between Washington and Clinton in the Huddy case was published, and it became evident that the general was disposed to accede to these demands For while the prisoners at York and Lancaster were protected by the capitulation of Yorktown, which in express terms provided against reprisals, and they therefore apprehended no injury to themselves, they feared that other captives, who had surrendered unconditionally, might be called upon to suffer

On the 24th of May, while Graham was on parole at York where his regiment was imprisoned, he received a somewhat unexpected visit from his friend Major James Gordon of the Eightieth regiment, the ranking officer among the British captives at that place, who said that he was the

---

[1] Washington Papers in Library of Congress, BXV pt 1, 303

[2] Graham's Memoirs United Service Journal, XVI, pt III, Chambers' Edinburgh Journal, January, 1835

ROYAL ARMS OF SCOTLAND.
Edinburgh Castle: 1566.

Nemo me
impune lacessit

Nemo me
impune lacessit

IN DE · VINCE ·

"Lord Jesu Christ that
Crownd was with thorne
Preserve the Birth quhais
Badgie heir is borne.
And send her Sonne Successione
to Reigne still
Lang in this Realme, if that
it be Thy will.
Als Grant O Lord quhat
ever of Hir progeni
Be to thy Glorie Honor
and Praise eobiei."

Lord Jesus Christ, the
crowned was with thorne
Preserve the birth whose
body heir is born
And send her sonn successioune
to reign still
Long in this realm, if that
it be Thy will.
Also grant O Lord, whate'er
of her proceed
Be to thy glory, honour, and
Praise indeed.

Quen Mary presents the infant Prince to Divnity.

bearer of a message from General Hazen to the officer in command at York to send all the British captains on parole there to Lancaster They were each directed to take a servant and spare necessaries, and to meet at Gordon's quarters in Lancaster, but the major did not tell Graham for what reason they were to be thus assembled, explaining that he had pledged his word not to divulge certain facts which had come to his knowledge

In accordance with these instructions, thirteen British officers who were confined at York and Lancaster gathered the next afternoon at Major Gordon's quarters They were Captains Alexander Arbuthnot and William Hawthorn of the Eightieth foot, David Barclay and Samuel Graham of the Seventy-sixth, James Ingram of the Thirty-third, Lanford Mills of the Seventeenth Thomas Saumarez of the Twenty-third (Royal Welsh Fusileers), and Bulstrode Whitlock of the Twenty-sixth, attached to the Queen's Rangers, and Lieutenants (Acting Captains) Charles Asgill, George Eld, H Fulke Greville, George Ludlow and John Peiryn, all of the First Foot Guards, or Grenadier Guards as they are now called Major Gordon, whom they found pacing the room in uncontrollable agitation immediately informed them for what purpose they had been called together "You have all seen the correspondence which has for some time been carried on between General Washington and the Commander-in-chief at New York," he continued, "and you therefore know that Washington is determined to revenge upon some innocent man the guilt of a set of lawless banditti Gentlemen, you will scarcely believe that in the face of the capitulation and in defiance of the strong remonstrances which I have felt it my duty to make, both to the American and French authorities, one of you is doomed to suffer I have told Washington that he will be answerable for this foul deed to all posterity, but I might as well reason with the air! I wish to God they

would take me in your place, for I am an old worn-out trunk
of a tree, and have neither wife nor mother to weep for
me   But even to that they will not consent so all that I can
undertake to do is, to accompany the unfortunate individual,
whoever he may be, to the place of his martyrdom, and to
give him every consolation and support while life remains,
and obey his wishes after it is taken away "

He also assured them that he would spare no exertion
to save the life of the victim, and read to them letters containing protests, or appeals for intervention, which he had
written to General Washington, to the President of Congress, to the Count de Rochambeau, to the Chevalier de la
Luzerne, French Minister at Philadelphia, and to Sir Guy
Carleton   Graham adds that the major, though a man of
great self-control, could not restrain his tears upon con-
templating the cruel fate which was about to befall one of
their number, and that there was not one of the younger
officers who did not feel a thousand times more for him
than for themselves   Nevertheless, they kept up their
spirits, chiefly on the major's account, and spent a tranquil
and even lively evening at his table

On the following morning (May 26th) at nine o'clock
the captains presented themselves at General Hazen's headquarters in the Black Bear tavern at Lancaster, there to
draw lots for life or death, and, despite their anxiety, they
repaired to the appointed place talking together as calmly
and cheerfully as if they were going to a ball   In the yard
of the inn they found a party of twenty dragoons already
mounted, who, it was understood, had been detailed to act
as the victim's escort upon his journey, and a large number of townspeople had gathered in front of the building
to learn the result of the lottery   In one of the rooms of
the tavern, to which the prisoners were directed, they were
met by General Hazen, who was attended by Captain
White, his aide-de-camp, and by Mr Witz, the commissary

of prisoners all of whom appeared to be considerably agitated Hazen evidently found the ordeal a trying one, and his voice faltered as he addressed the prisoners, informing them for what purpose they had assembled, and reading aloud the two letters of instructions which he had received from Washington

He earnestly requested the captains to decide among themselves who the victim was to be in order to save him the painful necessity of drawing the lots, but this they of course refused to do Major Gordon, who acted as spokesman for the group, entered a vigorous protest against this breach of the treaty of Yorktown, which contained a provision against reprisals Finding his protest of no avail, he raised the point that the captains there present were only a small proportion of the total number who had surrendered at Yorktown, and that if such a deed were to be done, it would be more fair and just if all of them were assembled He assured Hazen that none of the absent ones would shrink from the ordeal, but that, if sufficient time were allowed, they would be willing to come forward even from England to stake their lives with their comrades, and he asked that the matter be postponed at least long enough to summon a captain who had been left in Virginia when the captured army was removed to the prison camps But the brigadier replied that his instructions particularly mentioned such captains as were in Pennsylvania and Maryland, and as he was directed to send the victim forward immediately, he could not consent to any delay

"When all is over," said he, "and the lot has been declared on whom the blow must fall, then you may rely upon it that every indulgence shall be shown which you could expect, or my own feelings dictate" Then, turning to his aide and the commissary of prisoners, he requested them to withdraw to an adjoining room and prepare the lots

Captain Graham affirms that it would be quite im-

possible to describe his sensations, which were doubtless
experienced in like degree by the others, during the brief
pause which ensued   The prisoners for the most part remained silent, though all kept up a good countenance,
apparently without effort   Their courage was exemplified
by the conduct of Captain David Barclay, who, when informed by Hazen that Washington had given orders permitting him to go to New York, and that, in consequence his
name would not be included in the lottery, insisted that his
name should be added, and that he might share the danger
which menaced his comrades [1]

Perhaps ten minutes had elapsed when the aide and the
commissary re-entered the room, each carrying a hat in his
hand   They were followed by the officer commanding the
dragoons who were drawn up outside the building, and by
a drummer boy who had been called in to draw the lots   In
the hat held by the aide they had placed thirteen slips of
paper of equal size and shape, each of which bore the name
of one of the British captains, the hat carried by the commissary contained thirteen similar slips, twelve of which
were blank and one marked "unfortunate '   The drummer
thrust his hand into the first hat, drew out a slip of paper,
and read aloud the name written upon it, then from the
other hat he drew a slip which proved to be blank, thus
leaving in safety the officer whose name had just been read
Ten times was this process repeated, but at the eleventh
drawing the fatal slip "unfortunate" came forth, following
the name of Charles Asgill, to whom General Hazen
pointed while he said to the officer of dragoons, "That
gentleman, sir, is your prisoner "[2]

[1] Graham's Memoirs Appendix, Note A, B
[2] Graham's Memoirs, United Service Journal, 1834, XVI, pt 3

CHAPTER XVIII

The Asgill Case continued—Asgill is conveyed to Philadelphia and from thence to Chatham—Attempt to secure an Unconditional Prisoner as a Victim—Asgill's Execution delayed—He is admitted to his Parole and resides at Dayton's Headquarters in Chatham—Correspondence relating to his Case

CHARLES ASGILL, the British officer who was selected to be the victim of retaliation, as described in the last chapter, was a member of a distinguished family, and heir to an extensive fortune and estate. He was the only son of Sir Charles Asgill, baronet, a successful banker of London, who had been Lord Mayor of that city in 1757. The son was born in 1763, and was therefore about nineteen years of age at the time of which we write. He entered the army in 1778, joining the First Foot Guards with the rank of ensign. In 1781 he became a lieutenant and acting captain in the same regiment, and was ordered to America in the spring of that year[1] Being possessed of an amiable disposition and many engaging qualities, he was very popular with his comrades in arms, who were filled with sorrow when it was determined by the lottery that his life was to be forfeited

"The excitement of the scene was now over," writes Captain Graham after describing the drawing of lots, "and we gazed upon poor Asgill with a bitterness and intensity of feeling such as defied control   To know that his days, nay his hours, were numbered—that was a demand upon the fortitude of those who loved him, such as they could not meet   We all lifted up our voices and wept, and while a warm pressure of the hand was exchanged with

[1] Stephens' Dictionary of National Biography, Hamilton's Grenadier Guards, II, 252

each in his turn, the object of so much commiseration found it no
easy matter himself to restrain his tears   Nor, to do them justice,
were the Americans either within or without the house, indifferent
spectators to the drama   The crowd, too—and a dense multitude was assembled around the house—evinced their sympathy by
such exclamations of pity as crowds are wont to offer   Their observation was   'What odd people these Britishers are! they went in
all cheerful and chatting before they knew which one of them was
to suffer for our good friend Captain Huddy, but now when they
know, they all come out in tears, except the young man himself who
has been selected'   And so, in fact it was   There was not a dry
eye among us, except that of Asgill himself, as we proceeded from
the Black Bear to Major Gordon's quarters"[1]

Hazen's report to Washington was contained in a letter
of May 27th, which read as follows

Sir,
On the Evening of the 25th Instant I received your Excellency's Letters of the 4th and 18th Current, as I had to collect the
British Captains Prisoners of War, at this Place and York-Town,
it was 10 o'Clock this Morning before I could assemble those Gentlemen together at the drawing of Lots, which was done in the
presence of Major Gordon and all the British Captains within the
Limits prescribed,—the unfortunate Lot has fallen on the Honourable Capt Charles Asgill, of the Guards, a young Gentleman of seventeen Years of Age, a most amiable Character, the only Son of Sir
Charles Asgill, Baronet, Heir to an extensive Fortune, an honourable Title, and of course he has great Interest in the British Court
and Armies   The British Officers are highly enraged at the Conduct of Sir Henry Clinton, they have solicited my leave to send an
Officer to New-York on this Occasion, or that I would intercede
with the Minister of War to grant it   Being fully convinced that
no Inconvenience could possibly arise to our Cause from this Indulgence, but on the contrary, good Policy and Humanity dictates the
Measure   I was pleased at the Application, and with Cheerfulness

[1] United Service Journal, 1834, XVI, 318, Chambers' Edinburgh Journal,
January, 1835

CAPTAIN ASGILL.

CAPTAIN CHARLES ASGILL.

have recommended to the Minister of War to grant the Honourable
Capt Ludlow, Son of the Earl of Ludlow, leave to carry the Representations of those unfortunate Officers who openly declare to have
been deserted by their General, and given up to suffer for the Sins
of the Guilty   I must here beg to remark, that since my Command
at this Place, as far as I have been able to discover, those unfortunate
Officers have conducted [themselves] with great Propriety, and as I
sensibly feel for their disagreeable Situation, I hold it as a Part of
my Duty to endeavour to alleviate their Distresses by such Indul-
gences as may not be prejudicial to our Service

*   *   *   *   *   *   *   *

As your Excellency was pleased to direct that every possible
Tenderness should be shewn to the unfortunate Officer whose Lot
it should be to suffer on this Occasion, I have in Consequence of a
Joint Application by Capt Asgill and Major Gordon, permitted the
latter to accompany the former to Philadelphia, where he will of
course receive and follow the Orders of the Minister of War

Since I wrote the above Majr Gordon has furnished me with
an Original Letter of which the enclosed is a Copy, by which you
will see we have a Subaltern Officer and unconditional Prisoner of
War at Winchester Barracks   I have also just received Information
that Lieut Turner, of the 3rd Brigade of Genl Skinner's New
Jersey Volunteers is in York Gaol—but as those Informations did not
come to Hand before the Lots were drawn, and my Letters wrote to
your Excellency and the Minister of War on the Subject, and as I
judge no Inconveniency can possibly arise to us by sending on Capt
Asgill, to Philadelphia, which will naturally tend to keep up the Hue
and Cry, and of course foment the present dissentions amongst our
Enemies, I have sent him under Guard as directed   Those Officers
above-mentioned are not only of the Description which your Excellency wishes, and at first ordered, but in another Point of View are
proper Subjects for Example, being Traitors to America, and having
taken refuge with the Enemy, and by us in Arms   It having fallen to
my Lot to superintend this melancholy disagreeable Duty, I must
confess I have been most sensible affected with it, and do most sincerely wish that the Information here given may operate in favour of
Youth, Innocence, and Honour

I have the Honour to be, your Excellency's most obedt and most devoted humble Servant

MOSES HAZEN

His Excellency Genl Washington [1]

Now that the identity of the victim had been deter-mined, Major Gordon filled some blank spaces which he had left in the letters previously written to the American and French authorities, and obtained General Hazen's permis-sion to forward them without delay   His letter to Sir Guy Carleton, which was sent by the hand of Ludlow, read as follows

Lancaster 27th May 1782

Sir,

I am sorry to inform Your Excellency, in Consequence of an Order from General Washington, directed to Brigr Genl Hazen, commanding Officer at this Post, that Captain Asgill of the Brigade of Guards, has this day been made close Prisoner, and is to be escorted under a Guard tomorrow to Philadelphia, where it is said he is to suffer an ignominious Death in the Room of Captn Huddy, an American Officer, who was murdered some time ago, by a lawless Banditti calling themselves Refugees

I have done everything in my Power to prevent it, which I hope will meet with Your Excellency's Approbation

The Honble Captn Ludlow of the Guards will have the Honor of delivering this to Your Excellency, and will inform you of every Application I have made. Lots were drawn for the Captains of Lord Cornwallis's Army present here, and when the unfortunate Chance fell to Captn Asgill, he received it with that firm Coolness that would have reflected Honor upon any Officer in His Majesty's Service

The delicate Manner in which General Hazen communicated his Orders to the British Officers, shews him to be a Man of real Feelings, and the mild Treatment that the Prisoners have met with since we came to this Place deserves the warmest Acknowledgments of every British Officer   I shall expect with Impatience Your Excel-

[1] Washington Papers in Library of Congress, 114, 2

lency's Commands, and I have the Honor to be, Sir with the greatest Respect,

Your Excellency's &c

JAMES GORDON
Major 80th Regt & Field Officer
with British Prisoners

His Excellency
Sir Guy Carleton K B [1]

Following is his appeal to the French Minister

Lancaster May 27th 1782

Sir,

I beg leave to acquaint Your Excellency, that in Consequence of an Order from His Excellency General Washington dated the 18th of May directed to Brigadier General Hazen commanding at this Post, that Captain Charles Asgill of His Majesty's Guards has been made close Prisoner and is to be sent to Philadelphia, where it is said he is to suffer an ignominious Death in the Room of Captain Huddy, an American Officer, who was murdered by a Party of Refugees As this is in direct Violation of the Articles of Capitulation settled and agreed upon between His Excellency George Washington Esqr Commander in Chief of the combined Forces of America and France His Excellency Count de Rochambeau, Lieutenant General of the Armies of the King of France, Great Cross of the Royal and Military Orders of St Louis, commanding the Troops of his most Christian Majesty in America, and His Excellency the Count de Grass, Lieutenant General of the Naval Army of France commanding in the Chesapeak, on the one Part, And The Right Honorable Lieutt General Earl Cornwallis, commanding His Brittanic Majesty's Forces in the Garrisons of York and Gloucester, and Thomas Symonds Esqr commanding His Brittannic Majesty's Naval Forces in York River, Virginia on the other Part, I must therefore beg of Your Excellency, as Minister Plenipotentiary to His Most Christian Majesty Lewis the 16th King of France, who guarantees that Capitulation to Britain, that You will be pleased to order him

[1] British Public Record Office copy in Library of Congress

to be released from his Confinement on his giving the same Parole
with the rest of the Officers taken with Lord Cornwallis   If the
Law of Nations was to allow of so inhuman and barbarous a Method
of carrying on the War, as that of Retaliation, it never could extend
to Officers taken by Capitulation, nor would it ever be permitted by
the Subjects of our respective Sovereigns

The fourteenth Article of Capitulation expressly says, No Articles to be infringed on Pretext of Reprisals &ca

The Honble Captain Ludlow of His Majesty's Guards will
have the Honor of delivering this to Your Excellency, and receive
Your Answer

I have the Honor to be, &ca &ca

JAMES GORDON
Major 80th Regt and Field
Officer with British Prisoners

His Excellency
  Monsr de'Luzerne
    &ca &ca [1]

His letter to General Washington was couched in these
terms

Lancaster 27th May 1782

Sir

It is with astonishment I read a Letter from your Excellency,
dated 18th May, directed to Brigadier General Hazen, Commanding at this Post, ordering him to send a British Captain, taken at
York-town by Capitulation, with My Lord Cornwallis, Prisoner to
Philadelphia, where 'tis said he is to suffer an ignominious Death,
in the room of Capt Huddy an American Officer, who was murder'd
by a Lawless Banditti, calling themselves Refugees

As this is, in Direct Violation of the Articles of Capitulation of
the Garrison's of York and Gloucester, which Your Excellency
signs first, as Commander in Chief of the Combin'd Forces of Amer
ica and France, the 14th Article of which, expressly says "That
no Articles of the Capitulation are to be infring'd on Pretext of Reprisals, and if there be any doubtful Expressions in it, they are to
be interpreted, according to the common meaning and acceptation of

<hr>

[1] British Public Record Office, copy in Library of Congress

the Words " I, therefore in the Name of my Royal Master George the Third, King of Great Britain, Demand of Your Excellency, that you will order Captain Asgill of the Brigade of Guards, to be discharged from his Confinement, and admitted to the same Parole as the other Officers of my Lord Cornwallis' Army

I have the Honor to be Your Excellency's Most Obedt & most Humle Servt

JAMES GORDON

Major 80 Regt & Field Officer

with the British Prisors

His Excellency General Washington,

Commander in Chief of the Combin'd Forces

of America & France [1]

Gordon seems to have written more than once to Washington upon the subject, but the general, in accordance with the determination he had expressed in his second letter to Hazen, declined to reply

ASGILL TO CARLETON

Lancaster 27th May 1782

Sir,

General Washington having ordered Lots to be drawn for the Captains of Lord Cornwallis's Capitulated Army that One might be secured as amenable for Captain Huddy's Death, who was hanged by some Refugees the unfortunate Chance fell to me   Conscious of my own Innocence, and firmly relying that I shall receive every Support & Assistance my unnecessary Circumstances may need from your well known Justice and Humanity I shall patiently wait Your Excellency's Resolves

I have the Honor to be your Excellency's most obedient humble Servt

CHARLES ASGILL

Lieut 1st Regt Foot Guards

His Excellency

Sir Guy Carleton

&ca. &ca [3]

[1] Washington Papers in Library of Congress, 114, 4

[2] Ford's Writings of Washington, XI, 60

[3] American Manuscripts in the Royal Institution, Vol 26, No 206, copy in Library of Congress

ASGILL TO WASHINGTON

Philadelphia May 30th 1782

Sir

As I conceive myself under the Protection of a Treaty in which the Honor & Faith of Nations are the Pledges, I have nothing to apprehend but from Hasty resolves   I must therefore trouble your Excellency with those reasons that induce me to wish any final determination may be deferred untill Sr Guy Carleton can be thoroughly informed of the circumstances of my Confinement   From the Orders your Excellency sent to Genl Hazen it appears that a British officer being an unconditional Prisoner with the Rank of Captain or Lieutenant, was to be delivered up, that he might be retaliated with for the Death of Captain Huddy, that if no Officer under that Description could be found, this Order then extended to the Captains (British) of Ld Cornwallis's Capitulated Army—in consequence Lots were drawn for those Captains who were present of that Army & the decision fell upon me   Perfectly innocent of Captain Huddy's Death, & even at this moment uninformed of the circumstances & ever having acted consistently with the Tenor of my Parole I am certain in Justice his Death can never effect me, nor do I know why my Life should be an Atonement for the Misdemeanors of others   I claim protection under the 14th Article of the Capitulation & from your Excellency's known Character I have every Right & Reason to expect it

The same motives that prevailed with your Excellency to require an Officer who was not under the Sanction of a treaty of Faith, will I hope *once more* induce you to enquire if there are no such Officers at this time of the Denomination *unconditional* Prisoners

I shall at present trouble you with no further representations, what other Arguments I may have to urge in my favor are such self evident Truths as require no Elucidation   To your Excellency I again make my Appeal for Justice & repeat my request that no sudden or hasty proceedings may be held against me

I have the Honor to be, your Excellency's Most Obedt Humle Servant,

CHARLES ASGILL
Lieutt 1st Regt Foot Guards

His Excely Genl Washington
     commander in Chief of the American forces [1]

---

[1] Washington Papers in Library of Congress, 114, 6

Although Washington had directed that the victim should set out on his journey to New Jersey as soon as the selection was made, Hazen consented, at the earnest request of Major Gordon, to delay Asgill's departure until the next morning, in order that time might be allowed to perfect Gordon's arrangements for dispatching his letters Hazen insisted, however, that Asgill should be held in custody, and should no longer be admitted to his parole

The major, having learned that the party of dragoons who were to act as the prisoner's escort had arranged for regular stopping-places on the road, where forage was to be obtained, and that the intervening distances were so great that they would reach their destination very promptly, prevailed upon Hazen to allow him to choose his own stages, upon condition that he himself would provide the forage His object was to delay their progress as much as possible, in order to allow time for the delivery of his letters, it being understood that the prisoner would be executed as soon as the journey's end was reached By thus arranging more frequent stops, he succeeded in lengthening the journey several days, and, considering this to be a service of a public nature, he drew £500 from the British paymaster-general to pay for the forage and for similar purposes This expenditure, by the way, was regarded with disfavor by the auditors of the public accounts, who probably could not understand why the British government should be expected to provide forage for troops of the enemy, and for a long time they hesitated to ratify it [1]

The next morning Captain Asgill set out on his journey in the custody of the dragoons, accompanied by his friend Major Gordon General Hazen, whose sympathy for the young officer impelled him to take all possible steps to insure his personal comfort and alleviate his distress, rode with the party for several miles, and upon leaving them, he charged

[1] Graham's Memoirs, preface

the dragoon officer to pay strict attention to Gordon's wishes, and to implicitly obey any order which he might give, not inconsistent with the safekeeping of the prisoner When Philadelphia was reached, Gordon immediately applied to the French minister, to several members of Congress, and to other persons high in authority, entreating them to intervene in Asgill's behalf, but his efforts were in vain Indeed, Captain Graham adds the improbable statement that certain persons in that city who seemed disposed to move in the matter, received a sudden order to leave town—"a fatal sign," says he, "that the resolutions of the government were irrevocable "[1]

About this time General Washington learned from Hazen's letter the falsity of the information previously given him that the Americans had no unconditional prisoners who were available for the purpose of retaliation. Perceiving that the sacrifice of a capitulation prisoner was not necessary, he promptly dispatched a letter to Hazen in an endeavor to rectify the mistake The general wrote

Head Quarters, 4th June, 1782

Sir,

I have received your favr of the 27th May and am much concerned to find, that Capt Asgill has been sent on, notwithstanding the Information, which you had received, of there being two unconditional Prisoners of War in our possession I much fear, that the Enemy, knowing our delicacy respecting the propriety of Retaliating upon a Capitulation officer in our Care, and being acquainted that unconditional prisoners are within our power, will put an unfavorable Construction upon this Instance of our Conduct At least, under present Circumstances Capt Asgill's application to Sir Guy Carleton will, I fear, be productive of remonstrance and Recrimination only, which may possibly tend to place the Subject upon a disadvantageous footing

To remedy therefore as soon as possible this mistake, you will

[1] United Service Journal, XVI, pt 3, 318

be pleased immediately to order, that Lieut Turner, the officer you mention to be confined in York Gaol, or any other prisoner who falls within my first Description, may be conveyed on Phila under the same Regulations and Directions as were heretofore given, that he may take the place of Capt Asgill

In the mean Time lest any misinformation respecting Lt Turner, may have reached you, which might occasion further Mistake and Delay, Capt Asgill will be detained untill I can learn a Certainty of Lieut Turner's or some other officer's answering our purpose, and as this Detention will leave the Young Gentleman now with us in a very disagreeable State of Anxiety and Suspense, I must desire that you will be pleased to use every means in your power, to make the greatest Despatch in the Execution of this order

I am, dear Sir, &c &c [1]

For some reason which cannot now be ascertained, the above order was not obeyed   Turner was not sent forward to take Asgill's place, and the only effect of the correspondence respecting him was to delay the execution of the prisoner

After leaving Philadelphia, Asgill was escorted on his journey by a detachment of Olney's Rhode Island troops Washington's order, dated May 15th, and addressed to "Major Olney or the Commandg Officer of the Rhode Island Regt in Philadelphia," reads in part as follows

Sir

Immediately upon receipt of this, you will put the Rhode Island Regt in motion, and conduct it by easy marches, & the most convenient route, to join the Army on the North River   You must take care to bring on with you every man who is able to march, except such a Detachment as the Secry at War may think proper to order as an Escort for the British Officer who is to be sent to the Jersey Line for the purpose of Retaliation, this Detachment which ought to be composed of picked men under a careful Officer is to join the Regt, where ever it may be as soon as that duty is performed [2]

[1] Washington Papers in Library of Congress, B, XV, pt 1, 383
[2] Washington Papers in Library of Congress, B XV, pt 1, 295

Much of the correspondence in the Asgill case from this time forward is of especial interest because of its close relation to Chatham   The letter given below contains Washington's instructions to Colonel Elias Dayton, commanding the New Jersey line, to whom was intrusted the painful duty of carrying the execution into effect   The New Jersey troops at that time were encamped in the Loantaka valley, near Morristown,[1] occupying a number of rude cabins or huts, but Dayton had his residence at Chatham, and it was to this village that his instructions were sent

Head Quarters, 4 June, 1782

Col Elias Dayton,
    2nd New Jersey Regt
        Chatham

Sir,

I am just informed by the secretary at war, that Captain Asgill, of the British guards, an unfortunate officer, who is destined to be the unhappy victim to atone for the death of Captain Huddy, had arrived in Philadelphia, and would set off very soon for the Jersey line, the place assigned for his execution   He will probably arrive as soon as this will reach you, and will be attended by Captain Ludlow, his friend whom he wishes to be admitted to go to New York, with an address to Sir Guy Carleton on his behalf

You will therefore give permission to Captain Ludlow to go

---

[1] In the *New Jersey Journal* of February 6, 1782, Daniel Pierson advertises a farm for sale, three miles from Morristown on the road to Chatham, where the Jersey troops are hutted This phraseology, like that often found in newspapers of the present day, is somewhat ambiguous, but the author understands it to mean that the Jersey camp was three miles from Morristown Some of the New Jersey troops, however, were stationed at Chatham during the following summer, as thus reported in Rivington's *Royal Gazette*, of New York, under date of August 14 "We are informed that the Rebels have their artillery at Burlington, a party of Jersey troops at Chatham, and what they call the New York line at Pompton These are about 2,000, and the residue of their army (about as many) are in the Highlands The soldiers are in a mutinous temper for want of pay, and under the strictest watch and discipline and are paraded THRICE in every twenty-four hours "

by the way of Dobb's Ferry[1] to New York, with such representation as Captain Asgill shall please to make to Sir Guy

At the same time I wish you to intimate to the gentlemen, that, although I am deeply affected with the unhappy fate, to which Captain Asgill is subjected, yet, that it will be to no purpose for them to make any representation to Sir Guy Carleton, which may serve to draw on a discussion of the present point of retaliation, that, in the state to which the matter has been suffered to run, all argumentation on the subject is entirely precluded on my part, that my resolutions have been grounded on so mature deliberation, that they must remain unalterably fixed You will also inform the gentlemen, that, while my duty calls me to make this decisive determination, humanity dictates a tear for the unfortunate offering, and inclines me to say, that I most devoutly wish his life may be saved This happy event may be attained, but it must be effected by the British Commander-in-chief He knows the alternative, which will accomplish it, and he knows, that this alternative only can avert the due extremity from the innocent, and that in this way alone the manes of the murdered Captain Huddy will be best appeased

[In the draft of this letter the following paragraph is stricken out I wish you also to inform Capn Asgill, with all the tenderness possible, that no address from him or any of his friends can be admitted from them directly to me—that I can attend to no application but such as shall be made by the British Commander-in-chief]

In the mean time, while this is doing, I must beg that you will be pleased to treat Captain Asgill with every tender attention and politeness (consistent with his present situation), which his rank, fortune, and connections, together with his unfortunate state, demand

I am, dear Sir, &c &c

GO WASHINGTON [2]

In due time the party having Asgill in custody arrived

[1] Washington had previously ordered that no flag should pass to or from the enemy, under any pretext, except at Dobbs' Ferry —*New Jersey Gazette*, May 8, 1782
[2] Columbian Magazine, January, 1787

at their destination, and turned over their prisoner to
Colonel Dayton; but in compliance with Washington's instructions that he should be treated with the greatest kindness, the captive was not placed in confinement, nor even
required to remain at the camp, but was admitted to his
parole, and allowed to take up his residence at Dayton's
headquarters in Chatham   He arrived at this village early
in June,[1] and remained there (though perhaps not continuously) until the 17th of November [2]

GORDON TO CARLETON

Colonel Dayton's Quarters
Chatham June 3d 1782

Sir,

The last Time I had the honor of addressing your Excellency
was by Captain Ludlow, when I informed you of Captain Asgill's
being made close Prisoner   We are now here under Colonel Dayton, who commands the Jersey Line, and in all probability will remain here some Time   The disagreeable Situation we are under
will I hope plead my Excuse with your Excellency, for begging that
you will send your Commands as soon as possible   It is with pain
I repeat to your Excellency the Opinion of the People from Lancaster
to this Place, that Captain Asgill must suffer, unless one of the Perpetrators is given up

I have the Honor to be Sir
Your Excellency's Most obedt humble Servt

JAMES GORDON
Major 80th Regt

His Excellency
   Sir Guy Carleton K B[3]

The order for the execution, though daily expected, was

[1] Colonel Matthias Ogden, in a letter dated Bottle Hill, June 5, states
that Captain Asgill and his friend Major Gordon have arrived at Chatham
—*Washington Papers in Library of Congress, 57, 79*

[2] *New Jersey Gazette*, November 27, 1782

[3] American Manuscripts in the Royal Institution, Vol 27, No 3, copy
in Library of Congress

not issued   In view of the circumstances, Washington felt
justified in taking the proposed step, although conscious of
the impropriety of executing a capitulation prisoner, yet his
desire was not to sacrifice the life of the unfortunate victim,
but to compel the surrender of Lippincott, and he could not
bring himself to order the death of an innocent man   He
repeatedly declared that his purpose was unalterably fixed,
and his letters to Clinton and Carleton contained the solemn
assurance that Asgill's life would be forfeited if justice were
denied   But both Clinton and Carleton, although denouncing the murder of Huddy in the strongest terms, not only in
their letters to Washington, but in their official reports to
the British government[1] persistently refused to give up the
murderer, their obstinacy being probably due to pressure
brought to bear by influential tories in New York.

Growing impatient at the delay in learning the result of
Asgill's appeal to Carleton, Washington wrote to Dayton
the following request for information.

Head Quarters 11th June 1782

Sir

    * * * * * * * * * *

You will inform me as early as possible the present Situation
of Capt Asgill, the prisoner destined for Retaliation, and what
prospect he has of relief from his Application to Sir Guy Carleton,
which I have been informed he has made thro his Friend Capt Ludlow   I have heard nothing yet from N York in Consequence of this
Application   His Fate will be suspended 'till I can be informed
the Decision of Sir Guy but I am impatient least this should be
unreasonably delayed—the Enemy ought to have learned before
this, that my Resolutions are not to be trifled with

    I am Sr

Colo Dayton

P S ·

    I am informed that Capt Asgill is at Chatham—without

[1] Sparks's Writings of Washington, VIII 337 n

guard, and under no Constiaint   This, if true, is certainly wrong
I wish to have the young gentleman treated with all the tenderness
possible, consistent with his present situation, but, until his Fate
is determined, he must be considered as a close prisoner, and be kept
in the greatest Security   I request, theiefore, that he be sent immediately to the Jersey line, where he is to be kept a close prisoner,
in perfect security, until fuither orders [1]

Fiom the *New Jersey Jouinal* of Chatham, June 19,
1782

CHATHAM, June 19   Captain Asgill still remains at this
place, and we are informed an order has come from his Excellency
General Washington for his close confinement

ASGILL TO WASHINGTON

Coll Daytons Quarters
Chatham May [June] 17th 1782

Sir—

On the 30th of last Month I had the Honor of addressing
your Excellency in writing, stating the manner of my Confinement
& the Circumstances that induced me to claim your protection—
being ignorant of the fate of my letter, it would be very satisfactory to me, if your Excellency would be pleased to inform me if
it has been received   in consequence of your Orders, Coll Dayton
was desirous of removing me to Camp but being ill with a fever
I prevailed on him to let me remain at his Quarters close confined,
which Indulgence I hope will not be disapproved of   I cannot
conclude without expressing my gratitude to your Excellency for
ordeiing Coll Dayton to favor me as much as my situation would
admit of & in justice to him I must acknowledge the feeling &
attentive manner in which those Commands weie executed

I have the Honor to be with great Respect
Your Excellys Most Obedt Humbl Servt

CHARLFS ASGIIL,
Lieut & Capt 1st Regt Foot Guards

His Excy Genl Washington
Commr in Chief [2]

---

[1] Washington Pipers in Iibrary of Congress, B XV, pt 1, 415, et seq
[2] Washington Papers in Library of Congress, 114, 12

DAYTON TO WASHINGTON

Chatham, June 17th 1782

Sir

* * * * * *

Capt Asgill has been at Chatham hitherto, but not free from any constraint, as your Excellency has been informed   I have ordered him to the Huts to be confined agreeable to orders   He hourly expects letter from his friend which I expect will be delayed untill the sentence of the court is known, which has been sitting for some days in New York for the trial of Lipincut   Genl Paterson is president of the court who is said to have prejudged the matter unfavourable to Lipincut

* * * * *

I am your Excellys Most Obedient Very Humble servant
Elias Dayton [1]

DAYTON TO WASHINGTON

June 18th 1782

Sir

In my letter of yesterday I informed your Excellency that I had ordered Capt Asgil to the Jersey Huts but upon waiting on him today I found him in such a situation that humanity would have shuddered at the idea of his removal he has been in a fever for some time past and the agitation of his mind upon the apprehension of less agreeable quarters and perhaps more indelicate treatment have increased it to a very considerable degree   Presuming therefore on your Excellencys lenity, and that his safety was the only object, I have for the present confined him a close prisoner at my own quarters where he will be in perfect security until farther orders   I wish to make it my study at all times to obey literally every order from my superior officers and especially from your Excellency, but my feelings for the innocent & distressed urged me to take time to make representation

I have the honor to be

Your Excellencys most Hbl servant

His Excellency General Washington [3]   ELIAS DAYTON

[1] Washington Papers in Library of Congress, 57, 160
Washington Papers in Library of Congress, 57, 172

WASHINGTON TO DAYTON

Head Quarters 22nd June

Sir

I have recd your two Letters of the 17th and 18th Instant

The only object I had in view, in ordering Captain Asgill to be confined at the Huts, was the perfect security of the Prisoner— this must be attended to, but I am very willing, and indeed wish, that every indulgence which is not inconsistent *with that* may be granted to him. And so with respect to Captain Schaak [1]

[1] Captain John Schaak, of the 57th British regiment was captured in a small skirmish on the Shrewsbury river during the evening of May 25, 1782 —*New Jersey Gazette, June 5, 1782* Dayton, in a letter to Washington of June 17, says "Capt Schaak, of the 57th Regt, whom your Excellency mentions in your last letter, is now at the Huts in close confinement, he is not wounded as reported but was indulged by Mr Adams to continue at El[izabeth] Town until his servant & baggage could be sent him from Sandy Hook" On November 15th, about the time of Asgill's release, Schaak wrote to Sir Guy Carleton requesting his aid to extricate him from the prison where he had been confined the last five months without any reason assigned The letter is dated "near Chatham" and is marked "by Capt Asgill"—*American MSS in the Royal Institution, "Carleton Papers," III, 224* Colonel Tilghman, one of Washington's aides, wrote on November 21st to Lieutenant Rhea, who commanded at the Jersey huts near Morristown in the absence of Colonel Dayton 'You will be pleased to direct Capt Schaak to repair to Dobbs' Ferry, where he will meet Lt Coll Smith Commy of prisoners He will take his parole and permit him to go into New York"—*Washington Papers in Library of Congress* But this order, apparently, was not obeyed Carleton, on the 11th of December, wrote to Washington "The liberation of Captain Asgill was I trust founded on the equal principles of Justice and Humanity, and, I could wish, Sir, that Captain Schaak was also released, not only to close a question of such intricacy that justice cannot act upon it on either side without losing its quality, but as there are also circumstances of ill health and infirmities, I presume not unknown to your Excellency, attending that Gentleman, which may render his confinement to both sides perhaps, equally unpleasant and unbecoming" —*Papers of the Continental Congress, 152, v 47, in Congressional Library* On January 15, 1783, Washington wrote to Dayton, congratulating him upon his promotion to the rank of brigadier, and adding "If Cap Shaack is not yet gone in to New York I must request you to take measures to oblige him to go in"—*Washington Papers in Library of Congress, B XVI, pt 1, 159* Dayton replied as follows

Chatham Jany 20th 1783

Sir

Your Excellency's letter of the 15th came safely to hand I consider myself honored by your Excellency's congratulation on my late promotion & am highly indebted for the part your Excellency was pleased to take on that Occasion A little time will be requisite for some necessary preparations which shall not detain me longer than this week, when I shall repair to camp without loss of time Capt Schaak is still at bottle hill, where he has contracted debts to a considerable amount he pretends he expects money from New York to discharge them, but he does not appear to be very

When I first ordered on an Officer for the purpose of retaliation, I expressed my willingness that he should make any application
he thought proper to the British Commander in Chief in whose power
alone it lay to arrest his destiny, but I at the same time desired it to
be announced, that I would receive no application nor answer any
Letter on the subject, which did not inform me that satisfaction was
made for the Death of Captain Huddy

I immagine you was not informed of this circumstance, or you
would have prevented Major Gordons applications on the subject

I am Sir Your very humble Servant

Go Washington [1]

GREVILLE TO DAYTON

York Town, Pennsylvania,
July ye 27th 1782

Sir

I take the Liberty of enclosing of Letter for my particular
friend, Cap Asgill, the conveying it to him will be the addition of
one favour to the many I understand he has received from you

I have the Honour to be with respect and Esteem

your most Obedient Servant

Henry Grevilll
Lt and Capn Guards

[Addressed]
For Colonel Dayton
Chatham, Jersey [2]

WASHINGTON TO LUDLOW

Head Qrs. Augt 5th, 1782

Sir,

Persuaded that your desire to visit Capt Asgill at Chatham, is
founded on motives of friendship and humanity only, I enclose you a
Passport for the gratification of it

anxious about going into New York, owing I believe principally to a female
connexion he is said to have lately made

I have the honor to be yr Excellencys Most Hbl servant,

Elias Dayton
Ibid, 61, 90

[1] Dayton Papers in Library of the New Jersey Historical Society
[2] Dayton Papers in Library of the New Jersey Historical Society

The inclosed Letters for that Gentleman came to me from New York, in the condition you will receive them   You will have an opportunity of presenting them with yourself   Your own letter came under cover to me *via* Ostend

I have the honor to be Sir, yi most Ob Sv

GO WASHINGTON

[Addressed]

To Captain Ludlow,
        1st bat British guards, New York [1]

PASSPORT.

Captn Ludler of the British Guards, has my permission (with his Servant) to pass the American Post at Dobb's ferry, & proceed to Chatham   He has liberty also to return to New York the same way

Given at Head Qrs, 5th Augt 1782

GO WASHINGTON

The Commandg Officer at Dobbs's -

LUDLOW TO WASHINGTON

Dobb's Ferry August ye 14th

Sir,

I have the honor to acquaint your Excellency that I arrived this morning, according to your permission, at Dobb's Ferry, Sir Guy Carleton took the opportunity of my coming here to send some dispatches, which he wished me to have delivered in person to you; but finding that inconsistent with the orders, delivered to Major Clit the commanding Officer at this Post   I shall proceed to Chatham, & there wait your Excellency's Commands

I have the honor to be Sir, with the greatest respect your most Obed &c

GEORGE LUDLOW

His Excellency Genl Washington [3]

---

[1] Columbian Magazine, February, 1787, Washington Papers in Library of Congress, E 505

[2] Washington Papers in Library of Congress, E 507

[3] Washington Papers in Library of Congress, 58, 179

CHAPTER XIX

The Asgill Case continued—Efforts of the Prisoner's Friends to obtain his Release—Washington refers the Matter to Congress—Asgill's Correspondence—Intervention of the French Court—Asgill is released by Congressional Resolution

THROUGH the long and weary months of the summer of 1782 Captain Asgill remained at Chatham in a state of constant anxiety and suspense, dreading from day to day that the order for his execution would be issued. To add to his distress, it was erroneously reported in America during his captivity that his father, Sir Charles Asgill, who was known to be seriously ill, had passed away, and his captors unintentionally caused him a painful shock by addressing him with the family title, though later an express from New York gave him reason to hope that the report of his father's death was incorrect[1] The captive, however, was under little restraint. Colonel Dayton treated him as a guest rather than a prisoner, permitting him to ride on horseback for long distances about the surrounding country, sometimes passing within ten or twelve miles of the British lines,[2] and on more than one occasion allowing him to send his confidential servant to New York. But these privileges were doubtless curtailed after the receipt of Washington's order that greater care should be taken to insure the safekeeping of the prisoner.

During the whole period of Asgill's captivity at Chatham he seems to have been attended by his faithful friend Major Gordon who was untiring in his efforts to bring

[1] New Jersey Gazette, December 11, 1782
Ford's Writings of Washington XI 38
[2] Graham's Memoirs, 95

about the prisoner's release   The major exhausted every
expedient that his ingenuity could devise, even persuading
the relatives of the murdered Huddy to exert themselves in
Asgill's behalf, and Captain Graham alleges that, with the
assistance of some friends and sympathizers among the fair
sex residing in Chatham, he formed a plan for Asgill's
escape, which would have been attempted had the execution
been ordered—a plan which was so carefully laid that its
advocates were confident of its success

Asgill's unfortunate situation excited widespread
sympathy   The people desired that the murderer should be
brought to justice, and not that an innocent man should
suffer for the crime.   Captain Adam Huyler of New Brunswick, a warm friend of Huddy, made a daring attempt to
kidnap Lippincott out of the heart of New York, but was
unsuccessful, owing to the latter's absence from home [1]
Tom Payne, the famous essayist, published in the *New
Jersey Gazette* of June 12th a resumé of the Asgill case,
addressed to Carleton, in which he asserted that if the
captain died it would indicate that Carleton esteemed his life
of less value than the murderer's, and that his death would
be as directly chargeable to the British commander as if the
latter had himself tied the rope around the young officer's
neck

At length, however, circumstances arose which changed
the aspect of the case   While the matter was still pending,
and Washington was negotiating for Lippincott's surrender,
the preliminary articles of peace were announced,[2] and this
at once placed the affair in a different light, for, as the sole
object of retaliation was to prevent the repetition of the
enemy's crimes, the measure would be clearly unnecessary
and inoperative if, as then appeared, hostilities were drawing

[1] Sabine's Loyalists, II, 18, Lee's New Jersey as a Colony and as a
State, II, 250

[2] Boudinot s Elias Boudinot, 248

to a close   During the latter part of the summer Washington referred the case to Congress, and asked them to decide whether, in view of all the circumstances, it was their wish that Asgill should be put to death   He wrote to the president of Congress

Head-Quarters, Newberg,
19 Augt, 1782.

Sir,

Congress has been already furnished with Copies of all letters which had passed between the Commanders-in-Chief of the British Forces in New York and myself, respecting the matter of Captain Huddy, previous to the last of July. I now have the honor to inclose Sir Guy Carleton's letter of the 1st instant, (in reply to mine of the 25th ultimo,) and that of the 13th, which accompanied the proceedings of the General Court-Martial for the trial of Captain Lippincot   The proceedings, together with such other documents as relate to that unfortunate transaction, I also transmit by this opportunity

As Sir Guy Carleton, notwithstanding the acquittal of Lippincot reprobates the measure in unequivcal terms, and has given assurances of prosecuting a further enquiry, it has changed the Ground I was proceeding upon and placed the matter upon an extremely delicate footing

It would be assuming in me to ascribe causes to actions different from those which are ostensibly and plausibly assigned, but, admitting that General Carleton has no other object but to procrastinate he has, by disavowing the act, by declaring that it is held in abhorrence, by not even sanctioning the motives which appear to have influenced Lippincot to become the executioner of Huddy, and by giving the strongest assurances that further inquisition shall be made, so far manifested the appearance of an earnest desire to bring the guilty to punishment, that I fear an act of retaliation upon an innocent person, before the result of his inquisition is known, would be considered by an impartial and unprejudiced World in an unfavorable and perhaps unjustifiable point of view, More especially as the great end proposed by retaliation which is to prevent a repetition of outrages, has been in a manner answered, for, you will please to observe by the extract of General Carleton's letter of the 26 ot April to Govr Franklin, that he has expressly forbidden the Board of Directors to remove or exchange in future any prisoners of War in the custody of their Commissary without having first obtained his approbation and orders

The same reasons which induced me to lay the first steps I took in this affair before Congress, urge me to submit it to them at its present stage   It is a great national concern, upon which an individual ought not to decide   I shall be glad to be favored with the determination ot Congress as early as possible, as I shall suspend giving my answer to Sir Guy Carleton until I am informed how far they are satisfied with his conduct hitherto

I cannot close this letter without making a remark upon that part of Sir Guy s in which he charges me with want of humanity in selecting a Victim from among the British officers as early as I did   He ought to consider that, by the usages of War, and upon the principles of retaliation, I should have been justified in executing an officer of equal rank with Capt Huddy immediately upon receiving proof of his murder, and then informing Sir Henry Clinton that I had done so   Besides, it was impossible for me to have foreseen that it would be so very long before the matter would be brought to some kind of issue [1]

Annoyed by the failure of the legislative body to take action upon the case, Washington wrote a more insistent request for instructions, addressing this letter to James Duane, a representative from New York, and a member of the committee to which the Asgill matter had been referred

                                    Verplanks Point, 30th Septr 1782
Dear Sir,

I shall be obliged to you, or some friend in Congress, to inform me what has been, or is likely to be done, with respect to my reference of the case of Captn Wm Huddy [2]

I cannot forbear complaining of the cruel situation I now am, and oftentimes have been placed in by the silence of Congress in

[1] Washington Papers in Library of Congress, A VI, pt II, 263

matters of high importance, and which the good of Service, and my official duty has obliged me to call upon them (as the Sovereign power of these United States) to decide

* * * * * * * * * * * * * * * * * * *

The particular cause of it [his disquietude] at this time arises from two things   first, while I am totally silent *to the public* waiting the decision of Congress on the case of Huddy, I see publications on this head importing reflections in one of the Pennsylvania Papers, which no man could have made, that had not access to my official letter of the 19th of August to Congress, and secondly, because I feel exceedingly for Captn Asgill, who was designated by Lot as a victim to the Manes of Captn Huddy

While retaliation was apparently necessary, however disagreeable in itself, I had no repugnance to the measure   but, when the end proposed by it is answered, by a disavowal of the Act by a dissolution of the Board of Refugees, a promise whether with or without meaning to comply with it, I shall not determine that further inquisition should be made into the matter   I thought it incumbent upon me to have the sense of Congress, who had most explicitly approved, and impliedly indeed ordered retaliation to take place before I proceeded any further in the matter

The letter of Asgill, (a copy of which I inclose) and the situation of his Father, which I am made acquainted with by the British prints, work too powerfully upon my humanity not to wish that Congress would chalk a line for me to walk by in this business   To effect this, is the cause of the trouble you now receive from, Dr Sir, Yr Most obedt and Most Hble Serv

Go WASHINGTON [1]

Still Congress did not act   On October 7th the general wrote to the secretary of war

The delay of Congress   places me not only in a very delicate but a very awkward situation with the expecting World   Was I to give my private opinion respecting Asgill, I should pronounce in favour of his being released from his duress, and that he should be permitted to go to his friends in Europe [2]

[1] Washington Papers in Library of Congress, A VI pt II, 603
Ibid, 36

DAYTON TO ASGILL

[September, 1782]

Sir

I took the first opportunity of making known your request &
Situation to his Excy Gen Washington, but am unhappy in being
obliged to acquaint you that the former cannot be complied with, nor
the latter changed, until the Sense of Congress (who now have
under consideration the letters from Sir Guy Carleton upon the
subject) is known   Whenever their Decision & that of the Genl
is made known, I shall take pleasure in relieving your anxiety by an
immediate communication of their determination to you, which I hope
will be a favorable one [1]

ASGILL TO DAYTON

Chatham, Septr 5th 1782

Sir

I am extreamly obliged to you for your early attention in
writing to me, & am very sorry my request cannot be complied with
when you first informed me that it was Genl Washington's Order
that I should be admitted on Parole I naturally concluded that
every Idea of retaliating upon me for the Murder of Capt Huddy
was given up by his Excellency, & my only remaining wish to compleat my happiness was, that you should procure Genl Washington's Permission for me to go to Europe, & in consequence buoyed
myself with the hopes of soon revisiting those, who must have long
mourned my unhappy confinement & since that time till the receipt
of yours I began to recruit my health & Spirits, which you with
pleasure seemed to notice, but now my dejection is equal to my late
Joy, and those Ideal pleasures are entirely vanished & the Prospect
of continuing much longer in this dreadfull suspense   I fear that
if at a future time the Decision proves favorable, it will probably
be too late to render comfort either to me or my aged Father As
soon as you become informed of the determination of Congress, I
hope you will be kind enough to communicate it to me

Being absent from the Inn at Morris Town, where your letter

[1] Dayton Papers in Library of the New Jersey Historical Society

was left, I did not hear of it until the next day & received it open

Permit me to entreat you to intercede with Gen Washington in my behalf & to assist in relieving my present anxiety.

Believe me with gratitude for your pity and humane conduct towards me,

Your ever oblig'd obed't serv't

CHARLES ASGILL

Col Dayton [1]

SAME TO THE SAME

Chatham, Sep'br 6th 1782

Sir,

Least by any accident you should not receive my letter of the 5th inst which an officer of the Jersey line took charge of, I judged it would be best to prevent your conceiving me remiss in answering yours to send this duplicate by the Post, thanking you for your very early attention in writing to me, tho I am sorry my request cannot be complied with—when you first informed me that it was General Washington's orders that I should be admitted on Parole, I naturally concluded that every Idea of retaliating upon me for the Murder of Capt Huddy was given up by his Excellency, & my only remaining wish to compleat my happiness was, that you would procure Genl Washington's permission for me to go to Europe, buoyed with the hopes of soon revisiting those who must have long mourned my unhappy confinement, & since that time till the Receipt of yours, my Health and Spirits, which you with pleasure seemed to Notice daily mended, but now how great & afflicting is the change, those pleasing Ideas are entirely vanished & the prospect of continuing much longer in this dreadful Suspense will I fear if at a future time the decision proves favourable, be too late, to render comfort either to me or my aged Father As soon as you become informed of the Determination of Congress I hope you will be kind enough to communicate the Resolve to me—being absent from the Inn at Morris, where your letter was left, I did not hear of it till the next day, & then it was received opened Permit [me] to intreat you to intercede with Genl Washington in my behalf, & assist in relieving my present anxiety

[1] Dayton Papers in Library of the New Jersey Historical Society

believe me Dear Sir with Gratitude for your feeling & Humane
conduct to me,

Your ever Obliged Obedient Servant,
CHARLES ASGILL

P S —The Inn at Morris is full & there is no Lodgings for us
yet a while, but as soon as we hear of any we shall immediately
return there.

[Addressed]
Col Dayton,
        Commg Jersey Line,
            King's Ferry [1]

SAME TO THE SAME

Chatham, Sept'r 12th 1782

Sir

I hope my great anxiety to obtain permission to return to Europe
will plead my excuse for giving you so much trouble   the more
I reflect on my present Situation the more desirous I am for the
accomplishment of my Wishes, as I conceive myself by being admitted on Parole in every respect as before this unhappy affair,
& not the Object of Reprisal

the Confidence I have in your goodness of Heart which
prompts you to assist the truly unfortunate, leaves me no doubt
that the consideration of the consequence that must follow much
further delay in this affair will weigh with you to use your utmost
endeavours toward procuring me Genl Washington's Permission to
revisit Friends in England   Believe me with Gratitude & Esteem,
Your Obligd Ser't

CHAS ASGILL

[Addressed]
Coll Dayton,
        Commanding the Jersey line,
            King's Ferry
if removed by this may be forwarded -

[1] Dayton Papers in Library of New Jersey Historical Society   Dayton
had been ordered by Washington on August 25 to move his command to
King's Ferry, leaving behind no officers or soldiers capable of marching
except twenty invalids from both regiments, with a proportion of noncommissioned officers under a vigilant subaltern, to guard the huts, regimental baggage, and other public property, Captain Asgill to be left on
parole at Morristown —*Washington Papers in Library of Congress,* B XV,
pt 2, 137

[2] Dayton Papers in Library of New Jersey Historical Society

ASGILL TO WASHINGTON

Chatham, Sept 27th

Sir

I hope my unfortunate situation will plead my excuse for being so Sollicotous to obtain your Excellency's permission to return to Europe As I am by your Command admitted on Parole I am naturally induced to suppose the motives for my late confinement are removed, therefore let me intreat your Excellency to give me leave to revisit my Friends in Europe, whose concern for my Misfortune & anxiety for my return, is beyond all power of Description

thro Long Suspense my health is greatly impaired, & unless your Excy will be pleased to indulge me in this request, or cause me even to be assured of my fate I fear fatal consequences may attend much longer delay I hope when your Exy considers that I am not in the situation of a Culprit, that while on Parole I never acted contrary to the Tenor of it that my chief motives for being so eager for turther Enlargement is on account of my Family, these facts I hope, will operate with your Excellency, to reflect on my unhappy Case, & to relieve me from a State, which those only can form any Judgment of, who have experienced the Horror attending it

I have the Honor to be Your Excellys Most Obedt Most Humbl Servt

CHARLES ASGILL
Lt & Capt 1st Regt Foot Guards

His Excellency Genl Washington
Commander in Chief of the American Forces [1]

WASHINGTON TO ASGILL

Headquarters, 7th October, 1782

Sir,

I have to acknowledge your Favour of the 27th of September

The circumstances which produced in the first instance your unfortunate situation, having in some measure changed their

[1] Washington Papers in Library of Congress, 114, 29

ground, the whole matter has been laid before Congress for their directions I am now awaiting their decision

I can assure you I shall be very happy should circumstances enable me to announce to you your liberation from your disagreeable confinement

I am, &c &c

Go WASHINGTON

[Addressed]

To Capt Charles Asgill,
    1st bat British guards,
        prisoner, Chatham [1]

ASGILL TO WASHINGTON

Chatham Octr 18th

Sir—

I have been honored with your Excellys Letter & am exceedingly Obliged by the attention to which mine received I will not intrude on your time by repetitions of my Distress, which has lately been increased by accounts that my Father is on his Death Bed I have only to entreat as it may be a long while ere Congress finally determine, that your Excellency will be pleased to allow me to go to New York on Parole & to return in case my reappearance should hereafter be deemed necessary—if this request cannot be granted I hope your Excellency will give orders that my Parole may be withdrawn, as that Indulgence without a prospect of further Enlargement affords me not the least satisfaction, I had rather endure the most severe confinement than suffer my Friends to remain as at present decieved, fancying ever since my first admission on Parole, that I was entirely liberated & no longer the Object of retaliation—if your Excelly could form an Idea of my sufferings I am convinced the trouble I give would be excused I have the Honor to be your Excellency's Most Obedt Hbl Servt

CHARLES ASGILL
Lt & Capt 1st Guards

His Excy Genl Washington [2]

[1] Columbian Magazine, February, 1787
[2] Washington Papers in Library of Congress, 114, 34

Intelligence of Captain Asgill's plight reached London on or about the 13th of July,[1] and it created a great sensation, not only on account of the dramatic circumstances of the case, but because of the young officer's high social standing and distinguished connections. According to Baron de Grimm, public prints throughout Europe rang with the affair, causing so much excitement that the interest taken in the Revolution itself was to a great extent submerged in that of the Asgill case, and the first question asked of the commander of every vessel arriving from any American port was an inquiry into the captain's fate.[2] The efforts which had been and were still being made in Asgill's behalf by his sympathizers in America were surpassed by the activities of his relatives and friends at home. Lady Theresa Asgill, his mother, immediately protested to Washington in a letter which she desired Lord Cornwallis (who had returned to England) to send to Carleton to be forwarded to the American commander.[3] Baron de Grimm is the authority for the statement that she applied to the king, who directed that the author of a crime which dishonored the English nation should be given up to the Americans, but, incredible as it may seem, his command was not obeyed.[4] Richard Oswald, a gentleman whom the British ministry had sent to Paris a short time before to sound the French government on the subject of peace,[5] endeavored to persuade Benjamin Franklin, our representative at the Court of Versailles, to exert his influence in Asgill's favor, but Franklin assured him that nothing but the surrender of Lippincott could save the prisoner's life.[6]

[1] Letter of James Jay to Washington, Washington Papers in Library of Congress, 114, 16
[2] Memoirs of Baron de Grimm and Diderot, II, 244
[3] American MSS in the Royal Institution, Carleton Papers, III, 52
[4] Memoirs of Baron de Grimm and Diderot, II, 244
[5] Franklin's Works, IX, 373
[6] Perkins's History of the United States, II, 123

Among the varied activities of Lady Asgill in her son's behalf the only step which proved efficacious was a direct appeal to the court of France—a country then at war with her own   On the 18th of July she addressed the following letter to the Count de Vergennes, prime minister of France, imploring him to bring the case to the attention of the king, and to urge the monarch's intercession

If the politeness of the French court will permit a stranger to address it, it cannot be doubted but that she who unites in herself all the more delicate sensations with which an individual can be penetrated, will be received favorably by a nobleman who reflects honor not only on his nation, but on human nature

The subject on which I implore your assistance is too heart rending to be dwelt on, most probably the public report of it has already reached you, this relieves me from the burthen of so mournful a duty

My son, my only son, dear to me as he is brave, amiable as he is beloved, only nineteen years of age, a prisoner of war in consequence of the capitulation of Yorktown, is at present confined in America as an object of reprisal   Shall the innocent share the fate of the guilty?   Figure to yourself, Sir, the situation of a family in these circumstances   Surrounded as I am with objects of distress, bowed down by fear and grief, words are wanting to express what I feel, and to paint such a scene of misery, my husband given over by his physicians some hours before the arrival of this news, not in a condition to be informed of it, my daughter attacked by a fever, accompanied by delirium, speaking of her brother in tones of wildness, and without an interval of reason, unless it be to listen to some circumstances which may console her heart

Let your sensibility, Sir, paint to you my profound, my inexpressible misery, and plead in my favor, a word, a word from you, like a voice from Heaven, would liberate us from desolation, from the last degree of misfortune   I know how far General Washington reveres your character   Tell him only that you wish my son restored to liberty, and he will restore him to his disponding family, he will restore him to happiness

The virtue and courage of my son will justify this act of clemency His honor, Sir, led him to America, he was born to abundance, to independence and to the happiest prospects[1]

Permit me once more to entreat the interference of your high influence in favor of innocence, and in the cause of justice and humanity Dispatch, Sir, a letter from France to General Washington, and favor me with a copy of it, that it may be transmitted from hence

I feel the whole weight of the liberty taken in presenting this request, but I feel confident, whether granted or not, that you will pity the distress by which it was suggested, your humanity will drop a tear on my fault, and blot it out forever

May that Heaven, which I implore, grant that you may never need the consolation which you have in your power to bestow[2]

King Louis was deeply touched by this appeal, and he directed Vergennes to comply with Lady Asgill's request The prime minister accordingly wrote to Washington

It is not in the quality of [the minister of] a King, the friend and ally of the United States, (although with the knowledge and consent of his Majesty) that I now have the honor to write to your Excellency It is as a man of sensibility and a tender father, who feels all the force of paternal love, that I take the liberty to address to your Excellency my earnest solicitations in favor of a mother and family in tears Her situation seems the more worthy of notice on our part, as it is to the humanity of a nation at war with her own, that she has recourse for what she ought to receive from the impartial justice of her own Generals

I have the honor to enclose to your Excellency a copy of a letter which Lady Asgill has just written me I am not known to her, nor was I acquainted that her son was the unhappy victim, destined by lot to expiate the odious crime that was a formal denial

---

[1] Asgill insisted upon entering the army contrary to the wishes of his parents His father offered to give him a house and £3000 per year if he would adopt some other profession —*Journal Politique de Bruxells, August 1782*

[2] Memoirs of Baron de Grimm and Diderot, II, 244

of justice obliges you to avenge   Your Excellency will not read
this letter without being extremely affected, it had that effect upon
the King and Queen to whom I communicated it   The goodness
of their Majestie's hearts induces them to desire, that the inquie-
tudes of an unfortunate mother may be calmed, and her tenderness
reassured   I felt, Sir, that there are cases where humanity itself
exacts the most extreme rigor, perhaps the one now in question may
be of the number, but, allowing reprisals to be just, it is not less
horrid to those who are the victims, and the character of your Excellency is too well known for me not to be persuaded that you desire
nothing more than to be able to avoid the disagreeable necessity

There is one consideration, Sir, which, though not decisive, may
have an influence upon your resolution   Captain Asgill is doubtless
your prisoner, but he is among those whom the King contributed to
put into your hands at Yorktown   Although this circumstance does
not operate as a safeguard, it however justifies the interest I permit
myself to take in this affair   If it is in your power, Sir, to consider
and have regard to it, you will do what is agreeable to their Majes-
ties, the danger of young Asgill, the tears, the despair of his mother,
affect them sensibly, and they will see with pleasure the hope of consolation shine out for those unfortunate people

In seeking to deliver Mr Asgill from the fate which threatens
him, I am far from engaging you to secure another victim, the pardon, to be perfectly satisfactory, must be entire   I do not imagine it
can be productive of any bad consequences   If the English general
has not been able to punish the horrible crime you complain of in so
exemplary a manner as he should, there is reason to take the most
efficacious measures to prevent the like in future

I sincerely wish, Sir, that my intercession may meet success, the
sentiment which dictates it, and which you have not ceased to manifest on every occasion, assures me that you will not be indifferent to
the prayers and to the tears of a family which has recourse to your
clemency through me   It is rendering homage to your virtue to implore it

I have the honor to be, with the most perfect consideration, Sir,
        Yours, &c

                                    DE VERGENNES

Versailles, 29 July, 1782 [1]

[1] Ford's Writings of Washington, X, 105, n

The letter of the Count de Vergennes, accompanied by a copy of Lady Asgill's petition, was received by Washington on October 25th, at which time Congress had still failed to reach a decision in the matter The general immediately forwarded the papers to the president of Congress, with these words

> I have the honor to transmit to your Excellency the copy of two letters from the Count de Vergennes which were sent out in the packet from England, and have just come to my hands by a flag of truce from New York They contain a very pathetic and affectionate interposition in favor of the life of Captain Asgill I lose no time to forward them by a special messenger to Congress without any observations, being persuaded that Congress will not hesitate to give a very early decision respecting his further treatment [1]

One of the members of Congress at that time was Elias Boudinot of Elizabeth, N J, who thus recorded in his journal the circumstances under which these letters were received, and the effect which they produced

> A very large Majority of Congress were determined on his [Asgill's] Execution, and a Motion was made for a Resolution positively ordering the immediate Execution Mr Duane & myself considering the Reasons assigned by the Commander in Chief conclusive, made all the Opposition in our Power We urged every Argument that the Peculiarity of the Case suggested, and spent three Days in warm Debate, during which more ill Blood appeared in the House, than I had seen Near the close of the third Day, when every Argument was exhausted, without any appearance of Success, the Matter was brought to a Close, by the Question being ordered to be taken I again rose and told the House that in so important a Case, where the Life of an innocent Person was concerned, we had (though in a small Minority) exerted ourselves to the utmost of our Power We had acquitted our Consciences and washed our Hands clean from the Blood of that Young Man That we saw his Fate was sealed That

[1] Ford's Writings of Washington, X, 87

we had nothing to do but request that the Proceedings should appear without Doors, as being equal to the Occasion, and the World should know that we had conducted the Measure with a serious Solemnity That great Warmth had been occasioned Some harsh language had taken Place The minds of Gentn had been irritated I therefore moved that the Question should be put off till the next Morning, on the Minority giving their Words, that they would not say another Word on the Subject, but the Question should be taken in the first Place, after the Meeting as of course This was unanimously agreed to The next Morning as soon as the Minutes were read, the President announced a Letter from the Commander in Chief On its being read, he stated the rec't of a letter from the King and Queen of France inclosing one from Mrs Asgill the Mother of Capt Asgill to the Queen, that on the Whole was enough to move the Heart of a Savage The Substance was asking the Life of young Asgill This operated like an electrical Shock Each Member looking on his Neighbor, in Surprise, as if saying here is unfair Play It was suspected to be some Scheme of the Minority The President was interrogated The Cover of the Letters was called for The General's Signature was examined In Short, it looked so much like something supernatural that even the Minority, who were so much pleased with it, could scarcely think it real After being fully convinced of the integrity of the Transaction, a Motion was made that the Life of Capt Asgill should be given as a Compliment to the King of France This was unanimously carried on which it was moved that the Commander in Chief should remand Capt. Asgill to his Quarters at Lancaster To this I objected, That as we considered Capt Asgill's Life as forfeited, & we had given him to the King of France, he was now a free Man, and therefore I moved that he should be immediately returned to New York, without Exchange This was also unanimously adopted, and thus we got clear of shedding innocent Blood, by a wonderful Interposition of Providence [1]

----

[1] Boudinot's Elias Boudinot, I, 245

CHAPTER XX

The Asgill Case concluded—Asgill leaves Chatham and returns to England—Accusations of harsh and cruel Treatment are made—Washington denies the Charge—The Asgill Case dramatized in France—Asgill's subsequent Career

AS soon as Washington learned that Asgill had been liberated by Congress, he wrote him this letter, conveying the welcome intelligence that his long captivity was at an end

Head Quarters, 13th November, 1782

Sir,

It affords me singular pleasure to have it in my power to transmit you the inclosed copy of an Act of Congress, of the 7th instant by which you are released from the disagreeable circumstances in which you have so long been Supposing you would wish to go to New York as soon as possible, I also inclose a passport for that purpose

Your letter of the 10th of October came regularly to my hands I beg you to believe, that my not answering it sooner, did not proceed from inattention to you, or want of feeling for your situation I daily expected a determination of your case, and I thought it better to await that, than to feed you with hopes that might in the end prove fruitless You will attribute my detention of the inclosed letters, which have been in my hands about a fortnight, to the same cause

I cannot take leave of you Sir without assuring you that in whatever light my agency in this unpleasing affair may be viewed, I was never influenced thro' the whole of it, by sanguinary motives, but by what I conceived a sense of my duty which loudly called upon me to take measures, however disagreeable to prevent a repetition of those enormities which have been the subject of discussion And that this important end is likely to be answered without the effusion of the Blood of an innocent person, is not a greater relief to you than it is to Sir

　　　Yr most obt and hble servt,[1]

From the *New Jersey Gazette,* of Trenton, November 27th

CHATHAM, November 20   Captain Asgill, who had been detained here some months, and was thought would be executed to expiate the murder of Captain Huddy, is discharged by a resolve of Congress   He set out from this last Sunday for London, via New York

From Rivington's *Royal Gazette,* of New York, November 20th

Yesterday arrived in town Capt Asgill, of the Guards, this Gentleman had suffered a most anxious and melancholy durance during the last summer amongst the Rebels

As appears from the above news-items, Captain Asgill left Chatham on November 17th, and he hastened to New York intent upon taking the first ship to England   Finding that the packet *Swallow,* Captain Green, of Falmouth,[2] had just sailed, he abandoned his servant and baggage, procured a row-boat, and succeeded in overtaking the vessel   He reached his native land in safety on December 18th [3]

Major Gordon, after Asgill's release, returned to the prison camp at Lancaster.   Before his departure from Chatham he addressed a letter to Sir Guy Carleton, of which the following is a copy

　　　　　　　　　　　　Chatham, November,　1782

Sir,

　　　Captain Asgill will have the honour to deliver this to Your Ex-

---

[1] Washington Papers in Library of Congress, F 511
[2] Rivington's *Royal Gazette,* October 23, 1782
[3] McKinnon's Coldstream Guards, II, 19, n
[4] *The Remembrancer,* 1783, 79

cellency, who is at last set at liberty by a Vote of Congress after a long and disagreeable confinement which he bore with that manly fortitude that will forever reflect honour upon himself

During the period that he was close confined he had frequent opportunities of making his escape, and was often urged to do it by annonymous correspondents, one of which assured him that if he did not make use of the present moment an order would arrive next day from General Washington that would put it out of his power forever. This letter he gave me to read, and at the same time told me (that unless I wou'd advise him to do it) he never wou'd take a step that might be the means of counteracting measures adopted by Your Excellency to procure his release, or might bring one of the officers of Lord Cornwallis' army into the same predicament, and that he had made his mind up for the worst consequences that cou'd happen from rebel tyranny

I shall expect Your Excellency's commands at Lancaster, for which place I set out to-morrow by way of Philadelphia, when I shall visit our prisoners in gaol at that place and I will take the first opportunity to transmit returns to Your Adjutant General

I have the honour to be, &c &c

JAMES GORDON [1]

Major Gordon seems to have been the chief sufferer from the threatened act of retaliation   He took Asgill's misfortune keenly to heart, and his health, which previously had been somewhat delicate, was permanently impaired by the anxieties of the summer   He returned to Lancaster a changed and broken man, a lively and jovial disposition which had formerly distinguished h n gave place to profound depression; and even his release from captivity upon the cessation of hostilities and subsequent appointment to a command at Kingsbridge, New York, with the brevet of lieutenant-colonel, failed to restore his health or revive his spirits   Captain Graham tells us that Gordon was later appointed president of a sort of military court at New York which was in session for several weeks, deciding, among

[1] American MSS in the Royal Institution, Carleton Papers, III, 224

other cases, various disputes between the whigs and tories,
and that the major had won so high a place in the respect
and esteem of the people of the Jerseys during the summer
of 1782 that every litigant from this State, whether patriot
or refugee, eagerly sought to have his cause decided by him
Gordon died soon afterwards in the Morris house, now
known as the Jumel mansion and during his last moments
he was greatly cheered and comforted by the knowledge
that his conduct in the Asgill case had won for him the
approval and commendation of the Prince of Wales [1]

In order that the motives which actuated Congress in
liberating Captain Asgill might not be misconstrued, and
that no doubt or misunderstanding should arise respecting
the views of that body on the subject of retaliation in general, the following resolutions were passed

Friday, November 8th 1782

Resolved   That the Commander-in-Chief be instructed to call,
in the most pointed terms, on the British commander at New York,
to fulfil his engagement contained in his letter of the 13th day of
August last, "to make further inquisition into the murder of Captain
Huddy, and to pursue it with all the effect, which a due regard for
justice will permit "

Resolved   That to prevent any misconstruction which may
arise from the Resolution directing Captain Asgill to be set at liberty,
it be declared, and is hereby declared, that the Commander-in-Chief,
or commander of a separate army, is, in virtue of the powers vested
in them respectively, fully authorized and empowered, whenever the
enemy shall commit any act of cruelty or violence, contrary to the
laws or usage of war, to demand adequate satisfaction for the same,
and in such case, if such satisfaction shall not be given in a reasonable
or limited time, or shall be refused or evaded under any pretense
whatever, to cause suitable retaliation forthwith to be made, and
the United States in Congress assembled will support them in such
measures [2]

[1] Graham's Memoirs, 104, 105
[2] Journals of Congress

In accordance with the above resolution, Washington wrote to Carleton on November 20th, reminding him of his promise, and asking to be informed of the probability of convicting the culprit Carleton however, declined to re-open the question, and the matter was permitted to drop [1] And so the murder of Captain Huddy was never avenged

Asgill's escape from the ignominious death which overshadowed him so long was due to a number of circumstances combining in his favor—to Washington's natural repugnance to the shocking measure of hanging an innocent man in expatiation of the crime of another to his doubt of the propriety of sacrificing a prisoner who was protected by a capitulation, despite the fact that no unconditional prisoner of equal rank was available· to his courtesy in awaiting the result of the inquiry prosecuted by the British general, which held the matter in abeyance until peace was in sight, and it became apparent that retaliation was no longer necessary as a means of preventing further crimes, and lastly, to the intervention of the French court, backed by the pathetic letter of Lady Asgill It is difficult, nevertheless to account for the procrastination of Washington in this affair ; he seems to have shown a vacillation and hesitancy quite different from the firmness and decision which generally marked his character In his letters written during the early stages of the case he repeatedly declared, in the strongest possible terms his determination to execute the captive if justice could not be otherwise obtained, yet his resolution plainly faltered as time went on His apparent willingness to sacrifice a capitulation prisoner in direct violation of a treaty which he himself had signed (a willingness which English historians have declared to be the one blot upon the otherwise irreproachable character of the American hero) may be accounted for by the circumstances of the

[1] Ford's Writings of Washington, X, 106

case, and his belief in the absolute necessity of retaliation, but it cannot be explained why, when he learned that the Americans had two British officers in their hands who were unconditional prisoners, he did not instantly stop all proceedings relating to Asgill, and insist that one of them should take his place   The general himself was unable to explain this point a few years later, when the details of the case had escaped his memory   In a letter to Colonel David Humphreys written in 1786 he says. "There is one mystery in the business, which I cannot develop, nor are there any papers in my possession, which explain it   Hazen was ordered to send an unconditional prisoner   Asgill comes Hazen, or some other, must have given information of a Lieutenant Turner (under the former description)   Turner is ordered on, but never came   Why? I am unable to say; nor is there any letter from Hazen (to be found) which accounts for the non-compliance with the order   If I had not too many causes to distrust my memory, I should ascribe it to there having been no such officer, or that he was also under capitulation, for Captain Schaach seems to have been held as a proper victim after this "[1]

The English historians Craik and McFarlane explain the matter by ascribing rather unworthy motives to Washington and his subordinates   They write

It is not quite clear that the designation of this gentleman [Asgill] was left to chance   When Hazen sent this victim to Philadelphia, Washington expressed his regret that an *unconditional* prisoner had not been chosen, and to remedy the mistake he ordered that one Lieutenant Tumer, a British officer then confined in York gaol, who had been taken prisoner without conditions, should be substituted for Captain Asgill   But Brigadier Hazen, it appears, never obeyed this order, or at least the substitution of the *unconditional*

---

[1] Ford's Writings of Washington, XI, 60   It is thought that Schaak was mentioned inadvertently and that Asgill was meant   There is no evidence that Schaak was held for retaliation

prisoner for the conditional one never took place As Washington
never submitted against his will to any disobedience of orders on the
part of his officers, the conclusion is inevitable—that he was not
anxious there should be any such change   The Americans,
no doubt, thought it proper and spirited to adhere to the principle
of captain for captain though Lord Cornwallis' capitulation stood
in their way, and they may, besides, have given their cruel preference
to young Asgill from the knowledge of his being a person of family
and superior consideration, whose fate would excite greater attention than that of a more obscure officer

Further comment by the same authors is contained in
the following passage

Of this strange affair Washington's most minute and best
American biographer [Chief Justice Marshall] says not one word
though numerous documents relating to it must have stared him in
the face, and though he must have known that most of these docu
ments were given to the world in many publications both French and
English, and that the story at the time excited almost as much interest and was as universally known as that of the unfortunate André
Judge Marshall's silence looks like a confession of the impractica-
bility of defending his character and conduct in this particular   In
our eyes few things in the course of this unhappy war seem more
dishonourable and indefensible, and we believe Washington, as at the
crisis when he put Major André to death and refused him the last
sad consolation he asked for, was rendered gloomy and irascible by
the constant and degrading troubles and mortifications in which he
was involved [1]

Whether Asgill entertained any gratitude toward his
captors for the kindness and forbearance with which he
was treated while a prisoner at Chatham is very doubtful; it
is more likely that he carried with him on his return to
England a feeling of resentment toward those who had
compelled him to pass through this trying period of anxiety

[1] Pictorial History of England, I, 489

and terror He returned no answer to Washington's courteous letter of the 13th of November, and he doubtless
regarded the commander-in-chief as the author of his misfortune, who would have been glad to put him to death had
not Congress been prevailed upon by the French court to
intervene The whole incident was calculated to intensify
the animosity which he naturally felt toward the enemy in
time of war Washington's apparent readiness to execute
a capitulation prisoner was doubtless considered by him, as
it was by the English people in general, an act of treachery
and dishonor, and he may have attributed the leniency
with which he was treated and the delay in carrying his
sentence into effect, to Washington's fear of the consequences of such an act, rather than to his tenderness and
humanity

A few years after Asgill's return to England, stories
of harsh and cruel treatment, which he was alleged to have
received while a prisoner at Chatham, began to be circulated in London, in time finding their way into print, and
spreading to the continent These stories were supposed
to have originated with Asgill himself, and they were given
due credence in England and France It was said that
upon being brought to the place assigned for his execution,
the captain was closely confined, and that a gibbet was
erected for his execution directly in front of his prison window, which was often pointed out to him in an insulting
manner by his jailors, and that he believed these and similar affronts to have been offered by the connivance of Washington, who was eager to execute him, and was restrained
only by the protests of Rochambeau It was further
alleged (and this last statement was accepted without question by Baron de Grimm, and published by him in his
memoirs) that Asgill was thrice led to the gallows for execution, but that on each occasion the commander-in-chief

shrank from the sacrifice of innocent blood, and ordered a reprieve [1]

These charges of illiberal treatment were brought to Washington's attention through a letter written to Colonel Tench Tilghman by a friend in London, which read in part as follows

I have had it in contemplation to write to you for some time past on a subject in which I find myself more and more interested, I have endeavored to strike it off from my mind, because I am persuaded that General Washington is too great in himself to be concerned at any calumny, and his character too fair and pure to need any defense of mine

I have the honour to be introduced to a party of sages who meet regularly at a coffee house where they discuss politics, or subjects to communicate useful knowledge This set of men often mention our great and good general, and commonly in a *proper* manner, but some give credit to a charge exhibited against him by young Asgill of illiberal treatment and cruelty towards himself He alleges, that a gibbet was erected before his prison window, and often pointed to in an insulting manner, as good and proper for him to atone for Huddy's death, and many other insults, all of which he believes were countenanced by general Washington, who was well inclined to execute the sentence on him, but was restrained by the French general Rochambeau I have contended that it was entirely owing to the humane procrastination of our general, that captain Asgill did not suffer the fate allotted him, and that it was most happy to general Washington's good disposition that the French court interposed so as to enable him to save Asgill, and at the same time keep our army in temper

This affair is stated by young Asgill, and canvassed at the British court as before related Now sir, not for general Washington's sake, who, as I observed before, is above it, but for mine, who take pride in him, as I believe every honest American must, I request the favor that you would inform me fully on the subject, that I may be

[1] Memoirs of Baron de Grimm and Diderot II, 244

able to parry the only bad thrust made at our hero in my
presence [1]

The letter was never received by Colonel Tilghman,
who died before its delivery, but it was read by his father,
and by him the paragraphs above quoted were referred to
Washington   The latter, in writing to Mr Tilghman,
condoling with him upon the death of his son, denied Asgill's
charge in these words

I had laid my acct for the calumnies of anonymous scribblers,
but I never before had conceived that such an one as is related, could
have originated with, or have met the countenance of Capt Asgill,
whose situation often filled me with the keenest anguish   My
favorable opinion of him, however, if forfeited, if being acquainted
with these reports, he did not immediately contradict them   That I
could not have given countenance to the insults which *he says* were
offered to his person, especially the *grovelling* one of erecting a Gibbet before his prison window, will, I expect, readily be believed, when
I explicitly declare that I never heard of a single attempt to offer
insult, and that I had every reason to be convinced, that he was
treated by the officers around him, with all the tenderness and every
civility in their power
          I would fain ask Captn Asgill how he could reconcile
such belief (if his mind had been seriously impressed with it) to the
continual indulgencies and procrastinations he had experienced?
          He will not I presume deny that, if he was admitted to his parole
within ten or twelve miles of the British lines,—if not to a formal
parole, to a confidence yet more unlimited—by being permitted, for
the benefit of his health and recreation of his mind, to ride, not
merely about the cantonment but into the surrounding country for
many miles with his friend and companion Maj Gordon constantly
attending him Would not these indulgencies have painted a military
character to the portrait from whence they flowed? Does he conceive that discipline was so lax in the American army that *any officer*
in it would have granted these liberties to a Person confined by the

[1] Columbian Magazine, January, 1787

express order of the Commander in Chief, unless authorized to do so by the same authority? and to ascribe them to the interference of the Count de Rochambeau, is as void of foundation as his other conjectures, for I do not recollect that a sentence ever passed between that General and me, directly or indirectly, on the subject

This concise account of the treatment of Capt Asgill, is given from a hasty recollection of the circumstances If I had time, and it was essential, by unpacking my papers and recurring to authentic files, I might have been more pointed and full It is in my power, at any time, to convince the *unbiassed mind,* that my conduct through the whole of this transaction was neither influenced by passion, guided by inhumanity, or under the control of any interference whatsoever I essaved everything to save the innocent, bring the guilty to punishment, and stop the farther perpetration of similar crimes With what success the impartial world must, and certainly will decide [1]

Not only was Washington annoyed, but his friends and admirers were considerably exercised by the aspersions thus cast upon his character, and he consulted his former aide-de-camp, Colonel David Humphreys, as to the most expeditious and efficacious means of disproving these calumnies Humphreys decided to publish all military correspondence on the case which could be found among Washington's papers, knowing that the reiterated instructions contained in the general's letters to treat the prisoner with all possible tenderness, completely refuted the accusation of undue severity He obtained permission to take copies of the letters on the subject which were contained in Washington's official files, and these he published in the *Columbian Magazine* for January and February, 1787

If, as commonly believed in this country, these charges of cruel treatment were invented by Asgill, the circumstance seriously reflects upon his character as a man of veracity and honor It seems well established by the correspondence of

_____
[1] Ford's Writings of Washington, XI, 86

the period that he was not confined in the cantonments, and
we may dismiss the assertion that a gallows was erected for
his execution in front of his window—that is to say, in the
immediate vicinity of Dayton's residence at Chatham—for
the place assigned for his execution was not in this village,
but at the encampment in the Loantaka valley It is possible,
however, that the story of the gibbet had at least a foundation of truth, and that Asgill believed it to be accurate   It
may perhaps be explained in this way Washington, in a letter to Dayton of August 25, 1782, directing him to march
the New Jersey brigade to King's Ferry, instructed him to
leave Captain Asgill on parole at Morristown until further
orders,[1] and Asgill in a letter to Dayton written at Chatham
a few days afterwards, spoke of returning to Morristown
as soon as accommodations in the inn at that place could be
secured Although no more definite record has been found,
it would thus appear that Asgill spent part of his captivity
in Morristown, and it is probable that while there he lodged
in the Arnold tavern, diagonally opposite which, in what is
now the park, stood the county court-house and jail with
the gallows near it [2] If it is a fact that Asgill was accommodated in this tavern, the gallows may have been in view
from his chamber window, and it is not unlikely that some
of the townspeople, enraged by the murder of Huddy, and
strongly favoring retaliation, gave expression to their anger
by calling his attention to the gibbet, and reminding him that
Huddy's death was soon to be avenged   In such case he
might easily receive the impression that the gallows had been
erected especially for him [3]

[1] Washington Papers in Library of Congress, B XV, pt 2, 137

[2] Sherman's Historic Morristown, 68, 176

[3] Hamilton's History of the Grenadier Guards, and McKinnon's Origin
and Services of the Coldstream Guards mention the erection of the gallows,
and add that Asgill was "removed from Lancaster to Chatham loaded with
chains" This latter statement at least was denied Edward E Hale, in
his Life of Washington, gives the following quotation from Asgill's autograph written in London in 1783 'In answer to your question if the Americans put me in irons during the term of my confinement, for their sake as
well as mine, I have the satisfaction to inform you that they never did "

Thomas Jones, the tory historian, gives a version of
the Asgill affair from the royalist point of view, in which due
emphasis is laid upon the alleged brutality of the American
officers His statement, though inaccurate and unreliable in
many of its details, possesses a certain interest as showing
the intense acrimony which the case aroused in the minds of
those in sympathy with the crown It reads as follows

Information of this [Huddy's murder] was soon given to Washington, who sent a flag to General Clinton, and demanded in peremptory terms, that the executioner of Huddy, or a person of equal rank,
should be sent out in order to retaliate upon for, is he termed it, the
murder of Huddy In this, Washington showed spirit decision,
and resolution But then, Washington knew his man Clinton was
one of the most irresolute timid stupid and ignorant animals in the
world It is really surprising that a great king should have trusted
such a man with the command of a great army to quell a great, a
dangerous and a stubborn rebellion, in which the welfare of the nation and the honour of the Crown were so imminently concerned
Clinton was at a loss what to do His counsil were consulted Little
comfort was obtained All was amazement all was terror, and all
was atright, at head quarters   What Clinton had to fear,
I know not New York was as strong as it could be made He
had in the city and its environs 20 000 men, and it was surrounded
by men of war Washington's army did not consist of more than
10,000 men and it was in the Highlands, sixty miles off Yet the
General appeared to be panic-struck at Washington's demand The
Board of Associated Loyalists met The whole affair was laid before them These gentry all shrunk from the charge Some declared
it a falsehood, some attempted to justify it as an act necessary and
politic by way of retaliation, and others pretended a total ignorance
of the whole transaction Governor Franklin of New Jersey however who was at the head of the Board, left New York, and came
to England while the business was transacting

Sir Guy Carleton arrived and took the command and Clinton
sailed for England Washington now renewed his demand in a letter
to Sir Guy, and peremptorily insisted upon a compliance with it

Washington had hitherto dealt with British Generals, whose irresolution, indicision, and timidity, were such that with 6,000 men and not a ship, he frequently bullied them when at the head of 30,000 veterans and a victorious navy Washington thought he could play the same game, dance the same jig, and with as much ease insult Sir Guy In this he was, however, mistaken   .   Washington finding that in Sir Guy he had neither Sir William Howe nor Sir Henry Clinton to deal with dropped the correspondence, but not his design When a man breaks through the ties of honour, abandons his king by violating his oath of allegiance and fidelity, he will go to any lengths to serve his purposes, show his power, or gratify his vanity As a specimen of this, mark the sequel

Sir Guy having refused Washington's demand, a different mode was adopted, as well to the scandal of rebels, as of their great and good allies, the French It is to be wished the record of it may be handed down to the most distant generations
Washington finding Sir Guy resolute and positive, took, to the surprise of all civilized nations, nay to the astonishment of all mankind, rebels excepted, this most extraordinary step He sent to Virginia, ordered all the British captains (then upon parole under a solemn capitulation) to be called together, and when collected, directed that they should cast lots which of them should be executed by way of retaliation for the execution of Huddy This the captains refused to do Upon this refusal Washington ordered an officer of his own to cast the lots He did so, and the lot fell upon Captain Asgill of the Guards, as virtuous, as honest and as brave a youth as ever bore a commission, the only son of Sir John Asgill, a prominent banker in the city of London

The British officers then prisoners in Virginia, sent an express upon this serious and extraordinary proceeding to Monsieur de Rochambeau, then at Williamsburgh, one of the generals who signed the capitulation, and of course a guarantor for the punctual, faithful and honourable performance of it The dispatch was delivered No answer was returned The French are remarkable for politeness In this instance, however, Monsieur de Rochambeau was a manifest exception He had served so long with rebels, the allies of his Sovereign, that he had imbibed all their principles, contracted all their habits, and was as deaf to feelings of humanity as the most obdurate and inveterate rebel within the thirteen revolted Colonies   In the meantime Captain Asgill was carried in triumph, escorted by a rebel guard above 200 miles, from Virginia to the rebel camp in New Jersey   Captain Asgill was not permitted to come into the presence of Washington, but instantly put into a prison, deprived of the liberty of pen, ink and paper, his servant refused admittance to him, and the diet allowed him bread and water, with once a week a scanty allowance of animal food   This bespeaks the humanity, the politeness, the virtue of Washington   Captain Asgill had but one window in his apartment, out of which he could peep at the sun, or drawn in fresh air   To punish the unhappy youth as much as possible, the rebel Chief ordered a gallows erected, 30 feet high, directly in front of, and at a small distance from the window, with this inscription in capitals, "ERECTED FOR THE EXECUTION OF CAPTAIN ASGILL "   This gallows and this inscription presented themselves to the Captain's eyes whenever he approached the window, which for the benefit of fresh air must have been often   This was murdering a man by inches   It was a piece of barbarity that none but a rebel could be guilty of   Instant execution would soon have put the youth out of his pain, it would have been lenity, mercy, kindness, nay, it would have been generosity   Instead of suffering one death by an immediate execution, the unhappy young soldier must, in contemplation, have experienced one every day   Every morning that he arose, he naturally supposed it was the last of his existence   He never looked out of his window but he saw this tremendous instrument of death, with the more tremendous inscription, "FOR THE EXECUTION OF CAPTAIN ASGILL "   At conduct like this all Christians must shudder, and execrate the unfeeling severity which could be guilty of so deliberate and wanton an act of cruelty

Whether Washington's real intention was to have executed Captain Asgill is a doubt   That his design was, at least, to frighten Sir Guy into a compliance with his demand as to the executioner of Huddy, there can be no doubt   In this he was, however, mistaken Sir Guy was not to be bullied, frightened nor insulted   To the surprise of everyone Captain Asgill continued in jail a long time, and no execution took place   The particulars at length reached England Lady Asgill applied to the Queen of France in behalf of her only son, her favorite child   The Queen listened to the tears of a dis-

consolate mother, she applied to her loyal consort, and he ordered his
ambassador at Philadelphia to demand his release   This had the desired effect   Neither Congress nor Washington dared trifle with
their great and good ally   The Captain was therefore discharged,
sent to New York, and returned, as from the grave, to his parents, his
relatives, and his friends in England [1]

Alexander Garden, who served during the Revolutionary War in "Light Horse Harry" Lee's partisan legion,
comments in these words upon the accusation of undue severity in the Asgill case

To what, then, but the deadly animosity of a nation instigated
by the successful opposition to their arms, and the threatening prospect of the loss of empire, can be attributed the falsehoods and scurrili-
ties with which the British prints, on both sides of the Atlantic, over-
flowed?   Notwithstanding so satisfactory a termination of this
eventful business, the British Gazettes continued lavishly to dissemi-
nate abuse, and even to assert, "that Captain Asgill himself was, on
all occasions, loud in proclaiming the unnecessary rigour extended
towards him by General Washington, and a scandalous want of
delicacy on the part of the American officers, with whom he came in
contact"   I was greatly surprised at these statements, and loth to
believe them   I had been a school-fellow of Sir Charles Asgill, an
inmate of the same boarding-house for several years and a disposition more mild gentle and affectionate, I never met with   I
considered him as possessed of that high sense of honour, which
characterizes the youths of Westminster in a pre-eminent degree   Con-
versing some time afterward with Mr Henry Middleton, of Suffolk, Great Britain, and inquiring, if it was possible that Sir Charles
Asgill could so far forget his obligations to a generous enemy, as to
return his kindness with abuse, Mr Middleton, who had been our
contemporary at school, and who had kept up a degree of intimacy
with Sir Charles, denied the justice of the accusation, and declared,
that the person charged with an act so base, not only spoke with
gratitude of the conduct of General Washington, but was lavish in

[1] Jones's New York in the Revolution, II, 227 et seq

his commendations of Colonel Dayton, and of all the officers of the Continental army, whose duty had occasionally introduced them to his acquaintance It may now be too late to remove unfavourable impressions on the other side of the Atlantic, (should my essay ever reach that far,) but it is still a pleasure to me, to do justice to the memory of our beloved Washington, and to free from the imputation of duplicity and ingratitude, a gentleman of whose merits I have ever entertained an opinion truly exalted [1]

The interest which the Asgill case aroused in France outlasted the American Revolution, and caused the incident to be repeatedly dramatized, the most successful of these plays being "Asgill," a prose drama in five acts, written by J S le Barbier-le-Jeune in 1785 It was dedicated to Lady Asgill, and concluded with a letter of thanks from her The play represented *Wazington* as deploring the necessity of executing the hero, though sternly refusing to interfere with the course of justice, but finally yielding to the intercession of *Vergennes*, and infolding *Asgill* in a fond embrace, with serio-comic enthusiasm The part of *Wazington* was taken by the celebrated actor Saint-Prix Butler, who in reality was a leader of the tories during the Revolution, was introduced in the play as the murderer of *Huddy*, the latter being transformed by the dramatist into a British officer Other leading characters were two American generals, *Lincol* (Lincoln) and *Macdal* (McDougall) an English envoy named *Ioston* (Johnson), *Mrs Nelson*, a widow, the step-mother of the commander-in-chief; *M, Ferguson*, and the ghost of *Wazington's* son

There were three other dramatizations of the Asgill case

1 "Abdir," a drama in four acts and in verse, by M de Sauvigny; produced in the French theatre in January, 1785

[1] Garden's Anecdotes of the Revolution, Ser 2, 30, 33

2 "Asgill, *ou l'Orphelin de Pennsylvanie,*" a melo-drama in one act and in prose, with ariettas—"pitiful ditties uttered at mournful epoch" Book by B J. Marsollier, music by Delayrac Presented in the Theatre de l'Opera-Comique in March, 1790

3. "Asgill, *ou le Prisonnier Anglais,*" a drama in five acts and in verse, by Benoit Michel de Comberousse Never presented in any theatre [1]

Asgill's subsequent career is briefly outlined as follows· Upon the death of his father, Sir Charles Asgill, in 1788, he succeeded to the baronetcy, and during the same year married Maria Sophia, daughter of Sir Charles Ogle, Kt Soon afterwards he was accepted equerry to the Duke of York, and in 1790 was promoted to a company of guards with the rank of lieutenant-colonel He became colonel in 1795, brigadier on the staff of Ireland in 1797, and major-general in 1798. He remained on the staff until 1812, and was promoted to the rank of general in 1814 In the course of his services in the field he distinguished himself in Flanders and in Holland, and later took an active part in suppressing the Irish rebellion of 1798, during which he participated in the famous battle of Vinegar Hill He died in 1823, and, having no children, the baronetcy became extinct [2]

Captain Richard Lippincott, having been acquitted by the court-martial, escaped the penalty of his crime After the close of the war, when most of the tories left the United States and established homes in Canada, he lived for a time at Pinefield, New Brunswick In recognition of his military services throughout the Revolution the British government granted him the half pay of a captain for life, and 3000 acres of land in Ontario A large part of the city of

[1] Memoirs of Baron de Grimm and Diederot, II, 244, Appleton s Cyclopædia of American Biography, II, 159, Balch's The French in America (Thos W Balch's Trans), I, 62, n, Wharton's Diplomatic Correspondence, 463, n

[2] Stephens' Dictionary of National Biography

Toronto is built upon this land   His only surviving child,
Esther Borden Lippincott, her mother's namesake, married
George Taylor Dennison of Toronto, in whose house the
captain died in 1826 at the age of eighty-one[1]

[1] Ryerson's Royalists, II, 193